Ballots and Barricades

Ballots and Barricades

CLASS FORMATION AND
REPUBLICAN POLITICS IN FRANCE,
1830–1871

Ronald Aminzade

PRINCETON UNIVERSITY PRESS

PRINCETON, NEW JERSEY

Library of Congress Cataloging-in-Publication Data

Aminzade, Ronald, 1949–
Ballots and barricades : class formation and
republican politics in France, 1830–1871 / Ronald Aminzade.
p.   cm.
Includes bibliographical references and index.
1. France—Politics and government—19th century.   2. Toulouse
(France)—Social conditions.   3. Saint-Étienne (France)—Social
conditions.   4. Rouen (France)—Social conditions.   5. Social
history.   6. Republicanism—France—History—19th century.
7. Revolutions—France—History—19th century.   I. Title.
DC252.A46   1993   944.06—dc20   93-18279

ISBN 0-691-09479-9 — ISBN 0-691-02871-0 (pbk.)

TO CHUCK AND LOUISE TILLY

Who taught me to ask big questions.

Contents

viii · Contents

List of Illustrations

List of Maps and Tables

Acknowledgments

FOR READERS, these words mark a beginning. For me, they are the end, final words written after an exhausting attempt, lasting nearly a decade, to make sense of nineteenth-century French politics. There are too many debts, incurred in both teaching and research, and not enough ways to say thank you. My journey led me across many boundaries, of nation-states and academic disciplines. During my travels through France, I was assisted by numerous friends and acquaintances, who guided me through the archives and introduced me to the many delights of French culture and cuisine. I am especially indebted to Madame Maillard and Vivien Miguet, archivists who share my penchant for French history, and Philippe Videlier, Yves Lequin, Maurice Garden, and Yannick Marec, French historians who provided encouragement, warm receptions, and intelligent guidance.

My teaching experiences at the University of Minnesota and the Institute of Sociology of the University of Amsterdam informed my research and challenged me to think in new ways. Students in my graduate seminars deserve a special thanks. Much of what I know about class analysis and historical sociology was learned from team-teaching courses with two close friends and colleagues, Erik Olin Wright and Barbara Laslett, both of whom provided critical comments on the manuscript all along the way.

Faculty and student participants in the biweekly History and Society Program seminars at the University of Minnesota challenged my disciplinary reflexes and encouraged me to think beyond the boundaries of sociology. Colleagues and friends from the Social Science History Association also contributed to my healthy disrespect for disciplinary boundaries. Although trained as a sociologist at the University of Michigan, I had the good fortune to work closely with a renegade, Charles Tilly. Our conversations, once face-to-face but increasingly via electronic mail, have shaped my thinking in many ways. Chuck's lengthy and insightful comments on an early draft of this book prompted drastic revisions and a much-improved manuscript.

The only person who may be happier than me to witness the completion of this book is Mary Jo Maynes. She provided support, encouragement, and critical commentary throughout this research project. Dorothy and Ben Aminzade taught me to love books and read voraciously. Although Daniel and Elizabeth Maynes-Aminzade share my love of books, they enable me to live a more balanced life by constantly reminding me that there are more important things in life than books.

My thanks to colleagues who took time away from very busy schedules to read and constructively comment on the entire manuscript: William Brustein, Craig Calhoun, Michael Hanagan, George Steinmetz, Eric Weitz, and several anonymous reviewers. Many others read and commented on selected chapters over the years, including Julia Adams, Fred Block, Harry Boyte, Johanna Brenner, Michael Burawoy, Dan Clawson, Jim Cronin, Geoff Eley, Joe Galaskiewicz, Allen Isaacman, Christopher Johnson, Richard Lachmann, Helga Leitner, Scott McNall, William Roy, William Sewell, Jr., Eric Sheppard, John Stephens, and Mark Traugott.

My colleagues in the Sociology Department of the University of Minnesota provided a supportive atmosphere for my research and teaching. The staff in the department enabled me to maintain a cheerful disposition despite a frantic schedule. My thanks to Gloria DeWolfe, Bill Laznovsky, and Kate Stuckert for copy editing; to Michel LeGall for his generous help in preparing photographs; to Karl Krohn for guiding me through the mysteries of computer technology; and to Hilda Daniels, Marie Milsten Fiedler, Kathy Frank, Gwen Gmeinder, and Dawn Lindgren for making the day-to-day tasks of a college professor more pleasant and rewarding.

PART ONE

Political Change, Early Industrialization, and French Republicanism

CHAPTER ONE

The Political Consequences of Early Industrialization

EARLY INDUSTRIALIZATION AND POLITICS IN FRANCE

"Sociology as a whole," observed Philip Abrams, "is about the transition [to industrialism] more than about any other historical process."[1] The European founders of the discipline—Karl Marx, Max Weber, and Emile Durkheim—developed general theories of social change in an effort to understand the consequences of this process, which was dramatically transforming their societies. Although England led the way in the growth of "modern industry," it was in France that the potential political consequences of industrialization appeared most threatening, or most liberating, depending on one's perspective. The French Revolution placed the democratic vision at the center of European political life. Socialism and working-class revolution initially burst onto the European scene in France.

During the middle decades of the nineteenth century, political conflicts repeatedly recast the form of government in France, from monarchy and empire to parliamentary republic. French workers first developed a political rhetoric rooted in the language of social class during these years. This was the time when male workers were first granted the right to vote; when mass political parties initially emerged; when socialism first made its way onto the political agenda; and when electoral politics displaced, but did not eliminate, nonelectoral forms of collective political action.

At the same time that these momentous political changes were taking place, industrialization radically transformed the French economy, altering the organization of workplaces and patterns of inequality. To many contemporary observers, the political innovations of the mid-nineteenth century were undoubtedly connected to these socioeconomic changes. "The development of modern industry . . . ," wrote Karl Marx, "cuts from under its feet the very foundation on which the bourgeoisie produces and appropriates products. What the bourgeoisie therefore produces, above all, is its own grave-diggers. Its fall and the victory of the proletariat are equally inevitable."[2] At first glance, the connection between early industrialization and the transformation of nineteenth-century French political life appears to be quite straightforward. Capitalist development, by proletarianizing growing sectors of the labor force, swelled the ranks of dependent wage laborers who formed the natural constituency for labor and socialist movements that challenged capitalism and fundamentally altered the political landscape. Economic change produced a more cohesive and politically organized working class, a political agenda increasingly dominated by issues of economic inequality and expressed in a language of class, and new forms of political participation centered around the expanded suffrage rights won by militant workers.

On closer examination, an account of the political consequences of early industrialization that posits a straightforward relationship between industrialization, class formation, and political change is inadequate. Nineteenth-century French cities like Rouen, which witnessed the rapid growth of mechanized factory production and the birth of a proletarianized workforce, did not produce the most politically active workers or the strongest socialist or republican movements. Nor did Rouen experience a revolutionary commune in 1871. Relative backwaters of industrial development, like Toulouse, generated the earliest and most militant working-class socialist and republican movements, as well as revolutionary communes in 1871. In short, a comparison of nineteenth-century French cities suggests that levels of industrialization did not closely correspond with the development of a politically active working class embracing a socialist vision or the growth of local political organizations that framed political issues in the language of class. Efforts by twentieth-century social scientists to account for such anomalies have fostered innovative theoretical developments, ranging from postmodernism to neo-Marxism to revisions of our understanding of the process of class formation.

CLASS ANALYSIS AND THE AUTONOMY OF THE POLITICAL

Political sociologists have typically regarded social class relations as a central determinant of a wide range of political attitudes and behaviors. A considerable amount of research on voting behavior, for example, has documented the way in which political attitudes and actions are shaped by class position.[3] Seymour Martin Lipset asserts that "under contemporary industrial conditions . . . classes have been the most important bases of political diversity."[4] Sociologists have often emphasized class relations in their explanations of political outcomes, highlighting the way in which class structures determine the material interests of individuals, shape their understanding of the political world, and determine the resources available to them in the pursuit of interests in the political arena.[5] Social class is also frequently invoked by historians to explain political outcomes, often by the use of terminology suggesting the class underpinnings of political events. Social historians, for example, sometimes label the French Revolution a "bourgeois revolution" and the Paris commune a "working-class insurrection." Such characterizations suggest that class relations provide the key to understanding these political phenomena. Nineteenth-century observers also noted close ties between social class and political dispositions. After visiting the handicraft workshops of his city, the central city police commissioner of Toulouse wrote in November 1849: "The worker has different opinions than his employer and is naturally socialist. I have made this observation after visiting several workshops, especially those of printers, bookbinders, hatmakers, and tailors. . . ."[6]

In recent years, social scientists and historians have increasingly questioned explanations of political behavior that portray people as acting out predetermined political roles consistent with their class positions. They have developed historically grounded explanations that emphasize the institutional and political determinants of political behavior. Research on nineteenth-century French politics has documented the divergent political identities of those sharing similar relations to the means of production. For example, Mark Traugott's study of the composition of the groups that participated in the June 1848 insurrection, on both sides of the barricades, found deep class divisions in the political loyalties of Parisian workers. Contrary to the traditional Marxist notion that the *lumpenproletariat* provided the forces of repression in June of 1848, Traugott found that members of the Mobile Guard, which led the repression of the uprising, had virtually the same social backgrounds as the insurgents. Workers who joined the Mobile Guard developed bonds of solidarity in the context of an organizational setting that forged new collective identities during the relatively brief period between February and June of 1848. The interests that motivated working-class political action, in this case, were not reducible to social origins or prior class experiences; they were constituted during the course of political conflicts. Traugott concludes that "any class-based propensities of actors are conditioned by a set of contingent organizational forces." He emphasizes "the decisive role of political and organizational variables in explaining the course and outcome of collective action."[7]

William Sewell, Jr.'s, study of nineteenth-century French politics makes similar claims. After providing evidence that privileged workers whose trades were not degraded by capitalist penetration joined the ranks of radical artisans, Sewell suggests that a wide variety of different experiences, such as migration, ethnicity, unemployment, or lowered income, may predispose workers to political radicalism. He attributes the absence of a close connection between occupational conditions and political predispositions to the role of state structures and political discourses in radicalizing workers.[8]

These historical studies have the virtue of highlighting organizational and ideological factors that reductionist Marxist analyses of politics have ignored. Traugott and Sewell explore the institutional mechanisms that frame the identities and perceived interests of social groups. Their work challenges a structural reductionism which presumes the centrality of class interests in any particular conflict. It suggests an alternative approach that takes the identities and perceived interests of actors as problematic, and as constituted through political activity, via organizational and ideological mechanisms that link social structures, including class structures, to political behavior.

Some scholars have responded differently to the problems encountered by class reductionist approaches to politics. Rather than suggesting the need to integrate institutional, cultural, and class analyses in order to understand the complex interdependence between state and society, they have proclaimed the "autonomy" of the political. For example, Tony Judt suggests that we can understand political conflicts and outcomes in nineteenth-century France without analyzing the economic context in which they occurred. He argues that "the class consciousness of the labouring population as it emerged in the 1840s and developed over two generations . . . owed virtually nothing to identifiable shifts in the nature or organization of production. To use the redundant vocabulary of an earlier generation of marxists, the consciousness of the French working class emerged out of encounters with the political superstructure, with the economic infrastructure quite absent from the equation."[9]

Other French historians have dismissed the utility of the concept of class. William Reddy contends that the historical record shows that "political movements draw on broad bands of support, coalesce around principles that transcend the concerns of specific positions in the social structure, and depend on the dedication of selfless innovators." He concludes that we should "set the concept of class aside entirely, with all that it entails."[10] For some scholars, this rejection of class analysis has led to poststructuralist analyses of discourse. François Furet contends that during the course of the French Revolution, language became a decisive determinant of politics, as "speech substitutes itself for power" and "the semiotic circuit is the absolute master of politics."[11] Joan Scott also questions the utility of class analysis. By privileging canonical texts, representations, and linguistic codes and adopting a poststructuralist epistemology, Scott marginalizes the socioeconomic and institutional dimensions of class relations.[12]

Although Judt, Reddy, and Scott correctly insist that all social identities, including class identities, are culturally constructed, they theoretically downplay the way in which these constructions are grounded in material interests, economic relations, and institutional dynamics. These scholars too readily abandon class analysis by regarding class relations and material conditions as irrelevant to an explanation of political change. They assume the relationship between material conditions and political forces to be purely conjunctural rather than systematically structured. This abandonment of class analysis makes it impossible to explain local political differences in a context of similar national political cultures and discourses. My research on local political life in mid-nineteenth-century France reveals that relations of production make a substantial difference to political action, with the intensity of class divisions and the vigor of class-based collective action varying systematically from place to place and over time.

A Non-Reductionist Class Analysis

A nonreductionist class analysis of politics acknowledges that there are always multiple causes at work. Class relations typically produce politically variable outcomes due to: (1) the complexity of class relations; (2) the different interpretations of interests that can be attributed to particular class positions; (3) the role of nonclass factors, including shifting political opportunity structures; and (4) the importance of contingency, that is, of temporally and spatially specific events.

The complexity of class relations has at least four dimensions. First, such structural positions, understood in terms of social relations of production, often define contradictory class interests.[13] For example, the class interests of nineteenth-century master artisans in small workshops were contradictory. Their positions within production, as employers, made them intent on resisting the demands of their workers. As producers who engaged in manual labor alongside their apprentices and journeymen, however, they had an interest in resisting the innovations of capitalist merchants and manufacturers whose activities threatened the demise of their small workshops. Second, the material interests attached to structurally defined class positions are often complex, with such interests rarely structured one-dimensionally. Any given group of workers, for example, has heterogeneous material interests based on their social relationship to the means of production—for example, short-run and long-term, individualistic and collective. Third, occupancy of class positions, and hence commitment to the interests they define, can vary temporally depending on the extent of mobility between positions. Workers experiencing routine mobility out of the working class to the petty bourgeoisie are less likely to develop strong commitments to interests defined by occupancy of working-class positions than workers with little opportunity for such mobility. Fourth, workers' families are often class-heterogeneous, containing both workers and household members whose incomes are not derived from wage labor.[14] In nineteenth-century France, the persistence of a household economy founded on multiple sources of income meant that worker households living on industrial wages alone were a minority.[15]

The interests that can be attributed to one's position as a worker are subject to multiple possible interpretations, in part because of the complexity of class relations. Workers have an "objective" interest in not being

exploited by capitalists just as women have an interest in not being dominated by men, but the perception of these interests and their translation into
political objectives and collective political action is neither spontaneous
nor unproblematic. For example, Rouen's textile factory workers faced the
choice, in June 1869, of voting for three candidates for higher office, each
of whom appealed to their interests as workers in different ways. The
wealthy textile industrialist Thomas-Auguste Pouyer-Quertier succeeded
in convincing many workers that the fundamental interests of workers and
capitalists were identical; they both benefited from industrial growth, made
possible by protectionist policies that would allow French textiles to compete with the products of British industry. Pouyer-Quertier appealed to
workers by arguing that the regime's tariff policies forced employers to
reduce workers' wages in order to remain competitive. His liberal republican opponent, the lawyer Louis-Philippe Desseaux, persuaded many workers that their interests as workers could best be pursued by electing liberal
representatives who were sympathetic to their plight but would not radically alter the existing system of production. Desseaux appealed to workers
by criticizing high taxes and unemployment within the textile industry. He
emphasized themes of liberty and order, rather than equality, praising
Rouen's workers for enduring the economic crisis "with an admirable resignation." "Today there is no longer any possible antagonism between
workers and the bourgeoisie," proclaimed Desseaux, "because these out-
of-date classifications have been forever erased under the rule of universal
suffrage."[16] Fewer workers voted for the socialist candidate Émile Aubry,
the local leader of Rouen's branch of the First International. Aubry attributed workers' problems to the "tyranny of capital" and defined workers'
interests as inherently irreconcilable with those of industrialists like
Pouyer-Quertier. "We are work and production!" declared one of his 1869
electoral tracts. "They are capital and non-production! Our interests are
diametrically opposed."[17]

People typically embrace multiple social identities, for example, as
worker, Republican, Catholic, French, and male. The interests they perceive as associated with their identities are not static and their interpretations of these interests are linked to occupancy of structural positions
within and outside of production. Workers may perceive and pursue interests such as higher wages or decent working conditions, which are derived
in a relatively straightforward manner from their position in production.
However, they also have other identities, for example, as parents and as
local residents.[18] These imply interests, such as the maintenance of families
and communities, that cannot be understood simply in economic terms.
Such interests, which are also subject to multiple interpretations, are actively contested; they cannot simply be imputed to actors as members of
social categories.[19]

The translation of class interests, based on one's position as a landowner, shopkeeper, worker, or capitalist, into subjective political dispositions and collective political action depends on a political process in which institutions, such as political parties, and ideologies, like republicanism, play a key role. These institutions and ideologies are not independent of material conditions and class forces, nor are they capable of simply creating interests out of discourses, unconstrained by material realities. Structural positions within production (i.e., class positions) define a constellation of interests that can serve as a potential basis for collective political action. Such action depends on the building of political organizations and creation of identities that are not simple reflections of objective positions in class structures or of the interests that can be imputed to such positions.[20] Definitions of class identities and interests are typically contested in a political arena with rules that constitute opportunities and constraints and with multiple possible enemies and allies. This means that class factors alone never fully determine just how such interests will be defined in political programs and coalitions or how politically salient class-based interests (rather than nonclass interests rooted in racial, ethnic, or gender stratification) will become.

Our inability to deduce political preferences and actions from relations of production alone is a mystery only if we view politics as emanating from individual interests established by relations of production. Once we see that political behavior is a matter of relations between interests and opportunities, the mystery disappears.[21] The institutional dimensions of politics depend to an important degree on economically grounded interests, but at the point of choice and action they also constrain the operation of class-based interests. For example, if only a limited number of political parties exist, none of which are led by workers, workers must choose among a set of alternatives that may not effectively represent their interests. Some workers may respond to this situation by choosing the least bad alternative. Others may take on the daunting task of creating a new alternative while many may simply complain but not act collectively. Since political opportunity structures depend in part on local conditions, we have no reason to expect that all metalworkers, for example, will make the same political choices at a national level. The diversity of working-class voting behavior at the national level does not provide evidence against the relevance of class analysis, as some historians have argued.[22] It does highlight the need to be attentive to both interests and opportunities in our efforts to explain political behavior.

Recognition of the institutional and cultural determinants of political behavior need not lead to an assertion of the autonomy of politics or to an abandonment of class analysis. One can reject a class reductionist understanding of politics yet still acknowledge the centrality of class relations in shaping political behavior. Even when politics are manifestly organized around nonclass divisions, such as ethnic divisions in Serbia and Bosnia or religious divisions in Northern Ireland, class relations still shape political behavior. If the class structures of these communities were radically different, then the political conflicts within them would also be different. In short, class relations shape political behavior, but there is considerable variation in the degree to which, and the way in which, they do so.

Contingency also helps to account for the varied importance of class relations for particular political outcomes. The relevance of class analysis for any given explanation depends on the level of abstraction at which one describes the phenomenon to be be explained. At a relatively high level of abstraction, contingent events do not loom very large. At a more fine-grained level of abstraction, outcomes become highly contingent. For example, capitalist development may explain the downfall of Absolutist monarchs in Western Europe, in the sense that there is no set of plausible contingencies which would have allowed absolutism to coexist indefinitely with sustained capitalist development. But capitalist development cannot explain the distinctive types of institutions which displaced Absolutist states in different countries or the specific events which precipitated their downfall.

Historical sociologists are less interested in fully accounting for all of the details of an outcome than in identifying which factors make it likely. Their explanations refer to causes that increase the probability of certain things happening. For example, when we claim that the presence of handicraft and household artisans threatened by the development of early industrial capitalism was a significant cause of the French urban revolutions of 1870–71, we mean that the presence of such groups in a city increased the probability of revolutionary upheaval, not that it completely explains these outcomes.[23] Other factors, including contingent causes such as defeats in particular battles of a war or miscalculations by prominent leaders, may have played an important role. Explaining the outbreak of revolution in a given city means identifying the causal factors which made this outcome likely, not identifying every factor that contributed to the proclamation of a revolutionary commune at a particular time on a given date.

The central argument of this book is that the outbreak and defeat of revolutionary communes in certain French cities in 1870–71 was a product of prior local histories of Republican party formation. These histories varied considerably, due to the intersection of a changing national political opportunity structure with divergent local patterns of industrialization and class formation. Local patterns of capitalist industrialization produced cities with very different class structures, paths of proletarianization, and divisions among workers. These differences were highly consequential for the creation of class identities and for political developments in each city.

They decisively shaped the struggle among liberals, radicals, and socialists for control of local Republican parties, offering each group varied opportunities and obstacles for mobilizing popular support. The triumph of alternative liberal, radical, and socialist visions of the republic prior to 1870 set the stage for different local responses to the events of 1870–71, providing, or failing to provide, Republicans with the institutional leverage that made possible a revolutionary seizure of municipal power.

THE REPUBLICAN PARTY AND THE WORKING CLASS

Once one recognizes the problematic character of creating shared political identities rooted in similar structural positions and of organizing collective political action in pursuit of interests defined by such positions, the organizational underpinnings of the diffusion of interpretations and ideologies becomes a central focus of historical research. This means paying attention to the ways in which political identities are constituted in a structured process of conflict that cuts across class lines. Understanding this process requires analysis of the organization of institutional arenas, the strategies and choices of political actors, and the cross-class alliances that characterize collective political action. It also requires analysis of the nature of the ideologies underpinning such alliances and the concrete historical conjunctures within which collective political action takes place. These concerns inform this study of mid-nineteenth-century French republicanism. My research explores how changes in local class relations resulting from early capitalist industrialization shaped the strategies of republican leaders and the alliances they forged; how changing forms of the state transformed opportunities and costs for collective political action; how the institutionalization of political parties altered the nature of contention for state power; and how the ideology and practice of republicanism shaped working-class formation and the character of local politics.

In mid-nineteenth-century France, the process of working-class formation was closely tied to the institutional transformation of the political arena wrought by the birth of political parties. Whether the term "party" accurately describes the mid-nineteenth-century organizations that emerged to contest elections and mobilize supporters depends upon how one defines party. The term has been used by historians to refer to a wide variety of different political institutions and divisions, which is why French historians do not agree on when the first political parties emerged in France.[24] Political scientists have offered a variety of definitions, most of which focus less on organizational structure, ideology, or ultimate goals than on functions (e.g., representation, expression). They typically include an electoral criterion and often some organizational criteria, such as the requirement that the group have a label, share some "general principles," or be cohesive enough to elect some of its leaders.[25] Mid-nineteenth-century republican organizations made competition for electoral office by candidates espousing republican principles a central element of their strategy of contention for power. According to these definitions, they qualify as a nascent, or proto-, political party, even though Republicans were a very heterogeneous political grouping that included liberals, radicals, and socialists.

Nineteenth-century French political activists frequently used the word "party," but the meaning of the term shifted during the middle decades of the nineteenth century. In 1848, the term still retained its perjorative association with divisive factions, thus prompting politicians like Louis Napoleon Bonaparte to portray themselves as "above" parties. Because the term referred to a group of people who shared similar political attitudes, the word was typically used with a wide variety of adjectives, such as "workers," "royalist," "conservative," "radical," "republican," and "revolutionary." By the late 1860s, the term was increasingly employed to refer to organizations rather than opinions. This shift, which reflected the early institutionalization of political parties, was accompanied by a narrowing of the range of adjectives used alongside the term.[26]

Much of this book is concerned with documenting the role that the mid-nineteenth-century French Republican party played in the early formation of the French working class, that is, in the process by which propertyless wage laborers developed social relationships that fostered a shared identity as workers and a capacity to act collectively on the basis of that identity. This emphasis is justified by historical evidence which suggests that the early Republican party constituted the key institutional terrain on which mid-nineteenth-century French class relations were actively contested and redefined. It is also consistent with developments in contemporary political theory, which have increasingly highlighted the institutional dimensions of the process of class formation. Giovanni Sartori refers to political parties as the "structural cement of class reality" and hypothesizes that "a thoroughgoing organizational network is a necessary condition of class consciousness and behavior, for the latter varies with, and follows the density of, organization."[27] In their study of Western European social democratic parties, Adam Przeworski and John Sprague identify political parties as central forces determining the saliency of different potential sources of political identity and voting behavior. They argue that the strategies of organizations and the struggles they organize are central determinants of the extent to which individuals experience their lives in terms of the identities and commitments of class.[28] Other scholars have questioned the power of organizations to create interests, and emphasized the constraints and opportunities imposed by class relations on the activities and strategies of political parties. Michael Burawoy argues that institutions like parties translate, rather than create, identities and shared meanings that are firmly rooted in workplace-based experiences. Party strategies, he argues, are not freely selected by autonomous party leaders seeking to maximize votes; they are contested and constructed in a context of shifting constraints and opportunities rooted in class structures. The lived experiences of workers, concludes Burawoy, set limits on the range of party appeals that can mobilize their support.[29]

A historical perspective on the role of political parties sheds light on this debate, suggesting a complex and varying relationship between political parties and working-class formation. The centrality of political parties in the creation of social identities, their ability to create identities independent of workplace relations, and whether they reinforce or undermine class identities varies over time and place. This variability is a product of differences in the timing of the emergence of political parties vis-à-vis trade unions, in the development of productive forces and accompanying declines in the length of the workday, in the growth of supra-local communication and transportation networks, in the relative stability of social identities, and in the timing of suffrage extension. In the nineteenth century, the ability of parties to shape identities was greater in countries like France, where the initial growth of national-level political parties incorporating workers preceded rather than followed the emergence of a national trade union movement. Whereas unions preceded and facilitated democratization in Great Britain, in France they did not become tolerated until twenty years after the institutionalization of universal male suffrage. But even in France, early parties did not create class identities independently of what went on at the workplace. The extent to which parties are able to create identities independently of workplace relations varies historically, with parties facing greater constraints in historical contexts, like nineteenth-century France, where most workers spent the vast majority of their waking hours—often fourteen or more hours each day—at their workplaces. Dramatic changes in transportation and communication facilities also create historical variability in the extent to which parties can shape the process of identity formation independent of what goes on at the workplace. Periods of rapid social and political change, like the mid-nineteenth century, are more likely to provide institutions like parties with opportunities to shape new identities than are periods of relative stability.[30] During periods of rapid social change, political struggles are more likely to encompass both competing claims for scarce resources and alternative definitions of identities and interests.

Whether political parties reinforce or undermine class, rather than ethnic, regional, or other identities, also varies across time and place. A key determinant is the timing of working-class formation vis-à-vis popular struggles for voting rights. In the United States, where the extension of the suffrage to the working class was relatively early, nineteenth-century political parties reinforced ethnic and regional rather than class identities. The situation was very different in European countries like France, where the persistence of class barriers to voting rights made the abolition of class privileges and appeals to class identities and antagonisms central to the mobilizing strategies of early political parties. In the case of France, the mid-nineteenth-century Republican party played a decisive role in working-class formation by fostering workers' capacities for collective action and by encouraging certain forms of political participation.

The emergence of mass political parties in mid-nineteenth-century France did not represent the triumph of representative and defeat of participatory forms of democracy. Given the nonbureaucratic and localized character of the early Republican party and the relatively primitive state of transportation and communication, Republican party formation in France initially stimulated participatory politics and reinforced definitions of democracy centered around popular participation. The triumph among Republicans of representative rather than participatory forms of democracy was not an inevitable result of electoral politics. It was a product of decades of struggle among French Republicans over the legitimacy of revolutionary action and the proper relationship between elected officials and their constituents. These were understood differently by liberal, radical, and socialist Republicans, who held very different views of democracy.

LIBERALISM AND DEMOCRACY IN NINETEENTH-CENTURY FRANCE

The couplet liberal democracy has assumed a central place in our current political vocabulary, yet it conceals a highly problematic relationship, readily revealed by the changing historical connections between liberalism and democracy. The creation of liberal state institutions and the establishment of democratic reforms, like universal suffrage, were distinctive achievements that followed different trajectories and mobilized support from different social groups.[31] Liberalism and democracy were at odds in France and elsewhere during the early decades of the nineteenth century. Most French liberals advocated a free market, the rule of law, a multiparty system, parliamentary control over the executive branch of government, and civil liberties. But they feared democracy as the "tyranny of the majority" and opposed universal male suffrage as a threat to property rights and public order. Most early French democrats opposed economic liberalism because they feared that market forces freed from government controls would create massive socioeconomic inequalities that would undermine democracy. After 1830, liberalism became closely associated with an undemocratic constitutional monarchy in France, thereby temporarily dissociating liberal and democratic traditions. After the extension of universal male suffrage in 1848, liberals remained wary of the consequences of giving the vote to propertyless workers, especially after republican socialists made impressive gains in the elections of 1849 and 1850. For example, Saint-Étienne's liberal republican newspaper *L'Avenir républicain* supported legislation to restrict the suffrage in May of 1850. "In the eyes of loyal and sincere Republicans," proclaimed its editors, "universal suffrage as it is now practiced in France dishonors the Republic and is therefore in need of legal reform. . . . Universal suffrage as it is organized promotes anarchy and communism. . . ."[32]

By mobilizing political participation, institutionalizing political opposition, and facilitating the accountability of governing officials, early French Republicans helped lay the foundations for democracy. Yet Republicans remained bitterly divided over the meaning of democracy. They advocated different understandings of political representation and, consequently, differed over whether the mobilization of popular support should remain confined within the boundaries of the electoral arena. Liberal Republicans regarded elected representatives as an enlightened elite entrusted with political power, who should be granted considerable discretion to interpret the best interests of the nation. In their view, the revolutionary tradition constituted a threat to democratic government. Radical and socialist Republicans considered elected representatives as mandated officials who were obliged to carry out the expressed wishes of their constituents. They regarded the failure of elected officials to obey their mandates as justifying recourse to revolutionary action.

The couplet liberal democracy was a historical creation, the product of a long conflict over the meaning of both liberalism and democracy. The union of liberalism and democracy in France emerged only after liberals became reconciled to universal male suffrage and after a representative rather than participatory vision of democracy came to dominate republicanism. This reconciliation of liberalism and democracy took place in a distinctive political context: a struggle for the establishment of a republic which brought together liberals, radicals, and socialists in an alliance that remained tense and precarious throughout the mid-nineteenth century. An understanding of this reconciliation requires an analysis of the institutional terrain on which alliances were forged and contrasting visions of republican government were fought out, that is, of the internal conflicts of the early French Republican party.

WHOSE REPUBLIC?

In most accounts of nineteenth-century French political history, conflicts among Republicans are overshadowed by the struggle against royalists to establish a republican form of government. Since the attempt to establish a republic was a precarious undertaking, given persisting staunch opposition from royalist and clerical forces, early historians of French Republican party formation—most of whom were committed Republicans like Georges Weill and I. Tchernoff—emphasized unity in the face of monarchists rather than division and disunity among Republicans. Contemporaries were well aware of the bitter divisions among those identified as belonging to the same party. "There are so many parties in France, and so many divisions within parties," wrote Jules Simon in 1868, "that there is no longer a single word in our political language that is perfectly clear."[33] A portrait of republicanism as a movement unified by the royalist threat fails to adequately explain the bloody political confrontations of 1848 and 1871, which did not simply pit Royalists against Republicans. During the June days of 1848 and the revolutionary communes of 1870–71, self-proclaimed Republicans killed one another with a ferocity that shocked many observers. These violent events can be understood only in the context of an ongoing struggle among Republicans over different visions of the republic.

Mid-nineteenth-century French politics are filled with dramatic and violent events in the streets and on the barricades. These overshadowed the less visible day-to-day struggles that took place among Republicans in localities throughout France to control organizations, newspapers, and candidate selection processes. The lack of attention by historians to these conflicts among Republicans is due to a variety of factors, including the tendency of orthodox Marxists to dismiss early mass parties as "bourgeois" in character, the interests of party leaders and government officials, and the organization of French archives. The attachment of class labels to particular parties or ideologies has led more orthodox Marxist historians to ignore the complex and contradictory character of class forces embodied by such institutions and the intense class conflicts contained within them. Given their interest in attracting voters, Republican party leaders were naturally quite anxious to present as unified an image as possible and to play down or render invisible to the general public internal conflicts that might hinder their electoral prospects. The tendency of government officials to discredit political opponents by uniformly labeling diverse tendencies as "red" has also inhibited recognition of diversity among Republicans. The relative paucity of archival documents on the subject, and the way in which they are catalogued, has undoubtedly contributed to the neglect. The relevant documents are scattered across the country in various local, departmental, and national libraries and archives, and are typically cataloged according to administrative origins rather than content.

Although they lack the drama and violence of the barricades, struggles among liberal, radical, and socialist Republicans to control newspapers, organizations, and processes of candidate selection are the focus of attention in this book. In the short run, the outcomes of these struggles shaped local political conflicts and agendas, including the likelihood that class-based grievances would become salient political issues and that alternatives to existing distributions of wealth and power would become issues on the political agenda. In the long run, these conflicts decisively shaped the structure of the French political arena for many future generations. By institutionalizing certain victories and defeats, they set the basic parameters within which future political action took place. The structural legacies of political conflicts among mid-nineteenth-century Republicans, including the liberal-democratic institutions and normative patterns defined by the French Constitution of 1875, are still with us today.[34] The political struggles among Republicans of this period produced an enduring republican form of the state and distinctive visions and practices of democracy that continue to shape contemporary French political life.

DEMOCRATIZATION AND CAPITALIST INDUSTRIALIZATION

The social origins of different forms of the state—from authoritarian dictatorships to democratic governments—have always been a central concern of political sociologists. Barrington Moore, Jr.'s contemporary classic, *Social Origins of Dictatorship and Democracy*, explains those origins in terms of antagonisms and coalitions among social classes. Moore defines democracy in terms of the presence of parliamentary institutions that protect citizens against arbitrary rulers and rules and ensure some degree of legislative control over the decisions of government.[35] Democratic institutions, argues Moore, were a product of bourgeois revolutions, like the French Revolution, that destroyed social obstacles to democratic development by violently attacking the power of the traditional landed aristocracy and preventing the emergence and triumph of an antidemocratic class coalition.[36] Moore's emphasis on the triumph of parliamentary institutions and legal standards leads him to focus on the period prior to the nineteenth century and remain silent about the role of the working class in the creation of democratic institutions.

Democratization entailed more than the creation of parliamentary institutions and the establishment of juridical equality. It also involved the subsequent extension of universal suffrage and the right to association, which made possible the creation of competitive mass political parties, a product of the nineteenth and twentieth centuries. Universal suffrage and mass political parties make possible, but not inevitable, public control over elected representatives, thus providing meaningful democratic content to representative institutions by ensuring popular input into public policies. Two important consequences follow from this expansion of the definition of democratization. First, nineteenth-century industrialization and the emergent working class must loom larger in an analysis of the social origins of democracy. Second, the struggle for suffrage reform, and the role played by early mass parties in this struggle, become central to an analysis of the process of democratization.

The historical record does not reveal any universal association between industrial capitalism and the creation of democratic institutions. The process of capitalist industrialization in nineteenth-century France, for example, was accompanied by diverse forms of political rule, ranging from a constitutional monarchy to an imperial regime to a democratic republic. Despite this variability, a number of quantitative cross-national studies have documented a strong correlation between the emergence of democratic regimes and capitalist industrialization.[37] How can we account for this relationship? Seymour Martin Lipset emphasizes the way in which industrialization creates a growing educated and literate middle class, which is by nature moderate rather than extremist in its politics, and which constitutes a key social force in the initial creation of democratic institutions. Lipset acknowledges the role of the working class in the process of democratization, but only in the latter stages of industrialization, after economic expansion and increased education allows "those in the lower strata to develop longer time perspectives and more complex and gradualist views of politics."[38] Historical studies of suffrage extension in Western Europe suggest a much more central role for the working class in early transitions to democracy than Lipset acknowledges. Only in the British case, argues John Stephens, did middle-class-based (and largely upper-class led) parties extend effective suffrage to substantial sections of the working class. Although Stephens notes some cases of early suffrage extension in which the working class played little or no role, and cases in which workers were part of a broader alliance, he concludes that "none of the other social classes were as consistently prodemocratic, both across countries and through time, as the working class."[39]

Goran Therborn's analysis emphasizes the way in which industrialization stimulated working-class organization, leading to the creation of parties and unions that constituted key social forces in favor of democratization. While contending that "the labor movement was the only consistent democratic force on the arena," Therborn acknowledges that "it was nowhere strong enough to achieve bourgeois democracy on its own, without the aid of victorious foreign armies, domestic allies more powerful than itself, or splits in the ranks of the enemy."[40] He acknowledges the diverse class forces that shaped the process of democratization, but focuses on the later phase in the process, after workers had created national parties and unions. His analysis sheds little light upon the earlier achievement of universal male suffrage, which occurred in France in 1848, prior to the development of a national labor movement or a national workers' party. To understand the role of workers in this early struggle for suffrage extension, we need to explore not just the growth of working-class parties and unions with industrialization, but the cross-class institutional terrain on which democratic class alliances were initially created and the way in which early political parties committed to democracy mobilized workers and members of other social classes into the struggle for suffrage reform.

Among scholars who acknowledge the centrality of the working class to early European struggles for democracy and suffrage rights, there is considerable disagreement about the motivations that led workers to demand access to the ballot box and a voice in parliamentary politics. Reinhard Bendix explains working-class participation in the struggle for universal male suffrage in nineteenth-century Europe in terms of status conflict and political rather than economic alienation. In his account, the struggle for democratic institutions by the European working class "expressed above all an experience of political alienation, that is, a sense of not having a recognized position in the civic community, or of not having a civic community in which to participate." The nineteenth-century working class, Bendix argues, was not struggling to create a new social order but was merely protesting against second-class citizenship, demanding the right of participation on terms of equality in the political community of the nation.[41] Bendix's argument leads us to expect early republican efforts to mobilize workers in support of the suffrage to have addressed more strongly workers' desire to become part of the national political community than their socioeconomic grievances stemming from the inequalities produced by early capitalist industrialization. Whereas Marxist accounts suggest that the ability of Republicans to link the struggle for suffrage reforms to workers' economic interests should have been more decisive, Bendix's analysis implies that nationalist appeals should have played a more central role in the mobilization of workers into the ranks of the movement for suffrage reform.

The following research on the ideology and rhetoric of the political organizations that mobilized workers into the nineteenth-century French struggle for suffrage reform suggests a central role for socioeconomic grievances in mobilizing workers behind the cause of suffrage reform. Egalitarian themes and socioeconomic grievances, not just civic aspirations, motivated mid-nineteenth-century French workers to demand suffrage rights. This is evident in the ideology and mobilizing strategies of the early Republican party. French workers' demand for suffrage rights was motivated by the vision of a social republic that would empower workers and remedy their economic grievances, not simply provide them with a sense of political community. Many workers embraced the ballot box after initially rejecting republicanism in favor of the antiparliamentary alternative offered by Icarian communists. This suggests an initial ambivalence about parliamentarism on the part of many workers, rather than integrative national aspirations.

The early struggle for suffrage reform in France was led by a nascent political party that embodied contradictory class interests and competing ideological currents. This party included liberal Republicans, who favored reducing property restrictions on suffrage rights in order to enfranchise most professionals, shopkeepers, and small producers but not propertyless workers, as well as radical and socialist Republicans who advocated universal male suffrage. Republicans competed for the political allegiances of workers, however, with other organizations, including those of "utopian" communists who questioned the utility of the suffrage and regarded the ballot box as a diversion. A key question, largely ignored in the existing literature, much of which assumes that workers were naturally drawn to the struggle for universal suffrage because of their class position, is how workers came to be convinced that suffrage really mattered. Workers are no more naturally disposed toward parliamentary democracy than the bourgeoisie is towards liberalism.[42] Laboring in a handicraft workshop or an early factory does not naturally dispose workers to seek remedies for their grievances via electoral politics. Why and how workers came to see their fate as closely tied to political parties and the ballot box is an important but neglected dimension of the story of democratization.

The consequences of the initial inauguration of universal male suffrage are also an important part of the history of democratization in France. The revolution of February 1848 was the unanticipated outcome of Parisian Republicans' refusal to obey a government ban on a planned banquet for suffrage reform. After National Guardsmen fraternized with troops, who then refused to fire on demonstrators, the orleanist regime suddenly collapsed. Working-class pressure from the streets of Paris forced liberal republican leaders, who seized state power, to reluctantly concede universal male suffrage and grant several cabinet positions to radicals and socialists. Previous restrictions on assembly, association, and the press were immediately removed by republican officials, who espoused the theme of liberty. What were the consequences of this sudden democratization and development of parliamentary politics?

The pluralist perspective on state and society regards the extension of suffrage rights as a key element in the process of democratization and an important victory for the working class. According to this view, suffrage rights give workers greater influence over government, allowing them to express their preferences and demands in elections and to participate, as an interest group, in the bargaining and negotiation that characterizes party politics and legislative activity. Suffrage rights are highly functional for the social system. By allowing workers to influence the decisions of govern-

ment officials and shape the formation of public policy, they serve an integrative function, fostering the spread of democratic values. Elite theorists
of politics take a less sanguine view of the consequences of popular political participation. In their view, the political incorporation of workers fails
to significantly alter the concentration of power in the hands of a small but
powerful group of elite decisionmakers. The political participation made
possible by suffrage rights serves a largely symbolic function, providing an
illusion of power in a system in which key decisions remain the prerogative
of an entrenched bureaucratic oligarchy.[43]

Marxist analyses of the consequences of democratization typically share
the negative assessment of elite theorists. They generally view electoral
and representative institutions as instruments that legitimate the status quo.
Marxists have portrayed parliamentary parties as vehicles of working-class
integration that mystify the nature of bourgeois class domination and legitimate economic inequalities, displace class conflict from the fundamental
to the more immediate interests of a class, individualize political action in
the isolated act of voting by transforming workers into citizens, and force
the working class to undermine its cohesion as a class by searching for
electoral allies and majorities.[44] Electoral parties, and more generally parliamentary institutions, function to stabilize and reproduce the capitalist
system, in large part by distorting the interests, and undermining the capacities, of workers.

These three perspectives on democratic politics share a functionalist
view of voting and parliamentary politics that fails to recognize that electoral politics may have differing, sometimes contradictory, consequences
depending on historical contexts. A comparative analysis of the consequences of suffrage expansion and the growth of mass electoral politics
should help us identify which features of a given historical context determine the consequences of working-class electoral participation. What are
the conditions under which electoral parties foster the salience of class
identities and heighten the ability of workers to act collectively to pursue
their shared interests? Under what conditions do they inhibit the development of class identities and capacities? Karl Marx's own political analyses
emphasized the form of the state within which electoral parties operated,
especially whether state apparatuses, such as the executive and military, are
subject to parliamentary control.[45] But Marx's analyses paid insufficient
attention to the role of mass political parties and electoral competition in
mediating the consequences of parliamentary politics.

In exploring the consequences of democratization for class formation at
the local level, we need to examine the distinctive character of the political
parties whose leaders wielded state power and organized the electoral
arena. In the case of mid-nineteenth-century France, this means examining
how republican leaders who seized power in 1848 altered local political

opportunity structures and how these changes affected the organizational capacities and collective political actions of workers and the saliency of class-based political issues. It also means analyzing how the strategies pursued, and alliances forged, by different local Republican parties, shaped the willingness of workers to embrace electoral politics or take to the barricades.

STUDYING LOCAL POLITICS IN NINETEENTH-CENTURY FRANCE

Students of comparative politics often regard France, which experienced decades of Napoleonic rule at the beginning and middle of the nineteenth century, as an example of a highly centralized polity. By the mid-nineteenth century, the process of nation-state formation meant greater administrative, linguistic, and political uniformity across French cities. Paris played a decisive role in the development of nineteenth-century French political life. Key shifts in political opportunity structures, which were highly consequential for local politics, originated in Paris with the revolutions of 1830, 1848, and 1870. Central state officials repeatedly intervened in local politics, redrawing electoral boundaries, dissolving city councils, and organizing the arrest of political dissidents. But the nationalization and centralization of politics during the course of the nineteenth century was a relatively slow, uneven, and conflictual process.

In the absence of well-developed national parties and mass communications, mid-nineteenth-century French politics remained rooted in the daily routines of neighborhoods and workplaces. It was at the local level, where politics involved face-to-face interactions and personal connections, that ordinary people first ventured into public life and gradually accumulated political experiences. Although national electoral organizations existed prior to the extension of universal male suffrage in 1848, the relatively small number of eligible voters in any given electoral district, typically less than one thousand, meant that political campaigning remained highly localized.[46] But local politics existed above and beyond the very small group of official voters who paid at least two hundred francs a year in property taxes, often mobilizing propertyless workers around issues such as tax and suffrage laws, that were of national significance. Local parties and governments, which were smaller in scale and less remote than central state institutions, were generally more accessible to ordinary people and more responsive to their demands. Local institutions were also less responsive to pressures emanating from national dominant class actors, the exigencies of international relations, and the interests of central state managers. Although local political institutions remained fiscally dependent on higher levels of government, they were more than functional administrative appendages of the central government. Local states responded to national policies in very different ways, sometimes challenging central state authority.

Mid-nineteenth-century French local politics, though often preoccupied with matters such as public works projects, clerical control of educational institutions, and the distribution of relief to the poor, did not remain confined to municipal issues. French Republicans often mobilized supporters around issues of local economic development, such as the effect of tariff and railway policies on their city's economy, but republicanism was an international ideology. Republicans saw themselves as defenders of local interests as well as enemies of monarchies and aristocracies around the world. During the July Monarchy, for example, Republicans in Toulouse mobilized opposition to central state power around the issue of municipal liberties. They also repeatedly took to the streets to demonstrate in support of the Polish struggle for national independence.

Large-scale and long-term processes, such as industrialization, proletarianization, democratization, and party formation, are spatially imprinted, given their uneven development and the reactions of people in different localities to their uneven development. The study of localities enables researchers to explore the geographically specific and context-dependent features of general processes that span localities in a manner attentive to the concrete settings of everyday life that shape political identities and political consciousness. "To insist upon the continuing importance of place," writes John Agnew, "is not to deny that processes beyond the locality have become important determinants of what happens in places. But it is still in places that lives are lived, economic and symbolic interests are defined, information from local and extralocal sources is interpreted and takes on meaning, and political discussions are carried out . . . information and social cues are meaningful only when activated in everyday routine social interaction. For most people, this is still defined by the locality."[47]

Although France remained a predominantly rural society throughout the nineteenth century, this book is concerned with urban rather than rural politics. Cities were focal points for the development of early industrial capitalism and for the emergence and development of early French republicanism and socialism. It was in cities that innovative political ideas and practices thrived, among concentrated populations of workers threatened by early capitalist industrialization. In contrast to their rural counterparts, urban workers were less dependent on patronage ties, which continued to connect wealthy notables to large rural political clienteles. Although republicanism had rural as well as urban roots, French republicanism remained a predominantly urban phenomenon prior to 1848. It was in cities that Republicans won their earliest electoral victories. Republicans typically established a loyal electoral base at the local level in the more class homogeneous working-class neighborhoods of large cities. When electoral competition moved beyond the locality to regional or national levels of representation, the weight of rural votes often meant poorer results for Republicans and Socialists.

Republican leaders gained their political apprenticeship and developed their initial understandings of political opportunities and constraints at the local level. As Sanford Elwitt clearly documents, the men who dominated French political life in the decades of the 1870s and 1880s and laid the foundations for a republican order received their political training and apprenticeship in local provincial politics during the 1860s.[48] It was at the local level that they initially elaborated the ideology and constructed the political alliances that brought them to power and led to the triumph of a liberal-democratic republic. It was also at the local level that Republicans most actively contested competing visions of the republic. Control over urban-based institutions, including newspapers and electoral committees, became the object of bitter contention among Republicans at the local level. This is where class antagonisms sometimes exploded into violent conflicts and where the temporary triumphs and defeats of different visions of the republic encouraged political experimentation and creativity.

METHODOLOGY: COMPARISONS, HISTORICAL CASE STUDIES, AND NARRATIVES

Political sociologists have often compared countries with relatively similar paths of economic development but different patterns of working-class electoral incorporation. This approach has provided the familiar argument that the difference between working-class politics in the United States and Western Europe can be explained largely in terms of the earlier incorporation of American workers into mass political parties and the electoral arena. This study takes a different approach by comparing three mid-nineteenth-century French cities—Toulouse, Saint-Étienne, and Rouen—that had very different paths of economic development but experienced suffrage extension at the same time and shared the same national political culture and national political institutions. These similarities enhance comparability and allow us to avoid some of the difficult methodological problems that plague international comparisons.[49]

Republican activists at Toulouse, Saint-Étienne, and Rouen shared a common political culture, language, and institutional context. Certain symbols, meanings, rituals, and repertoires of collective action provided them with a common cultural legacy, rooted in the heritage of the French Revolution.[50] These three cities were similar in that they all witnessed a number of important economic and political changes during the mid-nineteenth century, including the emergence of new forms of industrial production, growing ties to an international world market, the development of class solidarities among urban workers, the initial emergence of mass-based political parties, and the appearance and spread of new political ideologies such as socialism. All three cities developed local Republican party organizations that shared the same dominant goal—the establishment of a republican form of the state. These local parties operated within a similar institutional context in terms of the system of electoral representation, the number and identity of competing parties, and the role of elections versus administrative appointments. The same national laws governed the right to vote, as well as rights of assembly, association, and a free press, in each city. All three local Republican parties were characterized by a decentralized, nonbureaucratic structure, a predominantly local orientation, limited patronage resources, and close ties to informal centers of popular sociability.

The selection for comparison of cities and time periods relatively close in time and space was motivated in part by the need to develop historically grounded theory. By comparing three cities during the same time period, rather than, for example, social revolutions separated by centuries, we are assured a certain equivalence among cases in terms of world historical time. Proximity in time and space makes these cases more equivalent and suggests the possibility of a "quasi-experimental" research design. But this proximity undermines independence, the second requirement of an inductive experimental design.[51] Experimental strategies based on inductive logic assume an independence of cases, yet these three cases were not independent of one another. The repression of the April 1848 insurrection in Rouen, for example, influenced what subsequently happened in other cities in France. This does not imply the futility of rigorous comparison, but suggests a strategy of comparison focusing on sequences of events, which may reveal the unfolding of similar, or analogous, causal processes among cases that are not independent of one another.

Despite important similarities among my three cases, local Republican party formation at Toulouse, Saint-Étienne, and Rouen differed substantially. At the local level, struggles among liberals, radicals, and socialists produced Republican parties that campaigned on different issues, embraced distinctive alliances, and crafted different ties to their city's working class. My comparative strategy is designed to illuminate the sources of these differences and to explore their connection to processes of capitalist industrialization and working-class formation. The cities of Toulouse, Saint-Étienne, and Rouen were selected for comparison because they differed in terms of the timing of the integration of their local industries into national and international markets, the growth and centralization of productive units, and the relative importance of handicraft, household, and factory production. The southwestern city of Toulouse, an important regional administrative and commercial capital, remained a center of handicraft production during the first two-thirds of the nineteenth century and witnessed the relatively late and slow development of industrial capitalism. It never became an important center of mechanized factories. The eastern city of Saint-Étienne became a center of household ribbon production during the eighteenth century, and an important center of the steel and mining industry during the mid-nineteenth century. Unlike Toulouse and Rouen, which were both old medieval cities, Saint-Étienne was a new nineteenth-century city—one of the few in France. It was the only one of the twenty-five largest cities in France in 1851 that had not been a chartered city and a major center of commerce, administration, and handicraft production during the Old Regime. The northern industrial city of Rouen witnessed a relatively early and rapid growth of mechanized cotton textile factories, that employed large numbers of unskilled and semiskilled laborers.

The comparison is designed to demonstrate the ways in which specific patterns of industrialization transformed different dimensions of class relations, assess the impact of these transformations on the development of local Republican parties, and see whether different trajectories of Republican party formation can help to explain different patterns of working-class formation and different local political outcomes, in particular, the revolutionary communes of 1870–71. The comparison should allow us to answer a number of questions about how class relations shaped local Republican party formation. Were the outcomes of struggles for control of local parties among liberals, radicals, and socialists largely a product of each city's class structure, of the nature of working-class struggles, or of the character of divisions within the working-class and bourgeoisie? Did socialists play a larger role in republican politics in cities where the working-class was the largest, grew the fastest, or was the most economically militant? How did the incorporation of different groups of working-class and bourgeois activists in each city shape the local texture and success of republicanism? How did different local Republican parties, in turn, shape the process of working-class formation?

The preceding questions are addressed, in chapters 4–7, by presenting parallel narratives of the development of republicanism in Toulouse, Saint-Étienne, and Rouen during the middle decades of the nineteenth century. Each chapter documents the way in which tensions within republicanism were played out at the local level in three very different socioeconomic contexts. The focus of the narratives is on how nascent local Republican parties that incorporated contradictory class interests, competing ideologies, and many features of a social movement produced alternative party strategies, shifting political alliances, and different relationships between Republicans and urban workers. The narratives highlight the way in which local class conflicts and internal party struggles among liberals, radicals, and socialists intersected with national-level political events to help determine the initial consequences of democratization and its subsequent set-back and revival. Each story recounts the struggle to mobilize political support for a democratic republic from 1830 to 1848, the initial consequences of the establishment of republican government and universal male suffrage in early 1848, the impact of the victories and defeats of 1848–51 on ongoing class, ideological, and strategic divisions among Republicans, and the consequences of the political repression of the 1850s and subsequent liberalization of the 1860s for class and party formation.

Narratives with plots that culminate in logical outcomes constitute an important rhetoric for historians. Formal logical or mathematical proofs—often devoid of events and even of actors—play a more important role in sociological discourse than narratives of events. Many sociologists distrust narratives because of their ability to bury explanatory principles in engaging stories and their frequent ad hoc use of unexamined concepts.[52] Yet a stance in favor of overt rather than covert theoretical strategies, and the systematic rather than ad hoc use of concepts, need not lead to an abandonment of narratives.[53] Narratives allow us to apprehend the unfolding of social action over time in a manner sensitive to the order in which events occur. They make possible richer, more complete, explanations because they typically involve very concrete levels of abstraction, at which it becomes possible to see the operation of contingent effects more clearly. Narratives enable us to capture the meanings and intentions of social actors, which purely denotative scientific rhetorics cannot adequately convey.

The presentation of historical evidence in subsequent chapters takes the form of analytic narratives—that is, theoretically structured stories about coherent sequences of motivated actions. The narrative framework makes possible a more event-centered historical sociology, which treats events not simply as manifestations of large-scale processes but as key causal factors in trajectories of political change. These narratives are used to construct explanations based on systematic spatial and temporal comparisons, thereby integrating theory and history, logical and chronological analysis.

Mid-Nineteenth-Century French Republicanism: Organization, Ideology, and Opportunities

REPUBLICANISM AND THE FRENCH LEFT: THE ORIGINS OF AMBIVALENCE

The French Left has always maintained a certain ambivalence toward republican institutions. An acknowledgement of the importance of the civil liberties and citizenship rights acquired by the triumph of the republic has been mixed with a sense that republicanism has helped to co-opt fundamental challenges to the capitalist system. This ambivalence is evident in the pronouncements and practices of late nineteenth-century French socialist leaders, including Jean Jaurès, Jules Guesde, and Edouard Vaillant. These men offered shifting, often contradictory evaluations of the republic. They alternatively condemned it as a facade of bourgeois class rule and embraced it as the institutional terrain necessary for the ultimate triumph of socialism. They also adopted an ambivalent position toward the French revolutionary tradition, at times contending that the transition to socialism required a revolutionary rupture with established political institutions, but sometimes urging accommodation to the republican form of government.[1]

French socialists were much less ambivalent about republican institutions during the middle decades of the nineteenth century. Despite some notable dissenting voices, most socialists agreed that the republic provided an ideal context within which to struggle for socialism. Yet there was little consensus over the meaning of the republic. This was evident in bitter quarrels over the proper relationship between republicanism, liberalism, and socialism. Republicanism was reinterpreted and transformed in different ways during the course of the mid-nineteenth century, as liberals, radicals, and socialists fashioned alternative social and economic visions of the republic, using a shared political rhetoric derived from the French Revolution.[2] Decades of struggle among Republicans produced these alternative visions of the republic, which amalgamated elements of classical liberalism and early socialism in very different ways.

This chapter maps out the institutional and ideological context within which mid-nineteenth-century French republican politics took place. It documents the distinctive features of mid-nineteenth-century Republican party organization and the contradictory and shifting character of republican ideology, which blended elements of various discourses in different ways to create distinctive but evolving liberal, radical, and socialist visions of the republic. The first section provides a brief history of national republican organizations and then identifies three central features of mid-nineteenth-century republican organization: fraternalism; an ideological rather than patronage mobilization of supporters; and a bourgeois leadership with a predominantly working-class base. These features proved to be highly consequential for the ability of Republicans to mobilize popular support and for divisions within local parties. The second section analyzes the changing contribution of liberal and socialist discourses to the formation of republican ideology. It traces the emergence of a radical synthesis that laid enduring foundations for the establishment of a liberal-democratic republic during the 1870s and 1880s. The triumph of the radical vision, a creative synthesis of liberal and socialist ideas, produced institutions and practices that were the source of subsequent left-wing ambivalence about the republic. The final section documents the shifting national political opportunity structure facing French Republicans in terms of changes in suffrage rights, the relationship between executive and legislative power, and rights to association, assembly, free speech, and freedom of the press.

MID-NINETEENTH-CENTURY FRENCH REPUBLICANISM: NATIONAL ORGANIZATION

French republican efforts to create the organizational foundations of a national political party were evident as early as the 1830s. In November 1832, the liberal republican association *Aide-toi, le ciel t'aidera* selected candidates; published brochures; maintained correspondence with provincial republican newspapers; and organized committees in thirty-five departments, some of which were joined in regional federations. Radical Republicans also created a number of different political associations from 1830–34, including the predominantly working-class *Société des droits de l'homme*, which had a central committee in Paris that provided loose coordination for relatively independent regional branches in many departments.[3] These early efforts at party formation were soon destroyed by repressive legislation in 1834–35. In September 1837, with the formation in Paris of the *Comité central de l'opposition constitutionnelle*, Republicans renewed their efforts to create a national association. This organization encouraged the formation of over two hundred local electoral committees, coordinated local activities by relaying electoral news via letters and press dispatches, and provided legal expertise on the complexities of voter registration. It also persuaded the editors of over fifty local republican newspapers to send copies of their publications to Parisian headquarters.[4]

Despite efforts toward national coordination, which peaked during national electoral campaigns in 1837, 1839, 1842, and 1846 and then diminished, French Republicans did not create a political party in the modern sense of the term prior to 1848. Republicans actively competed for elected offices in all regions of France, but there was no national organization that selected candidates and enforced party discipline and adherence to a consistent political program. Prior to 1848, the national party was a loose collection of prominent local leaders of similar political persuasion. National party organization centered around the half-dozen or so prominent Republicans in the Chamber of Deputies and around those who gathered at the offices of the two national newspapers in Paris, the liberal *Le National* and radical *La Réforme*. "The role closest to that of the offices, committees, and headquarters of the twentieth-century political parties," writes Maurice Agulhon, "was played throughout the nineteenth century by the editorial offices of the newspapers. . . ."[5]

The repressive laws of the July Monarchy (1830–48) inhibited the development of a centralized national party organization. In 1833–34 the government sharply increased the prosecution of republican newspaper editors, who faced mounting fines. When Republicans then turned to leaflets and street criers to spread their message, the government responded by outlawing unlicensed street criers. Republican associations were banned in 1834 and in 1835 a strict press law was enacted as well as a bill outlawing even the use of the term republican. A poorly developed national system of transportation and communication also contributed to the party's decentralized and loosely coordinated character. The French Republican party remained an agglomeration of diverse organizations, dispersed over a wide area and only loosely linked by coordinating institutions like Parisian newspapers, traveling spokesmen, and elected parliamentary leaders who traveled to Paris when the legislature was in session.

After the revolution of 1848 instituted universal male suffrage, Republicans renewed their effort to create a national party organization capable of coordinating electoral activities across localities. The advent of universal male suffrage and relaxation of restrictions on association, assembly, and the press encouraged them to organize on a regional level for purposes of candidate selection, electoral propaganda, and voter mobilization. The shift in electoral rules in 1848, from the *scrutin uninominal d'arrondissement*, in which voters chose a candidate within relatively narrow geographic boundaries, to the *scrutin de liste du département*, in which voters selected an entire list of candidates within fairly large geographic boundaries, also fostered the growth of political parties.[6]

The first nationwide direct election of a president under a regime of universal male suffrage in December 1848 prompted the formation of an organization, Republican Solidarity, to support the presidential candidacy of Ledru-Rollin. This organization, which had a central committee in Paris, established branches in sixty-two of France's eighty-six departments and rapidly acquired an estimated total of over thirty thousand members in 353 branches. The Concerned with winning elections and providing administrative leadership for a new government, Republican Solidarity established a shadow cabinet in Paris, with various "ministries," including a ministry of Workers' and Farmers' Associations.[7] Republican Solidarity had a hierarchical and centralized organizational structure, with the General Council initially appointing all local officers, who were subsequently elected by local members and then approved by the Council. Under the direction of Republican Solidarity, urban-based party organizations began sponsoring electoral committees in rural constituencies where there had been no republican presence and republican electoral committees began to coordinate the campaigns of parliamentary representatives on a regional scale. The organization also provided a closer link between Parisian parliamentary and provincial republican leaders. Despite the centralized Jacobin character of Republican Solidarity, the direction of party activities and selection of party candidates still remained localized and centered around provincial newspaper offices. In contrast to "modern" political parties, the national committee did not distribute any campaign funds to local branches, issue papers to card-carrying members, or enforce discipline on the party's legislative personnel.

The initial effort to create a centralized national Republican party quickly succumbed to political repression. In early 1849, the government shut down Republican Solidarity's national headquarters, outlawed the organization, and arrested its most prominent leaders. Continued repression inhibited the development of a centralized party structure. The harsh repression that followed Louis Napoleon Bonaparte's coup d'état of December 1851 temporarily destroyed what remained of national Republican party leadership and organization. The persistence of universal male suffrage after the coup d'état stimulated continuing local electoral activities organized by republican activists, but these became even more independent of national leadership, retreating into the informal social networks of neighborhoods, workplaces, and cafés that had served as a base for earlier clandestine activities. Not until the revival of the Republican party during the 1860s did a national party leadership once again begin to coordinate local and regional electoral activities.

Early Republican party mobilization was based on what social movement theorists have labeled "bloc recruitment." It relied on the incorporation of preexisting workplace and neighborhood groups that already possessed high degrees of group identity and extensive interpersonal ties.[8] Anthony Oberschall's observation that "a still viable network of communal relations can be the foundation and breeding ground for the rapid growth of modern associational networks" is clearly illustrated by the case of French republicanism.[9] The pattern identified by Oberschall is especially evident in France after 1849, when Republicans extended their electoral efforts into the French countryside, politicizing traditional communal institutions like the village club (*chambrées*), communal ceremonies like *fêtes* and carnivals, and popular folklore.[10] Republicans used traditions of mutual aid and institutions of popular sociability to forge new patterns of political solidarity.

At the local level, the Republican party was composed of diverse forms rooted in a rich organizational heritage that included the Jacobin clubs of the French revolution, the secret conspiratorial societies of the Restoration, and informal centers of sociability like *cercles* and cafés. "At the base," writes Raymond Huard, "the Republican party remained a mosaic of disparate organizations. . . ."[11] The importance of these different organizational forms varied with changing levels of political repression. Intensified repression typically reinforced the role of secret societies and informal centers of sociability, like cafés, vintners' shops, and cabarets, while periods of political liberalization heightened the importance of electoral associations, circles, and popular clubs. During periods of intense repression, when republican militants were more likely to face jail or exile rather than fines or acquittals, and when the survival of local party newspapers was jeopardized, informal social networks and clandestine secret societies took on greater importance. Secret societies had a very different organizational structure than politicized circles, electoral committees, or clubs. Their clandestine orientation meant an emphasis on military discipline, elaborate rituals, and small cells linked in an authoritarian manner to the top leadership. The republican secret societies of 1850–51, however, had a much larger audience than those of the 1830s, recruiting both a highly politicized elite and a popular base, and creating what Raymond Huard describes as a "symbiosis with circles and public societies."[12] During the 1860s, Republicans created yet another new organizational form, the *Ligue*, a national federation of special purpose organizations. The *Ligue de l'Enseignement*, for example, established popular libraries and reading groups devoted to secular education throughout France.

KEY FEATURES OF EARLY FRENCH REPUBLICANISM: FRATERNALISM, IDEOLOGICAL MOBILIZATION, AND BOURGEOIS LEADERSHIP

The distinctive features of early French republicanism included a gendered organizational structure and ideology, an ideological rather than patronage manner of mobilizing supporters, and a predominantly bourgeois leadership and working-class base. Fraternalism was a central feature of the mid-nineteenth-century French Republican party. Although fraternity is one of the three key words in the republican motto, historians have remained remarkably blind to republicanism's fraternal features.[13] Fraternity was not simply a republican expression of community; it was a gendered socio-cultural form of solidarity and community that played a key role in the constitution of republican political identities. Fraternalism appealed to a particular vision of masculine camaraderie and male authority, allowing Republicans to construct cross-class solidarities based on shared defini-tions of manhood and rituals of male bonding.[14] The quasi-familial ties, rituals, and solidarities sustained by republican associations were based on a vision that was explicitly restricted to men. Republican secret societies, masonic lodges, electoral associations, social clubs (*chambrées*), and infor-mal café gatherings fostered cross-class male bonding, often in an atmo-sphere of danger. Secret associations, such as the Carbonari societies of the 1820s, the secret societies of 1850–51, and politicized associations of urban sociability such as masonic lodges, were fraternal forms of organiza-tion that helped shape the Republican party during its formative years. These years were marked by intense political repression that drove republi-can activities underground into these fraternal associations and encouraged Republicans to embrace revolutionary violence, which helped to valorize masculine virtues of physical bravery and combat. Prior to 1848, republi-can rhetoric included a militaristic nationalism that appealed to males who had experienced military service. Both before and after 1848 it encom-passed a patriarchal view of citizenship rights limited to men. Like the traditional artisans' organizations (*compagnonnages*), and the predomi-nantly bourgeois masonic lodges, the secret societies and conspiratorial organizations that became prominent features of republicanism during the intense repression of the 1830s and 1850s utilized secret oaths and elabo-rate ritual. These included oaths of regicide and the ritual stabbing of straw manikins symbolizing royalty.

Although republican rhetoric called for political equality, women were excluded from citizenship rights in the republican constitutions of 1791 and 1793, and denied rights of assembly and association under the First French Republic. Though denied the vote and assigned to the category of "passive citizens," women played an active role in the French Revolution, from their march on Versailles to participation in clubs, demonstrations, and the press.[15] But the Jacobin republican regime of the Convention, fear-ful of sansculotte popular upheaval in which women played a key role, suppressed all political activity by women and outlawed female clubs and political associations in October 1793. Despite some dissenting voices among Girondin Republicans like Condorcet, the vast majority of late eighteenth-century Republicans shared Rousseau's aversion to women in public and embraced a vision of the republic that excluded women from formal political life and asserted their natural domesticity.[16] The general argument against female suffrage concerned the danger of enfranchising anyone who was legally defined as dependent and was therefore likely to follow someone else's orders when voting, not only women but also children, servants, prisoners, monks, and apprentices. Nineteenth-century Republicans adopted traditional notions of civic virtue that relegated women to the private sphere as mothers and moral guardians of the home. They added to this an opposition to granting women the vote, based on arguments that women were too influenced by reactionary clergy to provide secure electoral support for the republic.[17] "The Republic was constructed against women, not just without them," writes Joan Landes, "and nineteenth-century Republicans did not actively counteract this masculinist heritage of republicanism."[18] This heritage was evident in mid-nineteenth-century republican discourse and propaganda. For example, Rouen's liberal republican newspaper, *L'Ami du peuple*, which claimed to be "the newspaper of the true interests of the workers," advertised a patriarchal vision on its masthead, where it proclaimed: "The people: it is all of us, strong men, timid women, and small children."[19]

A second key feature of mid-nineteenth-century republicanism was a reliance on ideological appeals rather than patronage or corporatist strategies to mobilize support. Unlike their major electoral competitors, Legitimist, Orleanist, and Bonapartist parties, the Republican party did not have access to systems of patronage. Government bureaucracies provided Orleanists, and subsequently Bonapartists, with resources for patronage politics, while Legitimists relied on the private wealth of royalist landowners to maintain patronage networks.[20] There were personal loyalties and rivalries in republican politics and some wealthy republican notables used personal networks of patronage to rally support, especially in rural areas, but these played a much less important role in mobilizing supporters than ideological commitments.[21] Republicans utilized an ideological appeal, which included egalitarian themes regarding voting, taxes, schooling, and credit.

The origins of the French Republican party help to explain this orientation. The Republican party was established by political outsiders who organized a mass following in an effort to expand access to the electoral system for their supporters and replace an existing constitutional monarchy with a republic. In their quest for power, Republicans denounced the public patronage of the orleanist regime as corruption and advocated recruitment to government office based on merit rather than connections. After his election as deputy in August 1847, Toulouse republican leader Jean-Pierre Pagès proclaimed to a crowd of supporters, amid cheers of "Long Live Reform!" and "Long Live Honest Men!": "My election is a moral protest by the city against the corrupt system that oppresses us."[22] After attaining state power in 1848, Republicans did not make use of their newfound power to develop extensive party patronage networks but continued to rely on ideological appeals.[23] The formal national Republican party organiza-

TABLE 1
Republican Militants—Second Republic

	Toulouse ($n = 496$)	Saint-Étienne ($n = 132$)	Rouen ($n = 136$)
Bourgeois	21%	19%	11%
Professionals	12%	12%	7%
Merchants	5%	5%	1%
Propriétaires/Rentiers/Bankers/Industrialists	4%	2%	3%
Petty Bourgeois	21%	23%	28%
Shopkeepers	10%	17%	22%
Master Artisans	7%	1%	1%
Clerks	4%	5%	5%
Working-Class	55%	56%	60%
Artisans	47%	42%	40%
Textile, Metal, and Arms Factories/Mines*	0%	8%	10%
Other	8%	6%	10%

Sources: (See list of abbreviations on p. 266)
    A.N.: BB[18] 1360, 1388, 1395, 1398, 1449, 1793, 1795; BB[30] 388, 415; F[1c] III 9.
    A.D.H.G.: 4M 47, 50–53, 55, 56, 58-60, 62–67, 69–74, 76, 77, 81–84, 94; 223 U 10, 11, 14, 15, 17, 25.
    A.M.T.: 2I 63, 64; 1K 21, 2Q 7; S.G. 126.
    A.D.L.: 10M 37.
    A.D.S.M.: 4MP 4237.
    Maitron, *Dictionnaire biographique*.
* Police records at Toulouse and Saint-Étienne fail to distinguish between metalworkers employed in small workshops and those employed in factories.

tion that emerged after 1848 remained under the control of bourgeois parliamentary notables, not party bureaucrats. In contrast with the situation in the United States, professional local party bosses never acquired independent political power based on the distribution of patronage resources.

A third key feature of mid-nineteenth-century republicanism concerns the party's leadership, which was not an accurate reflection of its base of support. At the base, the Republican party attracted a constituency from various social classes, but the working class remained at the center of the republican project in France throughout the mid-nineteenth century. French workers, mainly artisans, constituted the revolutionary force that put the Republican party in power in February 1848 and unleashed the violent conflict of June 1848. It was the struggles of urban workers, and their efforts to build an alliance with the peasantry based on republican socialism, that determined the subsequent trajectory of republicanism and the fate of the Second Republic. Table 1 presents data, based on Second Republic police surveillance records, identifying the most outspoken and active members of republican associations, clubs, secret societies, and propaganda networks in the cities of Toulouse, Saint-Étienne, and Rouen. These figures reveal that in all three cities workers, mainly artisans, were a majority of republican political activists, although republicanism attracted militants from diverse social classes, especially professionals, shopkeepers, and artisans. Master artisans played a larger role in cities like Toulouse, where handicraft production was more dominant. Even in cities like Rouen, where factory workers, not artisans, numerically dominated the working class, artisans played a leading role in republican agitation. High rates of literacy, relatively high levels of workplace autonomy and trade organization, and threats posed by the growth of sweated production and manufactories help to account for this.

The leadership of the French Republican party remained predominantly bourgeois throughout the mid-nineteenth century. Even republican socialist organizations such as the Society of the Rights of Man of 1832–34, which espoused the principle of power exercised "from below" and had a predominantly working-class membership, were led by bourgeois students, intellectuals, and professionals.[24] A similar pattern is evident in 1849 in the leadership of Republican Solidarity. The organization was headed by a sixty-four member General Council that included thirty-two parliamentary deputies, most of whom had practiced law; four ex-government officials; six doctors; three journalists; four men of letters; four engineers; one lawyer; one professor; five businessmen; and four workers.[25]

Bourgeois dominance of Republican party leadership was contested by workers, who launched independent candidacies in numerous cities during the legislative elections of the 1860s.[26] Bourgeois republican leaders responded to these challenges in a rhetoric that appealed to civic identities and the need for republican unity. At Rouen, for example, the radical republican newspaper Le Progrès criticized independent working-class political initiatives in 1869 by reminding its readers that "outside of the workplace, [workers] are above all citizens . . . in their eyes there is not a working-class democracy and a bourgeois democracy, but only a single democracy generously pursuing since 1789, in the face of various reactions, the working out of the social problem, the elevation of the humble by education, and the material improvement of the condition of the laboring classes. . . ."[27] That same year, the liberal republican newspaper, the Journal de Rouen, denounced the independent working-class candidacy of Emile Aubry, leader of the local branch of the First International, as divisive and counterproductive. It questioned the need for a working-class candidate by asking rhetorically if "we need a special candidate for workers, another for manufacturers, and others for clerks, day laborers, and rentiers?"[28]

The realities of a class-divided society ensured that professionals and intellectuals dominated the party's national leadership. National parliamentary institutions placed a high value on resources, such as oratory, legal skills, and an ability to organize beyond the local level, that were much more accessible to highly educated, well-to-do individuals than to workers or small shopkeepers. Whereas workers, shopkeepers, and businessmen often could not afford to abandon their economic activities for full-time political activism, professionals found it easier to combine their careers as lawyers, doctors, notaries, or journalists with the demands of party leadership. Only the most well-to-do Republicans could afford to abandon their jobs for a six-month visit to the capital as an elected deputy, and many local republican committees had great difficulty finding candidates for elected offices prior to 1848. Newspapers constituted the focal organizational points for local Republican parties. Given the intellectual capacities and aspirations of professionals, and the fact that entry into journalism did not require specialized professional training, journalism often served failed professionals as an occupational refuge.[29] The system of caution money, which required that newspapers deposit a hefty sum with the government as surety for future possible fines, made newspaper ownership the province of bourgeois not working-class Republicans.

Party candidates, especially for national office, were mainly professionals who were connected with workers and, in many cases, had acquired a reputation as defense lawyers in strikes or as doctors who served a working-class clientele. Professionals not only had the necessary resources to provide party leadership; they were also attracted to republicanism by programs such as universal male suffrage and reform of the corrupt state administrative apparatus. These appealed to their moral principles and idealism as well as to their socioeconomic interests. Less wealthy and less successful professionals were excluded from voting during the July Monarchy because they did not earn enough money or own enough property to place them in a tax bracket high enough to qualify for the franchise. In an era marked by an overabundance of educated men, and a corrupt and competitive system of recruitment to government posts, republican ideals of meritocracy and frequent republican attacks on the corrupt civil service appealed to less successful professionals. Many of them turned to the Republican party, which led the unsuccessful effort to reform the electoral eligibility laws of the July Monarchy so as to grant professionals the right to vote without tax requirements.

MID-NINETEENTH-CENTURY FRENCH REPUBLICAN IDEOLOGY

Mid-nineteenth-century French Republicans shared a commitment to constitutional government, a hostility to aristocracy and monarchy, a belief in progress and secularism, and a refusal to accept tradition as a legitimate basis of political authority. "The Republic," argues Maurice Agulhon, "was at the same time a new source of sovereign power set up against real monarchs; virtually a new cult opposed to established religion, and a popular force against the dominant powers in society."[30] Republicanism, however, was not an internally consistent and logically rigorous system of thought.[31] Different elements of the French revolutionary tradition were borrowed from evolving discourses of liberalism, socialism, and democracy, and integrated into the contested ideology of French republicanism in disparate ways, in response to shifting economic and political realities.

The articulating principles of republican ideology, summarized in the slogan of the French Revolution—liberty, equality, and fraternity—were subject to alternative interpretations throughout the nineteenth century. For liberal Republicans, the principle of liberty meant freedom from state interference in the economy and from the oppressive and arbitrary practices of an autocratic state. The principle of equality meant the extension of legal rights to all men regardless of their wealth or property. The principle of fraternity referred to the national solidarities that connected all inhabitants of France regardless of their social class. Socialist Republicans also adopted a language of rights but in a way that attached very different meanings to the terms liberty, equality, and fraternity. The principle of liberty was expanded to include the "right to work," that is, state-guaranteed employment. The principle of equality was extended beyond the boundaries of the political arena to the economy. Whereas liberal Republicans envisioned a republic that would promote class conciliation among all French citizens, socialist Republicans appealed to class antagonisms by challenging established property relations. The principle of fraternity was appropriated by republican socialists to foster the values of collectivism, mutual aid, and class solidarity.

During periods of social and political upheaval, such as the days following the revolution of February 1848, liberal understandings of the principle of liberty often clashed head-on with socialist interpretations of the principle of equality. For example, at Rouen socialist militants confronted liberal Republicans over the right of political clubs to charge high admission fees. On March 24, 1848 a crowd of over two thousand workers, many allegedly from the municipal workshops, invaded the bourgeois Club National, refusing to pay the required twenty-five centime entrance fee.[32] Club leaders justified the entrance fee by arguing that, unlike the city's predominantly working-class clubs which the new regime had granted free access to government buildings, they were forced to rent the premises where they gathered. After entering the meeting hall, leaders of the group of workers, who claimed to have the backing of radical republican official Frédéric Deschamps, declared the present association "insufficiently republican" and designated a new provisional leadership for the club. Club leaders subsequently asked Deschamps to take action to protect their meeting place, but he refused to do so. Liberal Republicans defined the issue as a question of liberty, a matter of the defense of free speech and private property. They viewed the disruption as part of a secret effort by the radical and socialist *Comité central démocratique* to bring all the city's clubs under its control. Republican socialists regarded the club's entrance fee as a bourgeois attempt to deny workers equal participation in the political process, a violation of the newly proclaimed principle of political equality.

Traditional historical accounts of French Republican party formation focus on prominent political personalities and their ideas and fail to adequately explore the social dynamics underpinning the process of ideological change.[33] The transformation of republican ideology during the mid-nineteenth century, however, was embedded in changing socioeconomic and political, not simply ideational, processes. The political ideology of mid-nineteenth-century republicanism was not autonomous or detached from class relations nor was it simply a class ideology, despite its close connection to the working-class struggles of the period. The class connotations of republicanism were not given by the nature of the ideology but actively contested in political struggles over the incorporation of elements of liberal and socialist discourses and practices into republicanism.

FRENCH LIBERALISM

Classical liberalism is typically associated with parliamentary government, judicial equality before the law, civil liberties, economic individualism, and limited state intervention in the economy. The dominant economic principle of classical liberalism is the rule of the marketplace, while its central political tenet is a secular laissez-faire state constrained by the rule of law and with limited power to intervene in the economy. Nineteenth-century French liberals emphasized the need to strengthen civil society and associational life against the growing power of the state. One way to limit state power, they argued, was to institutionalize a representative form of constitutional government, based on a system of checks and balances in which the executive branch was accountable to a parliament and the judiciary remained independent. The competitive, contractual, and individualist principles that informed liberal notions of the good society contrasted sharply with the corporatist principles of the Old Regime.[34]

Liberal views of freedom encompassed economic as well as political life. Freedom from government interference in the personal exercise of religious or political beliefs, argued liberals, should extend to the freedom of enterprising individuals to seek profit and gain without government interference. In the nineteenth century context of rapid economic growth, the meritocratic ideals of liberalism, which challenged the ascriptive principles and inherited privileges of the aristocracy in favor of an open society in which enterprising individuals were given opportunities to rise to the top, had great appeal among those aspiring to a better life for themselves or their children. Liberals disagreed about various political issues, including the proper form of the state, with some liberals embracing constitutional monarchy and others favoring an empire or republic. They were more united on economic principles, especially the defense of property rights and the virtues of unbridled capitalism.

Though ardent in their defense of individual liberty against the state when it came to the liberty of capitalists to control their enterprises, liberals typically placed public order above civil liberties. In the aftermath of the working-class insurrections of the early 1830s, for example, French liberals supported legislation restricting rights to association, freedom of speech, and a free press, in the context of what they perceived to be a heightened threat to private property and class privileges. Liberal Republicans routinely accompanied their use of the word liberty with a reminder of the need for public order. In July 1839, for example, the liberal editors of Toulouse's republican newspaper *Émancipation* proclaimed their fidelity to "the sacred principles of our glorious Revolution of 1789, confirmed by the revolution of 1830." They demanded the application of these principles "as far as can now be permitted by the needs of order which one must never detach from the needs of liberty. . . ."[35]

The interest group politics of the July Monarchy (1830–48) made it difficult for French liberals to remain true to their antistate ideals. Key issues—like where to build railroads or which tariffs to maintain—prompted liberal politicians to support state intervention to foster the local or regional economic interests of the propertied notables who put them in office. Liberals retreated selectively from liberal economic principles when the issues of free trade or railroad construction threatened the local or regional economic interests of their constituents. The nonliberal character of the French clergy, who controlled the nation's educational system, also prompted many liberals to support state intervention to provide a nationwide system of secular primary education.

In contrast to Germany, England, and other Western European countries, French liberals did not form their own political party. The failure of French liberalism to mobilize broad popular support and become institutionalized in a political party was due in large part to orleanist state repression of the French labor movement during the early 1830s. This repression by the "liberal" monarchy meant that the issues used to rally popular support for liberalism during the late 1820s, freedom of the press and civil liberties, were not available for popular mobilization behind the regime. The regime's pacific foreign policies, connected to France's distinctive location in the world economy and international state system at this time, meant that nationalist sentiments could not serve to mobilize broad popular support for the liberal monarchy. Whereas German liberals created a party of national unification that mobilized support behind the ideal of German nationality,[36] nineteenth-century French liberalism initially became closely associated with an orleanist state that pursued a pacific foreign policy in the face of nationalist opposition from Republicans. British liberals rallied popular support for their cause in the Anti-Corn Law League, denouncing tariffs and contending that free trade would result in lower food prices for workers at the expense of the landholding class. Such a popular alliance behind liberal economic measures was not possible in France, due to divisions within the bourgeoisie over free trade and the support of most French businessmen for protectionist trade policies.

The period from 1846–51 was a key turning point for French liberalism in terms of its relationship to democracy. Although wary of universal male suffrage before 1848, liberals who played a prominent role in the banquet campaign for electoral reform in 1846–48 expressed democratic sympathies that were alien to their predecessors. Liberal leaders of the constitutional opposition, including Alphonse de Lamartine and Odilon Barrot, incorporated elements of democratic thought into their programs. Although the class struggles of 1848 and socialist electoral gains in 1849 renewed liberal fears that democracy meant disorder, many liberals were won over to democratic politics during the Second Republic, after the results of the nation's first national elections under a regime of universal male suffrage convinced them that social conservatism was compatible with universal male suffrage.

Liberal support for democratic ideals was rooted in a distinctive view of democracy that considered elected officials as trustees for the nation, not as delegates of their constituents. This view, elaborated during the French Revolution by the abbé Sièyes, was consistent with the claims of deputies of the Third Estate to constitute themselves in a National Assembly representing a unitary national will.[37] Liberal Republicans advocated granting representatives considerable discretion in their parliamentary activities, viewing representation as the process by which an educated and enlightened propertied elite is entrusted with political power. The Constitution of 1789 proclaimed this liberal notion of representation, stating that the National Assembly embodied the will of the nation and that "the representatives elected in the departments will not be representatives of a particular department but of the whole nation, and they may not be given any mandate."[38] The parliamentary monarchy of the liberal orleanist regime adopted this same principle of representation, emphasizing the independence of elected officials from the electorate as necessary for "national sovereignty."[39] Liberals argued that direct democracy was inapplicable to an electorate of vast numbers, and that it would foster disorder by encouraging interventions from extraparliamentary bodies. Liberal Republicans feared that direct democracy would lead representatives to put local interests above the national interest and, by inhibiting compromise and bargaining among legislators, would produce endless parliamentary stalemates, thereby strengthening the power of the executive branch. These liberal denunciations were strengthened by the hostility toward direct democracy fostered among Republicans by Louis Napoleon Bonaparte's successful use of plebiscites and referenda during the 1850s and 1860s.

FRENCH SOCIALISM

Early French socialism was predominantly "federalist trade socialism," a vision of democratic self-governing skilled trades collectively owning the means of production via a federation of producers' associations or cooperatives.[40] The term socialist, in its nineteenth-century French context, referred to those seeking a social as well as a political transformation of society. Although socialism was not a single, unifying creed, French socialists shared a commitment to social equality and a common concern with the plight of workers. Socialists rejected liberals' rigid separation of the economic and political spheres and questioned the liberty of bourgeois property owners to exploit workers. They adopted a language of class to explain existing injustices and inequalities, targeting wealthy owners of the means of production as the source of workers' suffering. Rouen's republican socialist leader Charles Noiret, a handloom weaver, denounced the egoism of the idle rich, proclaimed labor as the source of all wealth, and espoused independent workers' production cooperatives supported by the state as the solution to the social question. He vehemently rejected any role for capitalists in cooperative enterprises. "Some speak of the association of capitalists and workers," wrote Noiret in 1841. "I can think of nothing more dangerous or immoral than this monstrous coupling; I would rather associate myself with the plague and leprosy."[41]

Despite certain unifying themes, socialism was a disparate blend of competing ideas.[42] The early socialist ideologies of Louis Blanc, Pierre Buchez, Étienne Cabet, Pierre Leroux, and Pierre-Joseph Proudhon differed in their view of what role markets, private property, and the state should play in a socialist society. Although most socialists condemned the anarchy of the marketplace and denounced the monopoly power to which it gave rise, they disagreed about the virtues of markets. Louis Blanc elaborated a cooperative vision of small-scale, self-managed workshops in which associational monopolies within each trade existed alongside market relations that provided a coordinating function. Étienne Cabet rejected market relations in favor of a collectivist vision of socialist society based on common ownership of property by the state and the subordination of individual liberties to the overarching goal of economic and social equality. Proudhon and

Buchez favored a less egalitarian and collectivist brand of socialism, which included competition among small-scale workers' cooperatives and market relations. While some socialists denounced property as theft, others regarded the spread of small property ownership as a vehicle for liberating workers. Saint-Étienne's socialist newspaper *La Sentinelle populaire* proclaimed in 1848: "Our rallying cry is the abolition of the proletariat. Republicans have only one goal [with respect to property], to allow the worker to enjoy the right to individual property, for without property there is no liberty or independence. . . ."[43]

French socialists also disagreed about whether state power should be used as a vehicle for change. Auguste Blanqui advocated a revolutionary seizure of state power, while Louis Blanc and Pierre Buchez favored the democratic conquest of state power to establish a "social republic" that would provide cheap public credit to workers' cooperatives. "Utopian socialists," including Fourier and Cabet, as well as libertarian socialists like Proudhon, were not concerned with capturing state power, by either revolution or elections. Proudhon rejected the authoritarian and centralist tendencies of Jacobin socialists, preaching federalism and class conciliation and chastising Louis Blanc for favoring reforms initiated "from above." He denounced Blanc as "the stunted shadow of Robespierre" while Blanc characterized Proudhon's position as "the most audacious negation of socialism ever produced."[44] Fourier rejected electoral politics, but his successor, Victor Considerant, abandoned Fourier's antistatist views and joined the republican socialist movement after the February 1848 revolution. In 1870–71, many socialist communards rejected the Jacobin legacy and called for a reorganization of state power along decentralized federalist lines. For example, Saint-Étienne's republican socialist newspaper *La Commune* called for a federation of communes to replace the centralized state, denounced the communist wing of the First International for its centralism, and praised the federalist system of the United States.[45]

Socialists were also divided over the issue of democracy. Some socialists, like Blanqui, emphasized the need for secret societies organized by a revolutionary elite who would institute a centralized popular dictatorship. Most socialists denounced such undemocratic conspiratorial approaches to social change, arguing that socialism meant the radical democratization of the state and revitalization of the public sphere. Writing in 1870, Jean Jolivalt, the republican socialist leader of Saint-Étienne's revolutionary commune, blamed the downfall of the Second Republic on the failure of its leaders to fully embrace the democratic ideal: "It was insufficient to declare a republic, even a democratic and social republic. They should have introduced democracy into all levels of government; democratized not only the Assembly, but the executive power, administration, army, courts, and municipalities. . . . They should have begun to boldly democratize the laws, taxes, and education and to correct [the problem of] centralization. They should have resolutely admitted socialism and solidarity into [public] life, by encouraging public meetings. . . ."[46]

Although early socialists challenged the liberal vision of social order and criticized possessive individualism, most did so in a language that adopted key elements of a democratic discourse of rights inherited from the First French Republic. After 1831, French workers increasingly expressed their grievances and aspirations in a language of rights and associationalism, which built on but transformed the corporate idiom that had previously been used to express workers' grievances. Workers creatively adapted the rhetoric of the French Revolution to extend the notion of liberty to include the right of propertyless wage laborers to find employment. Republican socialists reinterpreted the meaning of liberty to justify the formation of associations that would supplant private property with associative property and allow workers to collectively control the means of production.[47] They also transformed corporate notions of trade solidarity into a new class-conscious idiom of associationalism. Urban skilled workers saw associations as the means of emancipating their trades from the wage system, and they turned to republican leaders, whose political programs promised to provide the cheap credit needed for collectivization of the means of production in producers' associations.[48]

The republican socialist discourse of the early 1830s was not the product of backward-looking artisans seeking to restore the corporate solidarities of a precapitalist moral economy but the creative response of artisanal craftsmen faced with harsh new political and economic realities. These included a liberal but undemocratic state and an expanding market economy in which unapprenticed labor, ready-made piece-work goods, nonmechanized factories, and subcontracted prison and convent labor increasingly competed with the products of handicraft industry. Working-class economic grievances were given political force by socialist discourse, which arose largely as a product of the socioeconomic changes wrought by early capitalist industrialization. The earliest working-class insurrections, by the Lyonnais silk weavers in 1832 and 1834, were generated by changing relations of exploitation within urban household forms of production. These revolutionary artisans were motivated by economic grievances which republican militants, employing a rhetoric of cooperative socialism, succeeded in politicizing and channeling into the struggle for a republic.[49]

Democratic ideals increasingly permeated the socialist movement during the 1840s, as the issue of class barriers to suffrage rights came to dominate republican politics. For republican workers, the extension of the suffrage was a means by which they could resolve the "social question," a vague reference to the economic problems confronting workers, rather than an end in itself. For these workers, socialism was the fulfillment of the republican ideal. "Socialism," wrote the machinist J. Baux in Toulouse's newspaper *Civilisation*, "is the most logical and broadest road to all reforms, and the why and wherefore of any republic truly seeking the emancipation of the people."[50] Republican socialists denounced liberal Republicans who contended that political reform alone would improve the condition of workers, arguing that without qualitative economic change, continuing economic dependencies would undermine political reforms.[51] The social republic promised not only political equality but full employment, more equitable taxes, and free universal schooling, all of which would reduce economic inequalities. The "social republic" would eradicate poverty by guaranteeing workers "the right to work," eliminate unfair monopolies by nationalizing the railroads, canals, mines, and insurance companies, and abolish wage labor by providing cheap public credit to smallholders and producers' cooperatives. These goals were clearly elaborated by local republican socialist leaders, including Rouen's Charles Noiret, who combined a call for "the organization of work to end the exploitation of man by man" with a variety of democratic reforms, including universal suffrage, initiative and referendum, the right to public assembly, the election and accountability of all public officials, free legal aid, free and equal public education, and progressive taxation.[52]

Parliamentary institutions elicited support among republican socialist workers throughout the middle decades of the nineteenth century, but this support was based on a distinctive understanding of representation and democracy. This understanding involved the traditional notion of the imperative mandate, according to which elected officials were bound to carry out the expressed wishes of their constituents.[53] The sansculottes of the French revolution adopted this view of representation, which was elaborated in the Constitution of 1793 in the statement that the government was the property of the sovereign people and its officials their clerks. During the nineteenth century, this understanding was reflected in republican hostility toward executive power, in the opposition of most Republicans to the direct election of a president, and in the very language of republican politics, which termed the written platforms of candidates for elected office *mandats*. Republican socialist advocates of direct democracy did not deny the need for representative institutions in a country as large as France, but they regarded the principle of the imperative mandate as a way in which to ensure popular control of elected officials.[54]

The participatory vision of elected officials as delegates with binding obligations to the voters who elected them (*mandataires*) contrasted with the liberal notion of elected officials as representatives who followed the dictates of their own conscience and acted with a degree of independence from their constituents. The participatory vision implied the right of citizens to take nonelectoral collective political actions if their elected representatives were not abiding by their mandates. Whereas liberal Republicans insisted upon keeping politics firmly implanted within the electoral arena, socialist Republicans did not scrupulously respect this boundary. During times of political upheaval, such as the periods following the revolutions of 1830 and 1848, socialist workers took to the streets, formed revolutionary clubs, and made use of traditional nonelectoral forms of popular protest, including processions, demonstrations, petitions, banquets, political charivaris, and serenades, to chastise or put pressure on government officials. These practices reflected what Alain Cottereau identifies as a key feature of nineteenth-century, working-class culture, "a pragmatic of direct action" that predated the emergence of a syndicalist movement.[55]

Throughout the mid-nineteenth century, advocates of democracy and socialism had a difficult time reconciling two key elements of French republicanism: the right to revolution and the principle of majority rule. Republicanism was born amid revolutionary ferment, with both the First and Second French Republics installed by violent revolution. The republican Constitution of 1793 guaranteed the right to insurrection when the government violates the rights of the people. A key tenet of republicanism, enshrined in constitutions, was the principle of majority rule.[56] During the 1840s, this principle became indissolubly connected with the struggle for universal male suffrage, which many Republicans came to regard as a panacea that would solve the nation's pressing economic and political problems. Yet the implementation of universal male suffrage in April 1848 resulted in the election of a National Assembly with a conservative monarchist majority and the subsequent election of a nonrepublican president in December 1848. The principle of majority rule became suspect among Republicans because the fundamental issue of the institutional and legal framework within which majority rule should operate was contentious. When monarchists, who had only temporarily accepted the republic as a fait accompli, gained power during the elections of the early Second Republic, socialist Republicans viewed the electoral defeat as a threat to the very existence of the republic. Rouen's republican socialist newspaper *La Sentinelle des travailleurs* explained the June 1848 insurrection in Paris in terms of a royalist plot to destroy the Republic and warned, "You forget that we are in the midst of a social revolution, which you are turning into a social war. . . . Listen to what we are shouting to you from the heights of the barricades: We want bread and work and you give us gunshots! But we will fight for the defense of the Republic, which alone will give us bread!"[57]

Republican socialists were hesitant to accept electoral defeat in 1848 because there was no guarantee that their opponents would accept the institutional foundations of the republic, which had been inaugurated in February on the barricades. They faced a similar situation in early 1871, following the election of a royalist-dominated National Assembly. When republican socialists took to the barricades, in June 1848 and March 1871, they defended their recourse to revolution by interpreting electoral defeats as a repudiation of the republic, which was constitutionally guaranteed, not subject to majority rule.

THE RADICAL SYNTHESIS

Both liberalism and socialism represented internally diverse and changing discourses. Despite sharp differences in their understandings of liberty, equality, and fraternity, nineteenth-century liberalism and socialism constituted overlapping and mutually interacting practices, which transformed one another during the course of the nineteenth century. French socialists increasingly came to accept working within the electoral arena and a representative rather than participatory practice of democracy. The harsh repression they faced strengthened their commitment to civil liberties and parliamentary restraints on executive power. Republican socialists of the late 1860s called for a variety of liberal measures, including civil liberties, the election of mayors rather than their appointment by the central state, and greater municipal freedom. French liberals came to accept not only associational rights but various types of state intervention to remedy the social ills of the free market, from child labor laws to progressive income taxes. But this reconciliation was not the result of a natural or peaceful process of change. The creation of a radical republican synthesis that selectively incorporated elements of liberal and socialist traditions in a manner that made democracy safe for capitalism was the outcome of a bitter, sometimes violent, struggle among Republicans.

Republican ideology became dominant in France only after it incorporated contradictory elements of liberalism and socialism in a manner that neutralized their potential antagonisms. This ideological synthesis was the achievement of radical republicanism.[58] Although radical Republicans rejected socialism, especially its statist versions, and preached class collaboration, they parted company with liberals by calling for government intervention in the economy to improve the condition of the working class and guarantee workers the right to organize. Radicals defended the inviolable rights of property against socialist collectivism but rejected the liberal antipathy toward political authority. They acknowledged the intimate connections between economic and political spheres and shared with socialists a willingness to use state power to remedy social problems. Unlike socialists, they were less concerned with reorganizing production than with promoting a more equitable income distribution via tax reforms, government regulation of monopolies, the legalization of unions, and welfare policies.

While rejecting socialism, radicals were much more willing than liberals to collaborate with republican socialists. The radical republican leaders who directed *La Réforme* during the early 1840s, including Alexandre Ledru-Rollin, Godefroy Cavaignac, and Ferdinand Flocon, opened the newspaper's columns to socialists like Louis Blanc and Pierre Leroux. Though wary of the economic equality advocated by socialists, French radicals were firmly committed to social equality. French radicalism, observes Alain Cottereau, "maintained a populist appearance, showing little respect for middle-class styles and proprieties, which gives it a very different coloring than that of English or American radicalism . . . far from sharing in the quest for honorability and for moral recognition by other social classes, the style of the French radicals was very populist and perhaps even 'demagogic' in the eyes of the most 'honorable' social classes."[59]

The radical vision of economic equality emphasized equality of opportunity, with free secular education providing the central vehicle for bringing about a meritocratic economic order. Like liberals, radicals viewed economic inequalities as inevitable but strove to create a society in which everyone would have an equal opportunity to make it to the top, or fall to the bottom. Although radicals acknowledged the need for state intervention to prevent free markets from producing unacceptable monopolies of economic power, they joined liberals in recognizing the virtues of economic competition. Espousing what purported to be a classless and universalist doctrine of republican citizenship, they praised bourgeois virtues of competitiveness, manliness, and rationality. Prior to June of 1848, radical leaders called for the nationalization of the railroads, banks, and insurance companies, and for progressive taxation. By April 1849, as part of an effort to rally the support of small rural property holders, references to socialist measures like nationalizations were avoided by radical leaders in favor of an emphasis on issues like free secular education, tax reform, cheap credit, and the breakup of monopoly power. Radicals maintained their commitment to "the right to work" but separated this from earlier denunciations of the institution of private property.[60] Radical Republicans advocated government action to prevent concentrations of wealth acquired via monopoly pricing, not the collectivization of private property. They championed the rights of small property holders while calling for nationalization of the nation's most concentrated industries, the banks, railroads, and mines.

The radical approach to inequalities of income and wealth was clearly expressed by Émile Critot, the editor of Saint-Étienne's radical republican newspaper *L'Éclaireur*, in February 1869. In response to a statement by local workers that attributed the cause of workers' sufferings to "those who own too much," Critot insisted that the issue was not the level of wealth or income but the manner in which it was acquired. Those who insisted on economic equality, he argued, were espousing the unacceptable doctine of communism, which would destroy initiative and inhibit economic growth. Social reforms, he contended, were necessary "to assure the honest origins of wealth," via laws prohibiting the accumulation of fortunes by "privileges, monopolies, immoral actions ignored by the press, abuses of power, and violence. . . ." But "liberty rather than terror" would eliminate ill-gotten wealth and promote social justice. Critot concluded that "the suppression of monopolies and establishment of free competition will lead to just rewards for capital invested in enterprises. . . . Undoubtedly, there will still be inequalities, but they will not be those which discourage the poor. Because the origins of fortunes will be more moral, they may generate envy but will also give birth to honest and legitimate ambitions. . . ."[61]

Radicals joined liberals, and parted company with most socialists, in insisting upon the shared interests of members of all social classes as citizens and calling for class conciliation. Although radicals denounced idle aristocrats and greedy financial speculators, they criticized socialists for preaching class hatred and praised both workers and industrialists as productive citizens who contributed to the nation's economic growth. In 1847 Charles Sédail, an editor of the radical newspaper *La Réforme*, called for a "union of the bourgeoisie and the working classes."[62] During the 1860s, his words were echoed in the radical republican rhetoric of Leon Gambetta, who called for "cementing the union of classes, establishing the regeneration and greatness of France on a solid foundation of an alliance between the proletariat and the bourgeoisie."[63] Radical republican leaders supported the right of workers to organize unions, which they viewed not as instruments to challenge employers or transform the social order but "as vehicles to channel workers away from revolutionary class violence. . . ."[64]

Radical Republicans were more willing than their liberal counterparts to embrace revolutionary action, but they were more ambivalent than socialists about violating the principle of majority rule. Prior to the establishment of the republic, radicals joined conspiratorial revolutionary secret societies committed to the violent overthrow of royalism, breaking ranks with liberals like Hippolyte Carnot and Louis Garnier-Pagès who had renounced revolution. After the abortive insurrection of 1839, radical as well as socialist Republicans rejected violence in favor of petitions, banquets, propaganda, and the struggle for electoral reform. When the government refused to allow an electoral reform banquet at the beginning of 1848, radicals reaffirmed the right to use political violence when it was collective, spontaneous, and in defense of "the fundamental law of the nation."[65] Radical leaders, like Alexandre Ledru-Rollin and Ferdinand Flocon, refused to join workers on the barricades in June 1848, arguing that under a republic citizens should use the ballot box not the barricades. When confronted with civil war in June 1848, radicals faced what Peter McPhee labeled "an ideological crisis," caught between the "sacred principle" of majority rule and "profound and genuine sympathy for the insurgents."[66] Radicals took to the barricades in June 1849, when Louis Bonaparte violated the republican constitution by invading Rome. After their defeat, radicals, still ambivalent about the use of revolutionary violence, joined liberal republican leaders in repeatedly urging their followers to temporarily accept electoral defeat, in the hope that future elections would reverse the outcome. The political situation of 1870–71 once again exposed an ambivalence about insurrectionary violence, prompting some radicals to lead revolutionary communes and others to condemn the insurrections as violations of majority rule.[67]

A central element of the radical synthesis that emerged during the 1860s concerned an altered stance toward the Jacobin legacy of the French revolution.[68] During the Second Republic, radicals embraced the Jacobin heritage. Ledru-Rollin dressed in the style of Robespierre, condoned the violence of the Terror, and led an electoral coalition whose name, the Mountain, elicited memories of Jacobinism. During the 1860s, many radical leaders reassessed the legacy of Robespierre and the Reign of Terror of 1793. This reassessment was part of a wider debate within republican circles, spurred by the publication in 1865 of Edgar Quinet's defense of Danton and attack on Robespierre, and by the renunciation of Jacobin principles by prominent liberal Republicans, including Antoine Garnier-Pagès, Étienne Vacherot, and Jules Simon in the platform of Nancy in 1865.[69] Many radicals, including Jules Ferry and Alphonse Gent, rejected Robespierre as a legitimate part of the republican tradition and denounced the Jacobin legacy of "violence and brutal revolution."[70] Radical leaders of the 1860s adopted a perspective on Jacobinism that "obscured, or rejected, or considered as embarrassing, and explained by special circumstances, the ups and downs of the Terror."[71]

A second key feature of the emerging radical synthesis, which distinguished it from the radicalism of 1848, was an intense anticlericalism rooted in a firm belief that democracy required secularized schools. In 1849–51, in their efforts to win the electoral support of the rural population, radicals developed a populist ideology that appealed to rural religiosity in a rhetoric of Christian millenarianism.[72] By the 1860s, radicals adopted a very different stance toward religion, directing their fiercest polemics against the clergy and the church. Anticlericalism enabled radicals to mobilize urban workers and peasants alongside bourgeois Republicans without appealing to class antagonisms. Radicals used anticlericalism to appeal not only to urban workers but also to rural voters, many of whom sided with village mayors who challenged the power and prestige of local priests by supporting free and compulsory secular education.[73] The solution to electoral defeat became the reform of education to inculcate republican values and attitudes rather than revolutionary action. Free secular education would promote equality of opportunity and give meaning to majority rule by creating more autonomous individuals, less susceptible to the clientelistic influences of local notables and clergy.

Positivism was a third key element of the emerging radical synthesis of the 1860s. Radical ideology of the 1860s emphasized scientific understanding rather than morality and virtue, key features of the radicalism of 1848. The romanticism and moral overtones that permeated the populist rhetoric of radical republican leaders like Ledru-Rollin was missing from radical republican rhetoric of the 1860s, which appealed to reason not emotions. The new generation of radical Republicans, led by Leon Gambetta, were heavily influenced by Auguste Comte and his positivist faith in scientific progress.[74] Positivism strengthened the anticlericalism of radical republicanism and made radical ideology less open to the revolutionary tradition. The radical ideology of 1848, which absorbed the populist romanticism and millenarian spirit of rural republican socialism, was more willing to justify revolutionary violence than was the positivist radicalism of the 1860s. Whereas the former was capable of generating the moral outrage that might lead one to mount the barricades, positivism emphasized progress and order, not revolution. It asserted the triumph of science and reason. The inevitability of progress meant, among other things, the victory of the republic regardless of temporary setbacks. Given this inevitability, it was unnecessary to risk life and limb on the barricades when patience and faith in the triumph of reason would ensure victory.

A fourth key element of the radical synthesis was an emphasis on liberal political themes that had not played a central role in radical politics during the 1840s. The repressive political climate of the 1850s strengthened the liberal elements of radical thought. After the coup d'état of December 1851, Louis Napoleon Bonaparte subordinated the elected legislature to executive power and denied political opponents the right to association, a free press, and free speech. The repression fostered a shift in radical ideology and practice toward liberal political goals. Liberal themes, such as freedom of the press and association, the responsibility of ministers to the parliament, and the separation of church and state, became a more central part of the radical republican agenda. In elaborating their radical creed in the first issues of Saint-Étienne's newly created newspaper *L'Éclaireur*, the editors emphasized their commitment to "the impending triumph of genuine liberal ideas," for "individual liberty is the basis of all other freedoms." After calling for freedom of the press and assembly, the separation of Church and State, free public education, the transformation of armies into citizens' militias, more equitable taxes, and judicial reorganization, the editors proclaimed: "Believe us! Liberty will create peace and progress, not disorder." They concluded with an interpretation of the other two terms in the republican motto, defining "equality" as equality of opportunity made possible by free secular education and "fraternity" as the proliferation of associations dedicated to education, consumption, credit, and production.[75]

The liberal principle of strengthening civil society in opposition to state power found expression in a number of radical organizational initiatives of the 1860s. Radicals created secularized nongovernmental associations, like educational societies, that spread republican values. They adopted the associationalist themes that dominated early French socialism but devoted their energies to cross-class associations fostering secular education rather than workers' cooperatives. The split between the church and the Second Empire during the early 1860s provided radicals with the opportunity to establish new associations, such as the *Ligue de l'enseignement*, dedicated to popular secular education. These civic associations sponsored public lectures, financed popular libraries, and educated hundreds of thousands of workers.[76] These associational activities combined liberal commitments to a limited state and strong civil society with republican ideals of civic obligation, community, and participation. They enabled radicals to build cross-class solidarities abstracted from the class antagonisms of an industrial capitalist society.

Although radicals of the 1860s, like their predecessors of 1848, embraced an imperative mandate vision of democracy, they redefined the meaning of the imperative mandate. The earlier meaning was concisely summarized by Ledru-Rollin in 1841 as follows: "I am their leader, I must follow them." During the 1860s, radical leaders reinterpreted the doctrine of an imperative mandate to give it a distinctive capitalist tone, using the free market language of binding contracts rather than the sansculotte rhetoric of popular sovereignty. According to radical republican leaders of the 1860s, like Leon Gambetta and Jean Macé, voters were like clients who instructed elected officials to carry out their wishes, and these officials, like honest businessmen, were obliged to fulfill their contractual obligations. Jean Macé wrote: "Businessman or deputy, can an honest man be anything other than a machine for keeping promises?"[77]

The ideology and practice of radical republicanism, which blended liberal individualist and parliamentary democratic ideas while rejecting socialism, was not the product of either an omniscient bourgeoisie or an inevitable result of the functional requisites of capitalism. It was the result of a highly conflictual, often violent, political process of trial and error, of experimentation with alternative political strategies, especially at the local level, where Republican parties devised varied electoral platforms that integrated elements of liberalism, democracy, and socialism in different ways. But it was at the national level that the rules governing contention for power were formulated. Despite very different local political situations, Republicans faced the same national political opportunity structure.

The National Context of Local Republican Politics:
A Changing Political Opportunity Structure

The national political context that shaped local politics during the middle decades of the nineteenth century can be summarized as follows: the shift from a revolutionary to a conservative liberal monarchy during the years from 1830 to 1848; the brief establishment of a democratic republic in February 1848, which gravitated to the right and increasingly restricted the political liberties inaugurated by the revolution; and the establishment of an authoritarian Empire in December 1851 that was transformed into a liberal Empire during the 1860s. This summary suggests that shifts in the national political opportunity structure facing Republicans roughly followed abrupt transitions of regimes inaugurated by revolutions in 1830 and 1848 and by a coup d'état in 1851. Each regime was characterized by different rules concerning suffrage rights, the relationship between executive and legislative power, and rights to association, assembly, free speech, and freedom of the press. Although each regime marked an abrupt change in the national political opportunity structure, the gradual transformation of political regimes, for example, growing restrictions on civil liberties by the orleanist regime after 1834 or the liberalization of an authoritarian Imperial government during the 1860s, suggests that regime transitions are not the only markers of changing national political opportunity structures.

The ability of Republicans to contend for state power was shaped by three key features of a shifting national political opportunity structure: the exent of suffrage rights, which determined the ability of Republicans to successfully contest the established regime via the ballot box; the balance of power between the executive and legislature, which made contested elections meaningful or relatively inconsequential; and changes in laws governing civil liberties, especially shifting restrictions on rights to association, assembly, free speech, and a free press, which affected Republicans' capacities for organizing and launching collective political actions. These three dimensions affected the electoral fortunes and strategic decisions of Republicans in localities throughout France. The following account briefly surveys these aspects of the shifting national political opportunity structure during the July Monarchy (1830–48), Second Republic (1848–51), and Second Empire (1851–70).

The Revolution of July 1830 toppled the Bourbon dynasty and established an orleanist regime based on representative government with a limited electorate. The regime maintained property restrictions on the right to vote but expanded the eligible electorate in municipal elections far beyond the narrow limits imposed on national elections; instituted elections for municipal councils; and resurrected local citizens' militias (i.e., National

Guard units) whose officers were elected by their troops. Although national laws restricted municipal voting rights based on the payment of taxes, there were fifteen times more eligible voters in municipal elections than in national elections in 1834. The electoral law of 1831 enfranchised 20–25 percent of all French males over the age of twenty-one for municipal elections.[78] Many professionals, shopkeepers, and well-to-do artisans participated in the election of National Guard leaders and city councilors, even though they did not qualify to vote in national elections because they paid less than two hundred francs in taxes. These electoral rules had important consequences for republican politics. Although weak in rural France, and possessing only a tiny minority in parliament, with only ten deputies on the eve of the 1848 revolution, Republicans captured municipal council majorities prior to 1848 in several important cities, including Toulouse, Rouen, Grenoble, and Strasbourg. They also won control of local National Guard units in many cities, which led to their dissolution in Lyon, Grenoble, Marseille, and Strasbourg in 1834–35. Republicanism remained concentrated in urban areas prior to 1848. Given that France was a predominantly rural country, this meant that Republicans were very weak at the national level, where wealthy orleanist and legitimist rural notables retained power, but strong in the larger cities, where they took advantage of the opportunities offered by a more democratic municipal electoral arena.

Conflicts over civil liberties and the balance between executive and legislative power helped bring about the downfall of the Bourbon regime in July 1830. The precipitating event for the 1830 revolution was the proclamation of the king's *Ordinances* of July 25, 1830. These political decrees suspended freedom of the press, reestablished censorship, dissolved the newly elected Chamber of Deputies, and altered the basis of calculating voter eligibility in order to restrict the power of the urban bourgeoisie. The revolution that established a constitutional monarchy rallied popular support behind the slogan "Long Live the Charter!", a reference to the constitutional charter of 1815 and the threat to constitutional government posed by the king's edicts. The new regime adopted the general principles of the liberal opposition to the prior Bourbon monarchy, depriving the king of the power to suspend laws, abolishing censorship, tolerating demonstrations, and making press crimes subject to jury trials.

The initial liberal policies of the orleanist regime were followed by a variety of repressive political measures in 1834, in response to the strikes, working-class insurrections, and growing republican agitation that marked the period from 1832 to 1834. The Chambers passed national legislation in 1833 and 1834 to outlaw street vending of newspapers and limit the right to association and assembly. The laws, which prohibited any group from gathering without prior government authorization, were directed at both political clubs and working-class mutual aid societies, many of which had come under republican influence. In 1835, following an assassination attempt on Louis-Philippe that left eighteen dead, the legislature passed laws that further restricted the press, defined criticism of the king or form of government as criminal libel, and made it illegal to advocate republicanism. The orleanist regime also abandoned its liberal commitment to enhancing the power of the legislature vis-à-vis the executive branch. The government undermined the independence of parliament by offering deputies hundreds of administrative positions, as diplomats, magistrates, and public engineers. These *députés-functionnaires* challenged the executive branch at the risk of losing their lucrative positions in the state bureaucracy and endangering the flow of government resources from various ministries to their constituents. By 1839, those opposed to the regime, including Republicans, Legitimists, and different dynastic tendencies, made royal intervention in politics a central issue of contention.

The national context of local politics shifted dramatically in February 1848, with the revolutionary establishment of a republican regime. The revolution replaced a central government that had banned workers' associations, outlawed strikes, and excluded workers from voting or holding political office with a regime committed to universal male suffrage and freedom of association and assembly. Universal male suffrage did not produce the "social republic" feared by conservatives and anticipated by many Republicans. The implementation of an unpopular forty-five centime tax alienated the peasantry, whose anger was mobilized by conservative electoral rhetoric depicting unemployed urban workers living comfortably off government handouts. Rural voters turned out in large numbers in April 1848 to elect a National Assembly dominated by conservative notables. Many of these men were crypto-royalists who had reluctantly accepted the republic as a fait accompli. The election paved the way for the closing of the National Workshops, which provoked the June 1848 insurrection in Paris and bloody repression by liberal republican officials. The repression of the insurrection was followed by a series of laws which placed greater restrictions on the press, limited the right to association, and reestablished caution money for newspapers.

The national political opportunity structure shifted again after Republicans took up arms in June 1849 to defend the constitution, violated by Louis Napoleon Bonaparte's decision to send an expeditionary force to aid the papacy in its fight against Italian republican forces. The abortive insurrection was led by radical republican deputies, after the National Assembly failed to pass a bill of impeachment against Bonaparte. The failed insurrection was followed by a law of June 19, 1849 that severely restricted the right to association. It gave the government the right to prohibit secret societies hiding under the cover of legally authorized nonpolitical societies, circles, *chambrées*, fraternal orders, working-class mutual benefit societies, and newspapers. New press laws were also passed, which raised caution money for many newspapers. Banquets were outlawed on the ground that they might trouble public order. Despite the repression, Republicans continued their effort to mobilize popular electoral support in the cities and countryside, turning to the ballot box in the belief that eventually they could win over a majority of French voters.

The growing electoral success of Republicans prompted a conservative reaction that included a new electoral law, passed on May 31, 1850. The law disenfranchised 2.7 million voters, reducing the electorate by 28 percent by excluding those who had not paid taxes, had a police record, or did not reside in the same place for over three years. The end of universal male suffrage did not lead Republicans to abandon the ballot box, but it generated divisions over strategy, the revival of secret conspiratorial societies, and increasing electoral abstentionism.[79] The National Assembly's refusal, in July 1851, to approve a constitutional amendment allowing Bonaparte to serve another term of office as president of the republic set the stage for a coup d'état by foreclosing any legal path to his effort to retain power. The final roadblock to the illegal seizure of power was removed in November 1851, when the National Assembly voted not to grant the president of the Assembly the power to requisition troops. Three-fourths of the Assembly's republican representatives opposed granting the Assembly such power, out of fear that it might lead to a royalist coup d'état. As a result, the parliament was incapable of effectively resisting Bonaparte's coup d'état in December 1851, which marked the death of the Second Republic.

The coup d'état of December 2, 1851 inaugurated a new national political opportunity structure. On that fateful day, Bonaparte announced the dissolution of the National Assembly, the reestablishment of universal male suffrage, a new constitution that extended the president's term to ten years and sharply reduced the power of the legislature, and a plebiscite to ratify these changes. Over twenty-six thousand people were arrested for resisting the coup d'état, the largest wave of mass political arrests that France had ever witnessed. The coup was followed by an intensified political repression that destroyed opposition parties. The new regime expanded police powers, centralized policing activities, and imprisoned suspected republican opponents of the regime rather than waiting to arrest them for specific political actions. Ordinary laws and judicial procedures were temporarily suspended in favor of military laws that gave unrestrained powers to the police, the military, and the prefects. Special tribunals—"mixed commissions" composed of the prefect, attorney general, and commanding general—were established to summarily judge suspected political opponents, including many Republicans who took no active part in the resistance to the coup but were convicted of having been active in the republican opposition. New press laws were implemented that eliminated jury trials for political offenses, raised the stamp tax, granted prefects the power to suspend newspapers without authorization from Paris, and prohibited any discussion of "the political or social economy."[80] The new regime also targeted the informal networks of cafés, cabarets, and taverns that had become breeding grounds of republicanism and set up an extensive secret police network to keep close watch over suspected opponents of the new regime.

Louis Napoleon Bonaparte represented an ambiguous figure vis-à-vis democracy. Claiming to base his rule on popular consent, he embraced universal male suffrage yet rejected political parties as divisive factions, severely restricted associational rights, arrested or exiled republican leaders, and relied on administrative pressures and state patronage to win carefully managed elections. Although the regime preserved universal male suffrage, it eliminated the civil liberties and parliamentary power that made party competition and contested elections meaningful. The government subordinated elected representatives to a powerful executive branch, supplemented the elected National Assembly with an appointed Senate, and deprived parliament of the power to initiate legislation.

The national political opportunity structure began to shift in 1859, as a result of the regime's effort to develop support for its foreign and economic policies. The conservative political alliance that had initially rallied behind the regime in response to the "red threat" fell apart due to the elimination of this threat by the repression of the 1850s, a controversial foreign policy in Italy, and the implementation of the Cobden-Chevalier free trade treaty with England. Imperial candidates made a poor showing in the election of 1863, due mainly to Catholic and protectionist opposition. The government responded with an electoral strategy designed to broaden its base of support among workers and liberal Republicans and Orleanists through policies of political and social reform. After nearly a decade of highly repressive policies designed to silence organized political opposition, the Imperial government attempted to expand its support by implementing liberal political initiatives.

During the 1860s, the Imperial government enacted a variety of reforms to make the executive branch more accountable to parliament and remove restrictions on newspapers and on the right to assembly and association. The regime legalized strikes in May 1864 but maintained restrictions on the right to assembly and association. In March 1868, an Imperial edict decreed that [depoliticized] workers' organizations would be tolerated, provided they submitted their statutes for government approval, gave the authorities copies of the minutes of their meetings, and allowed police agents to attend their gatherings. The liberal reforms antagonized many conservatives, although some Orleanists and Legitimists supported political liberalization as a way to strengthen parliamentary control over the executive branch. The reforms gave Republicans and workers greater freedom to organize and to launch rebellious collective actions. The general amnesty of August 1859 allowed numerous exiled republican leaders, many of whom never forgave Bonaparte for his crime of 1851, to return home and join the opposition. The late 1860s witnessed a revival of working-class labor associations, an outburst of working-class strike activity, and growing republican electoral strength. In the elections of 1869, Republicans increased their representation in the *Corps législatif* from seventeen to thirty seats. Republicans carried all the larger cities and opposition candidates won 3.3 million votes, compared to 4.4 million for government candidates. The republican revival of the late 1860s remained concentrated in the cities, as made clear by the plebiscite of May 1870, in which French voters overwhelmingly approved the liberalized Empire.

The preceding discussion of the national context of local republican politics suggests a certain uniformity in the political situation facing Republicans throughout France. However, despite a shared national political opportunity structure, republican politics developed in very different ways across localities, due in large part to distinctive patterns of economic development and class formation. The ability of Republicans to mobilize the support of heterogeneous groups in opposition to the government varied across cities, because distinctive patterns of early industrialization created different conflicts between workers and employers as well as different divisions and solidarities among workers and bourgeois. The following chapter explores these differences.

PART TWO

A Tale of Three Cities: Toulouse, Saint-Étienne, and Rouen

FRANCE

TOULOUSE, SAINT-ÉTIENNE, ROUEN

Lille

Le Havre   **Rouen**

Seine   Reims

Paris   Marne

Meuse

Brest   Strasbourg

Moselle

Rennes   Rhine

Le Mans   Seine

Loire   Saône

Nantes   Doubs

Loire

Saône

Clermont-Ferrand   Rhône

Lyon

Saint-Étienne

Grenoble

Gironde

Bordeaux   Dordogne

Lot

Garonne   Rhône

Nice

Toulouse

Montpelier

Marseille

Toulon

Corsica

0   50   100   150   200 Mi.

0   50   100   150   200 Km.

N

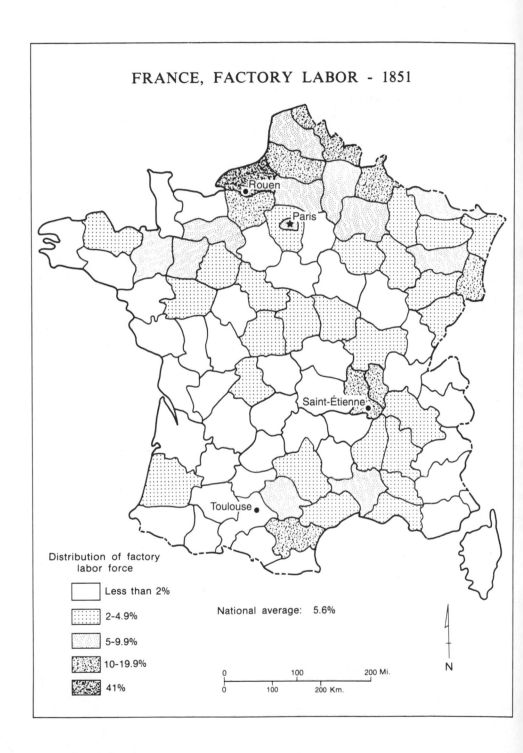

FRANCE, FACTORY LABOR - 1851

Rouen

Paris

Saint-Étienne

Toulouse

Distribution of factory
labor force

Less than 2%

2-4.9%

5-9.9%

10-19.9%

41%

National average: 5.6%

0   100   200 Mi.

0   100   200 Km.

N

CHAPTER THREE

Patterns of Industrialization and Class Formation

Recent research by economic historians of the nineteenth century has challenged the traditional view of early capitalist industrialization as centered around the growth of large-scale units of mechanized factory production. Small-scale, nonmechanized artisanal workshops have been portrayed as dynamic elements in the process of early industrialization rather than as archaic forms destined for extinction. Raphael Samuel writes of nineteenth-century England: "Capitalist growth was rooted in a subsoil of small-scale enterprise." Industrial production based on "the primacy of labor power" and on the "strength, skill, quickness, and sureness of touch of the individual worker rather than on the simultaneous and repetitive operations of the machine" was the "dominant pattern of growth" in Victorian England.[1] Gareth Stedman Jones's analysis of British industrialization challenges the assumption of a nearly automatic relationship between industrialization and increases in the scale of production. In nineteenth-century Britain, he writes, "because labor was plentiful and cheap, and demand was fashion-prone in addition to being seasonally and cyclically variable, increasing demand was met by the addition of new units of production rather than by economies of scale; and new technology was capital- rather than labor-saving."[2]

Studies of nineteenth-century French industrialization have added more voices to this chorus of revisionism. Patrick O'Brien and Caglar Keyder have documented very high levels of labor productivity in many industrial sectors that remained dominated by small-scale, nonmechanized enterprises. French industrialization, they argue, was different, not "retarded," in relationship to Britain, for it utilized the comparative advantages it had in the production of high-quality luxury artisanal goods to develop more productive workshops, but less productive factories.[3] The central features of nineteenth-century French industrialization, wrote Richard Roehl, included "a relatively high proportion of light, consumer-goods industries in the mix of total industrial production and the absence of a trend toward concentration in industrial organization, a tendency for scale to remain small. . . ."[4] T. J. Markovitch's quantitative study of nineteenth-century French industrialization found that during the middle decades of the nineteenth century small-scale household and handicraft production together accounted for a majority of French industrial output (59.9%) and employed the majority of French workers engaged in industry (70–75%).[5] Although workshop and household industry's share of total industrial production declined relative to capital-intensive factory production, small-scale industry continued to account for more than half the total value of industrial production.[6]

Most explanations of the continuing importance of small-scale, labor-intensive industrial production in nineteenth-century France emphasize France's relatively slow rate of urbanization, low proportion of industrial output sold abroad, and relatively high proportion of consumers with "middling incomes" who cared about high quality and design.[7] In focusing on these market factors, economic historians have failed to explore how the changing character of production relations within small-scale household and handicraft industries may have contributed to the persistence of small-scale production.[8] Household, handicraft, and factory forms of industry contained distinctive class relations that experienced dramatic changes during the course of the nineteenth century, as they were increasingly subordinated to the pressures exerted by an expanding capitalist market. Each form of production experienced technical innovations, which meant higher productivity and industrial growth, as well as explosive class conflicts between workers and capitalists.[9] The differing degree and pace of development of each of these forms of urban industrial production within particular cities generated distinctive divisions and solidarities among workers, which translated into varied opportunities and obstacles for local republican militants.

Recent historical research has challenged the notion that early European industrialization produced an increasingly homogeneous urban industrial labor force. Historians have carefully documented the diversity of living and working situations facing the growing number of people who were forced to sell their labor for a wage.[10] Industrialization simultaneously produced homogeneity and fragmentation within the urban industrial labor force, creating new skills while eliminating others, providing some workers with higher wages and more advantageous labor market situations and others with deteriorating working and living conditions.[11] In examining the diversity of situations facing wage laborers during the course of early industrialization, historians have focused upon a variety of different divisions within the working class. Proponents of the notion of a "labor aristocracy," for example, analyze differentiation within the working class in terms of a privileged stratum defined by the regularity and level of wages, workplace authority, or skill.[12] A labor aristocracy emerges, writes E. J. Hobsbawn, "when the economic circumstances of capitalism make it possible to grant significant concessions to the proletariat, within which certain strata of workers manage by means of their special scarcity, skill, strategic position, organizational strength, etc., to establish notably better conditions for themselves than the rest."[13] Gender was another basis for a clear and persistent division among nineteenth-century urban wage laborers. Women systematically received much lower wages and were assigned jobs with much less workplace authority than were male workers, as employers recruited and rewarded workers on the basis of their sex and marital status.[14]

Early industrialization proceeded very unevenly across different areas of France, with the growth of factory production concentrated in certain regions and cities (see map 2). This chapter examines how divergent patterns of early industrialization produced distinctive conflicts between workers and employers and divisions and solidarities among workers in Toulouse, Saint-Étienne, and Rouen. If we understand skills or gender not as a possession or attribute of certain workers but as a contested and continually renegotiated social relationship between employers and workers, then the connection between shifts in power wrought by changes within various forms of industrial production and divisions among workers becomes evident.[15] My account highlights the timing and character of industrialization in each city, especially the respective role of household, handicraft, and factory production, and the changes in class relations that took place within each of these forms of production as they became increasingly tied to an emerging capitalist order. The focus is on connecting different forms of industrial production to distinctive patterns of working-class solidarities and divisions that proved consequential for the efforts of liberal, radical, and socialist Republicans to mobilize popular support. Divisions among workers in each city are analyzed in terms of patterns of residential settlement, associational life, collective action, and informal social networks. The goal is to map out each pattern of early capitalist industrialization, delineate the consequences for class conflict and for divisions and solidarities within each city's working class, and examine how these conflicts, divisions, and solidarities created opportunities and obstacles for Republicans in their attempt to mobilize popular support.

THE INDUSTRIALIZATION OF TOULOUSE

Toulouse, the sixth largest city in France in 1851, was an important administrative, commercial, and educational center for the entire southwest of France. The city was the commercial center for the region's prosperous grain trade and it possessed numerous prestigious courts and educational institutions employing large numbers of judges, lawyers, and professors. A port city on the Garonne River, Toulouse was surrounded by a vast agricultural hinterland. Grains, wines, and woolen textiles passed through Toulouse's warehouses before being shipped along the *Canal du Midi* to numerous cities in the south of France. Although some local industries, producing shoes and carriages, sold their products overseas on an international market, the bulk of the city's commerce was oriented around local and regional trade. This meant that central state tariff policies designed to foster international commerce provided Republicans with powerful issues around which to rally popular support. For example, during the July Monarchy, state policies fostering the internationalization of the grain trade enabled liberal Republicans to mobilize electoral support among the propertied electorate, using a political rhetoric that made the defense of regional economic interests an issue of municipal liberties and decentralization.

The distribution of wealth at Toulouse reflected the character of the city's economy, especially the dominance of commercial rather than industrial capital and the close ties that the local economy had to regional agricultural production. Local inheritance records reveal that the city's wealth was highly concentrated in the hands of an urban aristocratic elite, which controlled approximately 33 percent of Toulouse's wealth in 1846.[16] This wealth was based primarily on large, landed property holdings in the wheat-growing Garonne valley and on the profitable grain trade they generated. Most of this wealth was invested in land and commerce and very little of it was devoted to industrial or financial ventures. The city's bourgeoisie relied heavily on commercial and administrative rather than industrial activities as a source of its wealth. Wholesale merchants were the wealthiest segment of the local bourgeoisie and industrial capital, based on investments in large-scale industry, accounted for a very limited proportion of Toulouse's property holding.

Toulouse never developed large mechanized steam-powered factories, in large part because of its distance from any major coal or iron fields. Whereas rich coal deposits fueled the iron, steel, and armaments industries in Saint-Étienne and numerous streams and rivers provided a relatively cheap source of energy for Rouen's early textile factories, Toulouse's industry was dependent on the water power of the Garonne River, along which the city's factories were established, and on expensive coal that was shipped in from Carmaux, ninety kilometers away.[17] Industry was less developed in Toulouse than in Saint-Étienne and Rouen, with 32.5 percent of Toulouse's labor force engaged in industry in 1830 and 38 percent in 1872.[18] Most of these workers (74% in 1830 and 65% in 1872) were handicraft artisans employed mainly in the production of food, clothing, and housing. The rapid growth of the city's population, from 60,350 in 1830 to 110,990 in 1872, created an expanded consumer demand for the products of local handicraft industry. In 1872, as in 1830, the ten largest trades in Toulouse were tailors, shoemakers, joiners, masons, metalsmiths, hatters, bakers, carriage makers, carpenters, and plasterers.[19] The construction, clothing, baking, carriage, and metal industries employed the vast majority of the city's handicraft artisans. All of these industries remained predominantly based on small-scale units of handicraft production, although they all witnessed either the penetration of manufactories, the growth of urban household production, or the development of merchant capitalist subcontracting during the middle decades of the nineteenth century. These three economic changes generated the grievances and class conflicts that led many of Toulouse's handicraft artisans to embrace republican socialism.

Some factory production did develop at Toulouse during the middle decades of the nineteenth century. Factory workers accounted for a small but growing percentage of the city's working class, increasing from 4.1 percent in 1830 to 11.3 percent in 1872.[20] These factories remained relatively small in scale, developed in a number of different industries, and relied heavily upon artisanal labor.[21] The largest factories in the city, the arsenal and the tobacco factory, were government-owned enterprises. Many of the factories listed in various industrial surveys of the period employed mainly artisanal labor. Most of Toulouse's factories existed within industries that remained predominantly handicraft in character. For example, although most of the city's hatters continued to labor in small handicraft workshops, by 1865 local hat factories employed 308 workers, or approximately 45 percent of the city's hatters. Most cabinetmakers also remained employed in small handicraft workshops, but by 1865 there were five cabinet-making factories employing 146 workers.[22] Although joiners, masons, and carpenters—the three largest construction trades in the city—also remained employed mainly in small handicraft shops, by 1865 there was a building-joining factory employing 135 workers and four marble-cutting factories employing 92 workers, and in 1868 there was a mechanized sawmill employing 32 workers.[23]

The joiners, printers, carriage makers, metalsmiths, hatters, cabinetmakers, marble masons, and bakers who found work in these manufactories faced foremen and factory discipline, which their counterparts in handicraft industry did not have to contend with. Although the growth of these factories entailed an increased scale and greater division of labor, they typically did not involve the use of steam power or the mechanization of production. Although they were wage laborers, artisans in these early factories, like their counterparts in handicraft production, typically owned the small tools they used in the factory. Despite their relatively small scale and their reliance on artisanal labor, Toulouse's nonmechanized factories differed from handicraft workshops in that factory employers, unlike master artisans, did not work alongside those they employed.

A second aspect of capitalist industrialization in Toulouse was the penetration of merchant capital into the city's two largest consumer-goods industries—tailoring and shoemaking—and into construction, the industry that employed the largest number of the city's artisans. During the 1830s and 1840s, ready-made standardized shoes and clothing increasingly challenged the custom-made products of small handicraft workshops. In Toulouse, shoe warehouses emerged as centers of organization for cutting leather and distributing leather pieces that were then assembled in the homes of local shoe stitchers. By 1858, this merchant-capitalist organization of shoe production yielded an annual estimated output of one million francs. The Toulouse Chamber of Commerce reported that "incessant activity reigns in the factories engaged in ready-made production of shoes and among the homeworkers (*ouvriers en chambre*) who supply them."[24] The de Planet industrial survey of 1865 lists three such factories, which were really warehouses that distributed cut leather to household workers, employing three hundred workers, or approximately 15 percent of the entire trade.

Urban household production made even earlier and greater inroads in Toulouse's garment industry. The city directories of 1840 and 1872 list three types of tailoring establishments: (1) small-scale master artisans (*tailleurs à facon*), shop owners with little capital who produced custom-made clothing from cloth provided by their customers; (2) artisanal tailors (*marchand tailleurs*) who had larger capital investments, including stocks of cloth that they usually bought in volume from suppliers on credit; and (3) large-scale merchant-capitalist producers of ready-made clothing (*maisons de confection*). The 1840 listing of Toulouse's tailoring enterprises includes forty-four small-scale master artisans, thirty-three larger-scale artisanal tailors, and eighteen ready-made producers. In the 1872 directory, there are listings for forty-nine small tailors, ninety larger artisanal tailors, and twenty-seven ready-made producers.[25] In other words, small-scale, custom-made tailoring dropped from 46 percent to 30 percent of local enterprises, while larger-scale artisanal tailoring and ready-made production organized by merchant capitalists grew to include a larger percentage of local firms.

In both tailoring and shoemaking, the incursion of merchant capital meant a transformation of the labor force as women and children household producers increasingly replaced handicraft artisans. This movement from handicraft workshops to household production did not increase the control employers exercised over the work process, but it did mean a more intensified division of labor than was the case in handicraft industry. It also involved an expansion of the scope of the market, since urban household industries, like local manufactories, produced for an international world market, exporting their products throughout Europe and overseas to the colonies.

Merchant capitalists also made important inroads, by other means, into the city's construction industry. During the 1840s, entrepreneurs increasingly hired subcontractors to organize different stages of the production process and provided credit, raw materials, or both to the subcontractors they hired. The subcontractor (*marchandeur* or *tacheron*) hired workers who executed the work given to them with materials and larger tools provided by the merchant-capitalist entrepreneur. Large entrepreneurs did not organize their own separate industry, but entered the fragmented local industry and engaged established master artisans as their subcontractors. Thus they split the small shops into independents and subcontractors, making the conflict all the more bitter. This system of subcontracting (*marchandage*) made the maintenance of uniform wage and working conditions extremely difficult and generated intense hostility on the part of masters and workers in the building trades.[26] In May 1848, small masters expressed their opposition to the disruption of standard hours of work within the industry. They sent a letter to the city council seeking approval for a request to enforce standard hours for starting, meals, and finishing throughout the construction industry. The masters affirmed their solidarity with their journeymen against local construction entrepreneurs, stating that "as workers ourselves, we will never abandon the cause of our brother workers; like them we have spent most of our lives with the hammer, trowel, and saw in our hands."[27]

The third key feature of early capitalist industrialization in Toulouse, the most important in terms of the number of workers affected, was the response of small-scale handicraft producers to the growth of newer forms of industrial production. The industrialization of Toulouse did not abruptly replace artisanal workshop production with mechanized factories staffed by unskilled proletarians, but it did transform handicraft production. Some artisanal masters, along with their workers, were deprived of their jobs because the custom-made products of small-scale production could not compete with the cheaper ready-made products of capitalist factory and household industry. Many other small handicraft masters responded to growing competition by enlarging the scale of their workshops, intensifying the pace of work, and ignoring traditional practices governing the use of apprentices and the division of labor. Faced with competition from factories or urban household production, they became capitalist masters; that is, they continued working alongside their journeymen and apprentices but enlarged the scale of their operations, hired apprentices to do work formerly done by qualified journeymen, increased the number of workers they employed, and intensified the division of labor. They thereby more efficiently exploited the artisanal labor they employed rather than introduce new machinery.

Small-scale handicraft production continued to exist in most artisanal trades, but these small handicraft workshops increasingly coexisted alongside handicraft shops owned by master artisans who had enlarged the scale of their operations as well as alongside larger-scale manufactories. This development is evident in the city directory statistics cited above on different types of enterprises in the garment industry. Other sources document this same trend in a variety of different trades. A city council commission report on Toulouse's baking industry in March 1848 noted that although most of the city's 250 masters owned only one or two ovens and hired only one or two workers, there were 20 masters who owned three ovens and 11 masters who owned more than three ovens and employed numerous workers.[28] A similar situation of the coexistence of large and small-scale enterprises existed in the city's cabinet-making industry, which was even more concentrated. In 1869 only 38 of the city's 100 masters regularly employed workers, but 6 employers hired 118 of the city's 343 workers.[29] Although shoemaking workshops also remained predominantly small in scale, by 1855 a number of masters, including Jean Guille, who employed 20 workers, and Jean Barbet, who employed 20 to 25, had greatly expanded the scale of their operations.[30] During the wheelwrights' strike of 1861, a local police report stated that the small masters in the industry were very jealous of the real carriage makers ("*véritable carrossiers*"), like Monsieur Mercier, a master carriage maker who had centralized the diverse operations of carriage construction under one roof in his own larger workshop.[31] Although disregard of traditional regulations that had previously governed their trades generated intense conflict between masters and journeymen, it enabled masters to maintain their relatively small workshops and to expand their production. Industrial capitalist development in Toulouse did not eliminate artisans; it transformed their work settings, made handicraft workshops more competitive, and generated class conflicts within handicraft industry that enabled socialist activists to mobilize working-class support for the cause of the social republic.

WORKING-CLASS FORMATION IN TOULOUSE

Early industrialization in Toulouse reproduced gender divisions separating the service and industrial sectors of the local economy as well as skill divisions separating proletarians from artisans within industry. It simultaneously reduced divisions among artisans based on trade loyalties, thereby fostering the growth of class solidarities among skilled male workers. Service workers, mainly domestic servants, accounted for 21 percent of the city's labor force. In contrast to Rouen and Saint-Étienne, the vast majority of female workers in Toulouse were employed in the provision of services, as domestic servants, laundresses, and street vendors, although some women found employment in local textile, tobacco, paper, and food processing factories, and as household garment workers. Dispersed into numerous households, working in their own homes, or peddling goods in local marketplaces, service workers did not organize, launch strikes, or join mid-century, working-class political movements. The city's numerous female service workers remained relatively isolated and excluded from the organizing and collective action of the predominantly male workers employed in industry, who provided leadership for the city's working-class Republicans.

The city's unskilled proletarians also remained marginal to the political mobilizations of the period, which were dominated by artisans.[32] Artisans, who were employed in the workshops, households, and factories of local industries, constituted 37 percent of Toulouse's working class in 1872, while unskilled and semiskilled proletarians employed in industry and transport accounted for 30 percent. Proletarians were employed as semiskilled and unskilled workers in factories, sometimes alongside artisans, and, in much larger numbers, as unskilled casual laborers in the construction industry and as haulers and carters in local commerce and transportation. Artisans received much higher wages than proletarians. Although artisanal wages varied across trades, most artisans earned an average daily wage between 2.5 and 3 francs in 1867, compared to only 1.75 francs for unskilled day laborers. The lowest paid artisans were those whose trades had witnessed an influx of female household producers—shoemakers and tailors—while the highest paid trades were highly skilled cabinetmakers, watchmakers, and ornamental sculptors.[33] Even within the walls of the same factory, artisans and proletarians earned very different incomes. For example, the Olin foundry, which employed 205 men, 22 women, and 15 children in 1840, paid its male employees wages ranging from 1.5 to 6 francs per day, depending on their skills, while the women received only .75 to 1.5 francs per day and the children .75 francs. A similar pattern was evident in the city's other factories, with a fairly wide wage range among male workers in factories employing both artisans and proletarians and with women and children earning a small fraction of male wages. Those manufactories that employed only proletarians, like the Moulin de Château grain mill and the Bazacle paper mill, paid uniformly low wages to their workers.[34]

The skills of artisans, which were the basis for higher wages and substantial workplace autonomy, also fostered craft pride and occupational subcultures that were absent among proletarian workers. Artisans were also far more literate than proletarians, which may help to account for their greater politicization, since literacy meant easier access to the numerous republican and socialist brochures and newspapers that circulated in local cafés, taverns, and cabarets.[35] Whereas most skilled trades had developed some form of labor organization by 1870, the vast majority of the city's proletarians remained unorganized. Artisans dominated the city's working-class associations, informal centers of sociability, strikes, and republican socialist movement.

The majority of artisans and proletarians migrated to Toulouse from the surrounding countryside during the mid-century, but patterns of residential settlement differed between these two groups.[36] Although a majority of proletarians settled alongside artisans in the rapidly growing faubourgs, a larger proportion of artisans than proletarians inhabited the older inner-city neighborhoods (of Saint Sernin, La Daurade, Arsenal, Saint George, La Dalbade, and Saint-Étienne), close to the hub of local economic and political life. A larger percentage of proletarians than artisans settled in the outer-lying sparsely populated areas of the city, some of which were located ten to fifteen kilometers from the city's center.[37]

The gender composition of the artisanal and proletarian labor force constituted another important difference between these two groups. Whereas the ranks of unskilled service and factory workers included large numbers of women, artisanal trades were much more sex-segregated. This difference between artisan and proletarian populations, along with differences in marital status, had political implications. A smaller percentage of male artisans than male proletarians were married in 1830 and 1872. In the 1872 census, 38 percent of the city's male artisans were bachelors compared to only 19 percent of male industrial workers. Bachelorhood typically meant that more time was spent in highly politicized centers of male sociability, including the city's numerous cafés, cabarets, and taverns. The greater percentage of women and of married men among the proletarian population meant lessened participation in the informal centers of sociability where republican and socialist political ideas spread and, along with the exclusion of women from associational activities that retained a fraternal character, may have reinforced the division between artisans and proletarians.

Among artisans, the growth of new forms of urban industrial production appears to have fostered class solidarities rather than creating new divisions. Although artisans were employed in a variety of different work settings, including factories, households, and small workshops, employment in different forms of productive activity did not become an important source of division. Factory bakers or joiners, for example, did not organize separately, or develop patterns of informal social interaction distinctive from members of their trade employed in small handicraft workshops. The same was true for those shoemakers and tailors who labored in their households and those who continued working in the shops of small masters. In June 1840, when approximately three hundred of the city's tailors went on strike for higher piece rates and a uniform citywide rate scale for the entire industry, they offered two francs per day to all household workers who joined them.[38] The diversity of productive relations encountered by members of the same trade did, however, help to make those who continued to labor in traditional workshops aware of the threat posed to their way of life by alternative forms of industrial production. For many artisans, republican socialist visions of cooperative production offered a potential defense against this threat.

Republican socialist themes of equality also appealed to artisans who, though much better off than proletarian workers, were by no means highly privileged workers. During times of crisis, they often found themselves thrown into the same destitute situation faced by less skilled proletarians. In the 1830 municipal census, 48 percent of the city's artisans were listed as living in poverty (*indigent, pauvre, vit de la journée*) along with 70 percent of the city's proletarians.[39] Vagrancy records for the late Second Empire also suggest that many unemployed artisans were also forced to live and beg in the streets. Although a majority of the 1,420 individuals arrested for vagrancy from November 1865 to December 1871 listed occupations as unskilled day laborers, a large proportion (30%) were destitute artisans whose skills were not a sufficient guarantee against homelessness and poverty.[40]

Republican socialist rhetoric appealed to workers in a language of class that resonated with artisans' experiences, due to the growth of solidarities fostered by capitalist industrialization. Although early industrialization in Toulouse reinforced divisions among workers rooted in gender and skills, it reduced divisions among artisans rooted in trade loyalties. Increasing numbers of artisans, though able to maintain strong craft communities, became subjected to deteriorating working conditions as capitalist development transformed their trades. As a result, artisans increasingly expressed their grievances and solidarities in a language and behavior that transcended trade boundaries and occasionally embraced nonartisanal workers. This change is evident in the associations, strikes, and political activities of the city's artisans.

During the early decades of the nineteenth century, the artisans of Toulouse were organized into *compagnonnages*, highly status-conscious journeymen's associations with elaborate rituals, status symbols, and internal hierarchies. *Compagnonnages* encouraged strong craft pride, promoting hierarchical status distinctions among trades. These distinctions were reflected in the refusal to admit bakers and shoemakers, who exercised what were considered to be less noble crafts, in the frequent roughing up of subordinate members, and in violent street brawls between rival orders (*devoirs*) to which the *compagnonnages* affiliated. Violent street fights pitting worker against worker over symbolic issues were common in Toulouse throughout the 1830s. By the end of the 1840s, violent confrontations among workers had disappeared from the scene, as a new spirit of solidarity emerged among workers in all trades. This emerging consciousness of common identity was reflected in the gradual disappearance of the *compagnonnage* during the 1840s and the parallel growth of mutual benefit societies. By 1862, there were ninety-six local mutual benefit societies providing unemployment, sickness, accident, and old age insurance to an estimated eighteen thousand workers.[41] Mutual benefit societies rejected the strict hierarchy, often oppressive rituals, and status-conscious spirit of the *compagnonnage*. These associations accepted skilled as well as unskilled workers, but trade communities often provided the basis of recruitment, although a few associations, like the Saint Saturnin mutual aid society, included both artisans and proletarians within its ranks.[42] Many of these organizations became centers of republican socialist propaganda and recruitment. "These societies," wrote the city's police commissioner in November 1850, "are really socialist societies that better disguise their revolutionary schemes. . . ."[43]

As artisans faced a growing threat to their control over access to their trades and over the pace and process of their work, they no longer found their identities in the status and privileges of their trade and its ritualized exclusivism. Traditional trade loyalties rooted in communal ties were not abruptly abandoned in favor of class solidarities; they were transformed to meet new needs and aspirations. Trade loyalties continued to underpin working-class social organization, but new forms of association increasingly fostered cooperation and community among skilled workers regardless of their trade. This decline of traditional divisions within the city's working class during the 1840s is evident in the political activities of Toulouse's workers. The rhetoric of the most politically active workers in the city identified the overcoming of craft divisions among skilled workers as a central task. The *Société des travailleurs*, a working-class republican electoral association founded in 1848 to ensure the selection of workers as candidates in the National Assembly election, had as its stated goal "the prompt and complete fusion of all trades (*corps d'état*) into a general association of workers."[44]

The growth of class solidarities bridging prior trade divisions, as well as divisions between artisans and proletarians, is evident in strike activities, which helped to construct classwide identities. Class solidarities came to play a more important role in strikes which, even when centered around the defense of trade interests, increasingly displayed a more general class character and a growing cooperation among workers of different trades. Acknowledgment of a common plight as propertyless wage laborers was reflected in the increasing exchange of strike support across occupational and city boundaries and even across the traditional barrier between artisans and proletarians. Collective action across trade boundaries was especially evident after the Revolution of 1848, when republican socialist militants encouraged the coordination of artisans' strike activities. In September 1850, artisans in the construction industry, joined by skilled clothing and carriage workers, met to discuss plans for a general strike for higher wages and shorter workdays. When construction joiners struck later in the month, local shoemakers, tailors, hatmakers, stonecutters, masons, plasterers, painters, and carriage workers met separately to discuss the possibility of a general strike. According to police, they decided instead to launch a series of successive strikes, out of fear that a general strike might provoke a state of siege.[45] Five bakers were arrested for soliciting money for the joiners' strike, and, after a meeting of joiners and bakers at the end of October, presided over by the republican socialist leader Jean Baptiste Astima, the bakers decided to strike as soon as the joiners won their strike.

Cooperation among striking workers in different trades and industries was also evident during the 1860s, when political liberalization encouraged workers to confront their employers. During the hatmakers' strike of January 1865, strikers circulated a resolution in the city to publicize their plight and gain the support of workers in other trades. In May 1868, striking carriage smiths received one hundred francs in aid from local hatmakers, and striking foundry workers received seventy-seven francs from workers at the arsenal, as well as promises of aid from foundry workers in other cities. During the strike wave in the summer of 1868, construction workers in different trades coordinated their strikes with one another in their struggle for a ten-hour day. Prior to their strike of May 1868, the masons met with other workers, including hatmakers and tawers, and during the strike they actively solicited aid from artisans in other trades. Proletarian factory workers, mainly women, appealed for aid from artisans in June 1866, when striking cotton print factory workers circulated pamphlets in the city to raise funds for their strike. When 1,000 of the city's 1,050 female tobacco factory workers went on strike over the increased fines and work discipline imposed by a new director in May 1870, none of their fifty fellow male workers joined them. Although their fellow male factory workers refused to support them, handicraft artisans demonstrated in support of the female strikers at the factory gates. When police dispersed the crowd, a young baker was arrested along with three of the strikers. Strike support funds were also collected by republican socialist militants in various handicraft workshops of the city.[46]

The gradual decline of trade divisions among artisans in Toulouse was fostered by political activists. A rhetoric of class solidarity was initially elaborated and spread in the context of political movements of republican socialists and Icarian communist militants during the 1830s and 1840s. The overcoming of craft divisions, and of divisions between artisans and proletarians, was not a direct consequence of economic changes, but a result of the spread of republican socialist ideas and practices, the popularity of which was tied to economic changes. The barriers separating artisans and proletarianized workers in Toulouse were bridged in a context of politicized struggles with employers in which republican socialist militants played a key role. Although Toulouse's mid-nineteenth-century republican movement excluded women and attracted few proletarians, it elaborated a political rhetoric that called on all workers to unite as propertyless wage laborers in pursuit of an alternative social order.

Divisions among workers arising from Toulouse's pattern of early industrialization created opportunities for republican socialists in their effort to mobilize artisans around a rhetoric of class solidarity. Craft solidarities cut across different forms of industrial production, uniting artisans employed in handicraft workshops, households, and factories. Grievances generated by changing production relations, which republican socialists used to mobilize workers, cut across different industries, including construction, clothing, hat-making, furniture, carriage-making, and printing. Industrial diversity was not a significant source of divisions within the working class because these industries experienced similar patterns of development, remaining dominated by handicrafts which were transformed in the face of competition from newer forms of production. Republican socialist rhetoric was grounded in a vision of cooperative trade socialism that resonated with the experiences and grievances of artisans across diverse industries. By reinforcing gender and skill divisions among workers, however, early industrialization in Toulouse also created obstacles for the political organization of classwide solidarities. The cooperative trade socialism espoused by working-class republican activists had less resonance and appeal for proletarians engaged in industry and commerce while the fraternalist organization and ideology of republicanism excluded the large number of women employed in services.

INDUSTRIALIZATION IN SAINT-ÉTIENNE

Saint-Étienne expanded from a small city of 24,342 inhabitants at the beginning of the nineteenth century to the seventh largest city in France by 1872, with a population of 110,814.[47] Unlike Toulouse and Rouen, Saint-Étienne was not an important center of commerce and administration before the nineteenth century. The city initially developed as a center of silk ribbon weaving during the eighteenth century and remained a center of industry, not commerce or administration, throughout the nineteenth century, when it was transformed by the growth of coal mining and metallurgy. The city's commerce was dominated by the products of industry, especially silk ribbons, which were sold on an international market. In contrast to Toulouse, Saint-Étienne was not an important religious, military, or educational center. Its bourgeoisie included few lawyers, judges, professionals, and administrators. The bourgeoisie of Saint-Étienne was sharply divided into industrial and commercial factions, with merchant capitalists in the ribbon, small arms, and hardware industries remaining socially separated from the industrial bourgeoisie, whose wealth was centered in the steel industry. The city's steel capitalists did not intermarry or launch business ventures with other segments of the local elite. Ribbon merchants did not invest their wealth in the city's prosperous and growing steel industry, despite its high rate of return on investments.[48] The distribution of wealth in Saint-Étienne reflected the economic dominance of silk ribbon merchants, as well as the growing economic power of steel industrial capitalists.[49] The owners of the city's coal mines did not reside in Saint-Étienne but in Paris and Lyon. These divisions within the capitalist class proved consequential for republican politics, enabling radical Republicans to win the support of several prominent steel industrialists in their battle against conservative silk merchants, who dominated local politics for decades, and to mobilize political opposition by targeting the wealthy nonresident owners of the region's coal mines.

Labor-force statistics for the Stéphanois region and for the city of Saint-Étienne reveal the continuing importance of the household-based silk ribbon industry during the mid-nineteenth century, despite the growth of mining and metallurgy.[50] The typical weaving household workshop contained one to four looms where the master, his family, and three or four hired helpers worked.[51] Wives, daughters, and sons played an important part in the production process. Eugene Bonnefous observed in 1851 that in Saint-Étienne "one no longer finds any women who know how to sew, since most of them have been working since infancy at cutting ribbons, preparing spools and warps, reeling, and the thousands of details of this industry."[52] Master weavers owned the looms and paid the costs of production, including rent, heat, lighting, and maintenance, but typically worked on raw materials belonging to the merchant capitalist, who sold the weavers' products on an international market.

During the middle decades of the nineteenth century, Saint-Étienne's silk ribbon industry was transformed by the growth of velvet ribbon factories and convent workshops and by the growing power of merchant capitalists within household weaving. Although factory production offered merchant capitalists a way in which to reduce the theft of raw materials and force weavers to work longer hours during periods of expansion, silk weaving factories did not rapidly displace household production.[53] Factories entailed high fixed capital costs in an industry in which capitalists strove to minimize fixed costs due to the highly volatile nature of the market for this luxury item. Investing in looms and factories would have shifted the cost of adjusting to frequent cyclical movements within the industry from the ribbon weavers to the merchants. The one branch of the local ribbon industry that did witness the early growth of nonmechanized factories was velvet ribbon weaving. Because the market for velvet ribbons was less subject to style changes and market fluctuations, merchant capitalists were much less hesitant to make fixed capital investments in this sector of the industry. By 1855, there were three thousand velvet ribbon looms in the city, owned by wealthy merchants, and over two thousand velvet ribbon weavers. Factory settings also characterized the city's six convent workshops, which, despite the use of hand looms, resembled factories in terms of the scale of production and the strict work discipline imposed on poorly paid adolescents.[54] The competition of the convent workshops and the workplace grievances of the velvet ribbon weavers provided working-class republican activists and radical republican leaders with powerful issues in their efforts to mobilize popular support.

Although the vast majority of Saint-Étienne's silk ribbon weavers remained employed in households, working on hand looms owned by master weavers, household production underwent important changes during the nineteenth century that altered the balance of power between merchant capitalists and master weavers. In particular, power shifted toward capitalists owing to the growing indebtedness of master weavers, increased merchant control over the preparatory and finishing stages of silk ribbon production, and the introduction of new nonmechanized hand loom technologies. During periods of prosperity, such as the years from 1818 to 1828, when many new arrivals from the countryside set themselves up as master weavers in Saint-Étienne, merchants often gave them a start by extending credit. This tied the master to a particular merchant capitalist, a seemingly temporary dependence that could easily become permanent. Merchant capitalists often sought to expand their power by extending credit to small producers against unfinished products, thus obligating the master to sell only to those capitalists. Merchants also increased their power by taking over the earlier stages of the ribbon production process, which had traditionally been the responsibility of the master weaver. During the 1820s, the preparation of the warp (l'ourdissage de la chaîne) and the weft (dividage des trames) increasingly took place in small workshops attached to merchants' warehouses.

The introduction of new weaving technologies also increased the power of merchant capitalists within household industry. The Jacquard loom revolutionized silk weaving by producing designs automatically from a perforated cardboard pattern, which raised and lowered the threads of the warp automatically. With this new hand loom, merchant capitalists, or more typically the skilled ribbon designers they employed, created designs that were punched into cardboard patterns that weavers simply followed. The Jacquard looms spread rapidly in the city after 1824, and especially during the years from 1829 to 1832, even though they cost three to four times as much as the older looms and required reinforced floors and ceilings. Masters were eager to acquire them because their lower labor costs and higher productivity enabled their owners to remain competitive. The adoption of the new looms increased the financial dependence of household producers on merchant capitalists. Because they were powered by hand, not water or steam, the spread of Jacquard looms did not transform the household organization of silk ribbon weaving, but it vastly increased the productivity of silk ribbon weavers, which prompted merchants to lower piece rates.[55] This led silk weavers to demand a uniform piece-rate scale from merchants, to launch production cooperatives to circumvent the merchants, and to embrace the cooperative vision of republican socialism.

The two other household industries in Saint-Étienne were armaments and hardware production, which experienced very different patterns of industrialization. The arms industry was divided into two branches: commercial and military production. While the small household workshops of the commercial sector stagnated and declined, the enormous state arms factory grew rapidly, employing a majority of the city's arms producers by 1872.[56] Mechanization and technological change rapidly transformed the expanding military sector of the armaments industry but had little impact on the declining commercial sector.[57] Although movement into the government-owned arms factory meant more intensified work discipline and some loss of autonomy with respect to the labor process, it also meant higher wages, more regular work, and exemption from conscription. The household-based hardware industry (*quincaillerie*), which produced a diversity of goods, including cutlery, locks, shovels, nails, screws, and files, also experienced stagnation and decline. The central threat to household hardware producers was the cheaper products fabricated by large-scale metalworking factories (*grosse quincaillerie*), which gradually replaced household production. Mechanized factories producing locks, bolts, files, nails, and scythes were established in Saint-Étienne during the 1860s, but they had trouble competing with national and foreign producers. Some former household hardware producers took jobs in these factories, but many more found employment in the expanding arms factory and in the region's steel mills. Their movement into armaments and steel factories meant stricter labor discipline but also higher wages, greater job security, and the preservation of skills. Opportunities for upward mobility meant that arms and hardware household producers were less likely than their counterparts in the silk industry to seek remedies for their grievances in the cooperative trade socialism espoused by working-class republican militants and more open to the appeals of radical Republicans.

The two "modern" industries in Saint-Étienne's local economy, coal mining and metallurgy, grew rapidly during the middle decades of the nineteenth century. The Stéphanois coal basin, which had the largest output of any coal region in France in 1844, was composed of three areas of extraction: Rive-de-Gier, Saint-Étienne, and Firminy. Prior to the late 1830s, there were thirty-eight companies in the basin, operating small mines that employed several dozen workers at most. During the 1830s, local mine operators sold their concessions to speculators and most of the mines in the Stéphanois basin were purchased by investors from Paris and Lyon. The production of coal almost doubled from 1831–36, resulting in a drop in coal prices during the late 1830s and a merger movement in 1840–42.[58] The merger movement culminated with the formation of the *Compagnie générale de la Loire* in 1844, which owned two-thirds of the basin's mines and controlled 85 percent of the basin's total production.[59] In 1844–45 there were further mergers as several smaller companies declared bankruptcy, and as the *Compagnie générale* gained control of the remaining mines in the Saint-Étienne area. By 1847, the *Compagnie générale* employed 3,875 of the basin's 7,217 miners (54%), operating thirty pits with 1,469 workers in the Saint-Étienne sector of the basin.[60] These economic changes provided powerful ammunition for radical Republicans, whose hostility toward inequalities produced by "monopoly" power led them to target the "coal monopoly" in efforts to mobilize popular support.

Capital concentration in mining was accompanied by important changes in the workplace, including new systems of wage payment, the imposition of more rigid work discipline, and mechanization. The leaders (*chefs de brigade*) of the small artisanal work teams that mined coal during the 1820s and early 1830s were replaced by company-appointed *gouverneurs*, whom workers accused of neglecting their safety.[61] During the early 1840s, the company eliminated the traditional system of wage payment, which entailed collectively paying a group of fifteen to twenty workers who contracted to extract a given amount of coal for a sum of money agreed upon in advance. The new system of individual rather than collective wage payments was accompanied by increased surveillance of the work process and increased fines.[62] The introduction of machinery to haul coal tubs to the surface during the 1840s further threatened the workers, given company rules governing the use of the machinery. Workers were required to supply, without payment, the coal needed to run the machinery, to work overtime without pay when machines broke down, and to pay for the previously free coal that heated their homes and the oil needed for the underground lamps.[63] The length of the workday increased from ten hours per day in 1830–37 to thirteen hours in 1844–47, and the pace of work intensified.[64] The introduction of interior rail transport during the 1840s eliminated coal haulers (*traîneurs*), who were replaced by low-paid children (*toucheurs*) who directed horses. In the 1848 industrial survey, Saint-Étienne's miners expressed nostalgia for the old days, when the workday was shorter and work rhythms were more flexible, when horses and machines weren't used in the mines, and when workers were accountable to *chefs de brigade* selected by their comrades rather than to company-appointed engineers and managers.[65]

A pattern of rapid regional but limited local growth characterized the second "modern" industry of Saint-Étienne, the production of iron and steel. By 1840, the region's steel industry accounted for 15 percent of French steel output, and by 1869 the figure reached 45 percent.[66] Most of this growth took place in the neighboring Ondaine and Gier valley towns of Rive-de-Gier, Le-Chambon, and Saint-Chamond, not in the Furens valley in Saint-Étienne.[67] Saint-Étienne was not receptive to the construction of blast furnaces or iron foundries within city limits, due to the fears of silk ribbon producers that smoke and pollution would ruin the quality of their ribbons. Iron and steel factories that did locate in the city were situated in the outer-lying east and northeast neighborhoods, and they employed a relatively small portion of the city's working class.[68] The city's biggest steel company, *la Compagnie des fonderies, forges, et aciers*, founded in 1865, employed seven hundred workers at the Barrouin factory in the suburb of Marais in June 1870. It was small compared to the region's giants, like Petin et Gaudet, which employed over nine thousand workers by 1866. During the late 1860s, the region's steel industry quickly adopted newer technologies, constructing nine of the sixteen Bessemer converters in France in 1869. None of these were located in the city of Saint-Étienne, which tried unsuccessfully to raise capital for a Bessemer steel plant.

Skilled workers in the region's iron and steel factories garnered relatively high wages and retained considerable workplace autonomy, but they faced long-term contracts and stiff fines for lateness, absenteeism, or insubordination. The regulations at the Terrenoire metalworks, located just beyond Saint-Étienne's city limits, included fines of one-half day's pay for being less than ten minutes late, a full day's pay for over ten minutes, and two day's pay for absenteeism without permission, drunkenness, or insubordination.[69] A system of inside contracting prevailed in heavy metallurgy, with highly skilled puddlers, forgers, and molders bidding on projects, hiring the work teams whom they supervised, compensating them with either a daily wage or proportion of the negotiated price, and setting work schedules.[70]

WORKING-CLASS FORMATION IN SAINT-ÉTIENNE

Divisions within Saint-Étienne's working class reflected a distinctive pattern of industrialization, marked by the coexistence of older household production and newer factories and mines. Industrialization created an important division between household artisans, who continued to numerically dominate the working class, skilled factory workers, and proletarianized miners. This division was manifest at the workplace in different wage levels, skills, and work settings as well as in residential segregation, associational life, and patterns of informal sociability.

The wages and working conditions of Saint-Étienne's proletarianized miners were a source of poverty and death. Although miners received relatively high average daily wages, frequent periods of unemployment meant that they typically earned subsistence-level wages for physically exhausting and often dangerous work.[71] They did so at the cost of high rates of death, disease, and injury.[72] Various estimates of the annual income necessary to feed a family of four suggest that, in the absence of other sources of family income, an adult male miner's wages were insufficient. In 1847 the estimated cost of living for a family of four was 956 francs per year, when the average mining wage was only 796 francs per year. This estimated cost rose to 807 francs per year in 1848, when the average mining wage was only 708 francs per year. Even in good years like 1854, when wages rose to 861 francs per year due to labor shortages, a miner could not by himself earn enough to feed a family of four, which cost an estimated 905 francs yearly.[73] According to the 1848 industrial survey (*enquête*), the city's miners were often living in poverty and were typically worse off than household silk weavers and arms workers.

Mine owners pursued policies of industrial paternalism, providing insurance funds, hospitals, schools, and low-cost housing for their workers. The *Compagnie générale* provided bread subsidies when prices rose to new heights in 1847, proposed a profit-sharing scheme and the creation of a retirement fund in 1848, and set up company-run butcher shops in 1851 when meat prices rose. The company initiated these paternalist policies to secure a more stable labor force, counter socialist propaganda, and gain political support against those calling for a dissolution of the coal monopoly. In commenting on the goal of these programs, company officials expressed their desire to "raise the intelligence of the working class and uproot from its heart the evil passions engendered by misery and anarchist preachings."[74] Employer paternalism was authoritarian in character. The coal company denied miners any control over their insurance fund even though all workers were required to contribute to it and, according to the decree of 1813, workers should have had legal control over the fund. Although miners received benefits in the event of disabling injuries, which were common, the companies distributed these small benefits sparingly and relied heavily on fines for work infractions, rather than company profits, to finance these funds. Company supervisory personnel, who also had discretionary power in job assignments and work discipline, decided what benefits to provide to which workers. Company policies stipulated that workers would lose pension benefits if they moved to another pit.

Skilled factory workers in the new and expanding steel, metalworking, and arms factories were much better off than miners. Factory metalworkers earned higher and more stable wages than other local workers.[75] Their daily wages generally translated into relatively high annual incomes because, compared to household hardware, silk weaving, and arms making, the expanding heavy metallurgy sector of the economy provided workers with more regular employment. During the 1850s and 1860s, an expanding and prosperous metal industry also provided local steel workers with a variety of benefits, including insurance and retirement funds. The most highly skilled male metal workers benefited from long-term contracts, lasting up to twelve years, and profit-sharing schemes introduced at the end of the Second Empire in a number of the larger steel companies. Most steel companies established insurance funds for their workers, although employers maintained strict control over these funds and staunchly opposed independent workers' funds. Some steel industrialists, like the radical republican leader Pierre-Frédéric Dorian, also provided model company housing and educational facilities for workers.

The wages and working conditions of armaments workers depended on whether they were employed in households or in the expanding state-run factory. Factory armaments workers, who were paid piece rates, could earn as much as 10 francs per day during the Second Empire, as well as a retirement pension of 200–360 francs after thirty years.[76] Those who remained in the household sector of the industry were much worse off, although, during periods of high demand, they benefited from the arms factory's growing demand for workers. Although household arms producers earned higher average daily wages (3.5 francs) in 1856 than silk weavers (1.75 francs) or hardware producers (2 francs), they also faced recurrent unemployment and frequent poverty.[77] The indigence of arms workers is documented by David Gordon, whose analysis of the death registers of 1852, 1862, and 1869 found that 75 percent of arms makers, along with 77 percent of ribbon weavers and 88 percent of hardware workers, left behind no property when they died.[78]

Workers in the city's household silk ribbon industry faced low wages, long working hours, and unsteady employment.[79] In 1848, male silk weavers earned an average daily wage of three francs while females earned one franc, but such daily wage figures tell us little about material conditions, given different types of looms and the irregularity of employment. Most weavers alternated between working intensely or not working at all, experiencing two to three months of unemployment each year. Household hardware workers, like silk weavers, suffered recurrent unemployment. They labored fourteen hours a day for meager earnings. In 1848, their average daily wage of 1.75 francs was even lower than household weavers and arms makers, and their average annual incomes of 600 francs were less than the proletarianized miners.

Divisions between household producers, skilled factory workers, and proletarianized miners are evident in patterns of migration and residential settlement. Most of the migrants who filled the city during the middle decades of the nineteenth century came from villages in the surrounding mountainous areas of smallholdings and rural industry, which deindustrialized during the middle decades of the nineteenth century. Most of those who arrived in the city seeking work in urban industry as silk weavers and arms, hardware, and metal workers were not uprooted agricultural laborers but workers with previous industrial experience in the countryside.[80] The most stable settled groups of workers within the city were household producers, who formed close-knit communities in which trade and kinship ties overlapped. Household arms producers and silk weavers had the highest levels of occupational endogamy and occupational inheritance, as well as a larger percentage of workers with local origins than was the case for miners and factory metal workers.[81] Skilled construction workers did not form a stable community, in part because they frequently returned to their rural communities of origin during the winter.[82]

Household ribbon weavers and arms makers formed relatively tight-knit communities in different neighborhoods than miners and metal factory workers. Ribbon weavers insisted on keeping their distance from the fumes produced by hardware and armaments workshops and metal factories. When the state arms factory was established in the Saint-Roch neighborhood during the early 1830s, there was a mass migration of ribbon weavers out of the area into the suburb of Montaud. The city council implemented zoning regulations which prevented newer steel and metal factories from locating in ribbon weaving areas.[83] In the silk weavers' neighborhood of Montaud, land contracts typically contained clauses prohibiting the establishment of ironworks. Because silk ribbon weaving required well-lit workshops, weavers settled in the more elevated parts of the city, which provided good light and eastern exposures. They formed stable communities on the slopes of Valbenoîte, Saint-Barbe, and Saint-François and in the suburb of Montaud. Since workers in the city's newer industries settled near the mines and factories that employed them, the more numerous ribbon weavers were residentially segregated from workers in the expanding metal and mining industries. A pattern of residential settlement by occupation created certain neighborhoods that were clearly dominated by particular occupations: the miners quarter of le Soleil, the arms makers' neighborhood of Villeboeuf, and the silk weavers' settlement of Valbenoîte. Metalworkers and coal miners resided on the outskirts of the city near the factories, railroad, and coal mines, beyond the limits of the *octroi* tax on consumer goods entering the city, where food and drink were cheaper.

Residential patterns inhibited the development of informal social ties between workers in older household industries and the newer factories and mines. Heavy metallurgy, like mining, required physical strength and teamwork, which fostered strong occupational communities among male workers. Outside of work, skilled factory metalworkers, like miners, spent their leisure time with coworkers in the cafés, taverns, shops, and dance halls of their neighborhoods, rather than with the predominantly inner-city silk weavers, whose leisure-time activities were more oriented toward the center-city neighborhoods where they lived and worked. Saint-Étienne's workers spent their leisure time pursuing different activities, with silk weavers forming blowgun (*sarbacane*) societies, arms workers gathering in rifle clubs, and miners joining gymnastic clubs.[84] The city's highly skilled household ribbon and arms producers generally looked down on the less skilled and less literate miners, many of whom were more recent migrants from the countryside. These patterns of residential and social segregation were an obstacle for republican socialist militants, whose initial base of support was in the silkweavers' community. They made it difficult for militant socialist silkweavers to mobilize workers in the mines and steel factories, where radical republican leaders were able to establish a strong base of support.

Skilled factory workers in the city's expanding steel and armaments industries did not create independent workers' associations during this period, in part because employer paternalism provided them with many of the benefits provided by the mutual aid associations of handicraft and household workers. Handicraft artisans in Saint-Étienne formed *compagnonnages* and mutual aid societies, but their relatively small associations remained confined to their trades and largely unconnected to political agitation. This was not the case for the city's more numerous miners and weavers. Miners initially developed occupational associations during the 1840s, at the same time that control over the mines was increasingly concentrated into the hands of fewer large companies. Encouraged by the advent of the republic, miners confronted employers in June 1848, occupying the mines, electing pit presidents to replace company engineers and directors, and forming a central committee with delegates in various pits who coordinated actions.[85] But this association proved short-lived. It was not until the 1860s that miners created an enduring association that effectively organized the entire Stéphanois basin. In 1866, miners formed a mutual aid society (*Société fraternelle des ouvriers mineurs*) that led the struggle for the creation of a unified workers' insurance fund for all mining companies in the basin. This association included five thousand miners by 1868. In 1869 it became the center of a strike involving fourteen thousand miners, which played an important role in winning miners over to the cause of radical republicanism.

Among household laborers, the silk weavers were by far the best organized. Although arms and hardware producers also possessed informal communal networks linking members of their trade, neither of these two groups formed strong or enduring associations.[86] Household silk ribbon weavers developed strong associations that confronted merchant capitalists. Although women constituted a majority of the ribbon industry's labor force, they were excluded from these associations. In early May 1833, master ribbon weavers formed a *Société mutualliste* and elected twenty leaders (a *conseil des syndics*) who sent a circular to the city's ninety merchants demanding the establishment of a uniform piece-rate scale for the industry. Male silk ribbon workers created their own association at the end of May 1834, following a meeting to discuss setting up an insurance fund. Their organization included a job placement bureau, and established wage rates for workers as well as piece rates below which masters would be forbidden to accept orders from merchants, under penalty of losing their workers. In order to avoid repression, there were eighty cells of eighteen members, who met separately and elected delegates to a central committee.[87] Subsequent organizing efforts included an attempt to create a cooperative association of production (the *Société générale des passementiers*) in 1841, which attracted over one thousand members. The cooperative was banned by the government in January 1842 as an "association of workers against merchants, of those who have nothing against those who possess something." One official expressed the fear that, if allowed to survive, this association would "submit to a single will the force of 40,000 workers."[88] In October 1848, silk ribbon masters and weavers founded a *Société industrielle* which recruited eight thousand members, but this association was dissolved by the government in June 1849, following the declaration of a state of siege. Weavers subsequently formed a mutual aid society, with over twelve thousand members, which attempted to control the placement of workers and prevent masters from lengthening the hours of work in response to periods of peak demand. When it was disbanded by the government in January 1852, this association had accumulated 26,320 francs in its treasury.[89] During the Second Empire (1851–70), ribbon weavers focused their collective energies on the creation of various consumer and commercial cooperatives.[90]

The barriers separating household producers, skilled factory metalworkers, and proletarianized miners were bridged in the context of politicized struggles with employers in which republican socialist militants played a central role. In March 1831, when troops were called in to disperse a group of arms workers who had destroyed a new steam-powered machine recently installed at the arsenal, silk weavers did not join in the protest. In 1834, however, republican hardware and arms workers joined the silk weavers on the barricades. Although the conflict began as an economic confrontation between weavers and merchants, it quickly became politicized, as Republicans embraced the cause of the weavers. Most of the 135 workers arrested during the 1834 insurrection were ribbon weavers, but among their ranks were 18 hardware producers, 10 miners, 9 arms makers, 6 shoemakers, and 5 tailors.[91]

The miners' strike of 1846 quickly became politicized as Republicans seized the opportunity to attack powerful outside capitalists whose pricing policies angered small producers in household hardware and arms industries dependent on coal as well as local consumers who used coal for heating their homes. Prior to the 1846 strike, republican activists led a campaign to persuade the central government to break up the coal monopoly. During the strike, groups of workers traveled through the coal mining areas singing the republican anthem, the *Marseillaise*. When troops opened fire on a crowd demonstrating in support of the strike, workers from various trades were present.[92] The politicization of an economic conflict by republican militants helped to break down boundaries between household workers and proletarianized miners.

The political agitation of the Second Republic fostered cooperation among workers across trade and industry boundaries. Silk weavers continued to dominate working-class political associations, but the members of these organizations came from a variety of trades. The most important working-class political association of 1848, the *Société populaire*, was led by a silk weaver and numerically dominated by silk weavers, but among its eight thousand members were arms makers, hardware producers, and coal miners. The organization of workers across occupational boundaries was also evident in the collective political actions of the period. In April 1848, local workers joined forces to burn and pillage the city's convent workshops, a persistent target of the silk weavers' hostility because of the workshops' role in driving down piece rates. Documents list the occupations of 134 of the 205 persons arrested during the 1848 attack on the convents; among their ranks were 36 ribbon weavers, 29 miners, 19 hardware workers, 16 arms makers, 13 day laborers, and 21 masons and locksmiths.[93] Politicized confrontations between workers and capitalists played an important role in bridging occupational divisions and forging class solidarities among workers in Saint-Étienne.

The political construction of classwide solidarities in Saint-Étienne faced greater obstacles than in Toulouse, due to divisions among workers along the lines of industry and an industrial paternalism, in mining and steel, that opened the door to political paternalism. In contrast to Toulouse, the emergence of newer forms of production in Saint-Étienne was more concentrated in particular industries—for example, mining and steel—and more geographically segregated from older forms of industry. The steel and coal industries remained spatially segregated from the city's older household industries, and the resulting consequences for working-class residential settlement and cultural life created obstacles to classwide political mobilization as well as political divisions between radical and socialist workers (see chapter 5).

The Industrialization of Rouen

Rouen was the capital of Normandy, one of the major cotton textile producing regions in France. By the time of the Second Empire (1852–70), Normandy had more spindles, hand looms, and workers employed in cotton textile production than any other region. Rouen's local economy contained spinning, weaving, printing, and dyeing factories as well as chemical and metal industries. The chemical industry produced the necessary chemicals for the bleaching, dyeing, and finishing of cotton, while the metal industry was geared mainly toward the production of machinery for the weaving, combing, and printing of cotton and for steam engines used in cotton textile factories. Rouen was also an important commercial center for Normandy's textile industry. Although long-distance ocean liners from North and South America increasingly used Le Havre as their port, coastal navigation (*cabotage*) connected Rouen with Bordeaux, Marseille, Algeria, and the rest of Europe. Linked with Paris by the Seine River, and by railway in 1843, Rouen was home to busy river traffic toward the capital. Despite the dominance of textile production and international commerce in the local economy, Rouen was also a regional administrative, religious, educational, and judicial center. These institutions employed considerable numbers of lawyers, professors, clerks, administrators, and professionals. Although Rouen's bourgeoisie was more heterogeneous than the bourgeoisie of Toulouse and Saint-Étienne, the city's wealthiest and most powerful men were prosperous cotton textile industrialists and merchants.[94]

Rouen's population expanded from 87,000 in 1801 to 101,265 in 1851, not nearly as rapidly as Toulouse or Saint-Étienne. This relatively slow urban growth was due to the dispersion of the cotton textile industry into the spinning towns and valleys of the region immediately surrounding Rouen and into the rural hand loom weaving area of the *pays de Caux*. The spinning factories of the region spread beyond Rouen, into the suburbs of Sotteville, Déville, Grand-Quevilly, Petit-Quevilly, and the nearby textile towns of the Andelle and Cailly valleys. The growth of steam-powered spinning and weaving factories during the Second Empire (1852–70) increased the city's importance as an industrial center at the expense of the surrounding industrial valley towns. By 1872, there were 28,000 factory workers in Rouen, 74 percent of whom were employed in cotton textile factories. Forty-seven percent of the city's 20,853 cotton textile workers were engaged in spinning, 34 percent in weaving, 10 percent in printing, and 10 percent in dyeing.[95] The timing of the introduction of factories, machinery, and steam power varied greatly across these sectors.

Cotton spinning in Normandy was almost completely mechanized by 1818, but the machinery was powered mainly by water, not steam. During the 1820s, many owners of spinning mills in the Rouen area purchased new mule jennies and installed more efficient drive shafts or pulleys in their factories, and a small number of owners made the costly transition to steam power. These employers attempted to maximize returns on their fixed capital investments by lengthening working hours, imposing tougher fines for lateness and absenteeism, and implementing a new payment system that provided higher piece rates to those who worked at a faster pace.[96] For spinners, these changes translated into a more dangerous and exhausting pace of work during a lengthened workday and a threat to established shop floor routines.

New technologies further transformed Rouen's spinning factories during the 1840s, when coal-powered, self-acting mules were adopted that could activate five hundred to seven hundred spindles compared to only three hundred for the mule jenny. The newer, more efficient steam-powered spinning mills were concentrated in the city of Rouen, which gave them access to imported coal, but the majority of the region's spinning mills continued to rely upon water power, though they too experienced technical changes during the 1840s, as many owners introduced larger mule jennies with more spindles.[97] Mill owners, who had previously paid a standard piece rate for thread, lowered piece-rate scales on the more productive mules with more spindles, which had a much higher rate of output per spinner. This meant that spinning factory workers were not rewarded for working on new machinery that required more effort, more experienced assistants, and a faster pace of work.[98] These transformations of cotton spinning during the 1820s and 1840s generated intense class antagonisms between workers and employers. These exploded into working-class collective protests in 1830 and 1848, which generated bourgeois fears that promoted socially conservative liberalism, produced sharp divisions between liberal and radical Republicans, and offered socialist Republicans opportunities to mobilize working-class support (see chapter 6).

It was not until the crisis of the 1860s that factories employing steam-powered, self-acting mules came to dominate Rouen's cotton spinning industry. The Treaty of Commerce of 1860, which lowered tariffs on imported British textiles, coupled with the American Civil War, which produced a sharp rise in the price of raw cotton, transformed the region's spinning industry. Many smaller firms disappeared, unable to compete with larger, urban, steam-powered factories that utilized self-acting mules. Between 1860 and 1870, fifty-three of the region's older factories shut down, while nine new large-scale steam-powered factories opened. The growth of mechanized steam-powered spinning created a proletarianized labor force that included growing numbers of low-paid women and children. By 1872, 62 percent of Rouen's 9,753 spinning factory workers were women and 12 percent were children.[99] Women typically earned one-half as much as men and children only one-fourth. In the large steam-powered spinning factories that utilized self-acting mules, like the La Foudre factory in the suburb of Petit-Quevilly, the six hundred to seven hundred workers were subjected to a work discipline imposed by the machinery, with meters attached to their machines to determine piece-rate wages.

The weaving branch of Rouen's cotton textile industry experienced the growth of factories and mechanization much later than spinning. Hand loom weaving in households, small workshops, and manufactories persisted throughout the middle decades of the nineteenth century alongside mechanized factories employing power looms. But the situation of the former deteriorated rapidly, as competition from mechanized weaving produced lower wages and longer hours, driving most hand loom weavers into desperate poverty but only slowly destroying hand loom weaving. As late as 1869, 78 percent of the region's weavers were employed in hand loom rather than mechanized weaving.[100] The main area of weaving in Normandy was the *pays de Caux*, a rural plateau north of Rouen that had been a center of household industry since the seventeenth century. The other center of cotton weaving was the city of Rouen, where five thousand weavers were employed in 1837.[101] These urban weavers, who were higher paid than their rural counterparts, specialized in better quality cloths, such as handkerchiefs. Mechanized weaving was first introduced in Rouen in 1816, but the second weaving factory in the region was not built until 1825 at Fécamp. By 1829, the region had three or four mechanized weaving factories with two hundred looms. Even though mechanical looms produced approximately four times the output of hand loom weaving, the mechanization of weaving was very slow, due to the high cost of machinery and coal.[102]

The situation of Rouen's weavers was carefully documented in a book written by the republican socialist hand loom weaver Charles Noiret in 1836. Noiret's survey of working conditions within the industry reveals the growth of nonmechanized manufactories using hand-powered Jacquard looms alongside urban household weaving. Most workers, he wrote, either owned their own looms and worked in their homes or labored in small workshops of two to eight workers where they rented looms by the year or for shorter time periods, while a small number of weavers were employed in the manufactories that used the more expensive Jacquard looms.[103] By 1847, the department had 7,790 mechanized looms employing 5,600 workers in forty-three factories.[104] This rapid growth of mechanized weaving had a disastrous effect on hand loom weavers, whose living conditions sharply deteriorated in the face of growing competition from mechanized production. The 1848 industrial survey documented the situation of the city's weavers, painting a picture of dire poverty, frequent unemployment, below-subsistence wages, slum housing, and inadequate diets.[105]

During the period of the Second Empire (1852–70), mechanized factories grew rapidly. The labor force employed in mechanized weaving factories increased from 5,600 in 1847 to 17,000 in 1869.[106] At the same time the number of hand loom weavers in the department dropped precipitously from 109,500 in 1847 to 61,000 in 1869. By 1872, there were 7,000 workers employed in mechanized weaving factories in Rouen. The vast majority of this labor force was composed of women (83%) and children (3%).[107]

The third major branch of the region's cotton textile industry was cotton printing. Although the printing of cotton cloth took place in large-scale factories, this sector of the industry was composed of relatively labor-intensive manufactories prior to 1830. The July Monarchy (1830–47) was a period of capital concentration and technical change for this sector of the industry.[108] The spread of steam engines, new rollers, and printing machinery capable of using several colors drove many of the smaller establishments out of business. By the 1840s, the ten largest firms in the industry employed 60 percent of the labor force of the region's cotton print factories.[109] By 1842, most of the cotton print factories of the region were equipped with steam engines, compared to only one-third of the region's spinning factories.[110] The Second Empire era witnessed further capital concentration, mechanization, and a general economic crisis for the cotton print sector.[111]

Dyeing was the one sector of the cotton industry that remained non-mechanized and highly dependent on artisanal labor throughout the middle decades of the nineteenth century. Unlike the other sectors of the industry, dyeing manufacturers did not employ women or children. The region's cotton dyeing industry, which was almost entirely located in the city of Rouen, employed a relatively small number of workers—1,200 in 1829, 2,000 in 1847, and 1,950 in 1869. By 1829, most dyeing establishments were manufactories rather than small-scale handicraft workshops. In 1829, dyeing factories employed an average of 22 workers. The figure rose to 33 by 1840–44 and to 43 by 1868. In 1840–44, only one employer had over 100 workers in his factory and only 9 out of 63 factories used steam engines.[112] The transition from small handicraft workshops to nonmechanized manufactories was nearly completed by the beginning of the 1830s. Charles Noiret noted the effects of that transition: "Dyers now work twice as long as before but receive less pay . . . they face the harshest and most humiliating treatment from employers and foremen."[113] Along with cotton printing, dyeing was the sector of the industry most severely hurt by the cotton crisis of the 1860s. Dyers faced widespread unemployment, lower real wages, and deteriorating working conditions. The development of artificial dyes and new chemical procedures during the 1850s also contributed to the elimination of many small dyeing firms and provided employers with an opportunity to reduce wages.[114]

WORKING-CLASS FORMATION IN ROUEN

The rapid proletarianization that marked capitalist industrialization in Rouen did not create a unified working class. Although industrialization produced a more homogeneous and undifferentiated mass of wage laborers than was the case in either Toulouse or Saint-Étienne, divisions within the cotton textile factory labor force of Rouen persisted due to the varied pace of proletarianization and feminization across the spinning, weaving, printing, and dyeing sectors of the industry and the uneven pace of mechanization within each sector. Divisions also existed between textile factory workers and skilled factory machinists and between the rapidly expanding factory labor force and the much smaller group of handicraft artisans, mainly construction workers.

Textile factory workers were divided along gender lines, with male and female laborers occupying different positions within the labor process and receiving different wages. Female workers were concentrated in the more highly mechanized spinning and weaving sectors where they were subjected to the most routinized working conditions and very low wages, typically less than half the wages of male workers. A strict gender division of labor existed within Rouen's spinning mills, with males assigned to better-paid tasks requiring special training (e.g., mule spinning, machine maintenance, carpentry, steam-engine operation), the exercise of workplace authority (e.g., foremen), or physical strength (e.g., beating raw cotton, moving stock). Women were consigned to the low-wage tasks of cleaning, carding, and stretching cotton.[115] In the water-powered spinning factories of the Rouen area, male mule spinners, who were paid by the piece at a per-kilogram rate, recruited their own helpers, often family members.[116] Whereas the older water-powered spinning factories that still dominated the region by 1870 typically employed one male spinner per mule jenny, in the newer steam-powered mills, two self-acting mules could be tended by one low-paid woman or child. By 1872, most workers in Rouen's spinning factories (74%) and weaving factories (86%) were women and children.

The varied pace of mechanization across textile factories created wage differentials among workers. Water-powered factories offered less secure employment than larger steam-powered mills, since they often shut down temporarily because of insufficient water power and the breakdown of old machinery.[117] Even within the largest and most mechanized factories, there were substantial wage differences based on skill and gender.[118] Since textile workers were paid piece rates for products rather than daily wages, even those workers with similar skills earned varied incomes depending on the size of their looms, the type (*numéro*) of thread, and the amount of uncompensated time they spent within the factory when their machines broke down.[119] Whereas workers in the largest steam-powered textile factories, like the modern La Foudre factory in the suburb of Petit-Quevilly, received a variety of paternalist benefits, including free medical care and accident insurance, those laboring in the more numerous dispersed water-powered mills of the region had no such benefits. During the election campaign of 1869, a group of workers at La Foudre published a brochure in support of their employer's candidacy, in which they asserted that their factory was directed with "the most equitable discipline allied with paternal concern."[120]

A detailed survey of average daily wages compiled by the police spy Antoine Philippon in December 1859 reveals substantial occupational differences among workers. Male factory spinners earned 2.5–4 francs per day and carders 2.5–3.5 francs, while female spinning factory jobs paid between .5 and 2 francs. Workers in the city's mechanized weaving factories earned higher wages, ranging from 4–6 francs per day for men to 1.25–2.5 francs per day for women. Wages for workers in local dyeing and cotton print factories were much lower, ranging from 2–3.5 francs per day, with frequent unemployment.[121] Skilled workers in the city's machine construction factories, as well as artisans employed in the building trades and chemical factory workers, earned higher and more stable incomes than local textile factory workers.[122]

Estimates of average daily or annual wage levels are problematic indices of textile workers' material conditions, since they translated into very different standards of living due to fluctuations in short-term unemployment and different family situations. Nevertheless, available estimates of average annual incomes for 1839 and 1848 suggest that most textile factory workers earned poverty-level wages. In the survey of 1848, the weavers' delegation, led by Charles Noiret, estimated that a single man living at a boarding house needed 750–800 francs to survive, while a family of four needed twice that amount. This was way above the maximum income they estimated a weaver could earn by working in a factory on a Jacquard loom, which provided 6.75–10.75 francs per week. Contemporary observers commented extensively on the dire living conditions of Rouen's textile workers, noting inadequate diets, poor health, slum housing, and ragged clothing.[123] Although most textile workers had trouble making ends meet on their meager incomes, some better-paid textile factory workers were able to earn enough to save money, but their small savings disappeared rapidly during periods of crisis. During the July Monarchy, 60 percent of the city's household heads were exempted from personal taxes as indigent, and, throughout the mid-nineteenth century, two-thirds of those who died left behind no inheritance.[124] Available statistics reveal high levels of alcoholism, consumption, and infant mortality, and a demographic pattern characterized by an excess of deaths over births.[125]

Divisions among cotton textile workers in different sectors of the industry are evident in collective industrial protests. Although workers in different factories within each sector often coordinated their actions, none of the industrial protests prior to 1871 involved spinners, weavers, dyers, or printers joining forces against employers. In 1839, at a time when crisis conditions within the industry led to wage cuts, more oppressive work rules, and reductions in the number of workdays per week, factory weavers and spinners in Rouen launched a number of short-lived strikes, but there was no coordinated action between these two groups. In March 1848, Joseph Potien, who began his career as a child laborer in a spinning factory and subsequently worked as a weaver and a foreman in a weaving factory, unsuccessfully attempted to create an association that would bridge divisions among the city's workers. He envisioned "a general association of all workers" that would include factory and nonfactory laborers from diverse occupations, "all of whom share the same interests, of working a reasonable length of time and being decently paid."[126] Even the increasing concentration of cotton textile operatives into large steam-powered mills, where spinning and weaving were done under one roof, did not readily produce coordinated action between workers in different occupations. In June 1865, when the 112 weavers employed at the de Loy factory walked off their jobs and demanded a wage increase, the spinners employed in the factory continued to work. The same was true in December 1868 when the 260 weavers at the Bertel factory went on strike to protest a wage reduction. The factory's spinners, who had not yet been targeted for a reduction, remained at work.[127]

Divisions also separated the well-paid, well-educated, and highly skilled workers laboring in the city's machine construction factories from proletarianized textile factory workers. According to the police spy Antoine Philippon, workers in the city's foundries and machine shops refused to socialize with textile factory workers, whom they looked down on with great disdain. During their leisure hours, these two groups of factory workers frequented different establishments. During his many years as a police spy in working-class neighborhoods, Philippon reported that he never once saw a cotton textile factory worker in the taverns and eating houses frequented by the city's machinists and metalworkers.[128]

Workers in the spinning and weaving factories of the Rouen area were largely recruited from rural households that had previously supplied labor for the region's household textile industry. Whereas migrants from the area immediately surrounding Rouen settled in the city's center and found employment in commerce, Cauchois migrants arriving from more distant areas of rural household textile production settled in the heavily working-class 5th and 6th cantons, where the largest textile factories were located.[129] Although these migrants encountered harsh working conditions, low wages, and unstable employment in the city's textile factories, they were typically less destitute than the friends and relatives who remained behind to eke out a living as handloom weavers in the Cauchois countryside. Many of the rural women who found employment in the city's steam-powered spinning factories retained their ties to the countryside. "The women," observed one factory owner in 1848, "come in small groups from the countryside, rent small rooms where they live together and return to their village from Saturday until Monday. . . ."[130]

Residential patterns of class segregation were quite rigid in Rouen. Workers were concentrated in the faubourgs surrounding the inner city and across the river in the industrial settlement of Saint-Sever, the two most rapidly growing areas of the city. The bourgeoisie continued to inhabit the western part of the inner city, which remained the center of commercial, banking, judicial, and administrative activities, and the slopes on the western area of the right bank, the Cauchois neighborhood, known to workers as the "gold coast." Workers inhabited the slums of the eastern section of the inner city (i.e., the 4th canton of Martainville and the faubourg Saint-Hilaire). During the middle decades of the century, workers increasingly deserted the inner city to inhabit the outer-lying factory areas beyond the boulevards. They settled in the faubourgs of the 5th canton, near the Darnétal and Maromme industrial valleys, and across the river on the left bank of the Seine, in the 6th canton of Saint-Sever, a working-class neighborhood adjacent to the industrial suburbs of Sotteville and Quevilly and itself the site of numerous large factories.[131] Workers preferred these neighborhoods, wrote the weaver Charles Noiret in 1836, because rents were lower and because "they don't have rich people, whose opulence insults their misery."[132]

Despite rigid social boundaries that fostered class antagonisms, the co-operative vision of republican socialism had less resonance with the experiences of Rouen's proletarianized factory workers than with the handicraft and household artisans of Toulouse and Saint-Étienne. Compared with the latter, Rouen's textile factory workers created few mutual aid societies prior to 1848 and no production cooperatives prior to 1870. Rouen's textile factory workers did form mutual aid societies during the 1850s and 1860s, designed to provide financial support for workers incapacitated by illness and accidents. These contrasted sharply with associations bearing the same title in Toulouse and Saint-Étienne. Whereas government officials in these cities repeatedly accused these local associations of serving as centers of strike mobilization and republican socialist agitation, officials in Rouen never expressed such concerns. The mutual aid societies that emerged in Rouen were paternalistic institutions of collective insurance fostered by church officials and bourgeois moralists rather than autonomous working-class institutions.[133] The loosening of government restrictions on the right to association during the 1860s stimulated the growth of workers' associations and, by 1872, there were fourteen mutual aid societies among Rouen's workers.[134] Cooperative societies of production, popular among French workers during the 1860s, were not feasible in the cotton textile industry of Rouen, where rapid mechanization and technical innovation meant high fixed capital costs. Although the handloom weaver Charles Noiret developed an elaborate scheme for a cotton textile workers' production cooperative in his 1836 book, no such associational effort was ever attempted by the city's factory workers.[135] Rouen's shoemakers and tailors formed production cooperatives in 1849, and local factory workers created short-lived consumer cooperatives.[136] Republican socialists renewed their efforts to create food cooperatives that would provide workers with lower-priced necessities during the late 1860s, but none of these associations lasted very long.[137]

In response to the 1848 survey question concerning the existence of associations among local workers, the weavers' delegation blamed the absence of workers' associations on widespread poverty: "There are no associations; but various attempts by workers have failed because their lack of resources makes it impossible to undertake anything."[138] The heightened pace of work and closer surveillance of workers that accompanied the mechanization of Rouen's factories also inhibited the creation of associations among factory workers. "All of these factories," wrote the police spy Philippon after inspecting the city's textile mills in 1859, "are run in a strict, very often brutal, manner. . . . Workers complain about their employers and foremen but stop there, only out of fear of punishment. . . ."[139] Poverty, employers' control over the workplace, and labor market vulnerability contributed to the limited capacity of textile factory workers to create autonomous enduring organizations. The relatively low levels of literacy among Rouen's textile factory workers, with less than one-third of the city's textile labor force able to read and write by 1872, also helps explain the relative absence of formal associations with their statutes, dues, charters, and elected officials.[140]

Although Rouen's factory workers were slow to create enduring formal associations, spinners developed an elaborate system of informal organization at their workplaces, which enabled older male workers to enforce workplace norms. Armand Audiganne, who visited several factories in the Rouen region during the early 1850s, reported as follows: "Every workroom, regardless of the number of spinning frames, has a leader who is always the oldest worker and who is called the priest (curé). . . . When the workroom has a large number of workers, the *curé* is assisted by a *vicaire*. The authority of this leader, which ends at the factory gates, involves the maintenance of order as defined by the workers and the execution of various measures decreed by them beyond the general regulations of the factory. In the case of violations, the *curé* pronounces punishments, which most often entail small fines. There is a more severe punishment, which consists of social isolation, that is designated by the bizarre words 'to cut one's stomach' (*couper le ventre*). No one speaks to the worker who is the target of this punishment; no one helps him in the thousands of small tasks that traditionally involve mutual assistance. Even outside the factory, no one has anything to do with him."[141]

During periods of political upheaval, as in 1830 and 1848, cotton textile spinners engaged in collective actions that built upon the informal organization already present within their mills. In August and September 1830, Rouen's factory spinners sent delegates to present their grievances concerning work rules, fines, and the length of the workday to the mayor and prefect. These delegates utilized the existing system of *curés* and *vicaires* within each mill to coordinate actions among dispersed factories. They created a "central administration," sent out letters inviting the *curé* of each mill to meet with them at a café in Rouen, and designated representatives charged with organizing the *curés* of the different suburbs and communes, including Déville, Maromme, Pavilly, and Darnétal.[142] These early short-lived efforts at organization quickly met with repression by the authorities, who considered the efforts of spinners to coordinate action across mills a violation of the law.

The initial growth of class solidarities among Rouen's textile factory workers was a product of politicized class struggles in which spinners played a leading role. In the aftermath of the revolution of July 1830, spinners in Rouen and surrounding textile towns engaged in a variety of collective actions to demand a modification of workplace rules, factory fines, and the new piece-rate system, all of which fostered a faster pace of work and longer hours. They marched from mill to mill, breaking factory windows, gathering in large crowds in the streets after work, tearing down newly posted factory work rules, and shutting down mills in the northwest communes of Déville and Maromme.[143] Spinners in Rouen's steam-powered mills marched on city hall to demand the abolition of new work rules while factory spinners in the nearby textile towns of Darnétal, after confronting the mayor and National Guard, marched to Rouen before troops dispersed them. "There exists in the working class, and especially among the spinners, a spirit of defiance and insubordination. . . ." observed the Rouen Chamber of Commerce in 1836.[144]

During the Second Republic (1848–51), intense class antagonisms within the textile industry were rapidly politicized by radical and socialist Republicans in a context of widespread industrial agitation. Rouen's textile workers took to the streets to express their grievances, pillaged factories, and petitioned the new prefect for shorter hours, higher piece rates, and better working conditions. As was the case elsewhere, Rouen's workers joined the political clubs that proliferated after 1848. Although many clubs provided republican workers with an opportunity to espouse a socialist ideology proclaiming the shared interests of all workers, Rouen's club movement also gave expression to existing divisions between artisans and the city's more numerous factory workers. According to one observer of Rouen's club movement, H. Dahubert, a liberal republican delegate from the Club of Clubs in Paris in early April of 1848, "The workers are divided into two groups; a very large one composed of factory workers and another group composed of the different trades, who are very democratic and understand the true meaning of liberty. The first group is not well educated, confuses liberty with license, and is capable of committing disorders in revenge for the sufferings that their employers have forced them to endure. . . ."[145] Factory spinners were in the forefront of the movement when Rouen's workers took to the barricades in April 1848. They were joined by day laborers and a small number of republican shopkeepers and intellectuals, but relatively few local artisans showed up on the barricades.

It wasn't until the end of the Second Empire, with the creation of the Rouen section of the First International, that an association composed of textile workers from different sectors of the industry emerged on the scene. In April 1868, Émile Aubry founded a federation of working-class associations under the title *Cercle d'études économiques*. Although this association cut across occupational and industrial boundaries, it attracted preexisting workers' associations whose members were recruited along occupational lines. This branch of the International grew rapidly in 1869, attracting the adhesion of Rouen's spinners and weavers associations, as well as organizations of local artisans.[146] In April 1869, Aubry estimated the number of members at three thousand, from at least ten different occupations, mostly in the textile industry.[147] Although hesitant to endorse strikes as a vehicle for action, Aubry used his connections with the Parisian section of the International to raise funds for Rouen's weavers and spinners during their strikes of 1868 and 1869. In contrast with earlier organizations of Rouen's workers, the First International recruited handicraft artisans as well as factory spinners, weavers, printers, and dyers, and its leadership included factory spinners and weavers.

The political construction of class solidarities faced different obstacles in Rouen than in Toulouse and Saint-Étienne. Widespread unemployment and fear of employer retaliation inhibited political activism among factory workers, while the rapid feminization of the industrial wage labor force made it difficult for fraternalist political organizations, like the Republican party, to mobilize support. The scale and concentration of textile production facilitated communication and organization among workers, but divisions across the spinning, weaving, dyeing, and printing branches of the industry constituted an obstacle to the political construction of classwide solidarities, as did the very different living and working conditions among textile factory workers and the much smaller handicraft labor force.

PATTERNS OF INDUSTRIALIZATION, WORKING-CLASS DIVISIONS, AND SOURCES OF CLASS SOLIDARITY

Toulouse, Saint-Étienne, and Rouen each experienced an expansion in the production of manufactured goods during the mid-nineteenth century, but local patterns of industrial growth were distinctive. Industrial development in Toulouse involved a variety of different consumer goods industries, but there was not much diversity with respect to forms of production, with a predominance of handicrafts and a relatively limited development of household and factory production. Saint-Étienne's pattern of industrialization exhibited industrial diversity as well as diversity in forms of production, with household production existing alongside mechanized and nonmechanized factory production. Rouen had the least industrial diversity as well as the least diversity with respect to forms of industrial production. Cotton textiles dominated the local economy throughout the mid-nineteenth century and the city's cotton textile industry was dominated by mechanized and, to a lesser extent, nonmechanized factories.

The social consequences of the transition to factory production varied across industries and cities. For the cotton textile industry of the Rouen region, the growth of factories meant routinized machine-paced work, feminization, and insecure employment for a low-paid labor force previously engaged in rural household production. The growth of steel, armaments, and metalworking factories in Saint-Étienne, however, meant higher pay, greater job security, and skilled labor for many former male household hardware producers whose industry was in crisis. The growth of a relatively small number of nonmechanized factories in the construction, printing, baking, furniture, metalworking, and carriage-making industries of Toulouse meant greater discipline and surveillance for traditionally independent male artisans who had previously exercised substantial control over the pace and process of their work in small handicraft workshops.

Although mechanization and dispossession of the means of production were a central feature of early industrialization in certain cities and industries, they were not the only means by which labor became subordinated to capital during the course of the nineteenth century. The separation of workers from the means of production was only part of a more general process of the subordination of labor to capital by various means. The dynamics and tendencies of local capitalist industrialization were diverse, with distinct patterns of capital accumulation giving rise to different means by which labor was subordinated to capital. In Rouen the mechanization of production and growth of semiskilled and unskilled propertyless wage laborers working under close surveillance in modern factories was central to the process of industrialization. But in Toulouse and Saint-Étienne, a more central feature of the process was the internal transformation of social relations of production within older forms of industrial production. In these cities, the factory was not the dominant site of proletarianization. The process did not entail the dispossession of workers from the means of production but the growing dominance of capital over labor, resulting from strategies of capital accumulation that altered control over raw materials, credit, labor recruitment, work organization, and product markets. In these two industrializing cities, many master artisans in household and handicraft production retained ownership of their small workshops and journeymen still owned the small tools they needed to ply their trades. Saint-Étienne's master silk weavers retained ownership of their looms, but were dependent on merchant capitalists who owned the raw materials and, in the case of Jacquard looms, the cardboard patterns that controlled them. Toulouse's journeymen in handicraft industry, even when employed in large workshops characterized by an increased division of labor, typically owned the small tools they needed to practice their trades; but they could make use of these tools only by selling their labor power to a master who owned the workshop and the raw materials they worked on.

Urban handicraft and household production were not static traditional forms that simply disappeared in the face of competition from more efficient units of factory production. In both Toulouse and Saint-Étienne, capitalist development produced important internal changes in the character of class relations between journeymen and masters in handicraft industry and between masters and merchants in urban household production. Both forms of production experienced critical changes during the nineteenth century that were not connected to dispossession of the means of production, mechanization, or the movement into factory settings. Older forms of industrial production were not simply vestiges of a precapitalist past destined to be rapidly eliminated or superseded by mechanized factory production; rather, they were linked in new ways to an emergent capitalist system and were internally changed. These internal changes, including the growing power of merchant capitalist entrepreneurs and of nascent capitalist artisanal masters, were an important part of early capitalist industrialization. Although they left intact the household and workshop, they dramatically transformed class relations.

The growing subordination of labor to capital that accompanied early industrialization generated intense class antagonisms in handicraft, household, and factory forms of production. For Toulouse's handicraft artisans, urban household production, manufactories, and protocapitalist masters within their trades posed serious threats to the traditional system of handicraft production. This generated numerous strikes by skilled workers determined to retain substantial collective control over the workplace and force their masters to adhere to a variety of regulations governing the trade. Since nascent capitalist masters played an important role in capital accumulation, master artisan employers became the targets of collective industrial protests. In Saint-Étienne, where capital accumulation within the silk ribbon industry was carried out by merchant capitalists rather than master artisan employers, a number of developments, including the introduction of new technologies, like the Jacquard loom, growing indebtedness, the development of convent workshops, and the rise of manufactories in the velvet ribbon sector, united small masters and journeymen workers in opposition to the growing power of merchant capitalists. The industrialization of the coal mines, owned by nonlocal finance capitalists, also generated intense class antagonisms and explosive, often violent, workplace conflicts. The pattern of industrialization in Rouen produced a more fully proletarianized labor force and more polarized class relations, which sometimes erupted into collective industrial protests. "Relations between employers and workers," stated Rouen's industrial survey of 1872, "are in general very strained. . . . The workers, propagandized by those claiming to be interested in improving the situation of the proletariat, are only interested in improving their condition and are envious, insubordinate, treat their employers like enemies, and agree that employers get rich at their expense. . . ."[148]

Although each local pattern of industrialization intensified class antagonisms and generated collective industrial protests, in no case did it automatically produce classwide unity across occupations and industries or a classwide political project that unified all wage laborers. Early industrialization created a variety of divisions among urban industrial workers. But heterogeneity within the working class was not an insuperable barrier to the creation of classwide identities and collective actions. Workers were often able to unite in collective defiance of their employers and, in some cases, express classwide solidarities that crossed the boundaries of workplace, occupation, and industry. Despite diverse and persistent sources of division within the working class of each city, growing numbers of workers in Toulouse, Saint-Étienne, and Rouen adopted a rhetoric emphasizing the unity of workers as a class. How can we account for the growth of shared identities among workers and classwide solidarities despite the persistence of divisions?

In classical Marxist accounts, the logic of capitalist development is assumed to provide the central source of working-class unity. As proletarianization creates more homogeneity among propertyless workers, and the centralization and concentration of capital facilitates their ability to communicate and act collectively, workers will develop classwide solidarities. The notion that proletarianization fosters working-class unity presumes that the separation of workers from the means of production creates propertyless wage laborers with shared interests and grievances. But the highly uneven character of proletarianization over time and across localities and industries produced extensive divisions, not unity, among nineteenth-century French workers. It created workplaces with very different labor processes, skill demands, wage patterns, and patterns of sociability off the job. The term proletarian, when used to refer to all propertyless wage laborers, is too broad to encompass the distinct ways that people earned wages and experienced their status as wage laborers. Although capital concentration and centralization facilitated greater communication among factory workers, this was often overridden by countervailing factors ranging from the creation of new hierarchies of authority within production to the establishment of high wages, paternalistic benefits, or mobility opportunities for certain groups of workers. How then can we account for the growth of class solidarities during the course of the nineteenth century?

"Class consciousness emerged in France," argues William Sewell, Jr., "as a transformation of the artisans' corporate understanding of labor under the twin impact of capitalist development and revolutionary politics."[149] This is an apt characterization of the emergence of a class-conscious workers' movement in Toulouse, and in other cities like Paris, where handicraft artisans dominated local industry and the transformation of an established corporate cultural and institutional heritage was central to the emergence of working-class consciousness. It is not an accurate account of working-class formation in either Saint-Étienne or Rouen, where household artisans and factory operatives developed class identities, understandings, and organizations in the absence of such a corporate heritage. The absence of corporate legacies among the miners of Saint-Étienne or the textile factory operatives of Rouen did not make them either politically quiescent or incapable of militant economic protest.

The movements and ideologies of artisans synthesized traditional and "modern" ideas and practices. Artisanal workers did not simply use traditional subcultures and communal forms of organization to defend themselves against the threats posed by capitalist industrialization; they combined communal and associational forms of organization and mixed traditional ideas and practices with newly emerging visions of republican socialism and Icarian communism. In doing so, they created new class understandings and identities that simultaneously built on and displaced older communal solidarities. Artisans did not live in static, self-contained, "traditional" communities, but in communities that creatively adapted to larger national and international political and economic realities. A focus on traditional communal ties and values as the source of grievances and capacities for collective action exaggerates the autonomy of artisanal communities and neglects the central role played by larger political forces, including state repression and republican political organization, in the collective protests of household and handicraft artisans.[150]

Explanations of the sources of classwide unity that focus on either proletarianization, corporate solidarities, or traditional communities are inadequate because they pay insufficient attention to the political arena. It was in the political arena that divisions among trades and across industries were broached, and that a language and consciousness of class was disseminated. Political ideologies, like republican socialism, played a central role in how workers interpreted their respective work situations. Neither communal traditions, proletarianization, nor conflicts with employers generated classwide solidarities among workers, for class identities and solidarities were ideologically and institutionally constituted by political processes. The solidarities linking workers of different genders, skill levels, and statuses across various firms, trades, and industries were actively forged by multiclass political organizations and ideologies in the context of economic and political struggles. For example, in leading the struggle for universal male suffrage, Republicans, by speaking to civic as well as class identities, extended their appeal across occupational and industrial boundaries to create forms of working-class solidarity that built on but went beyond the workplace. At the same time, their failure to include women in their vision of a democratic society reinforced gender divisions separating workers.

The socioeconomic forces that generated class conflicts and structured internal divisions among workers in Toulouse, Saint-Étienne, and Rouen did not determine the ideological and political consequences of these conflicts and divisions. These consequences were a product of the political arena, where the meaning of class and intraclass divisions for political identities was actively contested by liberal, radical, and socialist Republicans as well as by Bonapartists, Legitimists, and Orleanists. These political actors provided alternative explanations for workers' conditions and grievances, some invoking a language of class solidarity and others denouncing classwide solidarities in the name of citizenship and nationalism or appealing to victim-blaming explanations and individualist accounts of the workers' plight. The way in which these different political actors responded to the conflicts, divisions, and emergent solidarities fostered by different forms of early capitalist industrialization is documented in the following chapters.

1. An early nineteenth-century shoemaker's workshop, where conversation, smoking, and informal cooperation accompanied the production of custom-made goods. As the century progressed, many handicraft trades, including shoemaking, became increasingly threatened by the low-priced, ready-made products of large manufacturers and urban industry. In response, many handicraft artisans embraced republican socialism as a solution to their problems. Lithograph by C. Schultz. Reprinted with permission of Roger-Viollet, Paris.

2. A nineteenth-century Lyonnais silkweaver's household workshop. Silkweavers labored long hours in their homes, where family labor played an important part in production. Although master weavers owned their own looms, they typically worked on raw materials belonging to merchant capitalists. To remain competitive, they had to purchase expensive new looms, which often meant becoming heavily indebted to a merchant. Bibliothèque du Musée des Arts decoratifs. Reprinted with permission of Roger-Viollet, Paris.

3. A mechanized, steam-powered textile factory in mid-nineteenth-century Rouen. La Foudre, the largest textile factory in the Rouen area, was owned by the millionaire industrialist and politician Pouyer-Quertier. Built in 1859, this four-story brick factory covered four hectares and housed fifty-five thousand spindles, powered by five one-hundred-horsepower steam engines. Bibliothèque Municipale de Rouen, estampes.

4. Postcard of a nineteenth-century French coal miner with horse, Firminy. During the 1840s railways and horses were introduced into the mines of the Stéphanois basin, which included three areas of extraction: Saint-Étienne, Rive-de-Gier, and Firminy. Quoting a popular saying, A. Audiganne wrote in 1860: "Rive-de-Gier is heaven for women, purgatory for men, and hell for horses."

5. The interior of a nineteenth-century French coal mine. Reprinted from Turgan, *Les grandes usines*.

6. The operation of a Bessemer converter in a Saint-Seurin factory. Reprinted from Turgan, *Les grandes usines.*

CHAPTER FOUR

Toulouse: From Liberal Republicanism
to an Alliance of Radicals
and Socialists

WHEN THE DOWNFALL of the Bourbon regime was announced in Toulouse on August 2, 1830, crowds paraded through the streets, destroying all symbols of Bourbon rule. A violent confrontation erupted in front of city hall when the commander of the national police attempted to seize a tricolor flag from demonstrators. After they charged the crowd, which responded by throwing paving stones, police fired warning shots over the heads of the demonstrators. Although many people were injured, no one was killed in the confrontation. The liberal republican lawyers and merchants who led the protests tried their best to restrain the enthusiasm of the demonstrators, most of whom were artisans from the working-class districts of Saint-Cyprien and Saint-Étienne. Charles Chazal, a law student, dissuaded a crowd from burning down national police headquarters (the *gendarmerie*). Celestin Bert, a lawyer at the head of the crowd in front of city hall, claimed that he prevented the mob from killing the prefect and used his influence to prevent other violent actions.[1] The professionals and merchants who led the city's Republican party throughout the July Monarchy espoused the cause of parliamentary democracy but remained wary of workers who took to the streets to express their opinions. Public order ranked alongside liberty in their liberal vision of the republic, which placed political reform rather than socioeconomic change at the top of the agenda. These liberal leaders were aptly described by the prefect in 1844, in a report on the men who recently purchased the local republican newspaper *Émancipation*, as Republicans "whose hostility to the government is unquestionable, but whose social habits make them unsympathetic to the lower classes. . . ."[2] The liberal dispositions of the city's republican leadership were evident in the response of Adolphe-Félix Gatien-Arnoult, president of the republican city council in 1848, to the strikes and working-class club agitation unleashed by the 1848 revolution. At a meeting of the city's 214 wealthiest men, assembled in March 1848 to raise money for municipal public workshops, he declared: "The men who know so well how to die, weapons in their hands, in defense of liberty, also know how to die of hunger, out of

respect for order. And these workers, dreaming of liberty, asleep with im-
mortality, will also be seen dreaming of happiness, eternally at rest, envel-
oped in their virtuous misery as though it was a saintly shroud."[3]

Several decades later, in March 1868, workers took to the streets to express their political opinions. The Imperial government had recently revised the nation's draft laws as part of a larger project of military reform.
On March 9, 10, and 11, thousands of demonstrators gathered at city hall
and the prefecture to protest the reforms, amid chants of the republican
anthem, the *Marseillaise*. In various confrontations with police, angry
crowds invaded and pillaged the office of the central police commissioner,
attacked the residence of the mayor, and paraded through the streets behind
red flags. In one working-class neighborhood, the faubourg of Saint-Cyprien, young workers erected barricades, which were quickly dismantled by
troops, and covered walls with slogans like "Down with the rich!" and
"Jobs or blood!"[4] The bourgeois republican editors of *Émancipation* defended the predominantly working-class rioters, denouncing the government's reforms as preparation for a new war. That summer, these same men
actively supported the strike wave of the city's major artisanal trades, opening the columns of *Émancipation* to striking workers. The following year,
during the national election campaign of 1869, the city's most prominent
republican leader, Armand Duportal, espoused a Proudhonian socialist vision of the republic in his legislative campaign and proclaimed the Republican party to be the party of the working class. Duportal chastised his
Bonapartist opponent as follows: "You have done nothing for the working
class, nothing for its education, nothing for its spiritual development, nothing for its well-being, and nothing for its dignity. Your only concern has
been to stifle its independence and curb its freedom. Do not expect anything from the working class but demands and reproaches; prepare yourself
to either satisfy their demands or make way for those who have never de-
ceived them."[5] Duportal also criticized the city's liberal republican leaders:
"When the Republic is not supported by the required social institutions," he
wrote, "it is only an instrument of torture and wicked irony for men of
conscience and conviction who have dedicated their lives to the cause of
the poor and the outcasts of fortune."[6]

The preceding account highlights the tremendous change that took place
in republican politics in Toulouse during the years from 1830 to 1870. A
dramatic shift in the relationship between workers and Republicans was
accompanied by changing strategies of contention for power and shifting
alliances with other parties, all of which were a product of the displacement
of liberals by an alliance of radicals and socialists at the head of the city's
republican movement and party. The following narrative documents these
changes.

THE JULY MONARCHY IN TOULOUSE

Although workers in Toulouse did not launch any strikes or other industrial protests during the early years of the July Monarchy, and although electoral laws prohibited them from voting, the city's artisans were very active in nonelectoral republican political protests. On the evening of September 20, 1830, a crowd of approximately two hundred paraded through various neighborhoods amid shouts of "Down with the Ministers!" to protest the government's noninterventionist foreign policy in response to Russian military action in Poland. The following evening, after news arrived of the capture of Warsaw by Russian troops, an angry crowd of Republicans destroyed the printing presses of the city's two legitimist newspapers to protest their reporting of events in Poland. The local National Guard troops present on the scene, many of whom sympathized with the demonstrators, failed to prevent the attack. Most of those arrested during these riots were workers, mainly artisans. The prefect, when informing his superiors in Paris of these events, urged against the postponement of the upcoming municipal elections, emphasizing that recent working-class disorders would rally property holders, who were the only inhabitants eligible to vote, behind the new regime. The recent disorders, he wrote, "are a symptom of the dangerous excitation that the lower classes are susceptible to; on the other hand, they have served as a serious warning for industrialists and property owners. The consequences of these events have left quite an impression."[7] The Orleanists won the municipal election of 1830, garnering eight hundred votes versus five hundred for Legitimists and three hundred for Republicans.

Disenfranchised republican workers took to the streets to express their political views, despite the adverse effect this had on republican electoral prospects. On October 10, 1830, a crowd gathered to sing republican songs in public. Amid shouts of "Down with Louis-Philippe!" and "Long Live the Republic!" the crowd attacked the local tax offices in the faubourg Saint-Étienne and troops arrived to disperse them. During the summer of 1831, troops and National Guard units repeatedly dispersed crowds of Republicans on the place Rouaix, where demonstrators frequently gathered to protest the government's failure to close down a well-known legitimist café. In December 1831, a large crowd of workers, including many women and children, gathered in front of the mayor's home to protest the recent suspension of public works projects and to demand jobs. That same month, police and troops dispersed crowds gathered on the place d'Orleans to chastise the deputy Pierre-Catherine Amilhau for his support of the regime's increasingly conservative policies. The demonstrations continued the following year, as workers took to the streets to voice political opinions they were prevented from airing at the polls. In April and May 1832, police and troops dispersed crowds composed largely of working-class Republicans who had gathered to berate the orleanist deputy Amilhau with a noisy mock serenade (*charivari*) and to honor Republican party leaders with a serenade. Among the seventy persons arrested, fifty-one were identified by occupation, including three wholesale merchants, six shopkeepers, four clerks, twenty-three artisans, four nonartisanal workers, ten students, and one gardener.[8] Handicraft artisans were also very active in republican organizations. The local branch of the Society of the Rights of Man, founded during the summer of 1832, included several shopkeepers, master craftsmen, and students, but was dominated by about eight hundred to nine hundred artisans.[9]

The political repression of 1833–34, which included a ban on the Society as well as severe restrictions on the right of association, drove working-class political activities underground, put an end to street demonstrations, and eliminated the local republican newspaper. In August 1834, the prefect reported that the Society of the Rights of Man was "apparently destroyed . . . but fanatical Republicans are still trying to secretly maintain it. . . . It is in the lower class that they are trying to recruit. . . . Their meeting places vary and are usually on the street and sometimes in the cafés."[10] Radical and socialist republican militants responded to the intensifying repression of the 1830s with a conspiratorial revolutionary strategy. They abandoned earlier efforts to mobilize broad-based, working-class support through a program of cooperative socialism and an inclusive organization capable of leading a mass popular uprising. Instead, they created small secret conspiratorial groups dedicated to a violent overthrow of the government. The three secret conspiratorial societies in Toulouse—*La Praya, La Guerrière,* and *Le Sphinx*—were composed largely of soldiers, artisans, students, bourgeois, and foreign political refugees. Local police managed to infiltrate and destroy these groups in 1836, when sixty-eight alleged conspirators were arrested.[11]

The repression, by eliminating radical and socialist leaders from the scene and preventing nonelectoral political activity by workers, strengthened the position of liberals within republican circles. Liberal Republicans responded to the repression by pursuing a reformist electoral strategy, which meant an abandonment of any effort to mobilize broad-based, working-class support. Republican activities became increasingly focused around winning the electoral support of the small group of bourgeois and petty-bourgeois property owners entitled to vote—only 3 percent of the city's adult male population. Liberal Republicans hoped to win the support of those merchants, professionals, shopkeepers, and small employers who were qualified to vote. Many local small employers and shopkeepers were attracted by the party's educational, tax, and suffrage reform proposals, while lawyers, educators, and other members of the liberal professions were attracted by the republican vision of a secular parliamentary form of government, republican advocacy of rewards according to talent not influence, and republican attacks on corruption in the civil service.

Republicans also garnered electoral support from the city's commercial bourgeoisie, who were unhappy with orleanist tariff policies. The liberal leaders of Toulouse's Republican party included a number of wealthy grain merchants who shared with legitimist landowners an interest in the continuing prosperity of the regional grain trade. They joined together in opposing the orleanist government's agricultural and tariff policies, which were making foreign grains more competitive on the French market. In January 1835, republican leader Jean Gasc, a lawyer and city council member, joined nine grain merchants and landowners in signing a petition to the Chamber of Deputies calling for "greater protection than the existing law provides by soliciting more guarantees against this threatening and uninterrupted invasion of foreign grains."[12] Republicans also won the support of the propertied electorate by attacking the power of Parisian finance capital and the growing centralization of the banking system, which was making it increasingly difficult for local merchants to secure credit. In a letter to the Minister of Commerce and Public Works in 1836, the Chamber of Commerce urged the central government to alleviate the city's economic problems by "placing some obstacles in the way of this ruinous emigration of capital or by reducing the flow of tax revenues to Paris." "France is not Paris!" proclaimed the angry letter writers.[13] Republican abandonment of socialist economic programs, such as those advocated by the Society of the Rights of Man, and advocacy of communal liberties also helped them garner support from the propertied electorate.

Liberal republican strategy included the creation of an electoral alliance with the aristocratic-dominated Legitimist party. A wealthy, urban-based aristocracy inhabited Toulouse, providing the social base and economic resources for a relatively strong Legitimist party. In 1834, liberal leaders of the city's Republican party engineered an alliance with Legitimists, under the banner of municipal liberties. This electoral alliance proved quite successful, capturing two out of three contested seats in the 1834 Chamber of Deputies election, electing the Republican party leader Jacques Joly to the Chamber of Deputies in 1839, and gaining control of the city council in 1840. Republicans also scored impressive electoral victories in the local election of National Guard officers, maintaining control of the leadership of this citizens' militia throughout the 1830s.

The alliance of liberal Republicans and royalists met with continued opposition from radical party leaders and working-class militants from the very outset. Radical and socialist Republicans challenged the alliance after its victory in 1834, taking their politics into the streets. After the election, a group of Legitimists planned to serenade their leaders, but a crowd of republican demonstrators arrived on the scene singing songs and shouting slogans. A confrontational atmosphere quickly developed and a brawl nearly broke out, but police arrived and dispersed the crowd.[14] The alliance experienced another difficult moment in 1842, when the archbishop of Toulouse denounced the writings of liberal republican leader Gatien-Ar-noult, a popular university professor, as "neither Christian or Catholic" and as leading toward atheism. *Émancipation* defended Gatien-Arnoult, but, despite close ties between the clergy and local aristocrats, the legitimist newspaper *La Gazette de Languedoc* remained silent, not wishing to disrupt the alliance.[15]

Liberal dominance and pursuit of an electoral strategy meant an abandonment of earlier republican commitments to working-class issues (i.e., the "social question") and a decline in working-class participation in republican activities. Republican political propaganda of the late 1830s showed few signs of concern for the city's workers. The republican socialist schemes that had rallied workers to the cause of the republic during the early 1830s disappeared. Like the national liberal republican newspaper *Le National*, local party leaders studiously avoided discussing working-class issues, limiting their criticisms to political rather than social issues. Republicans did not actively support workers in either of the two labor conflicts that took place during the 1830s: a small but successful tailors' strike in March 1837, and a walkout of printers at the workshop of J. B. Paya, a prominent liberal republican leader, after he increased their workload without raising wages.

Workers joined the 1840 nationwide petition campaign for suffrage reform, although leadership of the reform committee in Toulouse was dominated by shopkeepers and master artisans. There were no workers among the five members of the central committee of the organization, but among the sixteen men leading the three subcommittees were four artisans, a baker, a marble worker, a metalworker, and a mechanic. The prefect noted, in a letter dated December 9, 1840, that only seven of the leaders of the organization possessed substantial wealth and social standing: a lawyer, three merchants, two property owners, and a tavern owner. The others, most of whom were shopkeepers and master artisans, "have no influence on the wealthy and educated population but several exercise considerable influence on a part of the proletarians (*prolétaires*) and workers (*ouvriers*) of this city."[16]

Though excluded from the electoral arena, handicraft artisans continued to play a decisive role in local political developments by taking politics into the streets. Although liberal republican leaders remained wary of threats to public order, they made use of popular protest during the census riots of 1841. In February 1841, the French Minister of Finance ordered a property assessment census to reevaluate the values of rental properties. Local republican and legitimist municipal officials denounced the census as illegal, claiming that only the city had a right to carry out such a survey. When Jacques-Alphonse Mahul, the new Prefect, was sent to Toulouse to implement the census, he was welcomed by a mock serenade organized by the police commissioner and the city council. The mayor, Armand de Perpessac, resigned in protest. His successor, the liberal merchant Benoît-Joachim Arzac, helped lead further resistance to the census. In the ensuing confrontation, on the evenings of July 7 and 8, crowds singing the *Marseillaise* filled the streets. Dozens of demonstrators, mostly artisans, were arrested, and barricades went up in the faubourgs of Saint-Étienne and Saint-Aubin. After a confrontation between troops and demonstrators in front of the prefecture on July 12, in which one demonstrator was killed and many were wounded, the mayor persuaded the prefect to recall the troops and allow the National Guard to police the city. National Guardsmen sympathetic to the insurrection freed prisoners and failed to protect the prefect from an angry mob. After the prefect and attorney general fled the city, groups of armed workers singing the *Marseillaise* paraded the tricolor flag through the city. Bonfires (*feux de joie*) illuminated all of the city's major squares.

The victory in the streets of the city was short-lived, but it was soon followed by the electoral triumph of those who led the insurrection. After heavy military reinforcements arrived, the central government placed Toulouse under a state of siege and dissolved the National Guard and city council. The mayor Arzac, along with liberal republican city councilor Jean Gasc, a lawyer, were arrested for their role in the insurrection. They were both convicted by the correctional tribunal at Pau in late November, but their sentence was only a fine of one hundred francs plus court expenses. The bourgeois and aristocratic leaders of the republican-legitimist alliance reaped electoral rewards for their role in supporting the resistance to central state power. In the local election of November 15, 1841, the republican-legitimist alliance won twenty-five of the thirty-seven contested city council seats, with Republicans capturing thirteen seats.[17]

Although victorious in its effort to win the electoral support of eligible bourgeois and petty bourgeois voters, the liberal republican strategy alienated local workers and fostered the growth of an Icarian communist movement. The carpenters' and tailors' strikes in June 1840 lasted for weeks and involved hundreds of workers from workshops across the city. The shoemakers' strike in October–November 1841, in which two hundred shoemakers from workshops across the city confronted forty-five masters in their demand for a uniform piece-rate scale, took place during the city council election campaign. These strikes, launched by the city's largest and most politicized trades, pitted artisanal workers in handicraft industry, who were by and large ineligible to vote, against their employers, who provided potential electoral support for republican candidates. The liberal editors of the republican newspaper *Émancipation* initially supported the tailors' strike but then reversed their position in favor of employers, out of fear of losing votes in the upcoming election. The republican-legitimist alliance won the November 1841 election, but the victory came at the cost of alienating workers from the Republican party. Many politically active artisans subsequently rejected bourgeois leadership in favor of more autonomous working-class activity, which took the form of an Icarian communist movement.[18]

Toulouse's Icarian communist leaders organized one of the largest branches of the first nationwide working-class social movement in France.[19] Local Icarian leaders played an important role in the census riots of July 1841, using the occasion to encourage workers to join their ranks. During the riots, the master stonecutter Étienne Rolland and joiner Joseph Sagansan actively recruited building trade workers to the movement. In July 1842, Icarian communist militants led a demonstration of approximately six hundred workers at the Daurade Church to demand a memorial service for Chavardes, who had been killed a year earlier in the census riots.[20] According to police, Toulouse's Icarians were planning for an armed insurrection, in a secret revolutionary group, known as the *Organisation méridional*, composed of five hundred to six hundred men organized into small sections of ten persons.[21] When local Icarian leaders were arrested and charged with an alleged insurrectionary conspiracy in 1843, they rejected bourgeois republican offers of legal aid and refused to allow the liberal republican deputy Jacques Joly to serve as their defense lawyer. They called on Étienne Cabet, whose visit to the city for the trial focused attention on the Icarian movement and increased the prestige and visibility of Icarian leaders. During the trial, defense attorney M. Detours warned the French bourgeoisie: "Look below you and see whether you are able to face the spectacle of the poor and the workers without feelings of anguish and fear." In response to the acquittal verdict, the prosecuting attorney lamented, "Oh, the poor French bourgeoisie!"[22]

Local Icarian leaders contended that bourgeois leaders of the Republican party were incapable of representing working-class interests and rejected republican contentions that the lot of workers could be improved by suffrage reform. Republicans, wrote the prefect in 1844, "want only a change in the form of government . . . [and] want to wait for the right moment" to act. The Icarians were described by the prefect as those who "would attack society in its entirety . . . [and] having less to lose, are more disposed to precipitating events and provoking opportunities so as to be more sure of seizing hold of them."[23] Although Republicans and Icarians maintained relatively harmonious relations between 1841 and 1843, they clashed with one another in June 1844. In making plans for a funeral procession to honor former liberal government official Jacques Lafitte with a funeral procession, liberal republican leaders failed to consult with Icarian leaders. Icarians organized a boycott of the procession, urging workers not to become pawns of bourgeois republican leaders. The Icarians, wrote the police commissioner on June 7, 1844, "are doing all they can to ensure the failure of this demonstration out of a hatred for the bourgeois, who appear to shove them aside when they are no longer needed."[24] The boycott was quite successful as word spread through the cafés and workshops of the city that Lafitte had betrayed the cause of the people in 1830 and was not worthy of a procession. Despite liberal republican plans to distribute two thousand printed invitations to local workers, only four hundred people showed up for the procession to the Daurade church.

During the final years of the July Monarchy, a period of severe economic crisis, an active republican socialist movement emerged that won the allegiances of workers, including many former Icarian communist leaders. Republican socialism spoke to the economic grievances of workers and promised a resolution to the so-called "social question" via the route of suffrage reform. Many former Icarian communist workers, discouraged by the failures of their own movement, came to see the goal of a mass mobilization to secure the vote for workers as a more promising strategy for change than the antielectoral stance of Icarianism.[25] Republican socialists argued that suffrage reform, by providing the vote to workers, could make possible the establishment of a new economic order that would guarantee full employment (*le droit au travail*), a cornerstone of the republican socialist program. Unlike the 1838–40 suffrage reform effort, the 1846–48 campaign for suffrage reform in Toulouse included working-class socialists in its leadership, and was accompanied by a concerted propaganda effort to link the issue of suffrage reform to workers' economic grievances. Most of the working-class leaders of the republican socialist movement in Toulouse were drawn from handicraft artisanal industries threatened by capitalist development, such as shoemaking, tailoring, joining, hatmaking, and metalworking.

The growth of republican socialism was marked by autonomous working-class political activity, for working-class leaders remained wary of liberal bourgeois republican leaders who had, for many years, ignored their interests and grievances. The central police commissioner, in September 1845, described the development of republicanism in Toulouse as follows: The city's Republicans are "divided into bourgeois and workers. . . . This latter class, which is now trying to organize itself, wishes to agitate independently of the former. . . ."[26] Although there was already a local republican newspaper, *Émancipation*, working-class republican socialists founded their own independent newspaper, *La Voix du peuple*, in February

1847. Although this paper printed articles by liberal bourgeois republican leaders like Joly, it was run by workers and it espoused a socialist vision of republicanism that emphasized the rhetoric of class solidarity and class conflict. The newspapers' editors, the shoemaker Antoine Rivière and the hat dyer Antoine Belou, included the following observations in their initial statement of principles: "Everything to the bourgeoisie, nothing to the people. Profits without work to the former and work without profit, even without bread, to the latter. Such is the distributive justice of the Solomons of the *juste-milieu.* . . . Able-bodied and well-intentioned men are not always able to find work to support themselves and, reduced to begging, they fall into the hands of the police and are arrested, prosecuted, and convicted, and punished for the faults of society. . . ."[27]

The rapid growth of a republican socialist movement in Toulouse strengthened the position of radical republican leaders, who opposed working within the narrow confines of the established electoral arena, and forced liberal Republicans to reconsider their electoral strategy and their alliance with Legitimists. Along with a revival of nonelectoral protests by workers, which alienated royalist voters, a rapprochement between liberal and radical republican leaders threatened to undermine the electoral alliance with Legitimists. In March 1846, riots broke out after a crowd at the local theater demanded a rendition of the *Varsovienne* to express solidarity with Polish Republicans in their struggle against Russia. The demonstration then spread through the streets of the city, with large crowds gathering to shouts of republican slogans and chants of the *Marseillaise*. In the rioting that followed, a crowd of workers attacked and pillaged the offices of the local legitimist newspaper. This event, along with the growing influence of radicals and socialists among Republicans, undermined the alliance with Legitimists. In the August 1846 legislative election, radical party leaders effectively opposed the effort of the liberal orleanist former mayor Armand de Perpessac to run for office. They actively supported the candidacy of Jacques Joly, a liberal Republican who was more willing to cooperate with radical and socialist Republicans. During his campaign, Joly received delegations of republican socialist workers, led by the hatmaker Paul Cazalas and tailor Amiel, and appeared alongside socialist leader Louis Blanc, who visited the city on July 27, 1846.[28] These events alarmed legitimist voters, many of whom refused to vote for Joly, who ultimately lost his seat.

Republicans blamed their defeat on the betrayal of the Legitimists and soon terminated their electoral alliance. At the end of August 1846, republican city councilmen joined Orleanists in an effort to remove Legitimists from positions on city council commissions. The following summer, on July 30, 1847, a special election was held to fill the seat vacated by the death of the orleanist deputy Jean Cabanis. The republican electoral campaign benefited from the economic crisis, as well as from scandals that revealed widespread official corruption. The liberal republican candidate Jean-Pierre Pagès won the election on the second ballot by twenty-six votes. Over three thousand people took to the streets to celebrate the victory. Pagès publicly thanked "not only the electors but the people of Toulouse who have deservingly associated with the triumph of the opposition."[29]

Republicans finalized the end of their alliance with Legitimists during the banquet campaign of 1847, after a dispute over what toasts should be made.[30] Legitimists objected to the increasing intrusion of the "social question" into the banquet campaign's toasts, a reflection of the growing influence of radical and socialist Republicans within the local party. The legitimist newspaper formally announced the end of the alliance by declaring that royalists should not dine with terrorists and communists. The banquet campaign provided the occasion for the Republican party's liberal leadership to jettison legitimist electoral allies by insisting on including several banquet toasts unacceptable to the royalists. Royalists rejected a toast "To the sovereignty of the people," arguing instead for "To national sovereignty." They also rejected a proposed toast "To the principles that brought 1789 and 1830." The breakdown of the alliance was publicized by an exchange of angry letters, published in local newspapers, between republican leader Jacques Joly and legitimist leader the marquis d'Hautpoul.[31]

Liberal republican leaders Joly and Gatien-Arnoult joined radical journalists from *Émancipation*, like Armand Duportal, and socialists from *La Voix du peuple* in the 1847 banquet campaign for universal male suffrage. Despite liberal Republicans' hostility toward socialism, and socialist workers' wariness of bourgeois republican leadership, these different factions united in opposition to the orleanist regime's restrictions on suffrage rights. *Émancipation* reminded its readers of the urgency of uniting "all true democrats."[32] Republicans organized a number of small banquets in favor of suffrage reform in July 1847, as well as a large banquet in January 1848. The January banquet, which attracted 750 participants, included several toasts by liberal party leaders, including one by Pierre Roquelaine to communal liberties, as well as a radical republican toast "to work and the laboring classes." The conservative newspaper, the *Journal de Toulouse*, pointed out class divisions among Republicans by chastising liberal leaders as "aristocrats of democracy" who drove to the banquet in the comfort of carriages while working-class Republicans trudged through the rain and mud to attend the banquet in the outer-lying neighborhood of Minimes. "Such conduct," observed the newspaper, "is very strange for men who claim to be partisans of equality."[33]

Police, judicial, and administrative records for the July Monarchy reveal the diverse class backgrounds of the city's republican activists as well as the predominance of artisans in working-class politics. Professionals, wholesale merchants, master artisans, shopkeepers, especially owners of cafés, taverns, and cabarets, and artisanal workers joined forces in the struggle for a republic. When this struggle moved into the streets, however, workers (mainly artisans), predominated. Artisanal workers dominated the ranks of those arrested during the political demonstrations of the early 1830s, the census riot of 1841, and the foreign policy riot of 1846. These artisanal militants were drawn from a variety of different trades, but those trades most affected by the growth of sweated production (tailoring and shoemaking), the spread of subcontracting (building trades), the growth of manufactories (metalworking and hatmaking), and repressive laws governing the press (printers) provided the largest number of militants.[34]

The trajectory of republican politics in Toulouse during the July Monarchy involved initial liberal dominance followed by growing challenges by radical and socialist Republicans. After an initial effort by radicals and socialists to mobilize working-class support met with harsh repression during the early 1830s, liberal Republicans make a successful effort to win the votes of the city's propertied electorate. They rejected conspiratorial revolutionary activities and socialist rhetoric in favor of an alliance with royalists, silence on the social question, and appeals to issues that would draw support from the ranks of bourgeois and petty bourgeois voters. This enabled liberal Republicans, in alliance with royalists, to capture power at the local level and win seats in parliamentary elections. But it also alienated a highly politicized male artisanate, who looked to Icarian communists for an alternative and developed strong capacities for autonomous collective political action. Though excluded from the suffrage and from the leadership of the Republican party, Toulouse's artisans agitated independently of bourgeois leaders, taking to the streets to collectively express their grievances, and putting pressure on liberal republican leaders to acknowledge their presence. After 1846, the growth of a republican socialist movement encouraged liberal Republicans to move beyond the electoral arena and join forces with radical and socialist Republicans to demand universal male suffrage. This led to an abandonment of their long alliance with Legitimists, but it enabled them to secure the allegiances of local artisans and temporarily unify liberal, radical, and socialist Republicans. This did not guarantee workers a strong voice within local party affairs or put an end to the autonomous political activities of workers, who remained ready to take to the streets to express their demands and extremely wary of bourgeois political leadership. The unity of Republicans based by the common goal of universal male suffrage proved to be short-lived. Once universal male suffrage was attained, with the revolution of 1848, divisions among Republicans rapidly surfaced.

THE SECOND REPUBLIC IN TOULOUSE

The advent of the Second Republic in Toulouse brought to power liberal republican leaders who had led the opposition to the orleanist regime. When news of the triumph of the revolution reached Toulouse, large crowds escorted liberal republican lawyer Joly to city hall, where he proclaimed the new republic. A telegram from the new Minister of the Interior, Ledru-Rollin, named Joly president of both the provisional departmental commission and the provisional municipal administration. Although working-class socialist leaders had played a central role in republican electoral reform agitation during the late July Monarchy, they were excluded from positions in the new government. The five deputy mayors (*adjoints*) who assisted Joly in directing the provisional city government were all well-to-do bourgeois republican leaders. They included four prominent liberal Republicans: Gatien-Arnoult (professor); Joseph Vivent (grain merchant); Bernard Mulé (grain merchant); and Pierre Roquelaine (property owner)— but only one radical leader, Jean-Baptiste Pégot-Ogier (merchant). The provisional municipal council and the provisional departmental commission also drew their members from the ranks of the city's liberal republican bourgeoisie.

The advent of the republic sparked the rapid creation of numerous political clubs. It transformed the streets of Toulouse, which suddenly became busy centers of politics, as orators, newspaper hawkers, and demonstrators filled public spaces. Clubs held frequent meetings where members debated various issues including unemployment, tax reform, reform of the National Guard, and the composition of the new government. Working-class club members, mainly artisans, took to the streets throughout March 1848 to protest government policies. When liberal republican deputy Pagès returned to the city in early March, he lectured a group of supporters, who had given him a welcoming serenade, about the need to maintain order in order to preserve liberty.[35] At the end of March, Pagès was the target of a charivari, by several hundred radical and socialist members of the Voice of the People club, who protested against his "lukewarm" republicanism.[36] After club members organized a political charivari at the home of former deputy and court of appeals president Adolphe Martin in late March, Joly removed this official from his post. At the end of March, 160 members of the *Club des droits de l'homme* unsuccessfully petitioned Joly to fire police commissioner Telmon, who had ordered police to tear down club posters announcing a demonstration to protest government policies, including the new forty-five centime tax.[37] Militant workers also took to the streets to protest the failure of the city's new public works program to provide decent wages.

The street politics of the clubs did not have a legitimate place in liberal republican visions of a democratic political order. They reacted to the clubs by denouncing demonstrations as a threat to public order and the stability of the fledgling republic. In requesting central government aid for a municipal public works program in March 1848, commissioner Joly noted that "unemployed workers gather regularly and are becoming more threatening" and that "the most incendiary proposals are being made in the clubs."[38] Gatien-Arnoult, president of the new republican city council, issued a declaration urging workers to maintain respect for order and blaming the recent club and strike agitation on misguided working-class leaders, many of whom, he claimed, were traitors to the Republic.

Workers aroused the hostility of liberal republican officials not only by taking their politics into the streets but also by launching strikes against their employers. At the end of March 1848, a strike by bakers threatened to disrupt the city's food supply in the midst of a severe economic crisis. The bakers walked off their jobs, demanding higher wages and shorter working hours, after meeting several times with Joly to discuss their grievances. Joly issued a threatening proclamation urging the bakers to end their strike, and then ordered the arrest of eight strike leaders. The arrests failed to break the strike, but on April 10, Joly ordered all striking workers who were not born in the city expelled from Toulouse if they did not return to work in twenty-four hours. This measure put an end to the strike.

The participatory democratic vision of Toulouse's radical and socialist club activists extended to the National Guard, which had been disbanded following the census riots of 1841 but reorganized after the February revolution. This local citizens' militia continued to exclude workers from its ranks. On February 28, 1848, at a meeting of over four hundred members of the *Voice of the People club*, orators criticized the government for its failure to arm its most ardent supporters, and urged Joly to arm the working class. Along with three of the city's other large clubs, they organized a demonstration on March 22 to demand, among other things, a reorganization of the National Guard. On April 9, 1848, the Voice of the People club, led by Jean Baptiste Astima, organized a demonstration to protest the exclusion of workers from the National Guard. That same day, an official review of the citizens' militia was scheduled to take place. While Joly was meeting with National Guard officers and bourgeois republican leaders at the prefecture, about four hundred members of the club arrived and demanded to meet with the authorities. Upon the refusal of Joly to meet with them, club members overcame National Guard resistance and forced their way into the courtyard and then into Joly's office. National Guard troops arrived on the scene, dispersed the crowd gathered in the courtyard, and arrested eighty-four club members. Joly ordered the dissolution of the club and accused club members of promoting the bakers' strike. The morning after the confrontation at the prefecture, a crowd of unarmed workers gathered at the prison in an unsuccessful effort to free their captured comrades. The day was marked by widespread agitation among the city's workers. Crowds gathered in several working-class neighborhoods, and police arrested several workers for attempting to incite them to action.[39]

The repression of the so-called "Astima affair" resolved two key issues of political contention: the role of clubs in shaping the policies of the government and the admission of workers into the city's National Guard. The banning of the most militant socialist club in the city, and the arrest and conviction of its leaders, put an end to working-class hopes that popular demonstrations organized by the clubs would be an effective means of exercising newly won political rights. The defeat of the Voice of the People club marked a turning point in the local development of the revolution, after which the clubs were relatively inactive. The repression also ensured that local workers, denied access to the citizens' militia, would not have weapons to pursue their political projects.

After failing to gain admission into the National Guard, socialist workers turned their attention to electoral politics, confronting liberal republican leaders over the class composition of the republican slate of candidates in the upcoming National Assembly election. Joly and other liberal party leaders formed the *Comité central*, which unsuccessfully tried to impose its list of candidates on the city's Republicans with little debate or discussion. A group of dissident radical Republicans, led by the accountant Joseph Balansac, a prominent club orator, formed an alternative group, the *Comité du sud*, which drew up their own list of candidates. Liberals whose support for the republic was belated and hesitant formed a third group, the *Comité républicain national*, centered around the formerly orleanist newspaper the *Journal de Toulouse*. Socialists created the *Comité central populaire*, headed by the shoemaker François Vincent, and inspired by the Society of Workers (*Société des travailleurs*), a political association which urged workers to organize independently rather than remain scattered in political clubs where they risked being dominated by the bourgeoisie, who were usually better orators. This association recruited workers from forty different trades. Its leadership was provided by artisans, including a metallurgist, a stove maker, a foundry worker, and a mechanic. The twelve candidates chosen by the committee included a locksmith, a mechanic, and a tailor, as well as nine bourgeois republican leaders, several of whom were excluded from Joly's list because of their radical views. Joly's name was included on the list of the *Comité central populaire* but he repudiated them, stating that he did not wish to share a slate with those whose socialist doctrines he rejected.[40] Liberal republican candidates, like the master locksmith Gilbert Castelbou, professed concern for the plight of the working class and campaigned for the abolition of regressive taxes on food and drink, but denounced socialist schemes of wealth redistribution and preached respect for private property. Liberal Republicans were thus able to simultaneously appeal to workers, especially those who were not active members of the club movement, as well as small property owners who attributed the economic crisis to the strikes and club protests that had followed the revolution.

Ten of the twelve liberal republican candidates on Joly's *Comité central* slate won seats in the National Assembly election of April 23, with the remaining two seats going to candidates of the *Comité républicain national* slate. The candidates who won the highest number of votes in Toulouse—Pagès (23,343); Joly (18,898); and Gatien-Arnoult (15,493)—were liberal Republicans. In the department, liberal Republicans also won the largest number of votes, with Pagès heading the list with 103,644 votes. Radical and socialist candidates were soundly defeated, with none of them placing among the top twelve vote getters.[41] Before leaving Toulouse for Paris, Joly was honored by a public celebration in which he received a crown of gold in appreciation for his services to the Republic. This ceremony angered radicals and socialists, who denounced the use of a "symbol of tyranny." In a meeting with National Guard officers prior to his departure, Joly expressed some misgivings about his recent actions, remarking, "Perhaps we have done too much for order and not enough for liberty."[42]

When news of the Parisian insurrection of June reached Toulouse, National Guardsmen prepared to leave for the capital to aid in the repression. News of the defeat of the insurrection arrived before their departure. Local workers gathered in response to news of the uprising, including a crowd on the place des Carmes that listened to a speaker who claimed to be carrying bullets from Paris and who read a telegram about the events. Despite an unsolicited citizen's report to the mayor that local workers were discussing revenge for the June massacre and planning an attack on the city hall, prefecture, and Arsenal, there were no incidents.[43] On June 29, the prefect Larouche reassured his superior in Paris that there was no threat of an uprising in response to the events in Paris because the clubs had been neutralized as centers of rebellion. "The clubs," he wrote, "do not present any danger. If they attempt any act of violence, even a demonstration, measures will be immediately taken to put an end to them. . . ."[44]

Divisions among Republicans continued during the summer of 1848. Radical Republicans, led by Marcel Lucet, formed their own newspaper, *Le Constituent démocratique*, rather than work alongside liberal Republicans at *Émancipation*. They also created their own electoral committee to draw up a list of candidates for the July 1848 municipal elections. These divisions on the left occurred at the same time that a conservative coalition, the Party of Order, unified the opposition around a political strategy that identified the republic with high taxes, unemployment, economic crisis, and class warfare. The conservative coalition won nineteen of the thirty-eight contested seats in the July 1848 municipal election and thirty-four of thirty-nine contested seats on the departmental council.

The electoral defeat of July prompted liberal, radical, and socialist Republicans to close ranks against the growing conservative threat. *Émancipation*, which had vehemently denounced socialism during the recent electoral campaign, commented on August 4 that although socialists "have done much harm to democracy . . . we esteem and respect their progressive ideas and revolutionary talent." Radicals and socialists responded by joining liberals in planning a large outdoor banquet to commemorate the founding of the First Republic. When a group of socialist workers urged radical leader Marcel Lucet to organize a rival banquet for the same day, he refused, arguing that Republicans were too divided. The banquet of September 22 attracted over four thousand diners along with approximately six thousand spectators. Party leaders were careful to exclude socialist orators from the podium, but a worker managed to mount the platform without authorization to shout a toast to the "Democratic and Social Republic." Banquet organizers quickly removed the ladder to the grandstand to prevent any further disruptions. The incident scandalized the conservative press and gave central government officials a pretext for replacing the mayor and prefect with more conservative men.

During the fall of 1848, the upcoming presidential campaign divided Republicans. Conservative Orleanists, Legitimists, and Bonapartists united in support of Louis Napoleon Bonaparte. Liberal Republicans supported the candidacy of General Eugène Cavaignac, denounced by radicals and socialists as "the butcher of June" for his role in defeating the insurrection in Paris. Radical Republicans, under the leadership of republican journalists Marcel Lucet and Armand Duportal, directed the campaign for Ledru-Rollin, rallying the support of the city's socialist workers. Radicals and socialists gathered regularly at the Club de la rue Lapeyrouse to discuss the electoral campaign. At its October 30 meeting, in order to elude laws on the clubs that required official authorization for each meeting, the organization changed its name to the *Comité central démocratique électorale*.[45] The leadership of the association included numerous workers and craftsmen, including the master shoemaker François Vincent, the printers Villette and Faux, the shoemaker Joseph Rivière, the hatmakers Bores and Henri Rouché, and the tailor Antoine Izard. The authorities kept a close watch on this club, which attracted over seven hundred persons to its October meetings. According to police spies, radical leaders adopted a revolutionary rhetoric in addressing their predominantly working-class audience. On December 2, Armand Duportal told club members that if Louis Bonaparte was elected, there would be a civil war, whereas if Cavaignac was elected, they would drive him from office as they did Louis-Philippe. But when the socialist hatmaker Henri Rouché suggested that they make concrete plans to take up arms in the event of an electoral defeat, he was ignored.[46]

Louis Napoleon Bonaparte won the election in Toulouse, capturing 15,544 (62%) of the city's 25,014 votes. Radical republican efforts produced 7,029 votes (28%) for Ledru-Rollin, while liberal Republicans had little success in rallying support for Cavaignac, who won only 2,441 votes (10%). In the department of the Haute-Garonne, Bonaparte won by a larger margin, with 73,947 votes (76%), compared to 15,852 (16%) for Ledru-Rollin and 7,222 (7%) for Cavaignac. The purge of republican officials that followed Bonaparte's election did not bypass Toulouse. The central government dissolved the city council, appointed a more conservative prefect, and, at the end of March 1849, dissolved the city's National Guard.

The conservative triumph and its aftermath prompted liberal, radical, and socialist Republicans to join forces in a Mountain electoral coalition that focused its attention on the legislative election of May 1849. At the beginning of 1849, the city's two republican newspapers, *Le Constituent démocratique* and *Émancipation*, combined into a single newspaper. Although workers maintained their own independent socialist organization, the *Association des travailleurs*, liberals, radicals, and socialists joined together to create a local branch of the Mountain electoral organization, Republican Solidarity. This organization attracted Republicans from different wings of the party, including liberals like Jean-Pierre Roquelaine, Bernard Mulé, and Isadore Janot; radical leaders Armand Duportal, Jacques Lucet, and Jean-Baptiste Pégot-Ogier; as well as socialist leaders Joseph Balansac, Gabriel Gaillard, and Paul Cazalas.

Despite growing unity on the left, working-class socialists remained hesitant to join an electoral organization that included the city's most prominent liberal Republicans among its leaders. Radical leaders Armand Duportal and Jacques Lucet presided over a club on the *rue Lapeyrouse*, which attracted a large number of working-class Republicans. They complained to working-class members that too few workers had joined Republican Solidarity, and that many workers who had joined later resigned to join the *Association des travailleurs*. They explained to working-class members that these two organizations shared the same political principles and that one could, in good conscience, belong to both. The presence of militant socialist workers willing to challenge the club's radical bourgeois leadership produced disruptive gatherings of the *Lapeyrouse* club. Duportal temporarily resigned his leadership at the meeting of March 5, in the midst of a raucous debate over methods of selecting candidates for the upcoming municipal election. At a subsequent meeting on March 8, Duportal walked out of a highly charged debate over whether or not to organize a banquet. At the following meeting of March 9, several working-class club members, angry about the omission of workers from recently revised electoral lists, suggested taking up arms, but other club members insisted that a legal strategy would ensure victory for the Republic and socialism.[47]

Despite tense relations between socialist workers and bourgeois republican leaders, members of Republican Solidarity agreed on a procedure for selecting Mountain candidates for the May legislative election. The committee responsible for selecting candidates included fifty people chosen by the various workers' trade associations, fifteen individuals chosen by the bourgeois and petty-bourgeois-dominated *Cercle de l'union démocratique*, and seventeen persons chosen by members of the liberal professions. Workers were given a majority voice in the selection of Mountain National Assembly candidates, in sharp contrast to their exclusion from the process of candidate selection a year earlier. Despite this reconciliation, divisions among Republicans persisted. In March 1849, prior to the election, republican socialists launched their own newspaper, *Civilisation*, abandoning the effort to collaborate with liberal and radical bourgeois party leaders in publishing *Émancipation*.

Divisions among Republicans played a role in the municipal electoral defeat of 1849. In the municipal election of late March 1849, a republican list dominated by radicals and socialists was defeated by a legitimist-dominated "party of order" slate. The conservative alliance captured a majority of city council seats, winning ten thousand votes, compared to nine thousand for the so-called "red" list. The attorney general blamed the outcome on the absence of conciliation between different wings of the Republican party, noting that the slim margin of victory for the "Friends of Order" list was very unstable, since "of the 19,000 voters, there are 2,000 who would vote otherwise if the [municipal] administration changed and others who, to please their employers or creditors, voted against their habitual friends. . . ."[48] In the May 1849 legislative election, Toulouse's "party of order" alliance captured all ten contested seats. In the department, the highest vote total for any candidate on the conservative list was 62,844, compared to only 33,155 for the top republican candidate. But in Toulouse, the leader of the Mountain slate, Ledru-Rollin, won 9,546 votes, outdistancing Charles de Rémusat, who led the party of order, with 9,373 votes. In the polarized political atmosphere of early 1849, a Republican party dominated by radicals and socialists had managed, over the course of only a few months, to win the support of a majority of the city's voters, who had recently supported Louis Bonaparte by a wide majority.

The Parisian insurrection of June 1849 prompted large crowds, numbering an estimated two thousand, to gather for several nights in front of city hall to protest the invasion of Rome by French troops. Although there were no violent confrontations between troops and demonstrators, authorities used the occasion to justify the arrest of the city's most prominent republican leaders, who were accused of a conspiracy to foment an insurrection.

The repression that followed the June 1849 insurrection, directed primarily against voluntary associations, newspapers, printed materials, and collective actions, drove republican activities underground into the informal networks of day-to-day sociability. The outlawed political clubs were soon replaced by informal political gatherings in the cafés, taverns, and cabarets of working-class neighborhoods and by secret societies. Most of these societies were headed by well-known, working-class republican socialists. They met in the cafés, taverns, and cabarets of the faubourgs; they tended to have working-class leaders and to be smaller in number and more working-class oriented than the clubs that preceded them. Their goal was not armed insurrection but propaganda and education, designed to win converts to the cause of the social republic. In 1849–51, police spies kept watch over eleven different secret societies. The attorney general, in January 1850, wrote: "Toulouse, which contains a large working-class population, is a hotbed of political excitement. . . . The closing of the political clubs and a certain economic revival have nonetheless calmed the political passions of many workers . . . but at the core of this class lies distressing desires; in the absence of the clubs, workers now gather in the cafés. . . ."[49]

Despite the growing repression, Republicans were incapable of putting aside their differences. The trial of those Republicans arrested for their role in the demonstrations of June 1849 exacerbated divisions among Republicans. During the trial, which took place in November 1849, working-class socialists accused bourgeois republican leaders of taking money from funds raised to aid political prisoners, and of seeking to ensure their own acquittal while failing to aid the workers arrested in connection with the events of June 1849.[50] Many socialists were further angered when, during the trial, Isadore Janot, editor of *Émancipation*, declared in court that he was "very red" but not a socialist. In the months that followed, divisions among Republicans became even more bitter. In January 1850, the editorial board of *Émancipation*, angered by an article published in *Civilisation*, sent a letter challenging the editors of the socialist newspaper to a duel.[51]

The May 1850 law restricting suffrage rights fostered a revival of conspiratorial secret societies among working-class Republicans, who were the principal targets of the proposed new electoral law, and a growing questioning of the party leadership's devotion to a parliamentary strategy. While not abandoning electoral activities, radicals and socialists prepared for the possibility of an armed insurrection. In April and May 1850, they created a secret militia, but conflict among Republicans soon took its toll. Police spies reported that the secret army (*la bataillon sacré socialiste*) was composed of eight hundred persons and divided into twenty-five sections. It was headed by the socialist leader Jean Baptiste Astima and the radical republican Joseph Bach. The highest-ranking officers in the secret militia were bourgeois and petty bourgeois Republicans chosen from among the ranks of former National Guard officers, while the lower-ranking leaders (*chefs de section*) were mainly workers. At the end of May 1850, internal dissension between a largely working-class rank and file and a bourgeois leadership led to the resignation of a large number of officers, including Bach, and a drop in the number of members to five hundred. Astima became the leader of the militia, which was then reorganized into ten sections, each headed by a worker.[52]

Political repression stimulated renewed efforts by Republicans to join forces. In October 1850, liberal, radical, and socialist Republicans formed an organization to aid victims of political repression. The president of the organization was liberal party leader Bernard Mulé, the vice-president was radical leader Jean Baptiste Pégot-Ogier, and the assistant secretary was the socialist militant Jean Baptiste Astima.[53] Bourgeois party leaders gathered regularly at the *Cercle de l'union démocratique*, on the *rue du Mai*, an organization whose leadership included radicals Armand Duportal, Isador Janot, and Jean-Baptiste Pégot-Ogier, as well as liberals Pierre Roquelaine, Bernard Mulé, and Joseph Vivent. Despite this short-lived attempt at republican unity, socialist workers continued to organize separately from radical and liberal bourgeois leaders. Working-class socialists created their own organization, gathering regularly at meetings of the *Société des travailleurs*. In November 1850, the authorities ordered the dissolution of the *Société des travailleurs*. A rumor circulated that bourgeois republican leaders of the *Cercle de l'union démocratique*, dissolved by order of the prefect several weeks earlier, had been responsible for the action. These men had allegedly complained to the authorities of the injustice of allowing the *Société des travailleurs* to continue meeting while their meetings were banned. Whether or not it was true, the rumor illustrates the intense suspicion that divided liberal and radical bourgeois republican leaders from working-class republican socialists.

Various police reports of 1851 reveal continuing divisions among Republicans. In October 1851, a police spy reported that the local republican newspaper *Émancipation* was on increasingly bad terms with the city's workers, because the latter had "turned to socialism" while the former, though "quite advanced," rejected socialist doctrines. The same agent reported that the *Café du sud* was no longer the center of left-wing activity due to a falling out between the bourgeois and working-class activists who frequented it.[54] That same month, the police commissioner Cazeneaux reported to the prefect that "the Republicans have split into factions—the workers, known as the pure democrats, which is to say socialists, have repudiated the bourgeois Republicans and no longer want to ally with them. . . ." Divisions between socialist workers and bourgeois Republicans, he wrote, had generated plans for a new republican socialist newspaper which would differ from *Émancipation*, which "represents a bourgeois

Republic," in that it would stand for "the pure democratic and social Republic in the fashion of Louis Blanc, Blanqui, Cabet, Pierre Leroux, and Proudhon."[55]

Despite intense repression, restrictions on the suffrage, and persistent divisions within their party, Republicans did not abandon the goal of winning an electoral majority. They hoped to win a major electoral victory in 1852 by mobilizing the support of the peasantry of the surrounding countryside and extending republican electoral strength beyond the city. In March 1851, republican socialists began publishing a special weekly edition for those who had neither time nor money to read a daily newspaper. This newspaper, *Le Travailleur*, raised issues of concern to the peasantry, and regularly carried agricultural information, including cures for various crop diseases. The newspaper's socialist editors remained convinced that a republican electoral victory was possible, despite the electoral law of March 1850. Liberal and radical republican leaders urged adherence to the law on their followers, renouncing the use of violence and expressing a firm belief in the triumph of their cause through electoral means. The year 1852 became a rallying cry for Republicans, who envisioned an electoral victory that would usher in the "social republic." In early May of 1851, Joly wrote to Bernard Mulé: "It is only in 1852 that the struggle must begin."[56] These hopes of electoral victory were abruptly cut short by the coup d'état, which inaugurated a police state that temporarily destroyed the Republican party and silenced the opposition.

The course of republican politics in Toulouse was dramatically altered during the Second Republic. At the outset of the new regime, workers and socialists were excluded from the liberal republican municipal government. Subsequent repressive measures in the face of the bakers' strike and club agitation fostered heightened distrust of liberal republican leaders on the part of workers, who shared a legacy of autonomous political activity rooted in the prior history of a strong Icarian communist movement. The class conflicts and political repression of 1848 helped to discredit liberal Republicans, polarize political relations, and give birth to a Mountain alliance. Despite their concerns for public order and liberty, liberal Republicans joined this alliance, rather than the conservative party of order. Within the Mountain, working-class leaders and republican socialist ideology played a prominent role, as is evidenced by workers' influence in the candidate selection process in 1849 and by the focus of the republican agenda on the social question. In sharp contrast to the Republican party of the 1830s and early 1840s, Republicans of 1849–51 targeted their electoral appeals to working-class interests and identities, utilized socialist rhetoric, and rejected an electoral alliance with royalist parties. The Mountain alliance remained unstable and fragile due to class and ideological divisions among

Republicans, which led to the creation of separate organizations and news-papers. Liberal and radical party leaders joined forces in the face of the intensified repression, but socialist workers continued to challenge bour-geois party leaders. These divisions hindered republican electoral efforts, resulting in narrow defeats in municipal elections and hampering the efforts of the Mountain alliance to mobilize republican support in the surrounding countryside, where conservatives maintained their electoral majorities.

THE SECOND EMPIRE IN TOULOUSE

When news of Louis Napoleon's coup d'état reached Toulouse, crowds gathered in front of city hall to protest. They were soon dispersed by troops after an unsuccessful attempt to storm the building. The city's two republi-can newspapers, *Émancipation* and *Civilisation*, published an appeal for insurrection. The rapid deployment of troops and arrest of prominent re-publican activists, including all those who had signed the appeal, quickly put an end to any threat of armed resistance. Local authorities banned all demonstrations and meetings, seized gunpowder from all of the city's gun shops, and suspended the two republican newspapers. One hundred and fifteen residents of Toulouse were arrested and tried by the department's mixed commission. Seventy of them were sentenced to punishments rang-ing from surveillance to deportation. The vast majority of the 105 victims of the repression who were identified by occupation were drawn from the same groups that had provided the bulk of participants in the republican movement throughout the Second Republic—professionals, merchants, shopkeepers, master artisans, and artisanal workers.[57] Liberal as well as radical and socialist party activists fell victim to the repression that fol-lowed the coup. Among those convicted by the mixed commission, the most severe sentences—deportations to Cayenne and Algeria—were re-served for working-class republican socialists and top bourgeois party leaders.

Working-class labor associations suspected of republican ties became targets of political repression. In 1853, the government dissolved several working-class mutual aid societies because too many of their members were known Republicans. Government officials refused to authorize an-other association because they feared that it might become a political club. Strikes prompted by the rising cost of living in the early 1850s—among shoemakers, carpenters, carriage painters, bakers, long sawyers, and tile workers—also met with harsh repression, including the arrest of suspected strike leaders. The repression succeeded in temporarily suppressing strikes and eliminating republican electoral activities and propaganda. Neither the liberals and radicals who had joined forces on *Émancipation* nor the republican socialists at *Civilisation* were able to sustain a newspaper during the early 1850s.

With their leaders in jail or exile, their newspapers shut down, and their associations banned, republican electoral opposition temporarily disappeared. "The Republican party," reported the prefect in April 1852, "has been forced to admit its impotence. . . . Socialism is defeated and buried, but its latent force remains among the lower reaches of society. . . ."[58] Republicans failed to run candidates in the 1852 legislative election, in which a majority of the city's voters (54%) stayed away from the polls. The official candidates supported by the administration were two former Orleanists who had rallied behind the new regime, the marquis Eugène de Tauriac and former mayor Armand de Perpessac. Abstentions ran as high as 80 percent in the predominantly working-class western canton of the city. The attorney general, writing in January 1855, dismissed the republican threat as follows: "This is a party whose supporters still exist and will always exist, but which is disorganized, without means of action, and which an energetic government has nothing to fear from."[59]

The repression was effective in the short run, in that Republicans remained disorganized and incapable of seriously challenging the regime throughout most of the 1850s. The repression severely weakened, but did not completely eliminate, the ability of Republicans to wage electoral campaigns. In the legislative election of 1857, Republicans ran two liberal candidates, François Arago and Jean-Pierre Pagès, against the regime's official candidates, the incumbent legislators Eugène Tauriac and Armand de Perpessac. Legitimist party leaders, who remained committed to a Bourbon restoration, refused to take the required oath of loyalty to the regime and boycotted the election. Despite police surveillance and the absence of a newspaper or electoral committee to direct their activities, Republicans won a majority of votes cast in the city. The two republican candidates won 6,660 (54%) of the 12,395 votes, in an election in which 42 percent of the city's eligible voters did not participate. The official government candidates won only 5,746 votes in Toulouse, but they won the departmentwide election with rural votes.

The political repression of the 1850s had the unintended consequence of strengthening working-class political autonomy. The repression channeled working-class economic and political activities away from formal Republican party organizations, in which the bourgeoisie played an important role, into the more exclusively working-class social networks of mutual aid societies, cafés, taverns, and workshops and into fraternally organized republican secret societies. In the absence of the Republican party and its bourgeois leadership, workers continued to gather regularly to discuss politics. Secret police reports of the summer of 1854 state that meetings of workers took place every evening in several homes in the city's working-class neighborhoods. Police were unable to gather sufficient information to take action and could not even acquire the names of the leaders. They reported that these clandestine gatherings were headed by men of little political stature, and that the really important leaders on the left had fallen victim to the repression which followed the coup.[60] It is in the cafés, wrote the attorney general in July 1858, that "the news of the day circulates and political party directives, especially for Republicans and socialists, are handed down."[61]

In their attempt to destroy the Republican party by eliminating its leadership, government authorities weakened the control of bourgeois Republicans and inadvertently fostered a stronger role for working-class leaders.[62] The temporary elimination of bourgeois republican leaders from the scene during the early 1850s encouraged the emergence of young working-class leaders who were unwilling to readily accept bourgeois political leadership. Due to the repression of the early 1850s, and temporary destruction of republican electoral activities, these men did not develop strong collaborative ties with local bourgeois republican leaders during their initial introduction to republican politics. In April 1859, the attorney general commented on the threat of a new, younger, and more militant leadership emerging from the rank and file of the left. "It is not the old leaders of the Republican party," he wrote, "who will pose the greatest threat when the occasion arises. Their names, like a flag, will initially rally the soldiers of demagogy, but then new men will emerge from the ranks, younger and more daring. Unfortunately, it is difficult to predict who they will be."[63]

The industrialization of the 1850s and early 1860s altered the character of artisanal production at Toulouse but did not dramatically transform the city's class structure or substantially alter the internal composition of the city's working class (see chapter 3). Local consumer goods industries expanded to meet the needs of a rapidly growing urban population and some industries, like carriage- and shoemaking, developed growing ties to the world market, but industrial growth did not produce a nascent industrial bourgeoisie capable of providing new political leadership. No prominent local industrialists emerged to vie for leadership positions within the city's municipal government or Republican party. The occupational composition of the Republican party's working-class base remained relatively unchanged, with the same artisanal trades continuing to provide the bulk of republican militants.[64]

The liberalization of the 1860s allowed Republicans to revive their newspapers and electoral committees, but the top leadership of the revived party remained in the hands of bourgeois rather than working-class Republicans. The small group who organized electoral campaigns and ran the local republican newspaper during the 1860s were merchants, lawyers, and journalists, almost all of whom were older men who had been active in republican politics during the July Monarchy and/or Second Republic. The republican city council contingent during the late 1860s included Gatien Arnoult (professor); Bernard Mulé (merchant); Antoine Monnié (merchant); Jean Beziat (merchant); and Joseph Bonnal (architect), all of whom had been prominent in the struggle for a republic during the July Monarchy, as well as Charles St. Gresse (lawyer); Edmond Valette (rentier); Jean Izard (merchant); and Jean Bonnet (master metal founder), who were republican activists during the Second Republic. All of these men were in their fifties and sixties. Armand Duportal, the most prominent party leader, who was fifty-four in 1868, had first become active in republican politics in 1832 as a writer for the local republican newspaper. The group of journalists who wrote and edited the republican newspaper *Émancipation*, which was revived in July 1868, included younger, more radical men like Jean Passerieu, Pierre Ducassé, Louis Dagé, and Jean Magre, all of whom were in their late twenties. A new generation of younger, radical, bourgeois militants gained a foothold at the party newspaper, but an older group of bourgeois Republicans, who shared different generational experiences, dominated the ranks of elected republican officials.

The repression of the 1850s and subsequent liberalization of the 1860s encouraged the creation of a liberal alliance (*l'Union libérale*) between Republicans and Orleanists in the legislative election of 1863. Liberal Orleanists and Republicans united in opposition to the regime's adventurous and costly foreign policies, including the Mexican war, and to the corruption and electoral manipulation that marred electoral politics. The liberal alliance was also united in support of greater civil liberties, a reduction of executive power, the election rather than appointment of mayors, free secular education, and greater decentralization and municipal liberties. Liberal republican candidates appealed to the city's small property owners and commercial bourgeoisie by condemning growing economic centralization and the monopoly control exercised by northern finance capitalists over the region's transportation network, which meant a competitive disadvantage for Toulouse's merchants. The railroad company, owned by the northern banking empire of the Pereire brothers, controlled the lines of the southwest. It wiped out its competition by purchasing control over the *Canal du Midi* and then raising regional transport costs, thereby making Toulouse's grains and other goods less competitive on the national and international market. Republican candidates urged the central government to intervene by purchasing the canal and prohibiting inequitable railroad rates. The candidates of the liberal alliance—Republicans Bernard Mulé and Alexandre Marie and the orleanist notable Charles de Rémusat—carried Toulouse by 9,008 to 7,421 votes, but opposition candidates were again defeated by conservative rural votes.

The liberal opposition alliance triumphed in the municipal elections of 1865, capturing thirty-two of the thirty-six contested seats. Republican city council candidates had campaigned against the government's urban renewal projects and denounced regressive consumption taxes and high food prices.[65] State-financed public works projects, including plans to build large boulevards through the center of Toulouse, provided powerful ammunition in the electoral campaign. Small shopkeepers opposed the construction projects, fearing both the costly threat of relocation and competition from large department stores that were likely to set up on the new boulevards. Republican candidates criticized the municipal government for raising the regressive consumption (*octroi*) taxes to their legal maximum to finance the projects and for contracting Parisian rather than local business firms to do the work.[66] Republicans also attacked the secrecy and corruption of the projects, pointing out that the city had purchased some properties at prices far above their officially estimated value and had leased city property, like the new livestock market, far below its market value. Although the government's public works projects created jobs for construction artisans, one of the largest and most politicized segments of the city's working class, Republicans were able to attack the projects without losing the support of these workers. Construction artisans maintained their traditional loyalties to the republican cause, attracted by republican support for the right to association, espousal of lower and less regressive taxes, and support of public works projects that would provide gas, street lighting, and water to working-class neighborhoods.

The victory of the republican-dominated liberal alliance in the city council elections of 1865 did not lead to the dominance of liberals within the Republican party. The growing political influence of workers, who turned up at the polls in increasing numbers throughout the 1860s, strengthened the socialist wing of the Republican party, which took advantage of the strike wave of the late 1860s to recruit workers. During the strikes of the late 1860s, the city's masons, tawers, carriage smiths, foundry workers, house painters, carriage painters, locksmiths, and bakers confronted their employers. Despite liberalization, local authorities kept a close watch over these collective actions, fearful that republican socialist activists might take advantage of the opportunity to politicize rebellious workers. If workers are allowed to meet too often, warned one police commissioner, they might "having nothing more to say about their situation vis-à-vis their employers, discuss other subjects, such as politics."[67] These fears were justified, as the city's handicraft artisans and their leaders came to play an increasingly important role in the revival of republican politics during the final years of the Second Empire. The strike wave of 1868–69 greatly strengthened the radical and socialist wing of the Republican party in its struggle with liberal party leaders, focusing attention once again on the "social question" and providing an occasion for the mobilization of growing numbers of socialist workers into a resurrected Republican party.

Local artisans became increasingly politically active during the late 1860s, forming new organizations, launching rebellious collective actions, and once again turning the city's streets into arenas of political contestation. After 1868, there were regular gatherings of workers in the faubourgs of Saint-Cyprien and Saint-Étienne, numerous working-class republican electoral gatherings to discuss issues and candidates, and many strike meetings to discuss grievances and plan strikes. Republican party leaders supported the artisanal strikes that swept Toulouse during the summer of 1868, voicing their support in the pages of *Émancipation* and sometimes providing financial aid to strikers. Police officials reported that *Émancipation* found "numerous adherents in the working class" and that free daily issues were distributed to workshops and working-class cafés.[68] The newspaper, which espoused a Proudhonian socialist political vision, had seven hundred subscribers in 1868 and sold several hundred issues each day on the streets. By the end of the Second Empire, it was the most widely circulated newspaper in the city, with a predominantly working-class readership of three thousand by 1871.

The republican electoral campaign of 1869 revealed the growing voice of workers within Toulouse's Republican party. No longer could the party afford to take a stand against striking workers, as it had during the tailor's strike of 1841 and the baker's strike of 1848. Republican candidates depended heavily upon working-class support for their electoral success and actively courted this support during their campaigns. One of the major issues of the 1869 campaign was which political party could best represent the interests of the working class. Napoleonic candidates contrasted the relative prosperity of the Imperial era with the economic crisis and high unemployment of the Second Republic, reminding workers of the recent liberalization of laws governing associational activities. The city's workers voted overwhelmingly for the radical republican candidate Armand Duportal. During the campaign, Duportal was the target of Bonapartist accusations that he preferred to shuffle papers rather than engage in honest labor like the workers he wished to represent. He responded to these attacks by questioning the regime's commitment to workers and emphasizing the link between republicanism and working-class interests.

Although Toulouse's workers showed up at the polls in great numbers to support republican candidates during the late 1860s, they did not abandon nonelectoral protests for the ballot box. Despite local republican electoral victories, workers continued to take their politics into the streets. In March 1868, workers responded violently to government efforts to reform conscription laws, which the city's Republican party portrayed as part of the Imperial government's plan to provoke a new war. Dozens of demonstrators, some of whom set up barricades in the working-class neighborhood of Saint-Cyprien, were arrested in violent demonstrations against the new conscription laws on March 9–11. The vast majority (89%) of the seventy-six persons arrested during the riots were workers, most of whom (71%) were artisans. The following year, in May 1869, workers once again took to the streets, to protest the electoral defeat of radical republican candidate Armand Duportal. Although he won Toulouse by a landslide, Duportal lost the election in the surrounding rural countryside. The announcement of election results in Toulouse touched off three days of rioting, marked by several confrontations between demonstrators and police. As was the case in the riots of the previous year, the majority of the 181 persons arrested (84%) were workers, most of whom (66%) were artisans.[69]

Toulouse's workers also demanded a greater voice in Republican party affairs and greater working-class representation in positions of party leadership. During the final years of the Second Empire, they denounced the party's failure to nominate workers as candidates and threatened to run independent working-class candidates. On April 1, 1870, over six hundred workers gathered at the *Grand Orient* dance hall in the faubourg of Saint-Cyprien.[70] The organizers of the meeting were a hatmaker, a joiner who was elected president of the gathering, and a currier, who had made arrangements for renting the meeting hall. Bourgeois leaders of the Republican party were not invited, and only those with written invitations were allowed into the hall. The assembled workers discussed the upcoming city council elections and resolved to support working-class candidates. They decided to withhold support from bourgeois candidates, regardless of their affirmations of republican principles, until after interviewing them. A twenty-member committee was elected and charged with seeking out suitable working-class candidates who would accept the political program approved by the assembly. This program included abolition of the death penalty, of taxes, of courts, and of the police, replacement of the army by a citizens' militia, the abolition of religious education, and the reduction of high-level government administrative salaries. The assembly also decided that the candidates selected by the committee would be presented to bourgeois republican leaders, and if these men refused to accept them, the workers would go their own separate way. These dissident republican workers negotiated a settlement with bourgeois party leaders and did not run an independent workers' slate in the 1870 municipal election. Their integration into the local party, under conditions of a greater say in party affairs, reflected both the political strength of the city's workers and the willingness of radical bourgeois leaders to cooperate with working-class socialists.

The small local branch of the First International, which had been established in 1866, attracted a number of men who later became prominent leaders of the revolutionary commune of 1871, including Jules Sarrans, Leopold Cros, Jules Ader, Jean Jacob, and Charles Pey.[71] But the International did not attract widespread support among the city's politically active workers, the majority of whom continued to pursue their goals within the Republican party. The Carol commission investigating Toulouse's revolutionary commune of 1871 reported: "All of the city's industrialists agreed that although the International was hardly known by name, it would receive support if it presented itself. . . ." "Although most of this city appears not yet affected by the International," concluded the commission, "its doctrines are almost everywhere among the city's working class employed in industry. . . ."[72]

The accommodation of working-class leaders was made possible by the defeat of liberals by radical bourgeois leaders in the struggle for control over Toulouse's Republican party. Prior to the legislative election of 1869, liberal and radical party leaders split over whether to maintain the party's electoral alliance with liberal Orleanists. Radical Republicans, led by Armand Duportal and Jean Passerieu, both of whom maintained close ties with socialist workers, urged an end to the alliance, labeling it "a dupery which benefits the royalists."[73] Violent street demonstrations by republican workers in 1868, in opposition to the new conscription laws, exacerbated existing doubts among Orleanist party leaders about the wisdom of an electoral alliance with a party that maintained close ties to militant socialist workers. One government official, the subprefect at Muret, de Rhoellerie, noted this concern as early as 1866: "Although the Republicans desire the ruin of the Imperial regime, the Orleanists and Legitimists only desire more liberty . . . and they tremble at the idea of overthrowing Napoleon, who may not embody their ideal but nonetheless protects their property. . . ."[74]

Republicans were also divided over the issue of candidate selection. Radical leaders of the party, led by the editors of *Émancipation*, held several meetings prior to the May 1869 election which were attended largely by socialist workers. Those attending these gatherings rejected the liberal candidates of the republican-orleanist alliance, Bernard Mulé, Edmond Caze, and Louis Picard. Liberal republican leaders, in turn, opposed Duportal's candidacy, fearing that his selection would endanger their alliance with the Orleanists. The liberals' failure to nominate Picard in place of Duportal signaled the defeat of the liberal wing and marked the end of the local republican alliance with liberal Orleanists.[75]

The factional strife that preceded the election of May 1869 intensified after Republicans gained control of the city council in the October 1869 municipal election. By the summer of 1870, a fierce confrontation erupted between leaders of rival wings of the party. A heated exchange of polemics in *Émancipation* eventually led to a duel between liberal party leader Bernard Mulé and radical leader Leon Castelbou. Although no one was killed or wounded in the duel, the factional bitterness that produced it continued to divide liberal and radical Republicans.

Liberal republican leaders, whom authorities referred to as "the Girondins of the party," threatened to found another newspaper that would compete with *Émancipation* if they failed to remove Duportal and gain a greater say in party affairs. In July 1869, they persuaded the newspaper's shareholders to set up a special committee to curb the militant revolutionary socialist rhetoric of *Émancipation*. The high cost of judicial repression probably helped to convince some of the newspaper's owners that a more moderate tone was necessary. In 1869 alone, the newspaper faced sixteen different court cases and was fined 26,102 francs. The new committee was charged with approving the content of the newspaper and revising articles judged to be too extremist. Radical leaders and socialist militants resisted such measures as unwarranted censorship and were eventually successful in eliminating the committee and gaining control of the newspaper. After losing the battle for control of the party newspaper, the liberal wing, led by Adolphe-Félix Gatien-Arnoult, Jean Gasc, and Théophile Huc, founded their own weekly publication, *Association républicain*. By the end of the Second Empire, radicals and socialists had gained control of *Émancipation*, the offices of which continued to serve as headquarters for electoral activities, put an end to the electoral alliance with liberal Orleanists, and won the battle over candidate selection.

Despite intense factional disputes, republican candidates carried the city in the national election of May 1869, winning 50 percent of the vote, compared to 27 percent for Napoleonic candidates and 23 percent for the orleanist and legitimist candidates. They lost the three contested seats, however, as rural votes once again annulled their urban victory. Conservative rural votes could not, however, keep Republicans from winning municipal elections. In the city council election of October 1869, Republicans triumphed, capturing eight thousand of the ten thousand votes cast.[76] Conservatives responded to the republican victory by re-creating a conservative alliance of Bonapartists, Orleanists, and Legitimists, in support of a regime dedicated to public order and the protection of private property. The board of directors of five of the city's six newspapers, *Le Progrès libéral* (orleanist), *l'Echo de la province* (legitimist), *Le Messager de Toulouse* (Bonapartist), *La Gazette de Languedoc* (legitimist), and *Le Journal de Toulouse* (independent), met to form an electoral committee that would choose a conservative slate for the next elections. This attempt to re-create a "party of order" floundered when orleanist newspaper editors refused to collaborate unless Bonapartists were excluded from the committee. The conservative alliance failed to mount an effective challenge in the municipal election of August 1870, in which Republicans again scored an impressive victory. Led by radicals and socialists, Toulouse's Republican party had already captured municipal power by September 1870, when the Empire was suddenly toppled by military defeats in the Franco-Prussian war.

During the Second Empire, the balance of power within Toulouse's Republican party shifted. In contrast to 1849–51, when radicals joined forces with liberals to confront the socialist workers of *Civilisation*, by the end of the Second Empire, liberals had lost their dominant position within republican circles to an alliance of radicals and socialists. Although the repression of the 1850s initially strengthened the role of liberal leaders and led to an electoral alliance with Orleanists in 1863, radical and socialist Republicans captured control of both the local newspaper and the process of candidate selection by 1870. This meant an end to the alliance with royalists, an electoral strategy emphasizing socialist rhetoric and working-class interests, and a willingness by radical party leaders to support nonelectoral forms of political action. Although the repression of the 1850s strengthened a strong tradition of autonomous working-class political activity, the willingness of radical leaders to accommodate working-class demands and acknowledge working-class socialist leaders meant heightened influence for workers within the Republican party, evident in the candidate selection process of 1869. In municipal elections, republican electoral strength grew steadily, enabling Republicans to win municipal elections by a wide margin by 1869, despite a continuing inability to garner an electoral majority in the surrounding countryside.

REPUBLICAN POLITICS AND CLASS RELATIONS IN TOULOUSE

Class struggles generated by early capitalist industrialization were key events influencing the development of republican politics in Toulouse, but strikes had different political consequences at different points in time, due to the shifting balance of power within the Republican party. Growing divisions between employers and workers in handicraft industries during the late 1830s and early 1840s, reflected in the tailors' and shoemakers' strikes of 1841, emerged after liberal republican leaders had committed the party to a successful electoral alliance with royalists. Because of the effort by liberal republican leaders to retain the electoral support of small employers during the strikes of 1841, these class conflicts fostered the development of autonomous, working-class political activity among artisans, which took the form of a vigorous Icarian communist movement. It was not until the end of the July Monarchy, after the rise and decline of the Icarian movement, that the Republican party altered its strategy of contention for power, abandoning the alliance with Legitimists and adopting a nonelectoral strategy based on popular mobilization in a banquet campaign for universal male suffrage. Like the strikes of 1841, the bakers' strike of 1848 also fostered working-class suspicions of bourgeois republican leadership. The strike, which was crushed by liberal Republican Joly, encouraged working-class political independence and continuing wariness of bourgeois political leadership. The strike wave of the late 1860s, made possible by the liberalizing reforms of the government, had very different political consequences. It provided Republicans with opportunities rather than obstacles for working-class mobilization, because the Republican party was no longer controlled by liberal leaders. These strikes enabled radical and socialist Republicans to place the social question at the center of the local political agenda and to mobilize the support of large numbers of artisanal workers, thereby strengthening the socialist wing of the party. The labor unrest of the late 1860s also helped to strengthen the role of workers within the Republican party, as radical leaders sought to politicize the class antagonisms expressed in the strikes of 1868 and 1869.

The contours of the struggle among liberal, radical, and socialist Republicans were shaped by the distinctive class structure of Toulouse. As an administrative, legal, and educational center for the region, the city contained a relatively large number of professionals, many of whom supported the radical demand for universal male suffrage. Toulouse was also an important center of handicraft production, with a large population of artisans, many of whom were drawn to republican socialism as a solution to the changes that were disrupting their industries and their lives. The persistence of a wealthy urban aristocracy meant a relatively strong Legitimist party, which provided liberal Republicans with an ally in their electoral battles against the orleanist regime.

The distinctive pattern of early industrialization in Toulouse, and the divisions it created within the city's working class, left its mark on republican politics. Artisans in handicraft industries, the workers most affected by the incursion of new forms of capitalist production, provided the bulk of working-class republican militants throughout the middle decades of the century. During the July Monarchy, Toulouse's handicraft artisans, though excluded from electoral politics, repeatedly took to the streets to express their republican political aspirations, launched a socialist newspaper, and created a republican socialist movement that played a key role in the campaign for suffrage reform. Republicans succeeded in mobilizing large numbers of skilled male workers employed in industry, and in rallying the electoral support of unskilled male laborers within the industrial and transport sector of the local economy. But proletarians did not play an important role in working-class republican politics and republican political mobilizations bypassed the city's female labor force. The political dominance of male handicraft artisans meant a working-class contingent within the Republican party with a long tradition of political autonomy, strong capacities for collective action, and an unwillingness to automatically accept bourgeois political leadership. This, in turn, meant a strong socialist wing within the party, which forged an alliance with bourgeois radicals that was capable of seizing control of the newspaper and candidate selection process and winning local elections.

The trajectory of republican politics in Toulouse was also the product of a dramatic shift in the national political opportunity structure. The revolution of 1848 and its violent confrontational aftermath made liberal and radical bourgeois Republicans suspicious of socialist workers who too readily took their politics to the streets at the same time that it fostered growing hostility toward bourgeois leadership on the part of socialist workers. The dramatic shift in the political opportunity structure that followed the coup d'état of 1851 also had enduring consequences for republican politics. Whereas the repression of the 1830s eliminated the conspiratorial activities of radical and socialist Republicans and strengthened liberal control of the party, the repression of the 1850s strengthened autonomous working-class political activities. When republican electoral politics resurfaced during the 1860s, this helped make possible a stronger voice for socialist workers within republican circles, a prerequisite for the effective challenge launched by an alliance of radicals and socialists to the party's liberal leadership.

CHAPTER FIVE

Saint-Étienne: The Transformation and Triumph of Radical Republicanism

DURING the 1830s, republican leadership in Saint-Étienne came to be dominated by bourgeois radicals who elaborated their vision of the republic in the context of a bitter struggle between local silk weavers and merchants. Radical leaders, like Martin Bernard, urged their fellow militants to translate republicanism into a language comprehensible to ordinary workers.[1] They joined workers on the barricades during the silkweavers' insurrection of 1834 and spent years in jail for their role in the uprising. When these men returned to active political life after the amnesty of 1837, their commitment to resolving the "social question" had not diminished. They provided leadership for numerous efforts by socialist ribbon weavers to establish a city-wide production cooperative, actively supported the coal miners' strike of 1846, and vociferously demanded universal male suffrage. Eugène Baune, a civil engineer, returned from exile in Belgium after the 1837 amnesty and wrote for the radical republican newspaper *La Réforme*, where he denounced the exclusively political focus of its liberal republican rival *Le National*. Blanc-Subé, the doctor for the silk weavers' association, became a vocal champion of the rights of workers, with whom he maintained very close contact. After being released from prison, Louis Marc Caussidière, formerly a silk ribbon designer, became an editor and traveling salesman for *La Réforme*. The lawyer Tristan Duché served as defense attorney for silk weavers arrested for illegal association as well as for striking miners while the merchant César Bertholon devoted his energies to the weavers' effort to form a production cooperative in 1841.

Strong radical republican support for working-class issues and interests was evident several decades later, during the legislative campaign of 1869, but by then the once fuzzy line dividing radical and socialist Republicans had become a clear divide. The radical republican candidate of 1869, Frédéric Dorian, rejected the socialist schemes of his opponent, Antide Martin, in favor of a market economy, but he appealed to workers by championing more equitable taxes, free secular education, an end to economic monopolies, and workers' rights to association and assembly. Dorian, who advocated a "union of capital and labor" rather than class struggle, soundly defeated his socialist rival in the working-class districts of the city. In the miners' strike that shortly followed Dorian's election, radical republican leaders, who controlled the local newspaper *L'Éclaireur*, supported the strikers. After soldiers opened fire on striking miners at Ricamerie, the newspaper's editors vehemently condemned the massacre, raised funds to support the families of the victims, and demanded the immediate removal of all troops from the city.

As the preceding account suggests, radical republicanism established strong roots in Saint-Étienne at an early date and remained the dominant force in republican politics for decades. But the character of radicalism was transformed during the middle decades of the century from a revolutionary to a reformist vision. This change is evident in the political biography of one of the most prominent radical republican leaders, Martin Bernard.[2] The son of a well-to-do printer, Bernard was heavily influenced by the utopian socialist ideas of St.-Simon, Fourier, and Leroux during the early 1830s. He joined the Parisian Society of the Rights of Man in 1833 and wrote articles for the *Revue républicaine* urging workers to resist the new "industrial feudalism" by embracing republicanism. After he was arrested, tried, and acquitted for his role in a revolutionary conspiracy in 1836, Bernard was convicted to life imprisonment in 1839 for helping to organize, alongside Auguste Blanqui and Armand Barbès, the abortive Parisian insurrection of 1839. Freed from prison by the revolution of 1848, Bernard returned to Paris where he played an active role in the city's club movement. Persuaded by Ledru-Rollin to accept a high-level administrative position in the new government (*commissaire générale*), Bernard returned to the Saint-Étienne region. Though attacked by liberal Republicans as "too radical," he managed to win a seat as a deputy in the Constituent Assembly in April 1848. Bernard remained loyal to the government during the working-class uprising of June 1848 but expressed strong reservations about using troops against the people. An active member of the Mountain in 1849, he was convicted for his role in the June 1849 insurrection and forced into exile until the amnesty of 1859, when he returned to Paris and found employment as a clerk in a gas company. Saint-Étienne's Republicans tried to convince Bernard to run for office during the 1860s, but he refused to take the required oath of loyalty to the Empire. In the struggle over who would represent Saint-Étienne's Republican party in the legislative election of 1869, Bernard supported the wealthy industrial Frédéric Dorian rather than the socialist candidacy of Antide Martin. Bernard's radicalism had taken on a reformist rather than revolutionary tone, as was evident during the revolutionary communes of 1871. Rather than back the insurrection, the former revolutionary urged conciliation between Paris and Versailles. Martin Bernard's life history reflects larger changes in French radical republicanism as well as in the evolution of Saint-Étienne's republicanism, which is documented below.

THE JULY MONARCHY IN SAINT-ÉTIENNE: 1830–1848

Announcement of the news of the downfall of the Bourbon dynasty during the summer of 1830 prompted public rejoicing in Saint-Étienne. Amid the acclamation of a large crowd, demonstrators hung the tricolor flag on the balcony of city hall, destroyed symbols of the fallen monarchy, and celebrated with public bonfires. Despite widespread unemployment among the city's silk weavers, the first few years of the new regime witnessed relatively few protests. The only major protest of the early years of the new regime took place on March 3, 1831, when a crowd of around two thousand men, women, and children attacked and destroyed a new steam-powered machine at the Girardel arms manufactory. National Guard units were called up to disperse the rioters, several of whom were arrested. One guardsman was killed during the confrontation. Republicans did not play an active role in this working-class protest nor did they make any effort to politicize the conflict. Among the National Guard officers commanding the troops who confronted the angry arms workers was the future radical republican leader, Louis Marc Caussidière.[3] With the exception of this event, Saint-Étienne's workers remained quiet during the turbulent years of 1830–32. Despite a large concentration of silk weavers in Saint-Étienne, the insurrection of Lyon's silk weavers in November 1831 found no echo in the city.

Government reports of 1831 dismiss the republican movement in Saint-Étienne as insignificant.[4] In July 1832, the prefect reassured his superior in Paris that "there are no known political associations in Saint-Étienne . . . our workers are not at all interested in politics."[5] There was a small local branch of the liberal republican electoral association *Aide-toi, le ciel t'aidera*, founded by the ribbon merchant Auguste Taber, but this organization had few members.[6] Republicans had little success in the electoral arena. Only 3.9 percent of the city's population was eligible to vote in municipal elections in 1831, but this electorate included a large number of small property holders.[7] In 1834, Orleanists held thirty-one of thirty-six city council seats, with only two Republicans and three Legitimists constituting the opposition. Republicans did make substantial electoral inroads in the suburban communes adjacent to Saint-Étienne, where a majority of council members (thirty-five out of the sixty-nine) belonged to what authorities referred to as the "moderate democratic" opposition.[8]

Radical Republicans made great efforts to rally the support of local silk weavers. Louis Marc Caussidière wrote a pamphlet entitled "The New Republican Catechism" in 1833, which became very popular among the region's silk weavers. The author contended that the exploitation of workers could only be remedied by political changes in taxation, voting, education, and inheritance rights. These initial efforts to politicize the weavers' confrontation with merchants were not very successful. The weavers' association explicitly prohibited any discussion of politics at their meetings under penalty of expulsion. Police reports of July 1833 dismiss local Republicans as "officers without any troops."[9] The subprefect in Saint-Étienne assured his superiors, in a letter dated August 10, 1833, of the "nonpolitical" character of the movement: "What do the workers want? Nothing political, I am sure, at least here. . . . What they want is a larger share of the merchants' profits."[10] In September 1833, a proposal for the weavers' association to affiliate with the local branch of the radical republican Society of the Rights of Man was rejected by the vast majority of the members of the weavers' association, but police reported that three hundred workers favored such an affiliation.[11]

Despite limited initial success, radical and socialist Republicans persisted in their efforts to politicize class antagonisms in the silk ribbon industry. In November 1833, after the weavers' association forced a master weaver to return an order that he had taken from a boycotted merchant, the subprefect issued a declaration offering support to anyone who wished to work for the boycotted merchant. Radical republican leader Caussidière responded with an attack on the subprefect's offer, in a pamphlet that was widely circulated among the city's weavers. Some government officials worried that government repression would drive the silk weavers into the camp of republicanism and warned against enforcing the law banning workers' associations for this very reason.[12] Government intervention in this economic conflict, warned the *gendarme* captain Dumas in August 1833, "will not be interpreted in terms of our desire to maintain public order but rather will identify us with the interests of the merchants, especially in a situation in which the working class is not very well educated and is thus disposed to see everywhere collusion between the government and the rich. . . ."[13]

Radical republican activists continued their efforts to politicize the silk weavers' struggle, winning over increasing numbers of supporters. By February 1834, there were fifty sections of the local branch of the Society of the Rights of Man, which was in close contact with the Lyon branch.[14] On February 19, 1834 approximately fifteen hundred ribbon weavers marched through the streets of the city in a funeral procession. When they arrived at the cemetery, Caussidière delivered a scathing attack on the government. The following day, members of the Society of the Rights of Man paraded through the center city singing republican anthems. On February 21, a large crowd gathered in front of city hall, amid shouts of "Long Live the Republic!" A brawl ensued when police tried to arrest some demonstrators, and a policeman was stabbed to death in the confrontation. Twenty people, including Caussidière, were arrested when police cleared the square. Radical

Republicans were more successful in mobilizing the support of ribbon weaving workers than of master ribbon weavers. In March 1834, local police reported a number of brawls, at various cafés, between journeymen weavers, "most of whom belong to the Society of the Rights of Man," and master weavers, who did not share their workers' republican political sentiments.[15]

The confrontation between weavers and merchants culminated in a violent insurrection on April 11–13, 1834. The uprising was inspired by economic not political grievances, but Republicans played an active role. The crowds that gathered in front of city hall during the insurrection chanted republican anthems, amid shouts of "Long Live the Republic!" Among the 135 workers arrested during the insurrection were 71 workers from various occupations whose republican convictions drew them into what was initially an economic conflict.[16] Although master weavers did not join in the street fighting, they expressed their sympathy for the insurgents by refusing to respond to the call-up of the National Guard, which was disarmed following the insurrection. The repression of the 1834 insurrection confirmed the expectations of some government officials, driving both master and journeymen ribbon weavers into the ranks of the republican opposition. When the weavers resumed their struggle against merchants for a uniform piece rate in 1840–41, the republican character of their movement was unmistakable.

A number of bourgeois republican leaders in Saint-Étienne, including Louis-Marc Caussidière (commercial broker and former ribbon designer); Eugène Baune (civil engineer); and Antide Martin (notary), were arrested and convicted for their role in the silk weavers' uprising. After years of imprisonment or exile, they returned to active political life after the amnesty of 1837. In sharp contrast to liberal party leaders in Toulouse, they did not abandon the "social question" in favor of an exclusive focus on political issues, nor did they direct their attention to the propertied electorate in an effort to win local elections. The city's most prominent republican leaders denounced class inequalities and spoke to the grievances of disenfranchised workers.

Newspapers provided the organizational nexus of republicanism and the character of the city's republican newspapers reveals the dominance of radical republicanism. In December 1836, Saint-Étienne's Republicans launched *L'Observateur de la Loire*, edited by professor Aimé Baune, younger brother of Eugène Baune. The newspaper espoused the cause of the workers and accused the government of "pursuing policies designed to keep the proletariat in their deteriorating condition." The government destroyed *L'Observateur* after only four months of publication by prosecuting and convicting the editor for press crimes.[17] In 1839, Republicans created another newspaper, the *Journal de Saint-Étienne*, founded by the printer Gonin and supported by radical leaders Tristan Duché and Alexandre Blancsubé. This newspaper, which espoused a position sympathetic to the ideas of Fourier and emphasized suffrage reform, soon gained six hundred subscribers.

The nationwide petition campaign for suffrage reform in 1840 provided Republicans with an opportunity to mobilize working-class support. The vice-president of the suffrage reform campaign was the silk weaver Laurent, and the campaign won widespread support from the city's silk weavers. Police reports of 1840 cite two silk weavers, Bayon and Jean Teyssier, as leaders of the local movement and the ribbon weavers' café (*café des passementiers*) as a center of republican activities.[18] In other cities, the campaign for suffrage reform generated divisions between republican and utopian communist workers.[19] In Saint-Étienne, where the utopian communist movement was very weak, Republicans dominated the suffrage reform drive, and the statutes of the reform committee refused admittance to members of secret societies, a provision directed against communist workers.[20]

Republicans in Saint-Étienne mobilized working-class support with little competition from the Icarian communist movement. The strong republican commitments of local workers, dating back to the insurrection of 1834, and their lack of sympathy with utopian socialist ideas, is evident in comments made by the utopian socialist feminist Flora Tristan during her eight-day visit to Saint-Étienne in June 1844. Tristan received a cool welcome. Unable to find ten workers willing to form a local committee to distribute propaganda, she attributed her failure to the influence of bourgeois Republicans who had convinced workers to emphasize political rather than economic issues. Tristan described the local workers she lectured to as familiar with political issues but ignorant of "social questions" and blamed the situation on radical republican leaders Tristan Duché and Alexandre Blancsubé. "Yesterday I spoke at a meeting of workers of all sorts," she wrote, "but none of them understood. It is evident that they are not used to social questions. A little political criticism, universal suffrage, they don't go beyond this. . . ."[21]

In contrast to their counterparts in Toulouse, Saint-Étienne's bourgeois republican leadership maintained close ties to the city's working class throughout the 1830s and 1840s. They embraced a radical rather than liberal vision of republicanism, staunchly advocated universal male suffrage, and supported local workers in their struggles with employers. In 1841, when Saint-Étienne's silk weavers renewed their attempt to impose a uniform piece rate on local merchants by creating a commercial cooperative, republican activists played a leading role. The plan was to create a commercial cooperative that would circumvent the ribbon merchants and set standards for the industry by purchasing raw materials and distributing the finished products of the weavers. The leader of this project was Laurent, who was also vice-president of the republican electoral reform association. The authorities refused a request to authorize the organization in August 1841, and maintained police surveillance. The Minister of the Interior pointed out, in a letter of March 5, 1841, that "such a project would place a considerable portion of the working class under the direction of [opposition] political leaders." The prefect noted in his correspondence on the matter that the inspiration for the association came from "the most ardent Republicans in the city" and voiced suspicions that the cooperative was really a secret republican conspiracy.[22] These fears were confirmed on May 17, 1841, when police in Paris intercepted a letter from Laurent, the president of the weavers' cooperative, to the republican deputy François Arago requesting financial support for the cooperative. "It is the duty and interest of political men," wrote Laurent, "to take control of this association. . . . My commercial project includes all of the improvements proposed by the reform movement: equality of work, equality of benefits, equality of science, equality of the elections. . . . All occupations thus organized would constitute a powerful force and when the proposal for electoral reform reaches the Chamber it would have to be accepted; otherwise, the struggle would be general."[23] Extraparliamentary activities like the cooperative, argued Laurent, when led by a well-organized workers' movement, would put sufficient pressure on legislators to bring about a change in suffrage laws. The authorities prosecuted leaders of the cooperative in a trial that took place in January 1842. The court banned the association, ordered all copies of its statutes destroyed, convicted Laurent to two months in prison and a fifty-franc fine, and convicted three others to fines while acquitting fourteen defendants. The defense lawyer for the weavers was the radical republican leader Tristan Duché.

During the 1840s, radical Republicans expanded their working-class support beyond the ranks of the city's silk weavers to encompass household arms and hardware workers and a growing number of proletarianized coal miners. They did so by attacking what they denounced as the monopoly power of the region's largest coal company and by supporting coal miners' strikes. After a series of mergers during the late 1830s and early 1840s, one coal company, the *Compagnie générale de la Loire*, managed to secure ownership of two-thirds of the mines in the region and control over five-sixths of coal production. The company antagonized Saint-Étienne's population by raising local coal prices to a level equal to that of exported coal, thus violating local custom and eliminating the previously favored treatment of local consumers. This policy angered the city's household arms and hardware producers, who depended on cheap coal to fuel the forges in their workshops. The company also alienated local industrialists by refusing to sign long-term contractual agreements of more than one year.[24] Since most of the coal company's stocks were owned by Parisian and Lyonnais banks, the struggle against the coal company became a broad-based popular struggle against Parisian finance capital. "The latest evidence," wrote the mayor of Saint-Étienne in May 1847, "reveals that the [coal] monopoly is a vast conspiracy by financiers against the industry of our region."[25]

In focusing on the issue of the coal company, Republicans were able to raise the social question, by denouncing the consequences of monopoly control for the living and working conditions of the growing number of miners. "The directors of the company," declared the city council of the Saint-Étienne suburb of Outrefurens, "promise dividends to shareholders that are obtained by crushing the workers and further oppressing all other industries . . . but beware, the workers will not remain inactive. We fear that their response may be brutal."[26] Similar expressions of hostility to the coal company were penned by Saint-Étienne's city council, which hired national republican leader Jules Favre to lobby government officials in Paris to break up the company. Although opposition to the coal monopoly cut across both class and party lines, Republicans were in the forefront of the agitation and raised the issue of the company's labor policies, as well as the issue of artificially high coal prices, to rally popular support. Republican city councilmen played a central role in drafting the city council report of February 1846 that denounced the coal monopoly. The report, which was sent to the Chamber of Deputies in Paris, criticized the company for "the elimination of small distributors of coal, the reduction of fees paid to local landowners, and especially the oppression of 6,000 workers subjected in an absolute manner to the caprices of their employers to work more at less pay." The report also condemned the skyrocketing price of coal and the "extortion of consumers" by the company, and concluded with a recommendation that the central government break up the monopoly.[27]

Radical, socialist, and liberal Republicans attempted to politicize the class struggles of the region's miners during the 1840s. During the miners' strike at Rive-de-Gier in 1844, which did not spread to Saint-Étienne, republican activists in Lyon collected strike support funds and circulated a number of socialist brochures, including Jules Leroux's "The Bourgeois and the Proletariat," among the workers. Both national republican newspapers in Paris, the radical La Réforme and liberal Le National, raised funds for the striking miners. Saint-Étienne's radical republican leaders, Tristan Duché and Pierre-Antoine Sain, served as defense lawyers for miners who were arrested during the strike.[28] During the strike, miners gathered in front of the homes of local notables and chanted republican anthems, the Marseillaise and Ca Ira.[29]

Republicans again made a concerted effort to win the support of the region's miners during the Saint-Étienne strike of March 1846, which took place in the context of a heated political controversy over the coal monopoly. This four-week strike culminated in a violent confrontation between miners and troops at Outrefurens that left five workers dead and seven workers seriously injured. Reports of central government officials point to "agents of communism" as inciting the miners.[30] In the Chamber of Deputies, radical republican leader Ledru-Rollin denounced the massacre and attacked the coal company.[31] The Saint-Étienne city council blamed the violence on the coal monopoly, which was responsible for "bloody clashes that bring grief and disturbances into a region formerly very peaceful under the legal system of free competition."[32] Although the local liberal newspaper, *Le Mercure ségusien*, remained silent about the massacre, out of fear of arousing working-class disorders and further violence, the Parisian radical republican newspaper *La Réforme* condemned the company and the government. The city's radical republican leader, Tristan Duché, served as defense lawyer for the twenty-two miners who were arrested and tried for their role in the strike. Government officials noted in their reports that opposition municipal leaders supported the miners' demands, and that in the city's cabarets, bourgeois political activists were buying drinks for the striking miners.[33] In the municipal elections that followed the strike, on July 6–24, 1846, opponents of the coal company were victorious. The mayor Jean-Joseph Tezenas, who failed to take a strong stand against the company, was defeated in his reelection campaign. Republicans on the city council joined forces with liberal opponents of the orleanist regime in attacking the coal monopoly and chastising the mayor for promoting public works projects that didn't benefit the entire population.

Newspapers constituted the centers of nascent party organization, yet Republicans in Saint-Étienne remained without a newspaper during the final years of the July Monarchy. Republicans had expressed their views in the liberal *Journal de Saint-Étienne*, but they abandoned this newspaper after it denounced the miners' strike of 1846 as "a barbaric travesty of association," and criticized the English Chartist movement for suffrage reform. During the confrontation over the coal company, the *Journal de Saint-Étienne* expressed sympathy for the company. By 1846, after changing titles to become the *Courrier* and then the *Union*, the newspaper abandoned the liberal principles it once espoused and became increasingly conservative. Republican party leaders Duché and Tardy switched allegiances to *Le Mercure ségusien*, which was a staunch opponent of the coal company but remained in the camp of the dynastic liberal opposition. Liberals of the left dynastic opposition supported a constitutional monarchy rather than a republic, but they shared with Republicans a desire to expand the suffrage to include more small property holders; eliminate restrictions on rights of association, assembly, and the press; and limit the powers of the executive vis-à-vis the legislature. Although the focus of local political attention on the issue of the coal monopoly temporarily allowed radicals and liberals to unite in opposition to a common enemy, the issue of suffrage reform soon forced radical republican leaders to part company with liberal Republicans and the left dynastic opposition.

The electoral campaign of 1846 provided the occasion for the city's radical republican leaders to clarify their differences with liberals, who supported lower property restrictions on voting rights but opposed universal male suffrage. In the election of August 1, 1846, for a seat in the Chamber of Deputies, radical republican leaders refused to support either the liberal dynastic candidate Hippolyte Royet, a wealthy silk ribbon merchant, or his orleanist opponent Joseph-Constant Lanyer. Rejecting liberal republican efforts to join forces with other liberal opponents of the regime, radicals contended that "neither one of the two candidates represents our opinions," and ran their own candidate, Camille Jacquemont. In a brochure written during the campaign but published afterward due to legal obstacles, Jacquemont and his supporters criticized Royet's silence on the issue of universal male suffrage. They argued that liberal opposition to clerical domination of education and the coal monopoly were insufficient grounds for their support. After chastising the city's two newspapers for failing to represent their viewpoints during the electoral campaign, Jacquemont asserted three guiding principles—"liberty of industry, liberty of conscience, and fair participation of all in political rights." Using language that referred to the issue that continued to dominate local politics, the coal monopoly, Jacquemont reproached the liberal candidate, Royer, for his failure to address the issue of suffrage reform: "M. Royet has not said a word about this immense question: it is therefore impossible for us to agree, because we have and will remain adversaries of the THREE MONOPOLIES of education, suffrage rights, and industry."[34]

The effort of radical republican leaders to place the issue of universal male suffrage on the local political agenda and to challenge the liberal dynastic opposition met with little success in the restricted electoral arena. Jacquemont's campaign received no attention in either *Le Mercure ségusien* or the *Journal de Saint-Étienne*. He garnered only 38 votes among the city's propertied electorate, compared to 184 votes for Hippolyte Royet and 325 votes for the victorious incumbent orleanist deputy Joseph-Constant Lanyer.[35]

The final months of the July Monarchy were marked by a struggle between the city council and central state officials over the issue of the coal monopoly.[36] In November 1847, after the subprefect ordered the council to cease all further discussion of the issue, the rebellious councilmen responded by prohibiting the discussion of any other issue. The prefect then issued an ordinance dissolving the city council commission charged with investigating the issue of the coal monopoly and annulling the council's recent decision to allocate ten thousand francs to this commission. The council continued to ignore the prefect's order, placing the issue of the coal monopoly at the top of its agenda in subsequent meetings, and listening to reports from the seven-member coal commission, which was headed by the radical republican leader Tristan Duché. At its meeting on February 7, 1848, after listening to a documentation of coal company abuses from Duché, the council voted once again to ask the government to either break up the coal monopoly, or, if it doubted the case against the company, to set up an independent government commission to investigate the issue. Continuing political debate over the coal monopoly was suddenly and unexpectedly interrupted by news from Paris of the revolution that abruptly ended the July Monarchy.

Republican party formation during the July Monarchy was characterized by the early mobilization of household workers, the dominance of radical leaders, strong ties between radical and socialist Republicans, a relatively marginal role for liberal Republicans, and little success in the electoral arena. The insurrection of 1834 enabled Republicans to establish a strong base of support among household silk weavers, the largest group of workers in the city. The subsequent focus of local politics on the issue of the coal monopoly enabled Republicans to expand their working-class support by appealing to household arms and hardware workers who were adversely affected by the coal monopoly and to proletarianized coal miners. The continuing dominance of radical leaders meant strong support for the cooperative socialist ventures of the city's silk weavers and a continuing emphasis on the social question. Close ties between radical leaders and disenfranchised working-class supporters were solidified by the active support of radical leaders in local economic conflicts. These ties meant a feeble Icarian communist movement as well as a relatively weak republican electoral presence. Although silk weavers made repeated efforts to form citywide cooperative associations during the 1830s and 1840s, in contrast to the handicraft artisans of Toulouse, they did not create independent working-class political organizations or launch a socialist newspaper owned and operated by workers. Since workers were denied the vote and had limited economic resources, their support for republicanism did not translate into electoral victories or strong electoral organizations. Saint-Étienne's Republicans remained without a newspaper throughout the 1840s. During the final years of the regime, liberal Republicans joined the dynastic opposition in support of Royet's campaign in 1846 and raised toasts for limited suffrage reform alongside liberal royalists in the banquet campaign of 1847. Despite their shared hostility toward the coal company, radical and socialist Republicans refused to join the liberal alliance and abandon the quest for universal male suffrage. They boycotted the liberal banquet campaign and did not support the candidate of the liberal alliance. The issue of universal male suffrage, a central component of radical and socialist efforts to rally working-class support during the 1840s, divided Republicans. The advent of universal male suffrage in 1848 exacerbated these divisions.

THE SECOND REPUBLIC IN SAINT-ÉTIENNE

The establishment of the Second Republic in Saint-Étienne brought to power a municipal government that included leaders of the diverse groups that had joined the opposition to the orleanist regime, including liberal and radical members of the bourgeoisie as well as working-class republican socialists. When news of the overthrow of the regime reached Saint-Étienne on February 26, 1848, a large crowd gathered in front of city hall. They burned in effigy a mannequin representing the coal company, and hung a large red flag on the front of the building.[37] Inside city hall, nervous members of the city council, elected under the previous regime, deliberated. They appointed radical republican leader Tristan Duché, the lawyer who defended striking miners in 1846, and Dr. Joseph Soviche, a liberal republican adversary of the coal company, as provisional subprefects. The council also appointed Hippolyte Royet, former leader of the dynastic liberal opposition, to head the new provisional local commission that replaced the municipal government. This commission was initially composed of seven prominent bourgeois leaders of the struggle against the coal company. In response to working-class pressures, it was expanded to ten persons by the addition of a mechanic, a weaver, and a mine supervisor. The commission issued a proclamation urging citizens to respect property and persons. It also ordered the replacement of the red flag that demonstrators had placed on city hall by the tricolor flag. The new municipal government quickly implemented a number of policies aimed at satisfying its working-class supporters, including creation of municipal workshops for the unemployed and appointment of a commission to study the grievances of Saint-Étienne's workers.

The February revolution prompted the rapid political mobilization of Saint-Étienne's working class. At the beginning of March, the *Société populaire*, an association composed largely of workers, mainly silk weavers, attracted over eight thousand members. The organization's central committee was led by republican socialist Pierre Chapuis, a former ribbon weaver who had become a cabaret owner. Other leaders included the socialist silk weavers Laurent Laroure, Moulinier, and Parane, as well as the doctor Martial, the notary Pierre Antide Martin, the rentier Pierre Tiblier, and the doctor for the ribbon weavers' association, Alexandre Blancsubé. The organization was divided into 280 groups of around thirty persons, each of which elected their presidents, who constituted the governing board of the association.[38] The leaders of the *Société populaire* cooperated closely with republican municipal authorities. The republican ceremony of April 9 to plant a liberty tree was largely organized by the *Société* in close collaboration with radical republican officials.

Radical republican leaders who took power after the February revolution envisioned a political order based on fraternalism, in which class antagonisms could be peacefully negotiated to the advantage of workers. On March 16, nearly one thousand people attended a republican banquet, led by Hippolyte Royet and Tristan Duché, at which 830 francs were collected to aid poor and unemployed workers. Duché toasted "the union of all classes of society into one single family," while socialist leader Antide Martin toasted "the realization of Fraternity." Republican visions of fraternity were quickly confronted with popular protests directed against the mining company. On February 27, a crowd composed largely of miners, but including other republican workers, demonstrated in front of city hall. They burned a mannequin representing Dr. Benoît Escoffier, an important shareholder and prominent political advocate of the company, amid shouts of "Down with the Monopoly!" The city council responded by promising that the coal company would be dismantled and competition restored in the coal industry, with the national government intervening to provisionally run the company.[39]

At the beginning of March, miners went on strike for higher wages. Groups of armed miners crossed the city to force those pits that remained open to shut down their operations.[40] Republican officials Tristan Duché and Eugène Baune issued declarations urging the striking miners to return to work immediately and to respect private property. They also warned the miners that any violation of the "liberty of work" would be punished by the government. Duché simultaneously notified company officials that they would be held responsible for any disorders. On March 1, socialist leader Pierre Chapuis, president of the *Société populaire*, issued an appeal to the miners to return to work while the new authorities negotiated a settlement with the company. On March 8, striking miners attacked and pillaged the home of Dr. Escoffier. Coal company officials responded to pressures from radical republican officials and militant workers with various concessions, including a proposal for a profit-sharing scheme and a decision to stockpile coal rather than lay off workers during the economic crisis of early 1848. The company director, Calley-Saint-Paul, declared on March 8 that "we must do everything to ensure that the workers are content."[41] The miners returned to work on March 11, after republican officials pressured the company into granting a twenty-five-centime wage increase. The focus of popular agitation then shifted to the silk weavers.

The February revolution was followed by an economic crisis that brought the city's looms to a halt, creating widespread unemployment among silk ribbon weavers. The new republican authorities responded by creating municipal workshops, organizing charitable efforts, and shutting down the city's convent workshops, which local weavers criticized as a source of unfair competition. On March 1, 1848, the provisional municipal government ordered door locks placed on the convent workshops to prevent them from receiving raw materials or delivering finished products. This action antagonized silk merchants as well as liberal Republicans, who condemned the measure as a violation of the liberty of work. On March 15, republican leader Eugène Baune, who had been appointed special commissioner by the central government, responded to these complaints by ordering the locks removed. On March 23, a large crowd of men, women, and children paraded a black flag through the streets of the city, demanding that the government close down the convent workshops. The demonstrators gathered in front of local religious establishments, shouted threats, and dismantled a building that was under construction. Troops surrounded the demonstrators when they passed in front of city hall, where twenty people were arrested before the crowd dispersed. The city council responded to the protest with an ordinance prohibiting public demonstrations, public singing in groups, and shouts that disrupted public order. This did not put an end to the agitation.

On April 12, 1848, rumors spread throughout the city that shipments of silk thread had been delivered to the convents, which were preparing to resume their operations. On April 13, a crowd of about fifteen women, gathered on the place Roannelle to protest the convent workshops, was soon joined by a large number of demonstrators. They proceeded to attack and pillage the *la Reine* convent workshop. The crowd then marched to the *Refuge* convent workshop, where they were met by a battalion of National Guardsmen who retreated in the face of stones thrown by angry demonstrators. Amid chants of the *Marseillaise*, the convent workshop was pillaged. Its looms, furniture, doors, and windows were destroyed in large bonfires. The crowd of weavers, joined by workers and club members from other occupations, then moved on to the *La Providence* convent where looms were removed and set on fire. That evening a crowd of men, women, and children attacked the *Saint-Famille* convent workshop. The National Guard opened fire, killing four women and a child. The next morning, another crowd attacked the *Dames de l'Instruction* convent workshop. At noon they moved on to the *la Visitation* convent, where republican leaders Tristan Duché and Antide Martin intervened. They persuaded the demonstrators not to destroy the looms, and promised that those arrested in the earlier disorders would be released. After the crowd followed Duché to city hall, the mayor Royet ordered the release of most of those who had been arrested.

During the course of these riots, five people were killed, many more wounded, and 205 people arrested, including weavers, miners, arms makers, hardware producers, day laborers, and construction artisans.[42] The so-cialist newspaper *La Voix du peuple* provided a sympathetic account of the convent riots, but nevertheless had urged workers to return to their looms and put an end to the violence.[43] Although radical leader Tristan Duché and socialist leader Antide Martin, an *adjoint* to the mayor, had intervened to put an end to the convent workshop riots and although a detachment of workers from the *Société populaire* had prevented further violence against the *Sourds-Muettes* convent on the evening of April 14–15, these events prompted bitter division among Republicans.

Liberal Republicans chastised radical officials like Duché for their han-dling of the silk weavers' uprising and claimed that socialist city officials, especially Martin, had openly supported the rioters.[44] The liberal republi-can newspaper, *L'Avenir républicain*, accused Duché of having forbidden National Guardsmen to use their weapons to defend the convents. Duché responded by pointing to the city council, which he claimed had informed him during the riots that they bore sole responsibility for policing the city. Liberal Republicans also condemned the city council for sending one of its members, M. Garnier, to participate in funeral services for those killed during the riots. A delegate from the Parisian Club of Clubs reported on April 17, 1848 that the laudatory funeral speeches made by socialist leaders in honor of those killed in the attack on the convent workshops had aggra-vated the situation, and that a young man who denounced Duché at a club meeting was stabbed.[45] Although radicals like Duché and socialists like Martin urged the rioters not to use violence against the convent workshops, they were hesitant to employ repression against the demonstrators. Radical and socialist leaders condemned the riots in *Le Mercure ségusien*, but they blamed the events on broken promises by authorities who failed to keep the convent's looms under lock and key. "The fear of sacrificing several looms," lamented the editors on April 14, "of simply halting their opera-tion, caused a very great evil. A little illegality would have prevented a much more disastrous violation of the law."

Despite criticisms generated by the way local authorities handled the weavers' riots, radicals and socialists affiliated with the *Société populaire* continued to dominate local politics. When the provisional city council was expanded and reorganized on April 15, after the convent workshop riots, the *Société Populaire* played a large role in determining its composition. Assisting the mayor Royet as *adjoints* were the association's two most prominent leaders, Antide Martin and Pierre Chapuis. Liberal Republicans were angered by the power of this organization, which they accused of fomenting disruptive demonstrations among workers, of initially exclud-ing nonworkers and liberal Republicans, and of seeking to clandestinely control the municipal government and the selection of Constituent Assem-bly candidates.[46] The liberal republican newspaper *L'Avenir républicain* criticized the *Société*'s organizational structure, claiming that it centralized power into the hands of a few leaders and did not allow its sections sufficient autonomy. "This form of organization," complained the editors on March 28, "is more suited to a secret society than to an association of voters under a free government."

Divisions among Republicans intensified during preparations for the Constituent Assembly election scheduled for April 23. On March 28, liberal Republicans formed their own electoral committee, the *Comités réunis*, whose motto was "Order in Liberty, Liberty in Order." They challenged the electoral list of the *Société populaire* with a slate that excluded both socialist candidates like Antide Martin, as well as radical republican leaders like Duché. The committee condemned the recent working-class agitation and appealed to "friends of order and liberty," proclaiming that its candidates were dedicated to the republic but "don't separate this cause from the great principles of individual liberty, the family, and property." Although dominated by liberal bourgeois Republicans, the committee appealed for working-class support, selecting a jewelry maker as its president, and the weaver Moulin as one of its vice-presidents.[47] The alternative republican list presented by the *Société populaire* included five of the same prominent republican candidates as well as a number of leaders identified with the party's socialist wing.

"Order," a codeword used to condemn the recent working-class disturbances, became a key issue in the Constituent Assembly election campaign, as socialists and radicals engaged liberal Republicans in a newspaper war of polemics. *L'Avenir républicain*, which organized the campaign for candidates of the *Comités réunis*, suggested that several of their opponents' candidates, including Tristan Duché, who had collaborated with Icarians during the final days of the July Monarchy, were communists. *Le Mercure Ségusien*, which supported the *Société populaire* list, accused its opponents of being Legitimists, noting that the editor of *L'Avenir républicain*, Auguste Callet, had collaborated with legitimist opponents of the July Monarchy during the 1830s.[48] While *L'Avenir* tried to pin the blame for the recent convent workshop riots on the socialist schemes of their opponents, *Le Mercure* responded that liberal Republicans' repeated condemnations of communism had generated hostility to the religious communities, which were organized along communist principles.

The results of the Constituent Assembly election revealed the strength of radical and socialist Republicans in Saint-Étienne but their weakness in the surrounding rural areas of the region. All five candidates who appeared on both lists were elected, but five of the remaining six seats were captured by candidates of the *Comités réunis*. Tristan Duché, whose candidacy had become a focal point in the split among Republicans, failed to win a seat, capturing only 28,970 votes, compared to 86,336 won by the leading candidate Joseph Alcock, the attorney general of Lyon. Radical and socialist candidates did well in Saint-Étienne and surrounding communes but were defeated by rural votes from the department's two other arrondissements, Roanne and Montbrison, where the nobility and clergy exercised considerable influence.[49]

The new prefect Pierre-Antoine Sain, appointed to replace Eugène Baune after his election to the Constituent Assembly, announced his intent to "maintain order and tranquility." He assured property owners that they had "no reason to fear any revolutionary measures on my part."[50] The election of a conservative National Assembly prompted the coal company to withdraw concessions it had made earlier. The company, which had been stockpiling coal to avoid laying off workers, decided that such sacrifices were no longer necessary given the altered political situation. It announced on June 8 that work in the mines would be reduced to only three days a week. Company president Calley-Saint-Paul acknowledged in his private correspondence that "a strike would be our salvation. When it is over we will probably reopen only certain pits and can limit the number of workers."[51] During the month of May, miners had created an organization (*Comité central de la société des ouvriers mineurs et charbonniers*) which held regular meetings to discuss the organization of work, shorter workdays, and the election of their immediate supervisors. They responded to the company's actions on June 9 by occupying the pits, and announcing their intention to work only six days a week without any supervisory personnel. The prefect Sain threatened to sequester company assets to force them to make concessions. He also ordered the arrest of strike leaders on June 10, after negotiating with the miners' central committee. On that day, numerous large gatherings of miners in the city prompted municipal officials to call up the National Guard to prevent an attack on the city's prisons, where strike leaders were being held.[52] On June 13, under pressure from the government, the company conceded a four-day work week.

The June insurrection in Paris did not generate demonstrations in Saint-Étienne. But the defeat of the uprising prompted Saint-Étienne's socialists to elaborate a political vision that denounced violence and advocated a parliamentary road to power. In early July *Le Mercure ségusien* went out of business and was replaced by *La Sentinelle populaire*, which became, alongside the *Société populaire*, the organizational nucleus of radical and socialist republican activities. *La Sentinelle* espoused a brand of socialism that glorified small property ownership, class conciliation, and workers' associations, condemned political violence and direct action, and espoused legality, gradual change, and a nonrevolutionary electoral strategy. "The goal of the Second Republic," proclaimed the editors on July 12, 1848, "is not in doubt for us: it is the progressive betterment of the fate of the poor, their moral and material liberation through education and property ownership." In a series of articles clarifying their vision of socialism, the editors condemned the June insurrection as the product of honest but poor and uneducated workers misled by royalist enemies of the republic.[53]

Republicans continued to criticize the central government for its failure to take action against the coal monopoly, and Saint-Étienne's city council continued to send petitions to Paris. But the issue, which had once dominated local politics, faded into the background as more divisive issues raised by the class conflicts of 1848 came to dominate the political agenda. Fears about public order and private property made "party of order" leaders hesitant to take any actions that might encourage agitation among the region's rebellious coal miners. "The political hatreds that have blossomed since February," declared *La Sentinelle populaire* on September 20, 1848, "have thinned out the ranks of the adversaries of the monopoly and reduced to a very small number those who can counterbalance the efforts of agents of the *Compagnie des mines* in Paris."

The municipal election campaign of July 30–31, 1848 revealed the growing political polarization that was to mark the remaining years of the Second Republic. Liberal Republicans of the *Association républicaine*, with the backing of the newspaper *L'Avenir républicain*, refused to collaborate with republican socialists of the *Société populaire*, whom they labeled "enemies of order." They joined forces with conservative Orleanists and Legitimists. *La Sentinelle populaire* supported the *Société populaire*'s list of candidates, whom it praised as "enlightened and honest men who know how to ally ideas of progress with ideas of order." This list, noted the newspaper, was drawn up in a spirit of conciliation to include socialist and nonsocialist Republicans, with only twelve of the thirty-six proposed candidates "especially representing progressive political opinion." The newspaper warned its readers that defeat in local elections could threaten the existence of the *Société populaire*, given recent legislative proposals to give municipal authorities greater discretion in regulating political clubs. In an election in which only 47 percent of eligible voters showed up at the polls, the *Société populaire* list won fourteen of the thirty-six contested seats, giving liberal republican candidates a majority on the city council.

In the presidential election of December 1848, liberal Republicans supported the candidacy of Cavaignac, while Orleanists and Legitimists rallied behind Louis Napoleon Bonaparte. Radicals and socialists backed Ledru-Rollin and created a local branch of Republican Solidarity, which held regular meetings at the homes of members and maintained close ties with leaders of the city's labor associations.[54] The departmental association that organized Ledru-Rollin's presidential campaign, the *Comité démocratique*, was headed by prominent bourgeois republican leaders from various cities in the department, including Saint-Étienne's Tristan Duché and Alexandre Blancsubé. There were five workers—a silk weaver, a miner, an arms maker, a tanner, and a day laborer—among its twenty leaders.[55] Louis Bonaparte carried the department by a wide margin (72%), but he won a smaller proportion of the votes cast in Saint-Étienne (51%), where Cavaignac won 23 percent and Ledru-Rollin, with 18 percent, made his strongest showing in the department.

The local Mountain included socialists and radicals, who cooperated on electoral activities but retained separate political organizations. It failed to attract liberal Republicans, who joined a "party of order" alliance with Orleanists, Legitimists, and Bonapartists in the May 1849 national election. At the beginning of January 1849, police agents reported that in addition to over thirty workers' associations, mostly of ribbon weavers, there were also "four purely political groups that remain clandestine." The two largest secret gatherings were divided into one predominantly working-class group composed of "former conspirators and several individuals who had seized positions in the government after the February revolution" and another "less exalted" group of Republicans who met at the home of city councilor Balleydier, a café owner, and "most of whom belong to a higher social class."[56] That same month, the subprefect reported on the local branch of Republican Solidarity as follows: "We can presume that members of this organization maintain close relations with the principal members of all sorts of workers' associations in Saint-Étienne and its suburbs, because the majority of these labor associations belong to the *Société populaire* and thus their relationship must continue. If this is the case, we can estimate their number at around 3,000 to 4,000."[57] Class antagonisms among Republicans emerged during the Mountain banquet of March 3, when socialist workers accused several bourgeois radical Republicans, who failed to attend the meager banquet which cost only fifty centimes, of behaving like aristocrats.[58]

The National Assembly election of May 13, 1849, witnessed a dramatic shift in voting patterns, with Mountain candidates making substantial gains. Mountain efforts to mobilize rural voters in the Montbrison and Roanne arrondissements, by appealing to peasant concerns with a Christian socialist rhetoric, were successful. Mountain candidates won five of the nine contested seats in the department. Tristan Duché, who had been defeated in 1848, captured an Assembly seat, along with four other Mountain candidates. Duché received far more votes than he had in the April 1848 election, increasing his total from 28,970 to 35,185. The liberal republican newspaper, *L'Avenir républicain*, estimated that the number of votes received by the "ultra-democrats" had increased by 20 percent since April of 1848.[59] In Saint-Étienne, the Mountain won by a landslide, capturing 78 percent of the vote.

After their victory in the May election, radicals and socialists continued their effort to attract more supporters, circulating propaganda throughout the city and countryside. "It is distressing," bemoaned one local police official, "to see and hear the working class, which is preoccupied only with newspapers and politics. Socialist ideas are making an alarming progress."[60] The abortive June 1849 insurrection in Paris and Lyon, to protest the French invasion of Rome, provoked large demonstrations in front of Saint-Étienne's heavily guarded city hall, but there were no violent confrontations between demonstrators and police or any attempt made to seize government buildings.[61] According to government officials, republican activists made plans to send an armed contingent to support the uprising in Lyon, as their counterparts had done in Rive-de-Gier, but the declaration of a state of siege the next day prevented them from carrying out this plan. The authorities arrested twenty-five prominent republican activists, most of whom were workers, and transported them to Montbrison. They also closed down seven cafés where Republicans gathered regularly, forbade all clubs and political meetings, banned the socialist newspaper *La Sentinelle populaire*, and shut down the ribbon weavers' association (*Société des ouvriers passementiers*). Although Duché signed an appeal to arms to protest the French invasion of Rome and Bonaparte's violation of the constitution, he was not arrested. But he was censured by the National Assembly when he criticized the declaration of a state of siege in Saint-Étienne.

The repression that followed the June 1849 Parisian insurrection did not alter the dominant role played by socialists in Saint-Étienne's Republican party. In July 1849, when a special legislative election was held, Republicans nominated socialist leader Pierre Antide Martin as their candidate. Martin was described in government surveillance reports as "the favored orator of the crowds," and "the director of the army of secret societies."[62] According to police agents, Martin's closest associate was the silk weaver Jean Baptiste Basson, a leader of secret societies in the weavers' commune of Valbenoîte.[63] Martin had intervened to prevent National Guardsmen from firing on convent workshop rioters in 1848, and had subsequently been an active supporter of silk weavers' efforts to win a uniform piece-rate scale. *L'Avenir républicain* denounced Martin and reminded voters of his role in the 1848 riots in a series of polemical exchanges with the candidate.[64] Martin carried Saint-Étienne by a wide margin, winning 9,350 votes (76%) with only 2,928 votes going to General de Grammont, who commanded the state of siege. He lost the election in the conservative rural areas of Roanne and Montbrison, winning 20,024 votes (41%) in the department, compared to Grammont's 28,970 (59%).

The growing electoral strength of the Mountain was confirmed by subsequent electoral returns. In the special election of March 10, 1850, to fill the seat vacated by Martin Bernard, who had been sentenced to deportation for participation in the June 1849 uprising, Republicans once again chose socialist leader Pierre Antide Martin as their candidate. Martin made an improved showing over his past electoral bid, losing the election by a slim margin of only 969 votes, or 1 percent of the votes cast. He won 35,138 votes compared to 36,107 for his conservative opponent Ernest Anglès. Rural propaganda had succeeded in increasing Martin's votes from 20,024 in July 1849 to 35,129 in March 1850, an increase of 43 percent. As in the previous election, Martin carried the city of Saint-Étienne and its surrounding communes by a wide margin, capturing 82 percent of the votes cast.[65]

The electoral law of May 31, 1850 encouraged many republican workers to question their commitment to an electoral route to change. The new law reduced the number of eligible voters in Saint-Étienne by 75 percent, from 12,747 to only 3,254. In the adjacent suburbs, which had become republican socialist strongholds, the number of eligible voters dropped by 77 percent, from 5,584 to only 1,262.[66] The first application of the new law took place on September 30, 1850, following the resignation of fourteen of twenty-six city council members, who refused to approve an official banquet to honor General Victor de Castellane, new commander of the state of siege. Socialist leaders urged Republicans not to vote in these elections, claiming that the election was illegal because the new law did not apply to municipal elections. In an election in which only 917 out of 2,629 registered voters (35%) participated, the party of order slate captured the city council.[67]

The restriction of suffrage rights revived working-class secret societies and conspiratorial revolutionary activities, but most bourgeois republican leaders maintained a continuing commitment to legalism. In August 1850, the attorney general reported that Republicans were postponing any agitation that might prompt further repression until after the presidential elections of 1852: "Their resolutions for the year 1852 explain the careful conduct of the working class and the lack of excitement aroused by the recent political measures. Although the revision of electoral lists have surpassed all forecasts, the workers have not given up the fight to use legal means against the effects of the electoral law. . . ." In the same report, the attorney general noted secret meetings by "men of action who know nothing of the wishes and tendencies of the party." Party leaders, he wrote, "accept their aid in combat but disavow them as soon as the authorities discover and attack them. In each locality there are a certain number of these men, drawn from the dregs of the population, suspected by the party leadership. The leaders allow them to continue because it is a way in which to divert the attention of the authorities, to conceal the real threat, and also because they are unable to discipline them. . . ."[68]

Police and administrative documents of 1851 reveal growing divisions within the republican camp between those favoring an insurrection and those advocating an electoral strategy. At the end of May 1851, the authorities reported that secret societies were deliberating on plans for an insurrection but that there was a division within the secret societies between "the impatients" and "the careful or cunning." The former were calling for an insurrection while the latter wished to wait for the right moment. But "the secret societies are in agreement on an insurrection in 1852, in the name of universal suffrage, which was sacrificed by the electoral law of May 31, 1850."[69] Police reports of August 1851 note that party leaders were preaching extreme caution in anticipation of the 1852 presidential election.[70] Amid rumors of an impending coup d'état, government officials reported in November 1851 that "the socialists are not very preoccupied with the idea of a triumph via universal suffrage. They generally believe that the elections will not take place and await an incident that will provide the signal for an armed insurrection. Orders have been given for them to be ready. . . ."[71] The coup d'état of December put an end to both republican electoral hopes and insurrectionary plans.

The path of Republican party formation in Saint-Étienne did not take a dramatic turn after the establishment of the Second Republic. Radical leaders remained in control of the party, maintaining the close ties with workers that they had forged during the previous decades. Despite the advent of universal male suffrage, workers continued to take their politics into the streets. Miners and silk weavers confronted their employers, hoping that the new republican officials would intervene in their favor. Though committed to maintaining public order, radical republican officials, unlike their liberal counterparts in Toulouse, proved hesitant to use repression against rebellious workers. This alienated liberal Republicans, who occupied a marginal position within the party, and drove them into the conservative party of order alliance at an early date. Liberal Republicans remained marginalized throughout the Second Republic, with socialist and radicals in control of the local newspaper and the candidate selection process. The Mountain alliance, which did not include liberal Republicans, won landslide majorities in the city and captured five seats in the National Assembly election of 1849. Within the Mountain coalition, socialists played a central role, as evidenced by the candidacy of Antide Martin. Martin won overwhelming majorities in Saint-Étienne in the July 1849 and March 1850 legislative election, suffering a narrow defeat in the department in 1850. Although class antagonisms occasionally disrupted relations between radicals and socialists, these divisions did not have the same intensity or political consequences as in Toulouse, where they produced separate newspapers and organizations. Despite their relatively strong electoral position, many Republicans boycotted elections and turned to revolutionary conspiracies following the restriction of suffrage rights in 1850, which disenfranchised a significant portion of Saint-Étienne's workers.

THE SECOND EMPIRE IN SAINT-ÉTIENNE

When news of Louis Napoleon Bonaparte's coup d'état reached Saint-Étienne, groups of workers gathered around the posters announcing the dissolution of the National Assembly and restoration of universal male suffrage. According to local police officials, militant republican silk weavers were convinced that any resistance would encounter military force, while other workers were pleased to receive news of the restoration of suffrage rights.[72] After news of armed resistance to the coup reached Saint-Étienne, the prefect posted a warning announcing that anyone found constructing or defending a barricade would be shot on sight. The subsequent repression included the dissolution of all fraternal associations, a measure directed against the silk weavers. Police gathered information on 146 suspected Republicans, but the ensuing repression was relatively mild, with socialist Republicans as its prime target. Fifty-one percent of the suspects were workers, with silk weavers constituting 32 percent of all suspects and 62 percent of all workers. Of the thirty-two suspects tried by the Mixed Commission, only nineteen republican militants, sixteen of whom were socialist workers, were convicted. The twelve activists who received the harshest sentences—deportation to Algeria—soon had their sentences commuted to internment.[73]

Although the repression that followed the coup made electoral opposition difficult, Republicans fielded both liberal and socialist candidates in the February–March 1852 legislative election. The official candidate Jules Balay, a ribbon merchant, was elected deputy, with 55 percent of the votes cast. In the city of Saint-Étienne and its surrounding communes, he won only 32 percent of 7,308 votes cast, compared to 46 percent for the liberal republican candidate Benoît Fourneyron, a wealthy engineer/inventor; 16 percent for the legitimist candidate Mathon de Fogères; and 4 percent for the republican socialist candidate Antide Martin. Only 34 percent of Saint-Étienne's 14,425 registered voters appeared at the polls.[74] Despite massive abstentions, administrative pressures, and continuing repression, Republicans elected two candidates, Pierre-Antoine Sain and Jules Favre, in the *conseil général* elections of August 1852. Unwilling to accept the coup d'état as legitimate, both men refused on principle to take the oath of loyalty to the Imperial regime, which was required to assume office. Republicans also made a strong showing in the city council election of September 5–6, 1852, despite the adoption of a new system of citywide rather than neighborhood representation and a turnout of only 23 percent. Republicans captured an average of 52 percent of 3,280 votes cast, electing several party leaders who had escaped arrest and exile, and defeating some of the city's wealthiest and most prominent ribbon merchants.[75] Fearing an even greater defeat in the second round of voting, scheduled for September 11–12, the government postponed the election until June 1853. The subprefect noted that an adjournment was necessary, given the danger of a republican victory, until after Louis Bonaparte's scheduled visit to the city.[76]

The political repression removed socialist leaders and working-class militants from the scene and destroyed the organizations of the most ardent supporters of republican socialism, the silk ribbon weavers. But Republicans continued to maintain an electoral presence in a city that had been won over to the cause of the republic. Widespread abstentions, continuing repression, government patronage, and a prefectoral decree expelling many workers from the city as vagabonds, led to a conservative victory in the municipal election of June 4–5, 1853. Only 2,456 voters, 15 percent of those registered, showed up at the polls. For the 1857 legislative election, the government divided the city into two electoral districts (*circonscriptions*), in order to counterbalance urban votes with more conservative rural ballots. In this election, the official candidate, the wealthy ribbon merchant Jules Balay, won a majority in the 1st district, but captured only 24 percent of Saint-Étienne's 6,425 votes. The frustrated attorney general's postelection analysis noted the ability of Republicans to mobilize voters in the absence of newspapers and formal organizations: "There was only one newspaper that even printed the names of the opposition candidates. Not a single proclamation was printed and nothing saw the light of day. . . . The names of the democratic candidates were practically unknown and not very attractive. Their only value was as protest candidates; but, nevertheless, appearing at the last moment with no newspapers or proclamations or personal worth, they won the majority of votes in all of the industrial centers. In one of the districts of Saint-Étienne, the government candidate won 1,500 votes while the democratic candidate had nearly 5,000. . . ."[77] This official attributed the alarming electoral results to Saint-Étienne's working class, which was still "obsessed with ideas of economic equality."

Republicanism remained strong among Saint-Étienne's workers but its character was altered by the internal transformation of the city's economy. Although silk weavers continued to constitute the largest portion of the region's working class by 1872, they declined relative to the growing number of workers employed in the expanding mining and steel industries. This shift in the occupational composition of the working class took place in a context of severe economic depression within the silk industry after 1857 and a crisis and decline within the city's household arms and hardware industry. Although falling ribbon prices exacerbated class antagonisms within the silk industry during the 1860s, economic crises weakened the organizational capacities of household workers, who responded by migrating, seeking private or public charity, or finding work in the expanding coal and steel industries. The economic changes of the Second Empire not only weakened the position of the most militant supporters of republican socialism, the silk weavers. They also strengthened the position of workers in the mining and steel industries. It was in these expanding sectors of the region's economy that radical bourgeois republican leaders mobilized working-class support based on an alternative to the republican socialism of the silk weavers.

Coal miners and steel workers experienced very different working conditions in industries that followed different trajectories than household silk weaving and small arms production (see chapter 3); they also gathered in different neighborhood cafés and taverns and pursued different leisure activities. Outside of work, factory metalworkers and miners spent their time with coworkers in the cafés and taverns of their neighborhoods, rather than with silk weavers, whose leisure activities were oriented toward the inner-city neighborhoods where they lived. As was the case in Toulouse, the repression of the 1850s drove republican politics underground into the informal networks of neighborhood cafés, taverns, and cabarets, but this had very different consequences in Saint-Étienne. It reinforced existing occupational divisions among workers and provided radical republican leaders with an opportunity to win working-class votes from growing groups of industrial workers who had not been won over to republican socialism. By reinforcing neighborhood rather than citywide patterns of political organization, the repression made it difficult for militant republican socialist workers, most of whom were silk weavers or small arms producers, to recruit new converts in the city's most rapidly expanding industries.

Economic changes also transformed the character of the Republican party's bourgeois leadership. The rapid industrialization of the 1850s and 1860s benefited the region's growing steel industry and augmented the wealth of the local industrial bourgeoisie, at the same time that a crisis within the ribbon industry weakened the economic power of the city's traditional merchant capitalist elite.[78] These economic changes intersected with an altered political situation to produce a change in republican leadership. The repression of the 1850s, by driving republican leaders into prison or exile, provided an opening for new party leaders, radical members of the city's industrial bourgeoisie who opposed the Imperial government's tariff and railroad policies. Although steel production expanded rapidly during the Second Empire, the high cost of iron imported from Sweden via England, as well as the better quality of English coke, made it difficult for the region's industrialists to compete with Britain. In 1855, the Imperial regime exempted all imported steel and iron destined for naval construction from existing tariffs. The city's Chamber of Commerce responded with a protest condemning the government's disastrous tariff policies, which they claimed had led to the shutdown of thirty blast furnaces in the Loire valley. During the Second Empire, the PLM railroad company, owned by Parisian-based industrial and finance capitalists and heavily subsidized by the Imperial regime, replaced the coal company as the target of radical republican attacks on the evils of monopoly power.[79] An Imperial decree of 1854 that divided the coal company into four smaller firms, as well as new company policies providing special rates and long-term contracts to the region's steel industry, diffused local hostility toward the coal companies.[80] Republicans attributed high transport costs to the monopoly control exercised by the PLM company and called for the repeal of the 1855 tariff decree, lower rail fares, and the construction of new railroad lines. The region's largest steel companies, including Petin and Gaudet, Jackson frères, and Terrenoire, benefited from large government contracts for railroad, naval artillery, and other military equipment; but smaller firms, like those owned by Hutter and Holtzer, were less dependent upon such contracts. It was the owners and managers of these smaller firms who provided new leadership for the Republican party, as well as financial backing for the radical wing of the party in its struggle against socialist Republicans.

Radical republican industrialists like Frédéric Dorian, director of the Holtzer steel company and owner of a scythe factory at Pont-Salomon, practiced workplace paternalism.[81] His steel company provided high wages, company housing, free education, and social insurance. These policies encouraged an ideology of class conciliation that, when transferred to the political arena, attracted industrialists as well as workers to the Republican party. The industrial paternalism of men like Dorian contrasted sharply with the labor policies of the wealthy ribbon merchants who served as the regime's official candidates throughout the Second Empire. Steel factory workers often voted in block for their employers, regardless of whether the candidate's sympathies were napoleonic, legitimist, or republican.[82] In contrast, when the wealthy ribbon merchants, who renounced paternalism in favor of higher profits, ran for office, they were unable to elicit strong support from the workers in their industry.

The legislative election of 1863 signaled the emergence of new republican leaders. In this election, Frédéric Dorian defeated the regime's official candidate and incumbent deputy, the legitimist compte de Charpin-Feugerolles, in a close election decided by only 678 votes. Although Dorian won only a slim majority (52%) of the 15,296 votes cast in the electoral district, he carried Saint-Étienne with 84 percent of the vote.[83] In the July 1865 municipal election, Republicans captured the city council, winning between 56 and 64 percent of the vote in the first round. Republican candidates had campaigned on a variety of issues including municipal liberties, the fiscal mismanagement of local administration by Napoleonic officials, corruption and waste in municipal public works projects, the rising price of housing and food, and inequitable tax policies. Their campaign mobilized strong support among shopkeepers and small manufacturers, who remained hostile to the politically dominant ribbon merchants and wary of the central government's public works projects. Republican candidates blamed high taxes and high rents on these projects, which destroyed low-rent housing and necessitated higher consumption (*octroi*) taxes. They also pointed to administrative incompetence in the public works projects and criticized the government for spending money on embellishing public buildings rather than on providing services to working-class neighborhoods.

Although the Imperial government made a continuing effort to win elections in which the votes of the countryside counterbalanced those of Saint-Étienne, after a very poor showing by the government candidate Félix Escoffier, director of the arms factory, in the *conseil général* election of 1867, government officials abandoned any hope of winning an election within the city. "In Saint-Étienne," wrote the attorney general in July 1867, "the working class listens only to leaders who caress their bad inclinations. They appear to have escaped all honest influences. We thus no longer have anything to hope for from the elections. . . . In reality leadership has escaped all government authorities. . . . The majority of the city council continues in its hostile disposition. . . ."[84] In the legislative election of 1869, the government did not field a candidate, unable to persuade its most prominent supporters, retiring deputy Francisque Balay and former mayor Christophe Faure-Belon, to run for office.

Divisions among Republicans resurfaced once the party captured municipal power in 1865. Liberal Republicans favored an alliance with nonrepublican opponents of the regime, criticized republican socialists as "the degenerated children of 1789," and rejected the suggestion that the party nominate workers as candidates for the National Assembly, contending that such positions should be reserved for better-qualified bourgeois candidates.[85] Government officials had noted the conflict over nomination of working-class candidates as early as July of 1864, but claimed that workers in Saint-Étienne were willing to accept bourgeois candidates because the electoral districts of the city included rural populations.[86] Radical and socialist Republicans rejected an alliance with liberal Orleanists and continued to raise the "social question." They were active in supporting the velvet weavers strike of 1865 and in subsequent efforts to raise money for a weavers' production cooperative.[87] The conflict intensified after Republicans captured control of the city council. "There is strife within the [Republican] party!" wrote the attorney general in December 1866. "One of the party's leaders has written to the newspapers to denounce his brothers, reproach them as pub-crawlers (*pilliers de cabarets*), as enemies of the true interests of the people."[88] Republican radicals and socialists responded to such attacks with equally hostile polemics, leading to the resignation of seven city councilmen, and provoking discussion of a new municipal election. In June 1867, a number of liberal Republicans were among the twenty councilors who signed their names on an address to the Emperor condemning the recent assassination attempt, but ten radical and socialist council members refused to do so.

Radical and socialist Republicans initially cooperated with one another but this proved short-lived. At the end of 1868, socialist leader Antide Martin joined forces with radical leader Frédéric Dorian to found the newspaper *L'Éclaireur*, which was financed in large part by the wealth of republican steel industrialists. Disagreements between radicals and socialists in 1869 led socialists to break ranks and create their own rival newspaper, *La Sentinelle populaire*. As in 1848, this newspaper was closely tied to an independent working-class association that also took its name from a Second Republic predecessor, the *Société populaire*. This organization challenged the exclusion of workers from the republican list of candidates and proposed candidates for the 1869 election. In February 1869, after the widely respected radical republican leader Martin Bernard announced his intention not to run for office, Antide Martin, who had been a National Assembly candidate in 1849 and 1850, declared his candidacy for the seat, with support from *La Sentinelle populaire*. The Republicans of *L'Éclaireur* refused to support Martin's candidacy and persuaded Frédéric Dorian, the wealthy steel industrialist, to run for reelection despite his earlier stated intention not to do so. Republicans directed their campaign attacks against one another, as well as against the government-backed legitimist candidate Vital de Rochetaillée. *L'Éclaireur* launched a personal attack on Martin, falsely accusing him of failing to remain an opponent of the regime during the difficult years of the 1850s, and of retreating to the safety and comfort of a well-paying job in Paris.[89] In fact, Martin was forced to leave Saint-Étienne by order of the police commissioner, and had to abandon his prosperous business as a notary. *L'Éclaireur* also recalled Martin's role in the 1848 silk weavers' attack on the convent workshops, labeling him a "liquidator candidate" and "an agent of destruction in 1848," thereby playing on fears of socialism among petty bourgeois and peasant voters.

Republican socialists had their own electoral committee, *L'Union démocratique*, which was led by the lawyers Victor Duchamp and F. Chapelle and the velvet ribbon foreman Canonier.[90] The most prominent working-class activists in Martin's campaign were leaders of the velvet ribbon weavers. The socialist weaver, Pierre Boissonet, an organizer for the First International, and the velvet ribbon weaver, Benoît Fontvielle, a leader of the local branch of the International who had served two months in prison for his role in the 1865 strike, were active in Martin's campaign. Martin's base of electoral support was largely confined to the city of Saint-Étienne, especially the ribbon weaving districts. When Martin campaigned in the mine workers' district of le Soleil, a large majority of the approximately sixty miners who showed up to hear him loudly expressed their support for

Dorian.[91] Martin's supporters at the poorly financed *La Sentinelle populaire* accused their radical republican opponents of using the same tactics as the Imperial regime to dictatorially gain control of the candidate selection process. They appealed to class antagonisms and attacked Dorian as a capitalist exploiter.

The cost of running a campaign beyond the local level meant that radical Republicans, who could rely upon wealthy industrial backers, had a decisive advantage. Dorian's candidacy found working-class support in the newer neighborhoods inhabited by miners and steel workers, and his financial resources allowed him to carry out a departmentwide campaign that won many rural votes. While socialist Republicans like Martin appealed to class solidarities and antagonisms to mobilize electoral support, Dorian touted an "alliance of capital and labor." Although Dorian appealed to small property holders by warning that only the republic could save them from the monopolies supported by the Imperial government, his campaign only cautiously raised the "social question" by advocating more equitable taxes. Since his opponent, the conservative baron Vital de Rochetaillée, was a former volunteer in the papal army and was closely identified with the clergy, Dorian emphasized anticlerical themes in his campaign. Campaigning as "free thinker," Dorian attacked the church and clergy, called for free compulsory secular education, and criticized the government's adventurous foreign policy, wasteful spending, and corrupt administration.[92] Although women were not invited to attend Dorian's electoral gatherings, they gathered outside on the street with their children and cheered the republican candidate when he entered and left the building. The police commissioner described the scene outside one electoral rally as "a sort of charivari, with women banging spoons against soup tureens they had brought to eat their soup while on the street."[93] Dorian handily defeated both de Rochetaillée and Martin in the May 23–24 election, capturing 62 percent of the 18,082 votes cast, compared to only 10 percent for Martin and 27 percent for the legitimist candidate.

The predominantly working-class crowd that gathered to celebrate Dorian's victory on the evening of May 24, amid chants of "Long Live Dorian!" and "Down with the Jesuits!" attacked the Jesuit college Saint-Michel, breaking several windows and setting fire to the concierge's chamber. The anticlerical polemics of the radical candidate had unintended consequences, sparking working-class street protests that carried politics beyond the ballot box.[94] Although *L'Éclaireur* downplayed these events, the legitimist *Le Mémorial* found them reminiscent of the revolutionary violence of 1848, and used them to denounce the "red specter" and the Republican party's "revolutionary candidates."[95]

Neither of the two candidates for the seat in Saint-Étienne's extramuros district, the radical Republican César Bertholon, and the government candidate, Hippolyte-André de Charpin-Feugerolles, won the necessary majority. A second round of balloting was scheduled for June 7. This district contained a large number of coal miners, who were divided in their support for the two candidates. Bertholon had been an active supporter of the silk weavers' cooperative in 1841, and had cosponsored a bill in 1849 to give public works contracts to workers' cooperatives. His campaign emphasized a variety of social issues, including a shorter work day, higher wages, and the legalization of trade unions. During the electoral campaign, leaders of the miners' mutual aid society (*La Fraternelle*) threatened to strike over the company insurance fund, which was financed in large part by work fines. They demanded a worker-controlled central accident fund that would allow miners to change jobs without losing benefits. The miners remained politically divided, with a conservative faction, the committee of fifteen, favoring the pursuit of Imperial government patronage to pressure company officials to make concessions, and a republican faction, led by Michel Rondet, pushing for direct negotiations with company officials.

The prefect met with delegates of *La Fraternelle* in May 1869 and promised to support their demands if they provided the regime with needed electoral support.[96] After the first ballot, the prefect sought a public declaration of support from the miners' leaders. On June 4 the secretary treasurer of *La Fraternelle* wrote an article for *L'Éclaireur* to encourage miners to vote for de Charpin on the second ballot. The newspaper's editors accused the miners' leaders of betraying the working class, and the next day six miners published a declaration of support for Bertholon. The support of the miners for the Imperial candidate was critical, for in the election the official candidate won by only 700 votes out of 29,015 ballots cast. Several days later, in response to rank-and-file militancy rather than the directives of their leadership, the region's fifteen thousand miners went on strike for shorter hours, higher wages, and control over a central accident and retirement fund, expecting tacit support, or at least neutrality, from the authorities. The leaders of *La Fraternelle* had planned to strike at a later date, after one more meeting with employers, but rank-and-file militants launched the strike earlier, taking their leaders by surprise.[97] The prefect, after meeting with strike leaders, tried to persuade his superiors in Paris that negotiated wage concessions, compensated for by lower railway rates, could provide an acceptable solution. But the Minister of the Interior took a harder line, ordering the prefect to arrest strike leaders and sending troops into the basin. On June 16, following the arrest of strikers who had prevented coal deliveries to the Holtzer metal factory, managed by Frédéric Dorian, troops at la Ricamerie opened fire on workers seeking to free their arrested comrades, killing fourteen persons, including two women and an infant of fifteen months.

The Ricamerie massacre put an end to the government's ability to win working-class support from the miners, consolidated the miners' support of republicanism, and strengthened the position of the radical wing of the Republican party. Radicals condemned the massacre not as an outcome of the inherent antagonism between capital and labor but as evidence of the regime's inability to promote class conciliation. The target of radical republican attacks was not the owners of the coal company but the Imperial government. *L'Éclaireur* accused the troops of murder and reported various atrocities committed by the soldiers. The newspaper later retracted these accounts, after the government seized one of its issues and threatened prosecution. But *L'Éclaireur* continued to condemn the massacre, to raise funds for the victims, and to denounce the widespread arrest of miners that followed the event. On June 23, 1869 fourteen republican city councilmen drafted a letter to the mayor, calling for the immediate departure of troops from the city and protesting the conduct of the soldiers implicated in the "inhuman repression." The prefect responded by dissolving the city council and appointing a municipal commission in its place.[98] The strike ended in defeat for the miners, in mid-July, with workers winning concessions only on the hours of work.

The 1869 election marked the triumph of radicals within the Republican party. It was soon followed by the disappearance of the socialist newspaper *La Sentinelle populaire*. But this did not signal the disappearance of local socialists. In October 1869, thirty socialists created a branch of the First International, which grew to include one hundred members by April 1870. Available information on the membership reveals that, despite the rapid growth of mining and metallurgy, household producers continued to dominate the ranks of Saint-Étienne's socialists. Of the fifty-seven individuals identified in existing records, fifty-five are identified by occupation. They include two clerks, a teacher, and a journalist as well as fifty-one workers. All but eight of the workers (84%) were velvet or silk ribbon weavers, with two arms makers, a miner, a hardware producer, a mechanic, a joiner, a baker, and a shoemaker among their ranks. The six leaders of the organization were all ribbon weavers.[99]

Once they had secured control of the candidate selection process and won the legislative election, radical party leaders were willing to seek reconciliation with socialist Republicans. After the 1869 election, divisions between socialist and radical Republicans temporarily subsided. On October 25, 1969 the central police commissioner noted that secret society members, who had been considering joining the First International, were slowly and cautiously rallying behind the Republican party.[100] While retaining control of the newspaper's board of directors, radicals allowed socialist activists, like the ribbon weaver Antoine Chastel and the journalist and future communard leader Adrien Duvand, to serve on the editorial board of *L'Éclaireur*. Though it avoided inflammatory rhetoric about class antagonisms, the newspaper published articles by socialists that addressed the economic concerns of workers. Radical party leaders joined socialist Republicans, in early October 1869, in a local reception in honor of national party leader Jules Simon. Socialist and radical Republicans also joined forces in the campaign over the plebiscite of May 1870, which was preceded by separate meetings of republican silk weavers and miners to discuss the plebiscite.[101] The socialist leader Adrien Duvand led the successful republican campaign to vote no in the referendum on the liberal Empire. This plebiscite on the regime's liberalizing policies generated the largest voter turnout of any election of the Second Empire, attracting 74 percent of Saint-Étienne's 23,486 registered voters. The majority (76%) voted against the regime, turning out the largest percentage of opposition votes in all of France.[102] In the August 1870 municipal elections, Republicans won all but two of thirty-six city council seats, capturing between 61 and 68 percent of the vote in the ten sections where the regime ran candidates.[103]

The republican resurgence encouraged conservative forces to reconstitute a "party of order" coalition after the 1869 election. Even before this election, Saint-Étienne's police commissioner reported that conservative opponents of the regime were moderating their opposition, with the threat of revolution forcing them to "admit that the peril they fear does exist."[104] Legitimists closed down their opposition newspaper, *La Loire*, in January 1870, joined forces with Bonapartists to mobilize support for the government in the May plebiscite, and supported the prefect's dissolution of the city council in June 1870. But a united conservative opposition failed to prevent the Republican party, dominated by radicals who had reconciled a weakened socialist wing, from capturing municipal power in August 1870, on the eve of the sudden fall of the Imperial regime.

The Second Empire was a decisive turning point in the development of local republican politics. The political repression that followed the coup d'état altered the balance of power within the Republican party. Although socialist Republicans managed to run a candidate in the 1852 election, the repression severely weakened their electoral capacities, temporarily helping to strengthen the electoral presence of liberal Republicans during the 1850s. But liberals remained relatively weak and marginalized within Saint-Étienne's republican circles throughout the Second Empire. The key change from 1849–51 concerned the displacement of socialists by radicals as the dominant force within republicanism. The victory of Dorian in the election of 1863 signaled the emergence of a new group of radical leaders, who were not as sympathetic to socialism as their 1848 counterparts. These men eventually gained control of the newspaper and the candidate selection process, but not without a fight from socialist Republicans. The conflict came to a head in 1869, when socialist leader Antide Martin, after failing to win the republican nomination, launched a campaign in which he was soundly defeated by Dorian. In the aftermath of this defeat, the republican socialist newspaper disappeared from the scene and socialist Republicans became reconciled to radical party leadership. By the end of the 1860s, radical leaders were firmly in control of the local newspaper and candidate selection process and the party they led was capable of winning electoral majorities in both the city and the region. In contrast to 1848 and 1849, liberal Republicans did not join the revived party of order coalition in 1870, but remained within the Republican party.

REPUBLICAN POLITICS AND CLASS RELATIONS IN SAINT-ÉTIENNE

The class struggles generated by early industrialization decisively shaped the development of republican politics in Saint-Étienne. The rapid introduction of new handlooms during the years from 1815 to 1832 altered the balance of power between weavers and merchant capitalists and generated the grievances that enabled radical and socialist Republicans to recruit Saint-Étienne's silk weavers. The economic struggles of the weavers created a situation in which the most politically active segment of the city's working class was closely integrated into the party of suffrage reform at an early date. But the city's weavers were by no means naturally disposed toward republicanism, as events prior to 1834 reveal. It was only after republican militants actively embraced the weavers' economic grievances and aspirations that these workers were won over to the cause of the republic.

Radical rather than liberal dominance of local republicanism militated against the strategy adopted by Republicans in Toulouse, who abandoned the social question in order to win the votes of the propertied electorate. Saint-Étienne's radical leaders repeatedly intervened in economic conflicts during the July Monarchy, including the miners' strikes of 1844 and 1846, to rally political support from disenfranchised workers. The Icarian movement, quite strong in Toulouse where Republicans failed to support the artisanal strikes of 1840–41, was very weak in Saint-Étienne, where Republicans established strong ties to workers during the class conflicts of 1834 and 1846. Because republican politics was dominated by radicals committed to universal male suffrage, rather than liberals pursuing an electoral strategy in the context of a restrictive suffrage, strikes provided Republicans with opportunities rather than obstacles for mobilizing working-class support.

Because radical and socialist Republicans held municipal power in Saint-Étienne in 1848, the political consequences of the class conflicts unleashed by the revolution were different from Toulouse. Whereas the up-heaval in Toulouse alienated radical and socialist militants from liberal republican officials and fostered autonomous working-class political activ-ity, in Saint-Étienne the popular protests of 1848 drove liberal Republicans into the conservative "party of order." To the dismay of liberal Republi-cans, radical municipal officials refused to use armed force to prevent the destruction of the city's convent workshops by socialist workers. The ini-tial willingness of these officials to shut down the convent workshops helped spark the riots, while their overt hostility to the coal monopoly en-couraged miners to confront their employers. The class conflicts of the period strengthened ties between radical bourgeois leaders and socialist workers while driving liberal Republicans into the arms of royalists. The class conflicts that erupted at the end of the Second Empire also helped to consolidate working-class support for radical republicanism. Although the miners who went on strike in 1869 initially had divided political loyalties, the Ricamerie massacre of 1869 solidified Republicans' hold over the workers of the region and destroyed the Imperial government's attempt to win working-class support through paternalist policies.

The trajectory of republican politics in Saint-Étienne was also shaped by the city's distinctive class structure. The absence of an urban aristocracy and presence of a powerful merchant capitalist class meant a weak Legit-imist but strong Orleanist party. The close ties of the latter to merchant capitalists, whose interests were linked to control over a household labor force, rather than, as was the case in Toulouse, control over product mar-kets, meant that orleanism took on a socially conservative rather than lib-eral coloration. It also meant that, in contrast with Toulouse, wealthy mer-chants were unlikely to embrace liberal republicanism. Because the local economy was based on industry rather than administration or commerce, there were relatively few professionals and intellectuals within the ranks of the city's propertied elite. This further limited the social base for liberal republicanism in Saint-Étienne. Unlike other major cities, like Toulouse and Rouen, which were located in predominantly rural departments where local notables and the clergy were very influential, Saint-Étienne was sur-rounded by large industrial cities, including Le Chambon-Feugerolles, Rive-de-Gier, and Saint-Chamond. This gave Saint-Étienne's radical Re-publicans the ability to win seats in departmentwide elections and allowed the socialist militant Antide Martin to come within one percentage point of winning the election in March of 1850.

The pattern of industrialization in Saint-Étienne, and accompanying di-visions among workers, had important political consequences. Whereas household producers, who embraced cooperative socialist visions, played the dominant role in republican politics during the 1830s and 1840s, the rapid industrialization of the Second Empire and the crisis of the silk and hardware industries meant an enhanced political role for miners and steel workers, who were more supportive of radical republicanism. Republican strategies of mobilizing support continued to center around appeals to workers, but new groups of workers, without a legacy of autonomous political activity, came to play a more central role. The political ramifications of divisions among workers wrought by industrial growth are evident in the electoral outcome of 1869. The electoral strength of the radical republican candidate was centered in the growing new industries of the region, among workers in the steel mills and mines, whereas the socialist candidate mobilized his strongest support within the old silk weavers' districts.

Although a distinctive local pattern of industrial development left its mark on politics in Saint-Étienne, changes in the national political opportunity structure also shaped the development of republican politics. The repression of the 1834 insurrection encouraged weavers to join the ranks of Republicans and helped establish a solid basis of working-class support for radical republicanism. The new opportunities for collective political action made possible by the revolution of 1848 unleashed working-class protests which alienated liberal Republicans and drove them into the arms of the royalist party of order. The political repression that followed the coup d'état of 1851 temporarily removed from the scene the radical professionals and intellectuals who had previously provided leadership for Republicans. This created an opening for a new group of republican industrialists whose radicalism emphasized anticlerical themes and rejected socialism. The repression also made it very difficult for socialist workers, most of whom were household producers facing deteriorating economic conditions, to recruit laborers in the expanding mining and metallurgy sectors of the economy. Political opportunities and constraints, as well as class relations, decisively shaped the local trajectory of republican politics.

CHAPTER SIX

Rouen: The Transformation of Radicalism and Triumph of Liberalism

DESPITE THE PRESENCE of large factories and an outburst of industrial protest on the part of factory workers in 1830, republican politics in Rouen remained divorced from the concerns of proletarianized factory workers throughout most of the July Monarchy. Widespread poverty and stark economic inequalities did not give the "social question" a central place on the agenda of local Republicans. In July 1834, Rouen's liberal Republicans joined forces with the dynastic opposition to help elect the wealthy liberal banker Jacques Lafitte. That same month, liberal Republicans gathered at a banquet to celebrate the anniversary of the July Revolution. The tricolor flag that adorned the room was inscribed with the words "Liberty and Fraternity." The word equality was conspicuously absent.[1]

Liberal control of Rouen's Pepublican party was challenged during the final years of the July Monarchy and early days of the Second Republic. Radical republican leaders, who had mobilized factory workers behind the banner of universal male suffrage in 1846–47, gained municipal power during the months that followed the February 1848 revolution. During their brief reign, radical leaders appointed socialists to positions of power and made a variety of important economic concessions to their working-class supporters. When these bourgeois radicals were defeated by conservatives in the April 1848 election, workers took to the barricades, where they faced the bullets and cannons of the "forces of order," whose ranks included liberal Republicans. In the polarized political situation that followed, radicals and socialists forged a Mountain alliance which liberal Republicans refused to join. In March 1849, when the government decided to arrest and try local radical and socialist leaders of the Mountain, the prosecuting attorney for the case was the prominent liberal republican leader Louis Philippe Desseaux.

When republicanism reemerged from the repression of the 1850s, relations among liberals, radicals, and socialists were very different. Radical leaders were no longer willing to support the demands of rebellious socialist factory workers. They campaigned for the election of liberal candidates and collaborated on a republican newspaper, *Le Progrès de Rouen*, that refused to open its columns to socialist workers. The editors justified this decision, in February 1869, as follows: "If it is a question of opening our columns to those favoring a suppression of interest [from investments], we say to those who would like to take our place: we are not apostles of this idea . . . we are in favor of liberty, even for capital. . . . Those who support ideas that we don't share should not be any more surprised by our refusal to become their rostrum than they are by our refusal to publish those who develop royalist doctrines. . . ."[2] When an independent socialist candidate, Émile Aubry, challenged the liberal republican nominee Desseaux in the 1869 legislative election, Rouen's radicals supported Desseaux. In response to their exclusion from republican politics, many socialist workers turned to the local branch of the First International. By 1869, radical leader Frédéric Deschamps, whose electoral defeat had helped spark the April 1848 insurrection, was espousing liberal principles and praising his former archenemy, liberal republican lawyer Jules Senard, as "an excellent colleague, comrade, and friend."[3] These changes in the relationship among liberal, radical, and socialist Republicans account for shifts in the local Republican party's platforms, strategies, allies, and electoral fortunes, which are documented below.

Workers and Republicans in Rouen: 1830–1848

The early days of the July Monarchy in Rouen were marked by widespread working-class protests against employers. During the summer of 1830, National Guard troops were deployed to confront rebellious textile spinning factory workers at Rouen, Déville, and Sotteville who were demanding higher piece rates, shorter working hours, and less oppressive workplace regulations. In August 1830, National Guardsmen dispersed a demonstration of workers in front of Rouen's city hall, and then arrested dozens of workers in the city's cabarets and cafés. In early September, Rouen's National Guardsmen were called on to free a textile industrialist from Bapeaume who had been taken captive by his angry workers and forcibly marched to Rouen to protest the arrest of two strike leaders. That same month, after a violent confrontation between a detachment of Rouen's National Guardsmen and working-class demonstrators at Darnétal, military authorities sent reinforcements of National Guard and army units to patrol the industrial valley towns of the Rouen region.[4]

Unlike the 1834 silk weavers' insurrection in Saint-Étienne, the factory spinners' struggles in 1830 did not create a group of bourgeois republican leaders who maintained close ties to workers, nor did it make the grievances of local textile factory workers central to republican politics. Those workers who became active in the local republican movement were artisans, not factory workers. Artisans, clerks, shopkeepers, and students animated the republican street demonstrations of the early 1830s. Factory workers were absent from the republican demonstration of July 30, 1833 to celebrate the anniversary of the revolution that inaugurated the regime, broken up by police after protestors shouted seditious slogans in front of the mayor's residence. They were also absent from the only other recorded republican demonstration in 1833, in the cafés near the *Théatre des Arts*, which resulted in the arrest of six people, including a goldsmith, three medical students, and a clerk.[5]

The local branch of the Society of the Rights of Man, which advocated universal male suffrage, tax reform, affordable credit, free education, associational liberties, and the democratization of the National Guard, recruited workers into its ranks, but they were artisans not factory workers. By January 1834, the Society had six hundred members. Police surveillance records list the names of sixty-four of the most active members, forty-one of whom are identified by occupation. Among this group were sixteen workers, all of whom were artisans, eight shopkeepers, nine clerks, two medical students, three actors, a professor, a lawyer, and a notary. The president of the central committee was a notary and the vice-presidents were a professor and a lawyer.[6] Police surveillance reports note discussion of a plan to send a delegation of workers to ask the prefect to forbid soldiers from working in local workshops, where they competed for jobs with artisans, but never mention any dialogue about the grievances of Rouen's factory workers. On October 3, 1833, police raided the homes of suspected leaders of the local branch of the association. Six men were subsequently tried and convicted in June and July 1834 for illegal association. The court also ordered the dissolution of the organization.[7]

Rouen's liberal Republicans remained committed to an electoral route to change and joined forces with the left dynastic opposition, led by former orleanist ministers Dupont de l'Eure and Jacques Lafitte. In January 1834, liberal Republicans formed a branch of the electoral association *Aide-toi*, which had only twenty members and, according to government reports, "admitted only men of wealth."[8] In the *conseil général* election of November 1833, a majority (55%) of the 1,101 voters from the six cantons of Rouen supported government candidates, but 23 percent backed candidates described by the prefect as "moderate democrats" and 13 percent cast their ballots for "pronounced democrats," while only 9 percent voted for legitimist candidates.[9] In the election of June 1834, the republican-liberal dynastic opposition alliance elected former orleanist minister and wealthy banker Jacques Lafitte as a deputy from Rouen.

Rouen's liberal electoral alliance appealed to small property holders, who constituted the majority of those eligible to vote in municipal elections, and to bourgeois merchants and lawyers dissatisfied with the regime's domestic and foreign policies.[10] The city's population included numerous lawyers and solicitors who were attracted to liberal republicanism because of its criticism of official corruption and advocacy of recruitment by talent rather than personal connections. The liberal opposition alliance appealed to the interests of Rouen's merchants, industrialists, master artisans, and shopkeepers, by criticizing government regulatory policies that fostered high interest rates, and by calling for a reform of the banking system to stimulate industrial development.[11] Although the orleanist regime's repressive labor policies won strong support among the city's industrial bourgeoisie, these industrialists were dependent on high protective tariffs to prevent lower-priced British textiles from flooding the French market. Their support for the regime wavered whenever the government considered tariff reforms. In October 1834, for example, rumors of an impending treaty with England to lower textile tariffs contributed to the growing electoral influence of the opposition.[12] Liberal opponents of the regime in Rouen abandoned their opposition to protectionism after the Chamber of Deputies election of 1837, when liberal banker Jacques Laffitte was soundly defeated.[13] By the 1839 election, opposition liberal candidates renounced reform of the regime's protectionist textile policies and acknowledged the need to protect certain industries, like textiles, from foreign competition.

The electoral alliance between Republicans and liberal monarchists aroused the opposition of radicals and socialists affiliated with the Society of the Rights of Man. Prior to a banquet in honor of the recently elected deputy Lafitte on September 23, 1834, a delegation from the Society met privately with Lafitte at his hotel, but they were not well received. The banquet attracted around five hundred participants, about half of whom were members of the propertied electorate. According to police surveillance reports, members of the Society of the Rights of Man showed up but were disappointed with Lafitte's "extremely moderate" speech, which focused on the prosperity of industry and commerce.[14]

After the destruction of the Society of the Rights of Man by repressive legislation in 1834, local republican activities became more dominated by liberals who favored working alongside the dynastic liberal opposition within the restricted confines of the electoral arena. The alliance between liberal Republicans and the left dynastic opposition was consolidated in 1837 when national Republican leaders joined forces with the left dynastic opposition to create a joint electoral committee for the 1837 election.[15] In 1838, Lafitte was president of the committee that organized a petition campaign, not for universal male suffrage, but for extending the suffrage to all National Guardsmen and allowing all electors to run for office. None of the government reports of the late 1830s on the local Republican party mention workers. In response to an inquiry from the prefect concerning a purported Parisian conspiracy, the central police commissioner insisted that the working class of Rouen was not at all interested in politics and that the national election of 1839 did not attract their attention.[16] The liberal alliance was successful in the 1842 Chamber of Deputies election, capturing three of four contested seats.

During the early 1840s, some of Rouen's workers became active in the Icarian communist movement, but local participation remained confined to artisans and failed to attract the city's more numerous textile factory workers. Close proximity to Paris, where the movement was headquartered, made it easier for the capital's activists to organize in Rouen, but by 1846 there were only 61 subscribers to Cabet's newspaper, *Le Populaire*, compared to 136 in Toulouse. Icarian communist and republican socialist workers in Rouen collaborated closely in the struggle for suffrage reform. In July 1840, the socialist weaver Charles Noiret presided over two working-class banquets for suffrage reform, at which toasts were made to electoral reform, fraternity, the equality of all men of all colors, and the abolition of exploitation. Speakers called for "organizing work along egalitarian lines," and argued that unless political reform was accompanied by social reform, "the numerous class of proletarians, of workers . . . will continue to vegetate in isolation and servitude. . . ."[17] A police raid on Noiret's home discovered a letter, dated August 17, 1840, from a group of communist workers in Rouen to Parisian communists congratulating them on the Belleville banquet, which marked their split with Republicans.[18] When Étienne Cabet visited Rouen in December 1843, he dined with nine of his local followers, discussed plans to move the newspaper *Le Populaire* from Paris to Rouen, and made plans for speeches to gatherings of workers during a subsequent visit.[19] Cabet also had lunch with radical republican leader Frédéric Deschamps, who maintained cordial relations with Icarian communists.

Radical and socialist Republicans cooperated with Icarian communists in efforts to mobilize the city's factory workers after 1844. They created an association in April 1844 to simultaneously solicit subscriptions and shares for *Le Populaire* and the radical republican newspaper *La Réforme*. This was accompanied by a plan, initiated by Noiret, to start a local monthly newspaper, *Le Journal des ouvriers rouennais*, which was never realized.[20] Republican socialists and Icarians also cooperated during the petition campaign promoted by *La Réforme* in 1844, gathering signatures among the city's textile factory workers. The petition, addressed to the Chamber of Deputies, called for the central government to conduct a nationwide survey to determine the "causes and extent of suffering" of the working class. The central police commissioner estimated that activists were likely to obtain ten thousand signatures from workers in the city and surrounding area.[21] Radical leader Frédéric Deschamps gained local prominence in May 1846 for his role in defending the striking textile factory workers of Elbeuf.

Rouen's radical Republicans and Icarian communists maintained cordial and cooperative relations despite growing hostility between Icarians and radical Republicans at the national level after 1845.[22] In April 1847, the Icarian newspaper, *Le Populaire*, financially pressed by the large security deposit required in Paris, moved to Rouen, where it was published as a weekly.[23] In July 1847, after the editor was arrested for submitting a false declaration in registering the newspaper, Deschamps came to his aid, volunteering his services as defense attorney and winning the praise of Icarian leaders for his role in the case. Liberal republican leaders distanced themselves from the Icarians and from the proclamations of radicals like Deschamps. They feared that association with such elements would alienate members of the propertied electorate and offend their dynastic liberal electoral allies.

During the final years of the July Monarchy, radical republican leaders challenged the liberal republicanism of the *Journal de Rouen* and sided with textile factory workers in their struggles against employers. In December 1846, a group of radicals, led by Deschamps, unsuccessfully attempted to create a newspaper entitled *Le Travailleur normand* as an alternative to the *Journal de Rouen*. Although this initiative came from bourgeois Republicans, not workers, the plan called for the inclusion of a number of workers on the board of directors. The nine members of the board included a lawyer, a merchant, a rentier, a property owner, and a manufacturer, as well as four workers, chosen by Deschamps, one from each of the major textile towns of the region—Elbeuf, Darnétal, Déville, and Rouen.[24] When workers at the Aroux spinning factory in Elbeuf went on strike in May 1846, to protest dismissals of female workers following the adoption of new machinery, over four thousand demonstrators took to the streets amid chants of the *Marseillaise*, threatening to destroy the machinery. Among the eighteen workers arrested during these disorders were a number of republican artisans (a butcher, four masons, a carpenter, and a shoemaker) who had joined the struggle of the factory workers. Deschamps, defense attorney for the arrested strikers, mounted an impassioned defense that helped rally factory workers to the cause of the social republic.[25]

During the 1846 electoral campaign, radical Republicans formed a *Comité radical* which challenged the liberal republican alliance with the dynastic opposition. In a statement of principles published during the campaign, they called for "profound, immense, and complete reform of the parliamentary and electoral world." They also insisted on making the social question central to the republican agenda, declaring: "It is time to seek to eliminate this deplorable and frightening antagonism between the worker and the employer that our current laws only perpetuate; it is necessary to work without respite on the solution of an issue that threatens, if we do not take care to do something, to cover with blood all of our manufacturing towns. . . ."[26]

The economic crisis of 1846–47 provided new opportunities for Rouen's radicals to recruit popular support.[27] Workers bore the brunt of the crisis as poor harvests, high bread prices, and the threat of famine were accompanied by widespread unemployment. Some employers responded to the crisis by cutting wages. In October 1847, workers at the spinning factory of Albert Menage in Elbeuf went on strike in response to a wage cut. Amid chants of the *Marseillaise*, a crowd of around six hundred strikers demonstrated in front of the factory. The attorney general in Rouen insisted that the insurrectionary dispositions of these spinning workers were not a product of low wages or suffering but a result of "the pernicious influence of communist agitators who remain in the shadows. . . ."[28] Republican candidates benefited from the crisis, and from their attacks on the government's railway policies and official corruption, winning growing support from the city's 3,502 eligible voters. Republican electoral support was strongest among poorer members of the liberal professions, especially lawyers, professors, and doctors who earned more than the two hundred francs in taxes needed to qualify for the suffrage, and among small shopkeepers and artisans who barely qualified for suffrage rights.[29] In 1846, Republicans secured a majority on Rouen's city council. According to a secret government report, twenty-one of the thirty-nine members of the council belonged to the republican opposition, five of whom were newly elected.[30]

The issue of railroad policy enabled liberal and radical republican candidates to mobilize support across class lines by acting as defenders of local interests against both the orleanist central state and a powerful company owned mainly by Parisian finance capital. Republicans denounced the Laffitte-Blount company's poor service and high prices and called for greater government regulation of the railway companies. The liberal republican *Journal de Rouen* complained about insufficient service, poorly maintained equipment, and high rates due to the absence of competition. It denounced the Parisian speculators who owned the railroad and warned that their enormous power threatened to create "a feudalism of a new type."[31] In November 1846, the mayor, in response to a city council request, wrote the Minister of Public Works to inform him of the Paris-Rouen railway's plan to discontinue service at the Saint-Sever station, which meant the elimination of numerous jobs in this working-class neighborhood. In March 1847, after the company published its new schedule, the central government responded to a second protest by informing the mayor that the company had received provisional approval of its new schedule. The city council then sent a delegation of its members to Paris to protest government approval of what it considered to be a violation of the company's contract with the city. In June 1847, after failing to receive a satisfactory response from the central government, the city council threatened to resign. Twenty of thirty-five council members voted to withhold approval of further municipal funds until the mayor agreed to quickly convene the council's railroad committee, which would initiate legal proceedings against the railroad company. After city council members angrily accused the mayor of siding with the central government against the interests of the city, the mayor and his assistants (*adjoints*) handed in their resignation.[32]

Although radical Republicans did not have their own newspaper, they were well financed, due to generous contributions from wealthy bourgeois supporters like the millionaire Achille Lemasson. When fiscal pressures drove the radical republican newspaper *La Réforme* toward the verge of collapse, its Parisian editors, Louis Blanc and Marc Caussidière, came to Rouen, where they were able to quickly raise thirty thousand francs from radical republican leaders.[33] Radical Republicans gathered regularly in the evening at the café Dubuc, in meetings which attracted around forty participants—workers as well as bourgeois. Rouen's radicals collaborated with Icarian communist workers in the 1847 campaign for universal male suffrage.[34] But they broke ranks with liberal Republicans, who joined the dynastic opposition on the *Comité constitutionnel*, which led the banquet campaign for suffrage reform in Rouen.

The banquets organized by the liberal alliance were dominated by privileged members of the propertied electorate. The speeches given at these banquets were relatively conservative in tone, advocating suffrage reform rather than universal male suffrage and ignoring the social question. The largest banquet in Rouen, which took place on Christmas day of 1847, attracted eighteen hundred participants, fourteen hundred of whom were already eligible voters. The liberal republican lawyer Jules Senard was president of the banquet. Speakers called for a reform of suffrage laws, but not for universal male suffrage, a project which Senard relegated to "the very distant future." Rouen's radicals and socialists boycotted the banquet after Senard refused to replace a toast to "the institutions of 1830" with a toast to "the revolution of 1830." Radical leaders Frédéric Deschamps, Buchet-Bellanger, and Félix Avril drafted a statement justifying their boycott and harshly condemning the liberal republican alliance with monarchists: "What can be the product of uniting heterogeneous elements, even on the question of suffrage reform, as in the rubbing of elbows between the dynastic left and the democrats? . . . Are there only slight differences between these two doctrines? No, there is deep-seated and visceral opposition. . . . According to one, the right to vote is a function assigned to a more or less restricted group of privileged [men]; according to the other, voting is a right that belongs to everyone. . . . This attempt at fusion between irreconcilable doctrines can only result in dealings unworthy of all men of serious and sound convictions. . . . No one can be so blind today as to believe that those who lead these demonstrations seriously want to extend to the so-called lower classes an equality of rights, of education, and of work. . . ."[35]

Although working within the narrow confines of an electoral arena that excluded workers, liberal Republicans and their dynastic liberal allies won three legislative seats in 1842 and captured municipal power in 1846. Though successful in the electoral arena, this strategy of contention for power meant the exclusion of workers from republican politics. This helped foster the growth of an Icarian communist movement, but the movement remained rooted in the relatively small local artisanate. It wasn't until after 1844 that textile factory workers became the targets of political mobilization, when radical Republicans mobilized them under the banner of universal male suffrage and the "social republic." Rouen's radical Republicans maintained good working relations with Icarian communists as well as strong ties to working-class socialists, but they were at odds with liberal Republicans. This division, which intensified after the Revolution of 1848, shaped the direction of the new republic.

The Second Republic in Rouen

The revolution of 1848 placed municipal power in the hands of radical and socialist Republicans, but only after a bitter struggle between liberal and radical party leaders. The *Comité radical démocratique* appointed five radicals and socialists to temporarily oversee the municipal government: the lawyers Frédéric Deschamps and Auguste Bachelet, the wealthy property owner Achille Lemasson, the Icarian communist tailor Victor Prosper, and the weaver Florentin Gruel.[36] After Deschamps refused to enlarge the delegation that he was leading to Paris to consult with the new government, the liberal republican *Comité d'opposition républicaine*, led by newly appointed attorney general Jules Senard, sent its own delegation. Deschamps was welcomed by the new Minister of the Interior, Ledru-Rollin, who appointed him to the region's highest post, special commissioner of the republic. Rouen's National Guard, which remained dominated by royalists, threatened to prevent Deschamps from taking office. They sent a delegation to Paris to protest the decision and tried to persuade central state officials to appoint someone else. Senard informed the royalist general Victor de Castellane, commander of Rouen's military division, that he had taken a number of measures to prevent Deschamps's return from Paris. Senard and other liberal Republicans distrusted the new commissioner because of his role in the boycott of their reform banquet of 1847 and his close ties to socialist and communist leaders. Their fears were quickly confirmed when Deschamps appointed a new municipal government dominated by radicals and socialists. Deschamps selected a mayor and four deputy mayors who were members of the *Comité radical*, allocated two-thirds of the seats on the city council to radical Republicans and workers, and named an Icarian communist, Victor Prosper, as central police commissioner.[37] Tensions between liberal and radical Republicans were further exacerbated by Deschamps's replacement of numerous administrative officials by radical club leaders whom Senard denounced as unqualified.[38]

On February 25, news of the proclamation of the republic was greeted by crowds of workers and large demonstrations. To avoid a violent confrontation between workers and soldiers, General de Castellane ordered all troops withdrawn from Rouen, leaving only four hundred National Guardsmen to police the city. The general justified his decision to remove troops to the northwestern heights of Mont-Riboudet as a measure that would prevent workers from the surrounding textile towns from descending on Rouen.[39] That evening, amid shouts of "Long Live the Republic!" and "Down with the English!" workers pillaged railway stations at Saint-Sever and la rue Verte and burned down the wooden supports of the Brouilly railroad bridge, known as "the English bridge." The following days were marked by attacks against textile factories owned by Englishmen in Sotteville, and a factory occupation that prompted the dismissal of fifty English and Irish workers hired to run the new machines at the La Foudre spinning factory. These actions expressed a hostility toward the railway company that had been encouraged by the Republican-controlled municipal government's agitation against the "rail monopoly" during the final days of the July Monarchy.[40] They also expressed strong anti-English sentiment, fostered by the role of English technicians and capitalists in technical innovations that proletarianized textile factory work, by the contribution of Englishmen to French railway development that threatened dock workers and boat operators, and by resentment against English workers and foremen during a period of high unemployment.

The initial days of the February Revolution were marked by factory workers' protests. In the textile town of Elbeuf, workers burned down the Grandin factory. Workers from the industrial valleys surrounding Rouen left their factories to demonstrate at the homes of their wealthy employers, parading through Rouen's wealthy *faubourg Cauchoise*, the neighborhood where most of the region's textile industrialists lived. On February 26, these incidents led the city council to request the return to the city of army troops, commanded by the royalist general de Castellane. Castellane, who had initially considered leading orleanist military resistance to the new republic, demanded the declaration of a state of siege in Rouen and control over the municipal government in return for "maintaining order."[41] Although the city council refused to accede to his demands, Castellane allowed his troops to return to Rouen and aid the National Guard in repressing working-class protests.

On February 27, five hundred textile factory workers from the Pavilly and Barentin valleys paraded through the region, demanding a shorter workday. Another column of rebellious textile factory workers in the Austreberthe valley northwest of Rouen marched to demand better wages and the reform of factory regulations.[42] A group of textile factory workers from Malaunay forced their employer, who was delinquent in paying their wages, to march barefoot to Rouen with a rope around his neck. At the beginning of March, the six hundred factory workers employed by Graindot at Lillebonne attacked their employer's home, breaking windows and destroying furniture. "The main effect of the February Revolution," wrote one official reflecting on these events nearly two years later, "was to arouse the lower classes of society and to abruptly and violently alter all relationships of subordination and hierarchy. . . ."[43]

The new radical republican commissioner, Frédéric Deschamps, hoped to put an end to the protests by persuading workers to express their grievances via petitions rather than in the streets. On February 29, he issued a proclamation urging workers to submit their grievances in writing to the government. The region's workers responded in large numbers, gathering thousands of signatures on petitions that carefully documented their economic grievances. They urged government intervention to ensure higher wages, shorter working hours, and better working conditions.[44] Deschamps's effort to seriously respond to these petitions antagonized Rouen's bourgeoisie, who viewed meddlesome government officials with the same hostility they had toward rebellious workers. Deschamps decreed a reduction in the hours of textile spinning and weaving factories, negotiated an agreement for shorter hours and minimum wages for dyers, established new rules governing work on the docks, strictly limited night work in factories, and ordered a uniform piece-rate scale for all cotton spinning mills. This last measure passed along the productivity benefits reaped by the recent introduction of larger mule jennies with more spindles to workers rather than their employers.[45] Rouen's factory owners resisted the measure as a socialist attack on private property that would eliminate incentives to invest in new machinery. Deschamps also organized departmental workshops to provide jobs for the region's numerous unemployed textile workers. He appointed a committee that raised sixty-five thousand francs to help the unemployed, approved a new ten-centime tax to help finance Rouen's municipal workshops, and ordered the release of all those imprisoned for debt.[46] In early March, Deschamps angered local church officials by forcing the archbishop to turn over 10,500 francs to the government, to aid the region's unemployed workers. The money had been collected as charity in 1845 to help the victims of a flood that destroyed three spinning factories and killed seventy workers at Montville, but church officials kept the funds to pay for an annual solemn mass for the victims.[47] Deschamps also acknowledged workers' right to organize and opened up the city's public schools in the evenings for workers' meetings, providing them with free paper, pens, and ink.

Deschamps's concessions failed to halt working-class protests, which continued throughout the month of March, a time of rising unemployment. Unemployed workers at the municipal workshops frequently paraded through the inner city, joined by large numbers of women and children, with music and tricolor flags leading the way. Thousands of workers gathered regularly in the city's more than twenty-three political clubs, which served as an arena for impassioned political debates. H. Dahubert, a representative from the Paris Club of Clubs, estimated that there were more than twenty clubs in Rouen. The three largest clubs were *La Tribune du peuple*, *Le Parisien*, and *Le Démocrate*, which Dahubert criticized for their socialist rhetoric and for rules prohibiting bourgeois participation.[48] The presidents, vice-presidents, and secretaries of fifteen of Rouen's radical and socialist clubs met daily at the *Club central démocratique*, led by the socialist shopkeeper Louis Durand, who directed the city's municipal workshops.[49] During the month of April 1848, Rouen's club leaders also collaborated with the former *Comité radical*, renamed *La Société égalité*, to publish a newspaper, *La Tribune du peuple*.

At the end of March, growing working-class protests further frightened an already anxious bourgeoisie. On March 27, a crowd of over two thousand workers from the textile centers of Sotteville, Déville, Maromme, and Quevilly, led by the republican socialist mayor of Sotteville, Leon Salva, and the son of Rouen's mayor, paraded along the docks and then marched to the Bicêtre prison where they demanded the release of workers arrested during the recent protests. Radical republican leaders, including deputy mayor Baudoin, city councilmen Delzeuzes, Lefevre, and Lemassson, and the working-class leader Charles Noiret, tried to dissuade the crowd from attacking the prison. The demonstrators, armed with hammers and knives, stormed the prison and forced guards to release a worker arrested for his role in burning down the railroad bridge. Troops and National Guardsmen arrived on the scene after the rioters departed.[50] The following day, a crowd of several hundred workers from the textile town of Maromme arrived in Rouen intent on freeing their recently convicted leaders. Deschamps persuaded the crowd to disperse, promising that he would expedite the appeal of their conviction.

The events of late March prompted republican officials to clamp down on working-class protests. In early April, National Guardsmen and soldiers were quickly dispatched to deal with agitation in the textile towns of Darnétal, Brionne, and Bernay. Deschamps declared all demonstrations illegal, proclaiming: "Order and authority must reappear. No authority and no form of government can tolerate such excesses."[51] On April 1, encouraged by recent events in Rouen, textile factory workers in the town of Lillebonne, carrying a tricolor flag and a liberty tree that they wanted to plant on the square where soldiers were stationed, threatened to hold officials hostage at city hall until their arrested leaders and comrades were released from prison. After demonstrators threw stones, National Guardsmen and soldiers opened fire, killing six workers, including two women, and wounding twenty-two. Local industrialists and liberal republican leaders blamed radical Republicans for inciting working-class agitation. The attorney general, Senard, in reporting on the massacre at Lillebonne, blamed agents of Rouen's *Comité démocratique* who, claiming to act under authorization from Deschamps, were "provoking and exciting the working masses against the manufacturers and, in general, against the rich and the bourgeoisie."[52] Rouen's *Comité démocratique*, wary of the official investigation headed by Senard, launched their own alternative inquiry of the Lillebonne massacre, but Deschamps criticized this challenge to established judicial authorities and refused to receive their report.[53]

Although liberal Republicans remained hostile to radical leaders like Deschamps, they were committed to a republican form of government. This was not the case, however, for many of the city's bourgeoisie, who regretted the downfall of the orleanist monarchy. Bourgeois opposition to the new republic focused around two key issues: working-class access to the National Guard and municipal workshops for the unemployed. On March 24, a delegation of club leaders met with Deschamps to request arms for the city's clubs, but Deschamps turned them down, promising to expand the city's National Guard to include workers. Deschamps failed to democratize the local militia, however, fearing that efforts to force the Guard to accept workers would result in violence.[54] Deschamps did not dismiss the National Guard colonel Bligny, whose commitment to the new republic was questionable, although he did appoint liberal Republican Auguste-Théodore Visinet, former director of the *Journal de Rouen*, as lieutenant-colonel of the militia, and radical leaders Mathieu d'Epinal and Henri Mesley as Guard commanders. Deschamps also requested two thousand rifles and one thousand swords from the Minister of War to arm new Guard members, and appointed radical leader Achille Lemasson to oversee the recruitment of new Guardsmen. But these plans to expand and democratize the citizens' militia were never carried out.

Rouen's bourgeois National Guardsmen resisted efforts to open the ranks of the citizens' militia to workers, and overtly demonstrated their hostility toward the new republic. When an official read the telegram announcing the appointment of Deschamps, several angry National Guard officers discussed using force to prevent him from assuming his post.[55] National Guardsmen welcomed Deschamps to the prefecture with jeers, whistles, and shouts of "Down with Deschamps!" They physically abused deputy mayor Auguste Bachelet, and routinely harassed other radical members of the council when they arrived at city hall. National Guardsmen shouted "Long Live the King!" during the early days of the revolution and refused to join in cries of "Long Live the Republic!" during the official ceremony of April 9 to inaugurate the new republic by planting a liberty tree. After this tree was mysteriously uprooted during the night of April 10–11, Rouen's workers organized their own unarmed brigade to protect the three trees that were planted in its place. They attributed the incident to National Guardsmen, who were widely regarded as enemies of the republic.

A second key issue that angered local conservatives concerned government efforts to deal with the growing ranks of the unemployed. The municipal workshops for the unemployed supported fourteen thousand workers by mid-April and placed a serious drain on the municipal budget. After borrowing half a million francs and lowering workshop wages, the government was forced to increase taxes by 10 percent on March 14. This measure alienated many small shopkeepers and master artisans and angered local conservatives, who regarded the workshops as publicly subsidized revolutionary clubs for lazy workers. The Rouen Court of Appeals, responsible for drawing up accusations against those charged with fomenting the April 1848 insurrection, characterized the municipal workshops as "a vast hotbed of insurrection" where "workers were incessantly incited against employers, where the most perverse doctrines were taught, which can be summarized by the following words: Hatred and death to the rich, to all those who own, to all friends of order and of true liberty. . . ."[56] Unemployed workers of the municipal workshops joined together in singing republican anthems, listening to speeches from radical orators and socialist members of the new city council, and discussing the "democratic and social republic" and the "right to work." The city council convened a special session on April 19 to investigate complaints of corruption and mismanagement of the workshops, and to interrogate the director, socialist club leader Louis Durand, who was also president of the *Comité démocratique*. Deschamps promptly intervened by declaring the session illegal, claiming that the city council was exceeding its authority, since the director of the workshops was responsible to him and not to the city council.[57]

The campaign that preceded the Constituent Assembly election of April 23–24 revealed deep divisions among Rouen's Republicans. There were four lists of nineteen candidates presented to the city's voters: the liberal republican *Comité central républicain* list headed by Alphonse de Lamartine and Jules Senard; the radical republican *Comité central démocratique* list headed by Deschamps; a slate of royalist sympathizers presented by the *Comité départemental des amis de l'ordre et de la liberté*; and a fourth list of candidates presented by Icarian communists who, because of their role in the attack on the Bicêtre prison, were expelled from the *Comité central démocratique* on April 7 and excluded from the radical and socialist slates.[58]

During the electoral campaign, liberals joined radicals and socialists in attempting to attract working-class voters. Liberal republican candidates, like the factory foreman Louis Demarest, called for lower taxes on basic necessities and a maximum limit on hours of work. Liberal Republicans proclaimed their support for "an improvement of the conditions of workers without injuring those of industrialists" and a rejection of "all theories that injure property or liberty."[59] Conservative candidates denounced Deschamps and depicted their opponents as socialist agitators who would increase taxes to support lazy workers and ensure a prolonged economic crisis by frightening investors. Preparations for the election included fistfights between those who hung rival wall posters. Rouen's workers, who had managed to win important concessions from employers due to the intervention of Deschamps, feared that an electoral defeat would mean an end to workshops for the unemployed and a retraction of Deschamps's concessions.

The April 23 election provided the occasion for the first large-scale bloody confrontation of the Second Republic.[60] Twelve candidates who appeared on both the liberal republican and royalist slates, and seven candidates who ran only on the royalist list, won seats. The radical list carried the textile factory towns of Darnétal and Maromme and did well in Rouen, but failed to win many rural votes. Deschamps won 13,073 (50%) of Rouen's 25,925 votes but did poorly in the rural areas of the department. When election results were announced on April 27, workers gathered in front of city hall, which was surrounded by armed National Guardsmen. Afraid that demonstrators would try to destroy the ballots or seize weapons stored at city hall, guardsmen evicted a group from the galleries of the building. In the courtyard surrounding the building, tensions mounted between the National Guardsmen and the predominantly working-class crowd, which included large numbers of women and children. After a group of angry guardsmen seized a flag from parading working-class children who were singing republican anthems, scuffles broke out and the crowd responded with stones. Demonstrators attempted to disarm National Guardsmen arriving at city hall, who then fired on the workers and killed one of them.[61] Troops cleared the square, as demonstrators retreated to the surrounding streets where they were pursued by troops.

Word quickly spread through the city of the killing at city hall. Workers began constructing thirty-six barricades in the surrounding Martainville neighborhood. There were soon over forty barricades in the city. The next morning, on April 28, troops and National Guardsmen dismantled barricades on the right bank, in Martainville, then crossed the river to confront those on the barricades in the working-class neighborhoods of Saint-Sever and Sotteville, where the city's largest textile factories were located. The barricade on the rue St. Julien, defended by around seven hundred textile workers, was blown up by cannon fire. The insurrection was defeated by nightfall. Thirty-four insurgents, but no soldiers or National Guardsmen, were killed in the fighting.[62]

The authorities were anxious to quickly put an end to the insurrection, before textile workers from the surrounding valleys could march to the aid of their Rouen comrades. Workers in Elbeuf built barricades to prevent their city's National Guard from departing for Rouen, and those of Lalonde, led by the mayor, tried to join the Elbeuf workers. Troops were stationed at Mont-Riboudet to prevent textile workers from the surrounding valleys from descending on the city. The general commanding the troops in Rouen reported that the decision to use artillery against the insurgents was largely motivated by the hope that the sound of cannons would frighten workers in the surrounding textile valleys.[63]

The repression of the uprising was followed by a right-wing reign of terror carried out by the National Guard. The liberal Republican, Hippolyte Dussard, who replaced Deschamps on April 30, described the Guard's behavior, which he characterized as "despotic," as follows: "They placed the city in a virtual state of siege. A large beard was cause for suspicion and a worker's smock was poorly regarded . . . they forced everyone to show them their hands and attacked a deputy mayor. There are even stories that they fired at people looking out of windows, wounding one woman in her bedroom. . . . After the victory, everything republican was suspect."[64] Five hundred and twenty-one suspected insurgents were arrested, including most of the city's club leaders. Two hundred of them were immediately released and only eighty-one insurgents were later brought to trial. Available records, which designate the occupations of seventy-seven of those tried, reveal the multiclass character of republicanism. A majority (77%) of the seventy-seven were workers. Alongside twenty-three textile factory workers were five building trades artisans, twelve metalworkers, thirteen day laborers, two dockers, three street vendors, and one domestic servant. In addition to these fifty-nine workers, there were nine shopkeepers, three master artisans, a professor, a journalist, a doctor, and three clerks.[65]

Rouen's republican socialists blamed the insurrection on the refusal of the bourgeoisie to accept the republic and grant workers their legitimate right to bear arms. "The bourgeoisie," proclaimed *La Sentinelle des travailleurs*, "did not want the republic, or wanted it for its exclusive benefit. . . . In vain the people tried to exercise citizenship by demanding arms as a guarantee of their rights. Equality demanded this. . . ."[66] The defense attorney for those arrested for their role in the insurrection blamed the uprising on republican hostility toward the conservative citizens' militia, which personified the continuing power of royalists despite the advent of a republic. "If there was an insurrection against anything," he argued, "it was against the uniforms of the National Guard."[67]

The defeat of Rouen's insurrection was followed by the withdrawal from office of the city's radical and socialist political leaders, and the repeal of programs they had implemented. Deschamps, who along with other radical leaders had unsuccessfully urged the city's workers not to take up arms, resigned his post on April 30. He was soon followed by radical and socialist republican municipal leaders, including mayor Charles Alexandre Leballeur-Villiers. The partial election, held on May 30 to fill three seats in the Constituent Assembly, generated divisions among liberal Republicans over the decision to include the royalist factory owner Eugène-Émile Loyer on their list. Dissident liberals, who opposed joining a party of order alliance, created their own *Comité de l'unité républicaine*, which replaced Loyer with liberal republican mayor Bobée. Many radicals and socialists urged abstention to protest the recent repression. In an election in which only 49 percent of Rouen's 28,954 registered voters participated, the liberal republican candidates supported by the *Journal de Rouen* were defeated by royalist candidates Eugène-Émile Loyer, Adolphe Thiers, and Charles Dupin. The radical slate won only 3,385 (26%) of the city's 14,183 votes. After the election, government officials retracted various concessions that had been made by Deschamps. The city council reorganized the municipal workshops, which were later dissolved on June 7. On June 16, the new prefect Hippolyte Dussard rescinded the decree raising wages for factory workers.

The Parisian insurrection in June did not generate any protests in Rouen, but it did prompt further conservative reaction, including the arrest of the editors of the city's two socialist newspapers, *L'Association libre des travailleurs* and *La Sentinelle des travailleurs*. These arrests put an end to their publication. Liberal republican authorities who rose to power during the summer of 1848 proclaimed their adherence to the republic and expressed a desire to improve the lot of the working class, but they were intolerant of demonstrations, strikes, and workers' associations. "Disorder and the republic are incompatible," proclaimed the new prefect Dussard on July 3, in a warning to Rouen's workers. "Those who foment disorder are not Republicans!" he asserted, in a proclamation threatening to severely punish all strikers and strike organizers.[68] The liberal republican *Journal de Rouen* urged its readers to join forces with other "men of order."[69] In the municipal election that followed on July 30, Rouen's radical republican candidates, supported by the *Comité d'égalité*, suffered yet another defeat. Eleven of the thirty-nine candidates on the liberal republican list also appeared on the royalist list, headed by legitimist leader Taillet and the orleanist former mayor Fleury. The Orleanist-dominated conservative slate swept the election, capturing twenty-seven of the thirty-nine contested seats.

Louis Napoleon Bonaparte was swept to power in the presidential election of December 1848, winning 79 percent of the votes in the department, with 17 percent going to liberal Republican Cavaignac and 7 percent to the radical candidate Ledru-Rollin. Louis Napoleon captured 78 percent of Rouen's 26,844 votes, compared to 3,654 (14%) for Cavaignac and only 1,851 (7%) for Ledru-Rollin.[70] Louis Napoleon's candidacy attracted substantial support among the city's workers, many of whom were won over by pro-working-class Bonapartist propaganda. In the heavily working-class district of the 6th canton, which had recently elected Deschamps to the *conseil général*, Louis Napoleon won 81 percent of the vote. Rouen was the only one of the eight largest cities in France to give Bonaparte more than the national average vote. Soon after the election, at the end of January 1849, the central government replaced liberal republican prefect Dussard with the Orleanist Ernest Le Roy.

During the presidential election campaign, radicals and socialists gathered regularly at the Club Nitrière, where between seven hundred and twelve hundred members heard orators denounce the violence of the barricades in favor of an electoral route to power. Speakers also condemned inequalities of wealth and inequitable taxes, praised the virtues of consumer cooperatives and workers' associations, exposed the dangers of free trade, and called for increased government intervention in industrial relations.[71] Club members expressed support for very different visions of socialism, espousing the ideas of Étienne Cabet, Pierre-Joseph Proudhon, and Louis Blanc, in a display of political diversity that often produced disruptive meetings. Although followers of Proudhon and supporters of Bonaparte spoke out against Ledru-Rollin's presidential candidacy in December 1848, the majority of club members and leaders actively supported his presidential campaign.

A local branch of Republican Solidarity was founded in Rouen at the beginning of 1849. The first meeting of the group, on January 14, attracted only two hundred people, mainly workers and leaders of the *Nitrière* club. It was broken up by police. Efforts to bring liberal Republicans into the Mountain alliance, in order to defeat the "party of order" slate in the May 1849 election, provoked sharp divisions that led to the dissolution of the *Nitrière* club. Following Frédéric Deschamps, the socialist shoemaker Pierre Letellier, who was the club's president, and club orators Leon Salva and Pierre Duboc allowed their names to appear on both the republican socialist ticket and the liberal republican slate headed by Jules Senard. This attempted alliance provoked bitter accusations of betrayal at a divisive final meeting of the club on May 12.

Prior to the 1849 election, liberal republican leaders joined conservative authorities in the prosecution of radical and socialist leaders of the Mountain. Five leaders of Republican Solidarity, two of whom were candidates in the upcoming election, were tried for illegal associational activity. At the trial on March 16–17, the prosecuting attorney, liberal Republican Louis Philippe Desseaux, insisted that the association was really a political club rather than a legitimate electoral organization. Although three prominent radical leaders were convicted and sentenced to several months in prison and fines of one hundred francs, Mountain organizers managed to launch a newspaper, *Le Républicain de Rouen*, on May 9, just before the National Assembly election. On May 12 and 13, police raided its offices, eliminating the central organizational nexus of the Mountain's electoral campaign.

Despite the polarized political atmosphere, Republicans remained divided for the election of May 13, 1849. The three electoral lists of candidates included a Mountain list headed by Ledru-Rollin and supported by *Le Républicain de Rouen*, a liberal republican slate headed by Senard and Cavaignac and supported by the *Journal de Rouen*, and a "party of order" list headed by Thiers and supported by *Le Mémorial*. Although four of the candidates on the Mountain list agreed to appear on the liberal republican slate, *Le Républicain de Rouen* denounced such an alliance as treasonous.[72] Mountain candidates appealed to class interests and antagonisms in soliciting the votes of workers and peasants, promising that a "democratic and social republic" would reduce inequalities of wealth and power.[73] In contrast to the 1848 electoral slate, the Mountain list of 1849, organized by the *Comité central démocratique*, included the Icarian communist weaver Dominique Gruel, although Mountain candidates distanced themselves from communism by preaching respect for property and the family.

Election results revealed the inability of the Mountain to mobilize support in the rural areas of the department, where conservative candidates triumphed. In an election in which 68 percent of the department's registered voters participated, the party of order slate captured all sixteen contested seats, winning between 71,085 and 108,510 votes (49–74%), compared to totals ranging from 34,865 to 40,775 (24–28%) for candidates on the Mountain list. The election also revealed the progress of radicals and socialists since April 1848, when Deschamps's slate won only 24,000 to 33,000 votes. In 1849, candidates on the liberal republican list won only 14,564 to 25,667 votes (10–18%), with Deschamps outpolling Senard by 40,700 to 19,000 votes.

After the election, at the beginning of June, authorities launched a series of prosecutions aimed at local leaders of the Mountain. Charles Furet, editor of *Le Républicain de Rouen*, was charged with insulting the generals who commanded the repression of the June 1848 Parisian insurrection and sentenced to two months imprisonment. Leon Salva, former mayor and National Guard commander of the working-class suburb of Sotteville, was sentenced to five months in prison and a five hundred franc fine for shouting "Long Live the Democratic and Social Republic!" *Le Républicain de Rouen* temporarily ceased publication on June 13, after authorities seized the paper for printing an appeal for armed resistance to the invasion of Rome and demanded an additional fifteen hundred francs in security deposit.[74] Although there was no armed uprising to support the June 1849 insurrection in Paris, the department was placed under a state of siege, and the city's most prominent radical leaders were arrested for voicing support for the rebellion.

After their defeat in the April election, and their replacement in key administrative positions by royalist officials during the summer of 1849, liberal Republicans dropped their vehement antisocialist rhetoric. Radicals joined the effort to unify Republicans, with *Le Républicain de Rouen* reminding its readers of the need for unity among "democrats of all nuances" in the face of the royalist threat.[75] In the partial election of October 14, 1849, radical republican candidate Deschamps ran against the former orleanist mayor of Elbeuf, Mathieu Bourdon. Though critical of Bourdon in the *Journal de Rouen*, and wary of a royalist victory, liberal Republicans failed to actively support Deschamps, who lost the election, which was marked by a high level (56%) of abstentions. Although Deschamps won fewer than the nearly 40,000 votes that the Mountain had garnered in May 1849, the left's proportion of the total vote increased from 28 to 34 percent. The region's rural voters once again elected the conservative candidate, who won 61,631 votes (66%) compared to 31,734 (34%) for Deschamps. In Rouen, the Mountain triumphed, with Deschamps carrying the city by a narrow margin of 8,787 to 8,310 votes.

Electoral defeat did not discourage Republicans from pursuing a parliamentary road to power, but it did prompt them to concentrate on mobilizing rural support under the banner of republican socialism. The biweekly Mountain newspaper, *Le Progressif cauchois*, published in Fécamp, attracted a large number of peasant readers. In November 1849, after a conviction for press crimes destroyed *Le Républicain de Rouen*, radicals and socialists launched the monthly newspaper *L'Émancipation normande*, which was edited by workers, including the former *Nitrière* club president Pierre Letellier. Espousing an associationalist vision of socialism, the newspaper made an effort to speak to the concerns and grievances of the region's peasants. By the beginning of 1850, it had become a weekly paper with a circulation of fifteen hundred to seventeen hundred. The motto on its masthead revealed Republicans' abiding faith in universal male suffrage: "Courage, perseverance, devotion, prudence. With education and universal suffrage, the future is the will of the people."

The restrictive electoral law of May 31, 1850 deprived republican socialists of their political control of the predominantly working-class municipalities of Sotteville and Elbeuf. On June 8, 1850, a new law further restricted the press and helped destroy *L'Union démocratique* and *L'Émancipation normande*. Both newspapers folded during the spring and summer
of 1850, following costly prosecutions and convictions. During the fall and
summer of 1850, Republicans organized a network of secret societies dedicated to defending the constitution and organizing the disenfranchised to
demand the right to vote in the 1852 presidential and National Assembly
election. Disunity within the party of order and rural propaganda by the
Mountain, during a time of falling agricultural prices and growing unemployment, made the authorities fear the approaching 1852 election. The
attorney general observed in June 1851: "In the National Assembly election, the issue will everywhere be stated as [a choice] between those who
own and those who own nothing, between the list of the employers and the
list of the workers, and the socialist slate will probably carry most districts.
Universal suffrage was able to function without entirely ruining us in 1848
and 1849, because, on the one hand, all the older parties abandoned their
quarrels and united their influence and, on the other hand, socialist influence hadn't yet invaded everything. But now that we are divided and our
enemies are indivisibly disciplined, chances look different."[76]

Rouen's Republicans anticipated the possibility of a coup d'état and
tried unsuccessfully to unify in the face of the threat. In July 1851, they sent
a delegation of five men to London to meet with exiled Ledru-Rollin and
organize resistance to an anticipated coup attempt by Louis Napoleon.
Growing fears of a coup prompted some liberal Republicans to entertain
the possibility of joining a republican alliance that included socialists. Rit-
tiez, editor of the *Journal de Rouen*, favored such an alliance. He resigned
from his position at the end of November 1851, after a bitter dispute with
the journalist Auguste-Théodore Visinet, whom he denounced for supporting the restrictive electoral law of 1850. Following his departure, the news
paper resumed its antisocialist polemics, eliminating the possibility of
unity among Republicans. The coup arrived before plans for resistance
were organized.

Although the Second Republic marked a turning point in republican politics, in that it witnessed the entrance of male workers onto the electoral
scene, divisions among Republicans that had marked the final years of the
July Monarchy persisted and intensified under the new republic. Liberals
and radicals remained at loggerheads throughout the Second Republic, despite a strong royalist resurgence. Radicals and socialists of the Mountain
alliance retained control of the candidate selection process but, despite
electoral majorities at Rouen, failed to win electoral victories. This was due
to the conservative votes of the countryside and to weak and hesitant liberal

republican support of radical candidates. The subsequent repression of the 1850s transformed the relationship among Rouen's liberal, radical, and socialist Republicans, producing a Republican party with a very different ideology, leadership, and relationship to the city's workers.

THE SECOND EMPIRE IN ROUEN

When news of Louis Napoleon Bonaparte's illegal seizure of power reached Rouen, a group of approximately one hundred local republican leaders gathered at the home of the radical lawyer Félix Limet to plan resistance. Unable to find a local printer willing to publish posters denouncing the coup, Limet and the weaver Eustache Beaufour traveled to Paris where they secured placards. Beaufour was arrested and the posters confiscated on his return to Rouen. While awaiting word from Paris, republican leaders sought to evade police but most were quickly arrested.[77] The city's textile workers did not respond to republican calls for armed resistance. The repression that followed the coup was relatively mild at Rouen. Only nineteen republican militants from the Rouen region were convicted by the mixed commission, with the most severe sentences, deportation to Cayenne and Algeria, reserved for thirteen socialist militants, most of whom had been former leaders of political clubs in 1848.[78]

The repression that followed the coup removed working-class socialist leaders from the scene. The repression that preceded the coup had already destroyed the city's socialist and radical newspapers, *Le Républicain de Rouen*, *L'Émancipation normand*, and *L'Union démocratique*. But radical republican leader Achille Lemasson, a wealthy property owner, managed to run for office in the February–March 1852 legislative election. The liberal republican newspaper, the *Journal de Rouen*, survived the coup, but it refused to support Lemasson's candidacy and did not even print his name. Political repression, administrative pressure and patronage, and widespread abstentions marked the election of 1852. Despite the absence of a campaign organization, Lemasson received 26 percent of the 13,578 votes cast in Rouen, compared to 64 percent for the official candidate, the Orleanist Charles Levasseur, who supported the new regime.[79] Lemasson lost the election by a wider margin in the district, garnering 23 percent of the total vote. The attorney general summarized the political situation in the region in July 1852 as follows: "The irritation of the working class against their employers is a powerful lever for the socialists in this area, but the affection of the workers for Louis Napoleon is also a heavy counterweight."[80]

During the early years of the Empire, government officials reported that the republican socialist agitation that had once aroused the region's workers had disappeared. The attorney general, in July 1854, noted that working-class socialists "have become isolated and form only weak groups without any coherence among them and with little influence on their surroundings. . . ." The following month, he reported that "the socialists, diminished everywhere, nevertheless conserve a certain force in the industrial centers; their old leaders have disappeared and their main organizations have been broken, but the same passions still animate them and new leaders will arise with the first favorable incident. . . ."[81] The most detailed accounts of working-class politics in Rouen during the years 1855–62 are provided by the police spy, Antoine Philippon, who regularly reported to the prefect.[82] Philippon noted that republican socialists had made inroads among skilled factory workers in the machine construction industry and among shoemakers and tailors, and that about one-tenth of the textile factory workers in the Rouen region were hard-core socialists, while another 10 percent were less ardent socialists. According to Philippon's reports, class divisions plagued Rouen's Republicans. Working-class activists criticized radical bourgeois leaders for keeping their distance and failing to inform workers of their plans, while bourgeois radicals worried about the revolutionary ardor of their working-class comrades.

In the 1857 legislative election, the regime designated the wealthy Rouen industrialist Thomas-Auguste Pouyer-Quertier as its official candidate, rather than the incumbent liberal orleanist deputy, Charles Levasseur, who was unpopular because of his authorship of a law raising taxes on alcohol (*eau de vie*), including Calvados, a staple product of this apple-growing region. Levasseur received the support of the region's liberal forces, including the *Journal de Rouen*. The Republican party, after much debate, rejected liberal Republican Senard, because of his role in the repression of April 1848, and decided once again to nominate Achille Lemasson. The continuing repression meant the absence of a radical newspaper or electoral committee, which once again made it difficult for Lemasson to run an effective campaign. Textile factory workers who were suspected of distributing republican electoral propaganda were dismissed from their jobs and had trouble finding work in other factories.[83] Radical leaders, most of whom were merchants and lawyers, met in small groups and maintained contacts with small committees of supporters, mainly artisans, shopkeepers, and spinning factory workers, who worked as electoral agents.[84] Although economic crisis had not yet hit the textile industry, the years preceding this election were marked by high bread prices, which reduced the purchasing power of the textile industry's working-class clientele. Republicans appealed to discontent over rising food prices, which they attributed to the regime's continuing protectionist policies. The official candidate, Pouyer-Quertier, defended protectionism and argued that high tariffs protected the interests of the region's factory workers and industrialists. In an election in which 53 percent of registered voters participated, Pouyer-Quertier was elected with 54 percent of the 16,746 votes cast. But opposition forces captured 45 percent of the vote, with Lemasson winning 31 percent and Levasseur 14 percent.

Unsuccessful legislative campaigns by the party's radical and socialist wing in 1853 and 1857 led liberal Republicans to once again challenge their control of the party. On April 10, 1863, the attorney general reported that the issue of candidate selection "threatens to become, in the bosom of the party, the subject of very lively disagreements."[85] Liberal Republicans succeeded in nominating their candidate, the lawyer Louis-Philippe Desseaux, for the June 1863 legislative election, even though Lemasson had outpolled Levasseur in the 1857 election. In contrast to the situation faced by Lemasson in 1853 and 1857, Desseaux campaigned in a much more favorable context for electoral opposition, including a severe economic crisis within the textile industry and a liberalized political situation. Republicans envisioned an electoral majority based on winning over liberal voters who had supported Levasseur in the 1857 election, while retaining the radical and socialist voters who had supported Lemasson. The economic crisis that gripped the cotton textile industry, following the free trade treaty with England in 1860 and the American Civil War, weakened support for the government and encouraged republican electoral hopes. It also weakened the position of radical and socialist Republicans, making it more difficult for them to mobilize textile workers, whose precarious material situation was coupled with the prospect of dismissal and unemployment for those identified as political agitators.[86] Industrialists who had supported the regime attributed the cotton crisis to the free trade treaty, while Republicans blamed the decline of Rouen's once thriving port on the government's promotion of railroads linking LeHavre to Paris, Dieppe, and Fécamp. Unlike the republican candidate of 1857, Desseaux rejected socialism and protectionism. He emphasized the liberal theme of "liberty" as "the most effective way to prevent a return of the upheavals of the past." Desseaux acknowledged the suffering of unemployed workers and called for a study of ways in which to aid the unemployed besides charity, but he did not propose any concrete measures of government intervention.[87] Republican party organization remained minimal, although the *Journal de Rouen*, which had refused to back Lemasson in 1857, supported Desseaux.

Liberal republican electoral prospects were weakened by a refusal to take a strong stand against free trade. Desseaux criticized the free trade treaty with England, not in principle but because it had been negotiated by the executive branch without consulting the legislature. He suggested that tax breaks for Rouen's textile industry would allow local industrialists to effectively compete on the world market. The *Journal de Rouen* continued to advocate liberal free trade policies, claiming that protectionism was harmful to the working class because it raised the price of basic necessities like clothing and constituted a barrier to industrial innovation and progress. Liberal republican advocacy of free trade alienated the city's powerful cotton spinning and weaving capitalists, who remained committed to protectionism and feared that the lower costs of coal in Britain and the more regular and numerous sources of waterpower in Switzerland would make it impossible for them to compete on the world market. Republicans won the support of some of the city's wealthy merchants and cotton print industrialists, like Charles Besselièvre, whose fortunes depended on foreign exports or the import of low-priced foreign goods. The region's textile workers remained divided over the issue. Some workers identified with their employers' hostility to English competition as a threat to their jobs and supported Pouyer-Quertier, who had broken with the Imperial regime over tariff policies.

Voter participation climbed to 74 percent in an election that the incumbent deputy Pouyer-Quertier won with 52 percent of the vote, compared to 39 percent for Desseaux and only 8 percent for Levasseur.[88] Although less radical than the republican candidate of 1857, Desseaux was able to rally the support of Rouen's republican socialists, given the electoral alternative of supporting a wealthy textile industrialist. In the city of Rouen, Desseaux won 5,917 votes (43%) and majorities (of 51% and 60%) in the textile factory districts and republican socialist strongholds of the city's 4th and 6th cantons. Pouyer-Quertier, a prominent opponent of the regime's free trade policies, won considerable support among the city's textile factory workers, especially those who had migrated to Rouen from his native region, the rural protoindustrial area of the *pays de Caux*.[89]

The triumph of liberal Republicans in the candidate selection process and the strong showing of Desseaux in the 1863 election paved the way for an electoral alliance that included liberal Republicans and Orleanists as well as radical Republicans. In the municipal election of July 1865, Republicans and Orleanists joined forces to create a liberal alliance that the attorney general later described, in January 1867, as follows: "The old Orleanist party remains what the coup d'état of 1851 showed it to be, officers without soldiers. These commanders have been rejuvenated by their alliance with the moderate Republicans and by the absolute liberalism that they parade . . . they have raised the banner of American and English theories on the unlimited liberty of the citizen . . . the liberal party, as they call themselves, has won over many adherents among the educated, the youth of the schools, the legal profession, in commerce and in industry. . . ."[90] In the 1865 municipal election, the opposition list included radical leaders Charles Cord'homme, Auguste Leplieux, and Charles Berthelot, as well as liberal Republicans like Louis-Philippe Desseaux and liberal orleanist leaders like Louis-Hippolyte de la Germonière. The liberal opposition list was defeated, with its candidates winning between 3,373 and 5,705 votes, compared to between 4,841 and 8,935 for candidates on the incumbent conservative slate. Although incumbents captured 33 seats on the first ballot, liberal candidates managed to win two out of three seats on the second ballot, due in part to the efforts of radical leaders Cord'homme and Leplieux to convince their followers to support liberal candidates rather than abstain. In the nearby working-class suburbs of Sotteville, Maromme, and La Londe, Republicans captured city council majorities.[91]

In contrast to the situation in Toulouse and Saint-Étienne, the liberal alliance in Rouen included radical republican leaders. Radical leaders like Charles Cord'homme and Frédéric Deschamps sought an accommodation with liberal Republicans, even though in 1848–51 they had previously maintained close ties to the city's socialist workers and an adversarial relationship with liberal Republicans. During the Second Republic, these men had worked alongside socialist workers as members of Republican Solidarity, leaders of the *Comité central démocratique*, and supporters of the socialist newspaper *Le Républicain de Rouen*. But in 1863, they supported the candidacy of Desseaux, despite his denunciation of socialism and his role in 1849 as prosecuting attorney responsible for convicting leaders of Republican Solidarity. Rouen's bourgeois radicals collaborated with liberal Republicans on the newspaper *Le Progrès de Rouen*, and failed to challenge the party's liberal alliance strategy or build an alternative base of electoral support by joining forces with working-class socialist militants. Their failure to challenge the exclusion of workers from the party's leadership or the alliance with liberal Orleanists alienated socialist workers from the Republican party, and encouraged the growth of more autonomous working-class socialist organizations, like the First International. The local leader of Rouen's branch of the First International, Émile Aubry, warned workers not to "compromise your growing power by dupe's alliances with bourgeois radicalism."[92]

Rouen's socialists challenged the liberalism of the city's bourgeois republican leadership during the late 1860s in a variety of organizational settings. The local branch of the *Ligue de l'enseignement*, an organization dedicated to fostering popular secular education through the creation of libraries and adult education courses, recruited Rouen's most prominent liberal and radical republican leaders as well as liberal bourgeois who supported the Empire. On the 1868 governing board of the organization were prominent partisans of the liberal Empire, including Senator Jean Clogenson and deputy Pouyer-Quertier, and several prominent members of the republican opposition, including the radical lawyer Frédéric Deschamps and liberal leader Louis-Philippe Desseaux. Émile Aubry, leader of the socialist *Cercle d'études économiques*, criticized the *Ligue* for abandoning its initial focus on empowering workers through education in favor of an emphasis on bourgeois philanthropy.[93] Aubry and other socialist leaders of the local branch of the First International organized an alternative series of public lectures. In March 1869, they invited the socialist feminist orator Paule Mink to address various social issues, including the role of women in the family and in society. These meetings were banned by the government, following hostile disruptions during her lecture entitled "Work and Poverty," but Mink returned to Rouen in July to give two private lectures.[94]

Republican leaders made no attempt to reconcile working-class socialists by offering them a greater role within the party, by collaborating with socialist leaders on issues that united Republicans, or by supporting the textile factory workers' strikes of 1868–69.[95] Although liberal Republicans appealed to workers for votes during their electoral campaigns, local workers remained excluded from leadership positions within Rouen's Republican party. Socialist workers created their own independent organization, a local branch of the First International (the *Fédération ouvrière rouennaise*), at the end of 1866.[96] The initial leadership of the organization was provided by artisans, the printer Émile Aubry, and the tailor Schrub, but by 1869 the group had expanded its leadership to include textile factory workers, including the Sotteville spinner Creusot and the Elbeuf weaver Eugène Pieton. By the beginning of 1869, the organization had twenty-five hundred members, mostly factory workers from various textile towns in the Rouen region, recruited from a variety of occupations including wool spinners, cotton spinners, weavers, dyers, calico printers, as well as skilled mechanics, tanners, printers, and carpenters. The main association created by the local branch of the First International was the *Cercle d'études économiques*, whose goal was to teach workers about socialist perspectives on contemporary economic issues.[97] The founding statement of the group, which attributed the cause of working-class sufferings to the "exaggerated development of capitalist monopoly," affirmed the goal of working to "peacefully liberate work from the subordination of capital." The group asserted its intention to avoid all "political questions."[98] Although the textile factory labor force experienced rapid feminization during the 1850s and 1860s, the Rouen branch of the First International remained entirely male in its leadership. It was dominated by workers and initially allowed only members of workers' associations to attend its meetings. This policy was abandoned in 1869 to admit shopkeepers, clerks, and professionals.[99] Although his principle appeal was to factory workers and radical artisans, Aubry's 1869 electoral campaign literature was addressed to "workers and shopkeepers (*petits commercants*)."[100] The rapid growth of the organization was due largely to its active role in supporting the strikes of textile factory workers, including the unsuccessful weavers' strike at the Bertel weaving factory of Sotteville in December 1868 and the spinners strikes at Elbeuf and Darnétal in October and November 1869.[101]

Republican liberals and radicals staunchly opposed this autonomous workers' organization, denouncing the socialist doctrines it espoused. Liberal Republicans Louis-Philippe Desseaux and Ernest Sottral joined radical bourgeois republican leaders Charles Cord'homme, Charles Berthelot, and Auguste Leplieux, in January 1869, to found a daily newspaper *Le Progrès de Rouen*. It took a more combative stance toward the government than the *Journal de Rouen*, and came to play a central role in Desseaux's successful 1869 legislative campaign.[102] Although the newspaper's director, Napoleon Gallois, had previously been associated with two radical and socialist newspapers in the department of the Sarthe, *Le Progrès* staunchly opposed socialist doctrines and denied socialist workers access to the columns of their newspaper.

Divisions between Republicans and socialists were further exacerbated by the May–June 1869 election campaign. Liberal republican candidate Louis-Philippe Desseaux altered his position on protectionism, belatedly abandoning his earlier advocacy of free trade in favor of selective protection for certain vulnerable industries, like cotton textiles. Socialist workers rejected Desseaux's candidacy. Given the absence of radical bourgeois leaders willing to challenge him, they put forth their own candidate, Émile Aubry. Aubry opposed the government's tariff policies but rejected the view that such opposition could serve as a source of unity between textile workers and their capitalist employers, whom he denounced as exploiters.[103] Unable to raise the 12,500 francs required as a security deposit for a newspaper, Aubry elaborated his program in a series of small brochures published by the *Cercle d'études économiques*, which were distributed in the factories of Rouen and Darnétal. These pamphlets denounced the continuing exclusion of workers from the legislature and elaborated an eighteen-point program that included the destruction of all industrial monopolies; the abolition of indirect taxes and of conscription; political decentralization; freedom of the press, association, and assembly; free secular education; the separation of church and state; and the election of judges. They attributed "the misery of the proletariat" to "the exaggerated development of capitalist monopolies" and the reign of "anarchy in the laws of exchange" and stated the goal of scientifically ascertaining the means to "peacefully emancipate work from the subordination of capital. . . ."[104] As candidate of the *Cercle d'études*, Aubry accepted the organization's imperative mandate view of representation, which required a pledge to adhere to its program and submit to its members any questions not addressed in its platform.[105]

The textile industrialist Pouyer-Quertier campaigned as the champion of protectionism and opponent of the monopolies produced by free trade. The regime's tariff policies, he claimed, forced employers to pay low wages in order to remain competitive. Pouyer-Quertier supported recent liberal political reforms and opposed government subsidies to the railroad companies. He responded to republican charges that he favored the regime's aggressive military policies by advocating sharp reductions in military spending and greater expenditures for public education.[106] Desseaux combined his advocacy of expanded civil liberties with criticism of the regime's foreign policies. He reproached Pouyer-Quertier for supporting the disastrous Mexican expedition and argued that a more pacific foreign policy could reduce taxes and revitalize the economy. Liberal and radical Republicans suspected that Aubry's candidacy was a plot by the authorities to siphon votes away from Desseaux and ensure the victory of Pouyer-Quertier. The *Journal de Rouen* argued that Aubry's candidacy would only divide the opposition to the advantage of the government.

The election of May 24–25, 1869 was extremely close, with Pouyer-Quertier edging out Desseaux by 10,777 votes to 10,548 votes on the first ballot. Aubry made a poor showing, winning only 826 votes, 75 percent of which came from the textile factory districts of Rouen and Darnétal.[107] Since no candidate received an absolute majority, a second round of voting was necessary. Pouyer-Quertier tried to win increased working-class support on the second ballot by personally visiting several large textile and machine construction factories, where he urged workers to support him as a protectionist candidate who could best defend their industries and protect their jobs.[108] The Bonapartist *Nouvelliste de Rouen* published a testimonial from 664 of the workers in Pouyer-Quertier's factory at La Foudre, praising his paternalist concern for their well-being.[109] Aubry refused to withdraw from the race or lend his support to Desseaux. He praised the republican candidate for supporting civil liberties and press freedoms but criticized him for failing to support social reforms and for practicing a paternalism that inhibited working-class emancipation. Aubry argued that the Bonapartist and republican candidates, though advocating contrasting political positions, were "in complete agreement on economic issues."[110] Aubry advised those who had voted for him to follow their consciences. Enough socialist workers who had initially voted for Aubry backed Desseaux on the second ballot, giving him a slim margin of victory, of 11,936 votes, compared to 11,450 for Pouyer-Quertier and 107 for Aubry. The defeat convinced Aubry that the electoral arena was the privileged terrain of the bourgeoisie. In opposition to other French leaders of the First International, Aubry subsequently advocated a focus on recruiting workers into labor organizations and organizing strikes, rather than diverting scarce resources into the task of changing the political regime.[111]

The plebiscite of May 8, 1870 to approve the regime's liberal policies generated widespread activity among Rouen's Republicans, including public meetings that attracted over three thousand people. In contrast to the situation in Toulouse and Saint-Étienne, Rouen's socialists did not join Republicans to campaign for a "no" vote. The socialist *La Réforme sociale*, published by the local branch of the International since early February 1870, advised its readers to submit blank ballots. The committee that organized republican opposition during the plebiscite campaign was led by liberal republican deputy Desseaux and included radical leaders Cord'homme, Berthelot, and Leplieux, as well as a member of the International, the Darnétal factory director Ernest Vaughan. In an election marked by a large turnout (86%), a majority (53%) of Rouen's 17,774 voters either voted no (8,653) or cast blank ballots (731). But the peasantry of the Normandy countryside remained faithful to the Empire, with 73 percent of the region's voters casting "yes" ballots. In the factory workers' neighborhoods of the 4th and 6th cantons, Rouen's voters cast "no" ballots by even larger majorities (58% and 64%, respectively). The socialist campaign for abstention and blank ballots resulted in only 4 percent blank ballots in Rouen.

After the plebiscite, the local branch of the International once again became active in electoral politics. It formed a *Comité électoral ouvrier* with the intention of running working-class socialist candidates in the June 1870 *Conseil général* and *Conseil d'arrondissement* elections. Plagued by inadequate resources, the committee decided to abstain from the election, advise its supporters to cast blank ballots rather than support the liberals and radicals of the *Union démocratique et libérale* slate, and focus its energies on the August 6–7 city council election. Despite the disappearance of its newspaper, and conviction of its leaders Aubry and Pieton in late July, the *Fédération ouvrier* participated in the municipal election but lacked the resources to launch an effective campaign.

The list of candidates in the municipal election suggests a rapprochement between radicals and socialists. The slate presented by the socialist *Comité électoral ouvrier* included thirty-six candidates, eleven of whom were members of the First International, as well as candidates from the radical and liberal republican tickets. Previously divided Bonapartists, Orleanists, and Legitimists united behind a "Friends of Order and Liberty" slate, while a second conservative slate (*liste de conciliation*) included bourgeois industrialists as well as merchants. The liberal republican slate of the *Comité libérale et démocratique*, which was supported by the *Journal de Rouen*, included a few radicals as well as several liberals who were also on the party of order slate. The radical slate (*Comité central démocratique*), weakened by the disappearance of *Le Progrès* in late July due to financial difficulties, included several liberals as well as seven socialist members of the *Fédération ouvrière*. Although twenty of the opposition candidates were listed on all three opposition slates, fifteen republican candidates issued a statement in the *Journal de Rouen* disassociating themselves from the workers' committee and its socialist platform. In an election in which only 47 percent of Rouen's registered voters appeared at the polls, Republicans and socialists suffered a decisive defeat. The party of order slate won by a wide margin, capturing twenty-six contested seats, with their candidates winning an average of 4,860 votes, or 50 percent of the total, on the first ballot. The candidates who ran on the liberal slate polled an average of 2,311 votes (24%). Candidates of the radical slate won an average total of 1,168 votes (12%) while those on the socialist slate captured an average of only 143 votes (1%).[112] On the second ballot, the remaining ten city council seats were won by the party of order slate, which outpolled the liberal republican list by 56 percent to 40 percent. Rouen's Republicans faced the final days of the Second Empire excluded from municipal power. The Republican party was now dominated by liberal Republicans, who faced a weak radical faction as well as militant socialist workers whom the party had failed to incorporate.

The balance of power within Rouen's Republican party shifted dramatically during the course of the Second Empire. Although radical Republicans continued to control the candidate selection process in 1852 and 1857, their relatively dismal electoral showings, attributable in part to the intense repression and widespread abstention, enabled liberal Republicans to challenge radical control of the candidate selection process. In 1863, in the context of a serious economic crisis within the textile industry, liberals finally managed to nominate their candidate. A much-improved republican electoral showing was followed by a successful municipal campaign in 1865 on the part of a liberal republican-orleanist alliance. Unlike their predecessors of 1846–47, radical republican leaders of 1863–70 joined the liberal alliance, rejecting the demands and aspirations of socialist workers. Liberal dominance produced autonomous working-class political activity, which took the form of a local branch of the First International.

REPUBLICAN POLITICS AND CLASS RELATIONS IN ROUEN

What role did the class struggles generated by early capitalist industrialization play in shaping the trajectory of republican politics in Rouen? The textile factory workers' protests of the early 1830s prompted a repression that helped to eliminate radical and socialist militants from the scene and give liberal Republicans control over the party. Fears generated by these protests among the property-holding electorate encouraged liberal Republicans to distance themselves from the "social question" and hesitate about extending suffrage rights to workers, a major issue of contention between liberals and radicals in 1846–47. The fears of the city's property-holding electorate, created by the violent textile workers' struggles of 1830, made Republicans hesitant to embrace the cause of Rouen's factory workers. In contrast to Saint-Étienne, Rouen's Republicans did not take advantage of the class struggles of the early 1830s, generated by the changes within the spinning sector of the textile industry, to mobilize working-class support. The factory, rather than household, context of these early class struggles meant that, in contrast to Saint-Étienne, they did not generate subsequent efforts at cooperative associations of production that could provide republican socialist militants with opportunities for political mobilization.

It wasn't until the last years of the July Monarchy, under the leadership of radicals like Deschamps, that Republicans made an effort to mobilize factory workers, under the banner of universal male suffrage and the social republic. The class struggles unleased by the revolution of 1848 polarized local politics and made liberal Republicans unwilling to accept radical leadership or a Republican party in which working-class socialists had a large voice. The intensity of class antagonisms in Rouen in 1848 meant that liberal republican officials and royalist National Guardsmen readily resorted to violent repression against socialist workers, after the efforts of radical leaders to keep working-class political activities confined to the electoral arena were undermined by a conservative electoral triumph.

The first barricades and bloodshed of 1848 took place in Rouen, a city with a highly proletarianized factory labor force. Was this political upheaval a reflection of the greater revolutionary consciousness of proletarianized factory workers? A close examination of the sequence of events leading up to the insurrection suggests that the uprising was more closely tied to republican politics than to the process of proletarianization. The insurrection was a response to the electoral defeat of April 1848, which took on great significance given sharp divisions among Republicans, the extensive concessions made to workers by radical republican officials, and the tense and polarized political situation. The presence of a radical rather than liberal government leader in 1848 was extremely consequential. The most powerful central government post was occupied by a radical republican leader who sympathized with the demands of socialist workers, made extensive concessions to factory workers, and defended socialist militants who led the clubs and municipal public works program. The victory of radical rather than liberal Republicans in the struggle to control the prefecture during the earliest days of the revolution resulted in a local political opportunity structure that fostered the capacities and collective actions of republican socialist workers. In short, the revolutionary consequences of democratization in Rouen cannot be understood outside the context of an ongoing struggle among liberal, radical, and socialist Republicans. The political consequences of working-class struggles can best be understood in terms of the way in which class forces were institutionally patterned by local Republican parties, rather than in terms of different levels of proletarianization.

Class struggles of the Second Empire also shaped local politics, but in a manner very different from Toulouse or Saint-Étienne, due to the different balance of forces within the city's Republican party. The textile strikes of the late 1860s offered an opportunity for socialists of the First International to mobilize support for an independent working-class politics at odds with the city's Republican party, from which socialists had been excluded. The political consequences of class conflicts, in short, were closely connected to the pattern of divisions among Republicans, which shifted dramatically during the Second Empire due to the political repression of the 1850s and economic crisis of the early 1860s. In contrast to Toulouse, where the repression strengthened the position of working-class socialists, and Saint-Étienne, where it provided an opening for radical bourgeois republican industrialists, in Rouen the repression helped foster the triumph of liberal republicanism.

The class structure of Rouen also shaped the character of republican politics. Like Toulouse, but unlike Saint-Étienne, Rouen was an important center of administration, commerce, and education, with a relatively large group of liberal professionals as well as a relatively large number of clerks, shopkeepers, and merchants. These groups provided a social base for liberal and, to a certain extent, radical republican politics, making possible the republican municipal electoral victory of 1846. But the violent protests of proletarianized factory workers made these groups wary of socialist workers and unwilling to support candidates whose commitment to public order and private property was questionable. The class structure of the city, with its wealthy industrialists and large numbers of clerks, shopkeepers, and merchants, all of whom feared the violence of proletarianized factory workers, made life difficult for radical Mountain candidates in 1849–51.

As was the case in other cities, Republican party formation in Rouen was a product of internal struggles among liberals, radicals, and socialists, whose relative strength was connected to the city's distinctive class structure. The radical faction of the party was strong due to the relatively large number of professionals and intellectuals and to financial contributions from a few wealthy supporters. But during the final years of the July Monarchy, radical Republicans succeeded in rallying popular support for republicanism beyond the ranks of the city's relatively small artisanate. They mobilized the much larger group of textile factory workers, who were attracted by a social vision of republicanism. By the end of the Second Empire, radical bourgeois Republicans were no longer willing to provide leadership for the struggles of socialist workers. This shift had important consequences for working-class politics given the legacy of bourgeois paternalism in local working-class politics. Unlike the handicraft artisans of Toulouse, Rouen's factory workers lacked a long tradition of autonomous political action. When first mobilized into republican politics during the late July Monarchy, they had looked to the radical bourgeoisie for leadership rather than develop autonomous bases of collective political action. The organizational bases for autonomous working-class politics emerged relatively late, during the 1860s, with the local branch of the First International.

Distinctive divisions among workers produced by early capitalist industrialization in Rouen also shaped republican politics. Divisions between handicraft and factory workers were evident in republican politics during the July Monarchy. Handicraft artisans, who were drawn to republican and Icarian politics at an early date, maintained weak contacts with the growing population of factory workers, many of whom were recent immigrants from the surrounding countryside. This division led to disputes over tactics among club members in 1848, when factory workers, though more open to the paternalist politics of a Deschamps or Bonaparte, proved more willing to take to the streets or barricades. Industrialization produced a geographic dispersion of the region's factory labor force, which posed a serious challenge for republican organizers. But radical and socialist militants managed to develop coordinated actions across factories throughout the region and to organize a relatively centralized club movement in 1848. A much more difficult obstacle was posed by the growing feminization of textile factory production. The fraternalist ideology and organization of republicanism, and the continuing exclusion of women from the suffrage, meant that a majority of the most important working-class constituency targeted by radical and socialist militants, that is, textile factory workers, never become the subjects of republican mobilization. Divisions among spinning, weaving, dyeing, and printing factory workers were overcome by a republican socialist ideology that claimed to speak for all workers in all trades and industries, but gender divisions proved more politically recalcitrant, given the fraternalist and patriarchal character of republicanism.

The national political opportunity structure also played an important part in shaping the trajectory of local Republican party formation. The relative weakness of the repression that followed the coup d'état allowed radical and socialist Republicans to maintain an electoral presence during the 1850s. In a context of rigid constraints on rights to assembly, association, and the press, they proved unable to rally strong electoral support from local workers, some of whom had been won over to Bonapartism and many of whom temporarily abandoned electoral politics in the face of disillusionment and repression. By destroying socialist and radical newspapers and organizations and weakening the ability of radical republican candidates to compete electorally, the repression helped the liberal wing of the party eventually gain control of the candidate selection process. Liberal Republicans proved far more successful in the electoral arena than had the socialist candidates, in part because their candidates campaigned during the 1860s, in the context of greater political freedom and an economic crisis in cotton textiles that helped to discredit the regime. Local struggles among Republicans intersected with a shifting national political opportunity structure to produce a political outcome that set the stage for municipal politics during the turbulent years of 1870–71.

Audition d'un Témoin devant la Cour d'assises

7. Trial of Icarian communists in Toulouse, August 1843. Although Icarian communist leader Étienne Cabet traveled to Toulouse for the trial of his supporters, he was not allowed to serve as defense attorney. Accused of a secret plot to foment an insurrection, the twelve alleged conspirators were acquitted. The prosecuting attorney's response was "Oh, the poor French bourgeoisie!" Lithograph by A. L. Soulié. Musée des Toulousains de Toulouse.

8. Proclamation of the revolutionary commune in Saint-Étienne. Saint-Étienne's communards repeatedly demanded new municipal elections and the establishment of a social republic. They called for a radical democratization of French society and politics as well as a federalist system of government. Reprinted with permission of the *Amis du Vieux Saint-Étienne*.

9. Barricade during the Rouen insurrection of April 1848. The first barricades and bloodshed of 1848 took place in Rouen, where a confrontation between republican workers and royalist National Guardsmen sparked an uprising. Lithograph by H. Bellangé.

10. Adolphe-Félix Gatien-Arnoult (1800–86). Liberal republican
leader, Toulouse. Lithographe de Romain Cazes, Musée Saint-
Raymond, Toulouse.

11. Armand Duportal (1814–87). Radical republican leader, Toulouse. During the late 1860s, Duportal engaged in hostile polemics with the city's liberal Republicans, who opposed his editorship of the republican newspaper *Émancipation* because of its revolutionary rhetoric. Although Duportal worked closely with republican socialist workers during these years, he refused to abandon the Versailles government when they proclaimed a revolutionary commune in 1871. Courtesy the Municipal Archives of Toulouse.

12. Martin Bernard (1808–83). Radical republican leader, Saint-Étienne. The son of a successful printer, Bernard urged his fellow militants to translate republicanism into a language accessible to ordinary workers. Bernard was sentenced to life imprisonment in 1839 for his leadership, alongside Blanqui and Barbès, of an abortive insurrection. After being pardoned and released from prison, he was elected deputy in April 1848. Convicted for his role in the June 1849 insurrection, Bernard was forced into exile from 1849 to 1859. After returning to France in 1859, he abandoned his revolutionary ways, backing the radical candidate Dorian rather than the socialist Martin in the 1869 election and refusing to support the revolutionary commune in 1871. Lithograph by Devéria. Collection de M. Bouasse-Lebel.

13. Pierre-Frédéric Dorian (1814–73). Radical republican leader, Saint-Étienne. Director of the Holtzer steel company, owned by his father-in-law, Dorian adopted paternalistic policies for the workers employed in his factories. Though hostile to socialism, he preached a radical republicanism that appealed to many workers by advocating free secular education, more equitable taxes, the right of workers to organize and strike, and social mobility through economic growth. Photo by Carjat.

14. Étienne Faure (1837–1911). Communard leader, Saint-Étienne.
Nicknamed Cou Tordu (twisted neck) because of his physical deform-
ity, Faure was an anarcho-socialist shoemaker who became central
police commissioner during Saint-Étienne's short-lived revolutionary
commune. Convicted in absentia after he fled to Geneva, Faure returned to Saint-Étienne in 1880 and resumed his political activities.
Reprinted with permission of the *Amis du Vieux Saint-Étienne*.

15. Jules Senard (1800–85). Liberal republican leader, Rouen. During the July Monarchy, Senard favored liberal reforms, including an expanded suffrage, but opposed universal male suffrage, a demand raised by Rouen's radical and socialist Republicans. As attorney general in 1848, Senard denounced working-class street protests, opposed the radical reforms introduced by Frédéric Deschamps, and advocated the use of military force to maintain public order. Lithograph by A. Maurin. Collection de M. Bouasse-Lebel.

16. Frédéric Deschamps (1809–75). Radical republican leader, Rouen. In 1848, as leader of the new provisional government in Rouen, Deschamps in-troduced economic reforms favoring textile factory workers, who sent him numerous petitions detailing their grievances. Deschamps's electoral defeat in April 1848 led to confrontations between republican workers and royalist National Guardsmen, which prompted the first barricades in 1848. Courtesy the Departmental Archives of the Seine-Maritime.

CHAPTER SEVEN

Failed Revolutions:
The Communes of 1870–1871

THEORIZING A FAILED REVOLUTION:
THE LEGACY OF REPUBLICAN PARTY FORMATION

The few successful social revolutions of the past three centuries have attracted considerable attention from students of social change. Most general theories of revolution highlight the "great revolutions" in late eighteenth-century France and early twentieth-century Russia and China.[1] In these successful revolutions, daring insurrectionaries violently seized state power, mobilized popular support, and used their power to institutionalize fundamental social and political changes. Failed revolutions are much less glamorous and have elicited relatively little scholarly attention. As is the case with the study of European state formation, such failures have been relegated to the dustbin of history.[2] The consequences of failed revolution seem derisory compared to the great social revolutions that radically transformed the day-to-day lives of millions of ordinary people. Such failures merit our attention, however, because their long-term consequences can be substantial. The French revolutionary communes of 1870–71, for example, are often ignored in discussions of revolution because insurgents failed to capture central state power and use that power to radically change French society. Despite their failure, the revolutionary communes transformed French politics and the French labor movement. The bloody repression of the communes eliminated many of the country's most militant republican socialist leaders, severely weakening the socialist wing of a nascent Republican party. This facilitated the triumph of radical republicanism, setting the stage for the subsequent emergence of an independent socialist party and the construction of an enduring liberal-democratic form of government.[3]

The emphasis on successful revolutions has encouraged social scientists to conceptualize revolution as an outcome rather than a process. A process-oriented view of revolution suggests the need to explore common sequences of connected events. If we envision revolution as a process, then what students of revolution often overlook or dismiss as mere rebellions appear as failed revolutions, as revolutionary processes that did not produce revolutionary outcomes. In terms of sequences of events, successful and unsuccessful revolutions look quite similar at the outset.[4] They both entail situations of multiple sovereignty, in which different contenders for state power make effective incompatible claims to control state institutions, such as the army, judiciary, police, or administration.

Theories of revolution typically have little or nothing to say about political party formation. Accounts of the failed revolutions in France in 1870–71, for example, acknowledge the central role of republican militants but do not trace the origins of urban revolutionary upheavals to prior histories of local Republican party formation. However, the sequences of events documented in the preceding accounts of Republican party formation from 1830 to 1870 provide the key to understanding the revolutionary events of 1870–71 in Toulouse, Saint-Étienne, and Rouen. Outside of this historical context, the events of the period appear as momentary eruptions explicable in terms of unusual circumstances, such as war defeat in 1870, rather than as the continuation, in dramatically altered circumstances, of a decades-long struggle among liberals, radicals, and socialists over different visions of the republic.

The key event that triggered a revolutionary crisis in France in 1870 was defeat in the Franco-Prussian War and the capture of Louis Napoleon Bonaparte by Prussian troops. Events at the national and international level explain the emergence of a revolutionary crisis that made possible the development of local revolutionary communes. The rhythm of revolution at the local level can also be understood in terms of supralocal forces, since in all cities it followed a pattern marked by major surges in revolutionary activity following the proclamation of the Third Republic in September, the war defeats of late October, the January armistice and subsequent February election of a conservative National Assembly, and the declaration of the Paris commune in March. The outcomes of the local revolutions that preceded the Paris commune of 1871 were also, in large part, determined by supralocal forces, especially the dispatch of Versailles troops to crush provincial municipal insurrections. But national and international factors cannot explain why revolutionary communes emerged in some cities but not others, because urban revolutionary upheavals were closely tied to different local histories of Republican party formation.

A cursory glance at the historical record reveals that revolutionary communes emerged in 1870–71 in cities that had been strongholds of republicanism during the late Second Empire. This suggests a certain continuity with prerevolutionary political developments, which implies a need to situate the revolutionary communes within the context of long-term processes of local party formation. The preceding chapters have documented important differences across cities in the shifting balance of power within local Republican parties. One of the questions addressed in this chapter concerns how these local political legacies shaped municipal politics during the revolutionary ferment of 1870–71.

The following account of the revolutionary events in Toulouse, Saint-Étienne, and Rouen during the early days of the Third Republic is preceded by a portrait of the national political context within which local revolutionary movements developed. This discussion of national politics sets the stage, briefly describing national conditions that generated a revolutionary crisis that made possible the municipal revolutions of 1870–71. The story then moves to the local level, documenting the three different sequences of events set in motion by the revolutionary crisis, the emergence of multiple sovereignty in some cities, and the outcomes.

THE NATIONAL CONTEXT OF LOCAL POLITICS

Although the political struggles of the late Second Empire did not bring about the downfall of the Imperial regime, they did help generate the international conflict that proved fatal to the Empire and gave birth to the Third Republic. The revival of republican and working-class opposition during the 1860s encouraged Louis Napoleon to implement additional liberal reforms to revive his popularity. In the plebiscite of May 8, 1870, voters overwhelmingly approved these reforms. But the plebiscite did little to stem growing urban republican opposition to the regime, the spread of strikes, and internal dissension within the Imperial court over the reforms. Although the liberal ministry did not want a war with Prussia, it was pressured by conservative Bonapartists to take a firm diplomatic stance with Prussia. Conservatives saw military victory in a brief war with Prussia as a chance to unite the nation, renew national glory, and create a less hospitable climate for liberal reforms. Diplomatic miscalculations lured the Imperial regime into a war that Napoleon III did not want and that his army was unprepared to wage. The war was sparked by a challenge to French influence in Spain, due to the succession of a Hohenzollern prince. When war began in July 1870, no one in France expected it to last very long nor did anyone anticipate military defeat and the ensuing revolutionary crisis.

Despite initial widespread support for the war, Republicans organized a growing campaign of opposition. A small group of republican deputies in the *Corps législatif* opposed government requests to finance the war, and republican workers took to the streets of Paris and Lyon to voice their opposition. After the military defeats of early August, antiwar protests spread rapidly. News of defeats at Froeschwiller and Forbach prompted revolutionary workers in Lyon and Marseille to launch brief uprisings on August 6–8, in favor of the establishment of a republic. Parisian workers gathered in the streets of the capital on August 9 in response to news of the war defeats, but liberal republican deputies of the *Corps législatif* failed to support their demand for an immediate proclamation of the republic. The deputies feared that an abrupt change of regimes would allow Parisian socialists to seize control of the situation in the capital and appoint a provisional republican government. They put forth their own narrower agenda in the *Corps législatif*, calling for a transfer of power from the executive to the legislature and the dismissal of the prime minister.

The defeat of the French army at the battle of Sedan on August 30 to September 2, and the capture of Louis Napoleon Bonaparte, sealed the fate of the Second Empire. Republicans were divided over what course of action to take in the aftermath of the capture of the Emperor. Liberal republican deputies were hesitant to declare a republic, and hopeful that a special session of the legislature would establish a new constitutional regime. A large crowd led by Parisian National Guardsmen broke through police and military lines into the *Corps législatif* and demanded the immediate proclamation of a republic. After the presiding officer refused to continue the meeting, the crowd marched to city hall, which was occupied by socialist militants intent on forming a new government. A confrontation over the composition of the new national government developed after the deputies arrived. Jules Favre offered a compromise solution, that only the deputies of Paris constitute the new government, since Paris had made the revolution. The compromise effectively excluded militant revolutionary leaders, such as Blanqui and Delescluze, from the government. General Jules Trochu, an Orleanist, was added to the provisional government in order to reassure conservatives and retain the loyalty of the army. The provisional government, Trochu later remarked, "saved the situation . . . [by] preventing the demagogues from taking over the defense of Paris and from producing an immense social upheaval throughout France."[5]

Although radicals and socialists were dissatisfied with the composition of the new government, as a patriotic gesture during a wartime crisis, they temporarily put aside efforts to establish a more "social" republic. Their reluctance to confront liberal officials of the new republic rapidly faded, however, due to disillusionment with the regime's timid defense policies that were motivated by fear of social revolution. The army, weakened by military defeat, was incapable of insuring internal order in the event of a popular uprising. The Parisian National Guard posed more of a threat than a safeguard for the new liberal republican regime. The government failed to adequately train and equip the 350,000 National Guardsmen of Paris for battle, out of fear they would be arming socialist opponents of the regime. Liberal republican government leaders were anxious to sign an armistice with the Prussians. This would allow National Assembly elections and a new government legitimized by universal male suffrage. Such a government would be in a better position than a provisional government inaugurated on the barricades to deal with the popular democracy of the clubs that arose during the fall of 1870.

The failure of French troops to break the siege of Paris, and the arrival of news that Jules Favre was secretly negotiating a treaty, angered radical and socialist Republicans throughout France. Their battle cry became the mass mobilization of the entire French population (*la levée en masse*). The French Revolution provided a precedent for such action. In 1792–93, volunteer battalions led by new commanders had driven foreign invaders from France. The revolutionary government that organized this popular mobilization resulted in Robespierre's Committee of Public Safety, and the revolutionary armies became agents of the Reign of Terror. This was precisely what liberal Republicans of the provisional government feared. Radicals and socialists also called for forced government loans from the rich to finance the war effort (*l'emprunt forcé*), an all-out effort to win the war (*la guerre à outrance*), and a refusal to negotiate with the enemy until all Prussian troops left French soil.

In addition to challenging central state policies on national defense, radical and socialist Republicans confronted the new government on issues of government personnel and class conciliation. Liberal republican leaders of the Government of National Defense were concerned with assuring the continuity of government despite the change of regimes. They resisted socialist and radical demands to break with the Imperial past by replacing all former Imperial officials and prosecuting Bonapartist officials who had played a role in the coup d'état of 1851. Although Minister of the Interior Léon Gambetta filled the prefectures with committed Republicans, the Ministers of Finance and Foreign Affairs retained officials who had served under the Empire. The upper reaches of the army and police also remained staffed by former Bonapartist officials. Radicals and socialists also challenged the government's policy of class conciliation to promote national unity for the war effort by calling for confiscation of the property of the clergy and traitors, and the levying of new taxes on the wealthy.

The defeat of the French army in Metz at the end of October 1870 marked a turning point, intensifying opposition to the central government and sparking massive protests, including abortive revolutionary communes in Marseille and Lyon. News of the defeat convinced many Republicans that the Government of National Defense was not committed to a serious pursuit of the war effort. Announcement of the surrender of 179,000 French soldiers at Metz by Bonapartist general François-Achille Bazaine coincided with the defeat of Parisian forces at Le Bourget and news that Thiers was negotiating an armistice with the Prussians. These events generated attempts by armed insurrectionaries to seize power in Paris. On October 31, working-class battalions of the Parisian National Guard, led by Auguste Blanqui, Gustave Flourens, and Charles Delescluze, stormed city hall, held members of the government prisoner, and spent the day debating the composition of a new government. After troops arrived, a negotiated settlement was reached, since neither side wished to start a civil war during a wartime crisis.

The best-organized challenge to the central government during the fall of 1870 came from a group of revolutionary leagues of the East, Midi, and Southwest, whose delegates gathered at Lyon, Marseille, and Toulouse. Their federalist program called for a reorganization of the state to rid it of all vestiges of the Imperial past, the election of judges, appointment of civilians to lead the army, and an arming of all citizens for the war effort. They also endorsed a variety of anticlerical and pro-working-class measures, including the secularization of schools, absolute separation of church and state, the drafting of the clergy, abolition of all regressive taxes, and implementation of a progressive income tax.

Agitation for revolutionizing the war effort continued through the winter of 1870–71, as Prussian troops began to bombard Paris and as food and fuel supplies needed to withstand the siege began to run out. A poorly organized attempt to break the siege prepared public opinion for an armistice, which liberal republican leaders were anxious to negotiate. Bismarck's threat to open negotiations with Louis Napoleon convinced members of the Government of National Defense that the alternative to an armistice was total defeat and a Bonapartist restoration. Socialists and radicals denounced the planned armistice as evidence of the government's treachery and defeatism.

Announcement of an armistice on January 28 was quickly followed by a national election on February 8. Rural voters elected a National Assembly dominated by conservative monarchists committed to signing a peace treaty with Bismarck. Republicans won only 200 of the 675 seats in the new National Assembly. Their electoral campaign was hampered by Prussian control of one-third of French territory, a capital city cut off from the provinces, communications in disarray, and a war-weary rural population. The election marked a turning point in the development of the republic, paving the way for a bloody confrontation between Versailles troops and the revolutionaries of Paris.

The National Assembly passed a variety of measures that aroused the hostility of Parisians, including abolition of Parisian National Guard payments, an end to the moratorium on overdue rents and debts, and transfer of the capital from Paris to Versailles. The government failed to affirm support for continuation of a republican form of government and appointed a number of Bonapartists to key military positions, thus raising questions about the Assembly's commitment to a republic. Asserting central government control over the organized means of coercion meant disarming the Parisian National Guard. The ensuing confrontation began with the government's unsuccessful effort on March 18 to capture Parisian National Guard cannons. Forced to evacuate the city, Thiers and his government fled to Versailles, leaving Paris in control of the Central Committee of the National Guard, a group of radicals and socialists who had been elected from predominantly working-class districts. Rather than march on Versailles and take advantage of the disarray of government forces, Parisian communards, afraid that such action would prompt accusations of fomenting a civil war, prepared for new municipal elections.

For Republicans throughout France, support or opposition to the events unfolding in Paris became the dominant political issue. The key question facing Republicans was: did the government in Paris or the one in Versailles exercise legitimate political authority? Radicals were hesitant to challenge a duly elected National Assembly and embrace revolution, but they were also wary of a National Assembly that had not yet expressed firm commitment to a republican form of government. The escalating violence, which included execution of captured insurgents by Versailles forces and the taking of hostages by communards, made a negotiated settlement increasingly unlikely. Republican socialists declared their support for the government in Paris and launched their own insurrections against Versailles. On March 23–26, revolutionary communes were proclaimed in Lyon, Marseille, Narbonne, Toulouse, Saint-Étienne, and Le Creusot. These uprisings were quickly crushed by Versailles troops, a prelude to the bloody week of May 21–28, when French soldiers marched on the Paris commune, killing an estimated 20–25,000 people.

Historical accounts of the revolutionary situation of 1870–71 often relegate the provincial communes to a minor role in the drama. Historians have focused their attention on the Paris commune, which lasted only seventy-two days but was the largest urban insurrection of the nineteenth century. They have paid relatively little attention to its provincial counterparts, typically dismissed as brief outbursts that were easily suppressed by the central government.[6] This focus on the capital is not surprising, given that the fate of the Paris commune shaped local politics throughout France. But the Paris commune was the culmination of a revolutionary process that began in the fall of 1870, in which provincial cities, not Paris, took the lead. Throughout the fall and winter of 1870, local insurrectionaries struggled for control of National Guard militias, police forces, and local governments in numerous French cities. Revolutionary communes were proclaimed in Lyon, Marseille, Nimes, Narbonne, Toulouse, and Saint-Étienne prior to the proclamation of the Paris commune on March 26.

Rather than view the provincial communes as responses to what happened in Paris, we need to situate them in the context of local republican politics. In comparing the sequences of events that unfolded in Toulouse,

Saint-Étienne, and Rouen in 1870–71, the following accounts focus on the way in which different patterns of cooperation and conflict among liberal, radical, and socialist Republicans shaped revolutionary processes in each city.

THE REVOLUTIONARY COMMUNE IN TOULOUSE

On August 7, 1870, a crowd of republican demonstrators, made up of young men from the working-class neighborhood of Saint-Cyprien, marched through the streets of Toulouse to protest the war against Prussia. Government officials reported that rumors were circulating throughout the city attributing recent military setbacks to the treachery of the rich, the clergy, and the nobility.[7] Popular unrest over war defeats was heightened by the Imperial government's decision to prevent the republican city council elected on August 6–7 from taking office. On August 12, the prefect proclaimed a state of siege and banned all public gatherings, except for the daily congregation of people in front of city hall to receive news of the war. When news of the defeat in Sedan and capture of the Emperor reached Toulouse on September 4, a large crowd accompanied the republican city councilmen who had been elected in August from the headquarters of *Émancipation* to city hall. The crowd forced open the doors of the building, and republican leaders proclaimed the new republic from the balcony. On September 8, radical republican leader Armand Duportal, who had been serving time in a Paris prison cell for press crimes, arrived in Toulouse to assume the post of prefect. Duportal immediately reorganized the police force and National Guard. He named the socialist Jean-Baptiste Cavaré as police commissioner and opened the citizens' militia to "all sincere Republicans," many of whom were working-class socialists. According to the Resseguier commission later appointed to investigate the revolutionary commune, Duportal "surrounded himself immediately with fanatical men who saw in the Republic only a regime of agitation. . . ." and turned over the city's police force to "the most dangerous men in the city. . . ."[8]

The advent of the republic spawned numerous political clubs, which provided radicals and socialists with a means to influence public opinion, mobilize popular support, and pressure republican officials. Many of the clubs were led by workers rather than respectable bourgeois. M. Proxy, a liberal republican law professor, reported to the Carol commission investigating the revolutionary commune as follows: "The clubs were actively followed at Toulouse. . . . No truly serious men agreed to lead these gatherings. I tried several times to persuade a number of honorable and sober men to chair these assemblies but failed. . . . In general these assemblies had at their head and as their leaders men perfectly unknown and déclassé. . . ."[9] According to the Carol commission, the issues discussed at club meetings were not "political questions properly speaking" but focused instead on class inequalities, especially "the unequal distribution of wealth and the riches possessed by religious establishments."[10] The law professor Proxy testified that habitual topics of club discussions were "the unequal distribution of wealth, the distinctions between rich and poor, and the fortunes of religious establishments . . . every time someone demanded forced loans from the rich, the taxing of landowners, or the seizure of church properties, they were loudly applauded. . . ."[11] On September 18, club leaders organized a rally that attracted four thousand demonstrators who demanded that the government refuse to negotiate until all enemy troops departed from French soil.

Alongside the clubs, the institution that provided workers with the organizational capacity to challenge the government was the National Guard. After September of 1870, the sole criterion for admission became one's good standing as a dedicated Republican. As a result, this citizens' militia was rapidly transformed into a predominantly working-class organization. The Résseguier commission of inquiry into the causes of the commune reported that only those with "radical opinions" were admitted into the National Guard, which "naturally elected an officer corps recruited from the most fiery club orators."[12] François de Carbonel told the commission that "persons from more elevated positions were carefully excluded in favor of arming the workers of the faubourgs."[13]

Armand Duportal, who had established close ties with the city's working-class socialist leaders during the final years of the Second Empire, justified revolutionary measures by pointing to the threat posed by royalist opponents of the new regime. On September 18, he reported that monarchist parties were "spreading fear of the enemy and of the instability of republican institutions." He criticized the central government for selecting several prefects whose orleanist sympathies were known, claiming that such policies encouraged royalist intrigues.[14] Duportal publicly urged his supporters to "Arm yourselves with scythes and rifles against the Prussians of Germany. Arm yourselves with suspicion, hatred, anger and rage against the royalists, these Prussians of the interior."[15]

The conflict among liberal, radical, and socialist Republicans that had marked the final years of the Second Empire erupted once again during the early days of the new republic, over the issue of control of the city council. On September 24, *Émancipation* complained that the composition of Duportal's recently appointed new city council "does not sufficiently represent the radical and socialist element" of the city's Republican party. In early October, radicals and socialists created a revolutionary Committee of Public Safety, which attempted to displace the city council. According to the Réssiguier commission of inquiry, the Committee of Public Safety "tried to replace the city council and took on the functions of intervening in all administrative services, keeping an eye on all government authorities, and directing the police and National Guard."[16] The committee, which expressed a determination to "resolve social questions in the best interests of the working class," called for revolutionary measures to strengthen the young republic in the face of royalist intrigues and foreign invasion. Evoking memories of the French Revolution, the committee proclaimed: "The situation is the same as in 1792. Think of what our forefathers did and use the examples they gave us."[17] The committee was chaired by the radical republican lawyer Gustave Cousin. Among its members were a number of workers, including the National Guard officers Esparbes (mason), Boudin (joiner), and Cantegril (butcher). Two members of the committee's executive commission were active participants in the Toulouse branch of the First International, the lawyer Jules Sarrans and the furniture maker Pierre Gaubert.

When the city council resigned in protest in response to this challenge to their authority, Duportal sided with the Committee of Public Safety. He telegraphed the following message to the Minister of the Interior on October 16: "The Toulouse city council is betraying us; its principal members are making common cause with the Legitimists and Orleanists. The council's unpopularity alone has given rise to a Committee of Public Safety, which has greatly aroused the population and created a conflict with the city government. I have accepted the resignation of the city council and formed a municipal government before which the Committee of Public Safety is dissolved or indefinitely adjourned. . . ."[18] Duportal failed to mention that the new city council had as its president the lawyer Gustave Cousin, former head of the Committee of Public Safety, and that most members of the new council were radicals and socialists from the Committee of Public Safety.

By the end of October 1870, the radical and socialist alliance that had gained control of the Republican party during the final years of the Second Empire succeeded in capturing key institutions of municipal power, including the local police, National Guard, prefecture, and city council. The defeat of the French army in Metz at the end of October led them to attempt to expand their control to the military. On October 30, when news of the surrender of Metz reached Toulouse, Armand Duportal addressed a large crowd at the prefecture, charging the army and its leaders with incompetence and treason. He called for the arming of all citizens, expulsion of the Jesuits from France, the dismissal of all generals, and absolute subordination of military officials to civilian control. According to the Résseguier commission report, Duportal proclaimed to the crowd: "Seize weapons in all the arsenals. . . . If civil war becomes necessary, I will be your captain for the civil war." After hearing Duportal's speech, a contingent of sixty National Guardsmen marched to the arsenal, which was guarded by only six soldiers, and seized control of the building. The commander of the arsenal, Gen. Courtois d'Hurbal, immediately went to city hall to protest the takeover. On his arrival, he was arrested by a group of National Guardsmen and surrounded by an angry crowd demanding a revolutionary trial and revenge for "the treachery of the generals." The general was brought before the city council, which also served as a revolutionary tribunal. He refused to honor the city council's request that he accept National Guard control of the arsenal. Duportal arrived at city hall, which was surrounded by a large crowd of protestors, and tried unsuccessfully to persuade d'Hurbal to grant the National Guard control over the arsenal. After Duportal persuaded the general to resign his command, the city council allowed Duportal to escort the general to the prefecture where he was temporarily held prisoner.

The next morning Duportal accompanied members of the city council and a delegation of club members on an inspection of the arsenal, which remained under National Guard control. After they discovered thirty thousand rifles in storage, Duportal dismissed Colonel Decroutte, who was in charge of arms supplies at the arsenal. He also named Dumay, commander of the National Guard, as the new commanding general to replace d'Hurbal, who fled the city after being released from custody. The central government responded by dismissing Duportal and appointing a new prefect named Huc. Duportal wired Minister of the Interior Gambetta that the entire officer corps of the National Guard had urged him to remain in office, and that any attempt to replace Dumay as commander of the garrison at Toulouse would meet with armed resistance from the National Guard. The entire city council resigned in support of Duportal and the city's clubs organized a mass demonstration to prevent Huc from taking office. The new prefect was greeted by a hostile crowd of about four thousand demonstrators. Since General Dumay had refused the new prefect's request for military protection, the crowd easily entered Huc's residence and made him promise he would not take office.[19] Huc then telegraphed his resignation to Gambetta. The central government backed down, allowing Duportal to remain at his post as prefect, and General Dumay to remain as armed forces commander.

During November and December, Toulouse's radical and socialist Republicans played a central role in organizing the League of the Southwest. Local Republicans also continued to meet regularly in the city's clubs. They elaborated their demands for radical measures against the clergy, price controls on food, and a *levée en masse* to come to the aid of besieged Paris. *Émancipation* called on the city government to prohibit landlords from collecting rents in advance, and the city council organized a bread coupon program to aid needy workers. On November 21, the city council voted to confiscate the property of the *Frères des écoles Chrétiennes*, a clerical teaching order, and turn over control of their school buildings to secular educators. Duportal supported this measure by issuing a decree relieving the *frères* of their functions as municipal teachers. On December 14, the royalist newspaper, *La Gazette du Languedoc*, criticized Duportal for participating in a republican funeral procession dominated by National Guardsmen and club activists, who marched behind a red flag. That evening, an angry crowd of club members, led by National Guard officers, attacked the newspaper's headquarters and destroyed their printing presses. The central government responded by trying to disarm the National Guard, but the entire city council resigned in protest. Duportal warned the central government that the disarmament measure was very unpopular and that a new municipal election would be ill-timed and dangerous. Club orators urged workers to keep their weapons in the event that armed resistance became necessary.[20] As in November, the central government backed down in its attempt to disarm the city's socialist workers, and the city council withdrew its resignation. Although liberal Republicans held power at the national level, radicals and socialists retained local state power in Toulouse.

The announcement of an armistice on January 28, 1871 provoked cries of outrage and betrayal by Toulouse's radicals and socialists. *Émancipation* responded defiantly to news of the armistice: "If we listened only to our first inspiration and followed only our first impulse, we could cry out for insurrection and immediately call for revolution. But who would hear us and who would respond?"[21] In the campaign preceding the National Assembly election of February 8, radicals and socialists denounced the armistice and called for the election of a National Assembly that would intensify the war effort. Liberal Republicans, alarmed by the revolutionary agitation of the clubs and National Guard, joined forces with Orleanists and Legitimists to form a conservative electoral alliance, *l'Union nationale*. Although Toulouse gave a majority of its votes to the radical republican slate, the surrounding rural voters of the Haute-Garonne voted overwhelmingly for peace, electing six Legitimists, two Orleanists, and two liberal Republicans. Duportal described the election results as "the triumph of the Prussians of the Interior," while *Émancipation* labeled the newly elected National Assembly the "Chamber of the Abdication of National Honor."[22]

Despite their electoral defeat, radicals and socialists still retained control of the city's National Guard, the only significant armed force in the city following the armistice. On March 12, National Guard troops marched through the faubourgs, amid cheers from working-class inhabitants. Then they defiantly paraded through wealthy royalist neighborhoods. This show of force by armed workers prompted the city's conservative newspapers to petition the Minister of the Interior to reorganize the National Guard. The central government responded with the following directive to Duportal: "The National Guard is composed . . . of many more workers and inhabitants of the faubourgs than of bourgeois and property owners. . . . The most honorable men have been refused weapons while those whom it would have been wise not to arm have received weapons. . . . Carefully adopt measures that will remedy this situation. . . ."[23] Duportal took no action to implement this directive.

After the outbreak of the Paris commune in March, the key issue facing Republicans was whether to support the government of Paris or Versailles. On March 19, news reached Toulouse of the insurrection in Paris and retreat of the government to Versailles. That same day, Duportal received orders from Versailles to replace National Guard troops at the arsenal with soldiers loyal to the Versailles government. Anxious to avoid a confrontation, Duportal tried to persuade the generals in command to postpone taking action, but he affirmed his loyalty to Versailles. In contrast, the socialist editors of *Émancipation* declared the Paris commune to be the only legitimate government, and appealed to soldiers to support the commune. Pressured by National Guard officers to declare his support for the Paris commune, Duportal threatened to resign. He rejected National Guard leaders' demand that he stop issuing public declarations containing bulletins from Versailles, but continued to resist government pressure to reorganize the National Guard.

News of Duportal's replacement as prefect by the royalist comte de Keratry reached Toulouse on March 23. The mayor and the entire city council immediately resigned in protest. Fearful of violence, and unwilling to lead an armed insurrection, Duportal decided not to resist his dismissal, even though he had successfully done so in November. On March 25, after holding maneuvers, about one hundred National Guard officers and several thousand guardsmen marched to the prefecture amid shouts of "Long Live Paris!" and "Long Live the Commune!" During a meeting with National Guard officers, Duportal argued that he was no longer prefect and refused their offer to lead a revolutionary commune. National Guard officers asserted their intention of proclaiming a commune. Duportal persuaded them that, since the proclamation was a municipal act, they should do so at city hall not at the prefecture. The revolutionaries obeyed his advice. National Guardsmen accompanied Duportal to city hall, surrounding him with an honor guard to prevent escape into the crowd. *Émancipation* reported that the prefect was escorted to city hall "more as a prisoner than as a victor."[24]

The legacy of autonomous working-class political activity that had marked decades of Republican party formation in Toulouse was evident in the organization of the city's revolutionary commune. The leadership of the commune included working-class leaders like Leopold Cros (upholsterer), Jules Ader (cabinetmaker), and Jean Jacob (stonecutter), who were active in the First International but kept their distance from bourgeois leaders of the Republican party. Duportal claimed that the leaders of the commune were "almost completely unknown" to him and that he knew only two of the National Guard's four battalion commanders. Since the commune was a product of National Guard members, available registers from this citizens' militia provide the best evidence about the social backgrounds of the city's communards. Seventy-three percent of the 866 individuals identified by occupation in these registers were workers, 15 percent were bourgeois, and 12 percent were petty bourgeois shopkeepers and small masters. The majority of working-class Guard members (73%) were artisans.[25]

The executive commission of the commune drew up a proclamation in support of Paris which called for the retention of Duportal as prefect. Duportal refused to preside over the deliberations, but he was persuaded to sign the final document declaring the commune. Officers of the National Guard proclaimed the commune from the balcony of city hall, in front of a large crowd. The Carol commission estimated the number of revolutionary communards at only fifteen hundred to two thousand but added that "the vast majority of our workers are ready to follow their lead. . . ."[26] The predominantly working-class National Guard was the key force engaged in efforts to take control of municipal institutions. After occupying the telegraph and post office, to intercept telegrams from Versailles and prevent the postmaster from carrying out the judicial order to confiscate copies of *Émancipation*, National Guardsmen tried to arrest judicial officials on March 26. The judges received advance warning and escaped to the arsenal, where the "forces of order" were gathering.

Liberal Republicans refused to join the royalist "party of order" coalition that was mobilizing a military response to the radicals and socialists who had siezed control of city hall. But they also refused to support revolutionary initiatives. The liberal republican *Association républicaine* urged its members not to join the military forces gathered at the arsenal. While expressing support for the Versailles government, the association advocated "sincere conciliation" and warned its members that "a majority of the volunteers are royalists," some of whom "favor energetic repression rather than conciliation."[27] Liberal Republicans played an important role in the negotiations that followed. A settlement was reached on March 27, which allowed troops to occupy the prefecture and temporarily left the guardpost at city hall to a detachment of National Guardsmen reinforced by a contingent from the *Association républicaine*. The radical republican mayor and communard leader Valette, who was also a National Guard battalion commander, reported immense difficulties in winning over the more militant socialist guardsmen to the idea of a negotiated settlement. He confided to captain Guillaume-Albert de Puybusque, who escorted him back to city hall after a negotiating session at the arsenal: "I am even threatened by some of these men. . . . If this continues, I shall have to place myself under your protection."[28]

The negotiated settlement which ended the commune specified that the executive committee of the commune would be dissolved but that National Guard commander Edmond Valette would be appointed provisional mayor. On April 8, after soldiers tried to regain control of the city hall guardpost from National Guardsmen, the city council called for dismissal of the newly appointed National Guard commander, François de Carbonnel, and then resigned in protest after the prefect refused. The prefect then ordered the temporary dissolution of the entire National Guard and the replacement of guardsmen by soldiers at all posts. A large crowd gathered at city hall to support the National Guard. When the cavalry dispersed them, barricades went up on the adjacent streets. An officer ordered the soldiers to fire on the demonstrators, but troops fired above their heads and cleared the barricades and the city hall square with little resistance.

The defeat of the commune in Toulouse was followed by efforts on the part of liberal Republicans to avoid a bloody civil war in Paris. At the end of April 1871, a delegation of liberal Republicans, including Bernard Mulé, Théophile Huc, and Jules Bibent, went to Versailles to argue in favor of conciliation with Paris, based on recognition of the Republic, communal liberties, and dissolution of the National Assembly now that a peace treaty was concluded. Though successful in Toulouse, they failed to prevent the subsequent bloodbath in Paris. Toulouse's most prominent radical and socialist republican leaders were subsequently arrested and tried for their role in the commune. The ex-prefect, Armand Duportal, and ex-mayor, Léonce Castelbou, as well as two police commissioners, Jean-Baptiste Cavaré and Jean Jacob, several National Guard officers, and the editors of *Émancipation*, were tried and acquitted of charges of attempting to overthrow the government and incite a civil war.

THE REVOLUTIONARY COMMUNE IN SAINT-ÉTIENNE

After the military defeats of early August, the central police commissioner in Saint-Étienne reported that the city's silk weavers "appear to have lost most of the patriotic spirit that animates the rest of the population. They are indifferent to our situation, displaying more bitterness than sorrow in their conversations."[29] As the military situation deteriorated, Republicans took to the streets to express their opposition to the war. At a rally on August 14, four hundred Republicans gathered to hear speakers call for an overthrow of the Empire and the drafting of the clergy and the rich.[30] When news of the defeat in Sedan and capture of the Emperor reached Saint-Étienne on September 4, Republicans who had been elected to the city council in August gathered at the offices of *L'Éclaireur*. After drafting a proclamation of the republic, they marched to city hall to proclaim the republic in front of a large crowd gathered in the square in front of the building. Later in the day, the prefect reported that a red flag was flying from city hall but that, despite agitation, there were no disorders.[31]

Upon assuming his new post as prefect on September 5, radical republican leader César Bertholon immediately replaced the conservative departmental council (*Conseil général*) with a republican departmental committee. Though dominated by radicals, there were several socialists on the council, including future communard leaders Barthelemy Durbrize, Jean Jolivalt, and Adrien Duvand. Bertholon also appointed a provisional city council for Saint-Étienne, drawn largely from the radical Republicans who had been elected in August. He ordered the red flag on city hall replaced by the tricolor. Bertholon busied himself with the task of organizing for the war effort and replacing compromised Bonapartist municipal officials. The city council devoted its attention to reorganization of the National Guard, making an effort to recruit workers at their workplaces.[32] These efforts paid off, and by September 9, over eight thousand men had registered for the local militia.[33] The city council tried to raise 1.5 million francs in municipal bonds to finance the armament of the National Guard, but these efforts to arm workers evoked a wary response from the local bourgeoisie and produced only 500,000 francs.

The tensions between radical and socialist Republicans that had marked the final years of the Second Empire erupted during the early days of the new republic. Socialist club leaders were determined to put pressure on radical republican officials to revolutionize the war effort. "The extremists are impatient and make me uneasy," wrote Bertholon, noting that his efforts to unite and conciliate were undermined by the journalists of *L'Éclaireur*, which included socialist militants Adrien Duvand and Antoine Chastel.[34] Socialists criticized the central government for not vigorously pursuing the war effort, and chastised the radical city council for failing to take action against the clergy. Their targets included the director of the arms factory, colonel Boigeol, whom they accused of failing to properly organize arms production. After the city council passed a resolution calling for the drafting of the clergy, but failed to take action against the Jesuits, socialists at *L'Éclaireur* denounced their actions as "more befitting the [clerical] Society of St.-Vincent-de-Paul than elected radical democrats."[35] The city council subsequently passed measures turning twenty-one congregational schools into secular schools and ending municipal subsidies to clerical education. The council also responded to these attacks by making sure that municipal workshops for the unemployed created in September did not become centers of socialist agitation. The measure creating the workshops stipulated that wages would be paid by the task rather than by the day, to prevent unemployed workers from spending their time listening to speeches by socialist club orators.[36]

The burgeoning club movement provided republican socialists with a strong organizational base. In numerous club meetings, socialists voiced their demands for social reform and a revolutionizing of the war effort. The most important club in Saint-Étienne was the *Club de la rue de la Vierge*, also known as the *Comité central républicain*, which had neighborhood branches throughout the city. Its meetings were open to women as well as men, although the leadership was exclusively male. Among the leaders of this club were the most ardent advocates of a revolutionary commune: the silk weavers Johanes Caton and Antoine Chastel, the hardware salesman Louis Coste, and the bookkeeper Barthelemy Durbize. Socialists hoped to replace radical Republicans in the municipal elections scheduled for September 25. Given their superior organization, in the form of numerous clubs, and the role of their leaders at *L'Éclaireur*, socialists anticipated a greater voice in municipal affairs after the elections. Much to their dismay, the government abruptly canceled municipal elections on September 24.

Faced with growing pressures from socialist club members, and fearful of a monarchist restoration, Bertholon envisioned a Jacobin solution to the crisis. On October 9, he urged Vogeli, a League of Midi delegate in Tours, to ask the government for "dictatorial authority for prefects, except for revocation in the case of abuse . . . otherwise the Prussians of the Interior will outflank us."[37] Bertholon faced growing pressure from the clubs to crack down on royalist opponents of the republic, who voiced their opinions in the newspaper *Le Défenseur*, edited by the former legitimist deputy Auguste Callet. On October 10, Bertholon ordered the suspension of *Le Défenseur* and prosecution of its editors. The Minister of the Interior overrode this action. He informed the prefect that judicial action against authors of inflammatory articles was acceptable but that he could not shut down the newspaper. Bertholon, who considered royalist attacks on the government during wartime as treasonous, obeyed his superior but warned that "the popular clubs (*sociétés populaires*), accusing the government and its representative of weakness, are already disposed to take justice into their own hands in the face of provocations."[38]

At the end of October, news of the military defeat in Metz led to renewed demands for revolutionizing the war effort and the election of a new city council. Socialist club leaders denounced the "powerlessness and inertia of the city council in the face of the invasion of our country" and called for the establishment of a commune.[39] On the morning of October 31, a large crowd led by Adrien Duvand, a socialist journalist at *L'Éclaireur*, occupied city hall and demanded the proclamation of a revolutionary commune. In the heat of the situation, Bertholon gave in and announced municipal elections for a revolutionary commission, to be held October 31–

November 1.[40] Duvand announced the decision to a large crowd gathered in front of city hall. In this speech, he called for intensification of the war effort, drafting the clergy, government measures to assure adequate food supplies, and adoption of the red flag rather than the tricolor.[41] Shortly after Bertholon signed the proclamation calling for new municipal elections, socialist militants raised the red flag in front of city hall. Bertholon immediately issued an order to replace it with the tricolor. The city council decided to meet in permanent session until new elections were held. The following day, Bertholon retracted his concession, indefinitely postponing municipal elections. On November 8, he received orders from the Minister of the Interior forbidding new municipal elections.[42] Although they controlled the local republican newspaper and the club movement, revolutionary socialists in Saint-Étienne, in contrast to Toulouse, never managed to gain control of the city council, prefecture, police, or National Guard.

During the month of December, socialist club militants continued to meet at gatherings organized by the *Club de la Vierge*. Club leaders called for the execution of the generals responsible for recent defeats and demanded the establishment of a revolutionary commune. In response to the challenge posed by socialists, and in an effort to rally conservative support for the war effort, Bertholon tried to reorganize the administration. At the beginning of December he appointed a number of royalist notables to the departmental commission, including the baron de Saint-Genest and Alfred de Meaux. Both men refused the offer, calling instead for the election of a new departmental council. The sudden death of the mayor, Tiblier Verne, at the end of November, provided the occasion for another confrontation between radical and socialist Republicans. At the funeral, which took place on December 23, club members demonstrated in favor of a revolutionary commune. Bertholon responded with a public declaration denouncing the agitation as unpatriotic, affirming that a majority of citizens rejected the idea of a commune, and warning demonstrators that they would face arrest.[43]

At the end of December, socialist leaders resigned their positions at *L'Éclaireur* to create their own newspaper, *La Commune*. The managing director of *La Commune*, which first appeared on December 29, 1870, was the thirty-year-old silk weaver Antoine Chastel, a member of the First International who had helped found *L'Éclaireur* in 1869. Another editor, Andrien Duvand, had previously worked at *L'Éclaireur*, and also belonged to the local branch of the First International. *La Commune* espoused a federalist socialist ideology, envisioning a society in which "workers will be called on to play an important role in social affairs. . . ."[44] The editors accused the city's radical Republicans of being "a little too aristocratic" to cooperate with socialist workers. They labeled the Jacobin republican leader Gambetta "a tyrant like Bonaparte or Robespierre" and demanded new municipal elections.[45]

Radical Republicans responded by creating their own political organization, the *Alliance républicain*, to counteract the influence of the socialist clubs. This organization, which was founded on January 22, 1871, recruited most members of Saint-Étienne's city council. According to César Bertholon, the goals of the new organization were to "defend the republic by all legal means, engage in electoral propaganda, and prevent disorders in the street. . . ."[46] Whereas socialist ribbon weavers provided a large majority of the members of the *Club de la Vierge* and of the local branch of the First International, the *Alliance républicain* attracted workers from various industries, including the city's newer mining, metal, and railway industries. Although bourgeois radicals like César Bertholon, Jean-Marie Boudarel, and Joseph Dorzat provided its leadership, workers constituted 66 percent of the members. Silk weavers constituted 18 percent of all members, arms makers 10 percent, miners 4 percent, steel workers 10 percent, railway workers 9 percent, building trades workers 5 percent, and workers from various artisanal trades 11 percent.[47] The social underpinning of these republican organizations reveals the continuing ability of socialists to recruit household silk weavers, and radical Republicans' mobilization of workers in the expanding metal and mining industries.

Advocates of a revolutionary commune continued to denounce the government for failing to adopt revolutionary measures in the face of impending military defeat. At the end of January, Bertholon responded by urging central state officials to shut down *La Commune* and ban the city's clubs.[48] The announcement of an armistice on January 28 led Bertholon and other radicals to demand a *levée en masse* and *guerre à outrance*, rather than a humiliating peace treaty. It also prompted renewed calls by socialists for the establishment of a revolutionary commune. On February 3, club members apprehended a police officer caught ripping down an announcement urging citizens to gather at city hall for proclamation of the commune. They took him to the *Club de la Vierge*, where about six hundred club members were discussing recent events. The mayor, prefect, and public prosecutor soon arrived and persuaded the group to release the officer. Bertholon, though hostile to the club members' demand for new municipal elections, agreed to call new elections if the city council resigned. He immediately notified the Minister of the Interior of "serious troubles" and threatened to resign if he was not granted "full powers to act."[49] The radical republican mayor, Pierre Boudarel, promised to raise the issue of elections with the council immediately. Declarations appeared on February 3 announcing that the commune would be proclaimed the next day. The following day, the city council met and refused to resign and allow new elections.[50]

In the National Assembly election of February 8, liberal Republicans of *Le Mémorial* joined forces with royalists under the banner "order and liberty" in a conservative electoral alliance, the *Comités réunis*. The radicals of the *Alliance républicaine* ran their own slate of candidates, while the socialists of *La Commune* had their own list, which included future communard leaders. The election heightened antagonisms between socialist and radical Republicans. After *L'Éclaireur* refused to print a letter from Gen. Gustave-Paul Cluseret concerning the elections, *La Commune* reminded its readers that the radicals of *L'Éclaireur* are "our enemies," denounced the *Alliance républicaine* as "the society for the exploitation of the popular vote," and warned that "with these men, you will be as exploited as with the Jesuits."[51] The conservative slate won all the contested seats, capturing the vast majority of rural votes and garnering 55 percent of the ballots, compared to 35 percent for radicals and only 10 percent for socialists.

In the aftermath of their electoral defeat, radicals and socialists failed in an attempt to create a united front. On February 16, Barthélémy Durbize, president of the *la Vierge* club, proposed to members of the *Alliance républicaine* that the two organizations create a joint central committee of forty members to coordinate their activities. Radical Republicans turned down the offer. In early February, communard advocates Antoine Chastel and Barthelemy Durbize joined the board of directors of *L'Éclaireur*. Chastel was expelled from the board on February 21 and Durbize then resigned. On February 26, *La Commune* accused the radical bourgeoisie of the *Alliance* and *L'Éclaireur* of "making advances to Orleanists behind the back of the working class."

The insurrection in Paris forced Republicans to take a stand in favor of either the Versailles government or the Paris commune. On March 22, *L'Éclaireur* denounced the insurrection in Paris as "discrediting Republicans," and urged Saint-Étienne's Republicans to remain calm and orderly. Though worried about the threat of monarchist restoration, the city's radicals were unwilling to condone revolution. Socialists at *La Commune* had no such hesitations, declaring their support for the Paris commune and urging their readers to follow its example.

News of the commune in Lyon reached Saint-Étienne on Thursday, March 23. The socialists of the *Club de la Vierge* central committee called a meeting to discuss the creation of a commune in Saint-Étienne. The city council met in emergency session throughout the day, and the mayor received a delegation of communard supporters who requested the resignation of the city council and immediate municipal elections. The mayor raised the issue with the city council, which voted seventeen to seven to resign but to remain in office until the election of a new city government. During these deliberations, several companies of National Guardsmen occupied city hall, and crowds filled the streets in response to news of the events at Lyon. At a large gathering at *la Rotonde* that evening, socialists of the *Club de la Vierge* called on the radical Republicans of the *Alliance républicaine* to join them in creating a list of candidates who would organize the proclamation of a commune. Radical Republicans rejected the offer.[52]

On March 24, *La Commune* declared that "the commune must be proclaimed everywhere, as in Paris . . . without violence, but with steadiness of purpose." *L'Éclaireur* published a proclamation by the prefect denouncing the communes as "open revolt against the sovereignty of the French people." In another proclamation, the city council announced its dissolution. Groups of club activists, led by red flags and drums, marched through the city to publicize a meeting at the *Club de la Vierge*. The meeting ended with a decision to march on city hall, which housed both the prefecture and city council, to demand the proclamation of a commune. When several hundred club members tried to force their way into city hall, Colonel Lagrive, commander of the National Guard, agreed to allow eleven delegates into the building. Negotiations followed with the prefect, mayor, and city council. Communard delegates requested the appointment of a commission, from among their ranks, to assist the city council in its deliberations. The prefect refused, claiming that such actions were beyond the scope of his authority. The mayor reminded them that he was awaiting a response from Versailles regarding the possibility of holding new municipal elections. The delegates then announced their intention to occupy the building and hold the mayor and city council captive until their demands were met. They moved to another room, where they were joined by a company of National Guardsmen. At midnight, the crowd that had gathered outside city hall forced its way into the building.

When news of the defeat of Lyon's commune reached Saint-Étienne early the next morning, the communards evacuated city hall after securing a promise from the mayor that he would ask the city council to consider whether to hold a referendum on the establishment of a Commune. The newly appointed prefect, Henri de l'Espée, had arrived in town that night, accompanied by two National Guard companies loyal to Versailles. In the morning, he occupied his office in city hall without resistance. De l'Espée immediately issued a proclamation urging all citizens to support the government of the Republic. At 9:30 a.m., he received a delegation of the city council, which assured him of their support for measures to maintain order. They presented a request for municipal elections on the issue of the commune and warned the prefect that stationing troops in front of city hall would provoke the crowds gathered in the streets. Against the advice of General Lavoye, de l'Espée ordered the removal of troops at city hall, mistakenly believing that loyal units of the National Guard offered sufficient protection.

Negotiations continued through the day on March 25. A delegation of National Guard officers met with the mayor early in the afternoon, to request that the citizens' militia be polled on the issue of a commune. The mayor initially responded that he did not have the authority to call such an election, but eventually agreed to do so in order to avoid a confrontation. The city council approved the proposal, and called on each National Guard company to elect two delegates to meet with elected authorities. The council was forced to retract this concession, however, after the prefect refused to accept the compromise. City council deliberations were then interrupted by National Guardsmen, who entered the building after one of their members, the silk weaver Lyonnet, was killed by gunfire from an unknown source on the crowded square in front of city hall.[53] The communards arrested the prefect, hung a red flag from a window overlooking the square, and established an administrative committee headed by Jean Jolivalt, a republican socialist freethinker and professional soldier by training.[54]

Available evidence on participants suggests that the Saint-Étienne commune attracted insurrectionaries from a diversity of class backgrounds, although all except Durbize and Jolivalt were men of relatively modest means. The most active workers in the commune were silk weavers. Workers from the city's newer industries—coal miners and steel workers—played a relatively minor role. Michel Rondet, who was arrested and convicted for his participation in the commune, testified that he saw none of the workers he knew from the mines of Ricamarie and Firminy among the crowd at city hall. The prefect Ducros confirmed his observation: "People attribute all sorts of ill deeds to the miners of Saint-Étienne, but . . . there weren't any miners present. . . ."[55] Of the fifty-six suspects later tried for participation in the commune, fifty can be identified by occupation. Among them were seventeen shopkeepers or merchants, seventeen silk weavers, five hardware or steel workers, four building trades workers, three arms workers, two miners, one soldier, and one police inspector who was a former miner.[56] Available records on Saint-Étienne's approximately three thousand–member National Guard also suggest that communard supporters were drawn predominantly from the inner city household silk weaving neighborhoods, such as Valbenoîte and Montaud.[57]

National Guardsmen occupied strategic points throughout the city, including the telegraph station, the Chateaucreux railroad station, the gunpowder factory, and the arms factory. The prefect remained a prisoner in a large room at city hall, where he was surrounded by National Guardsmen, many of whom were purportedly drunk. Guardsmen questioned de l'Espée about his previous official activities, demanded his resignation, and asked him to proclaim the commune. De l'Espée agreed to resign as prefect but refused to authorize the proclamation of a commune. Later in the evening, around 10:00 p.m., a new group of guardsmen entered the crowded room where the prefect was held prisoner. When Fillon, who was in charge of guarding the prefect, was pushed back by the growing crowd, he drew his pistol. After falling on the ground, Fillon fired several shots. In the ensuing fusillade, two National Guardsmen and de l'Espée were killed. News of the death of the prefect weakened support for the commune, reinforcing conservative accusations that a commune meant the reign of disorder, pillage, and violence.

The next day, March 26, the communards busied themselves with the trial of the deputy public prosecutor, Jean-Baptiste Gubian, and another official, DeVentavon. Both men were acquitted by a revolutionary tribunal headed by Jolivalt and Durbize. The communards also issued a proclamation announcing the establishment of the commune by the National Guard, and setting March 29 as the date for new municipal elections.[58] In the meantime, military forces under the command of General Lavoye prepared for an assault on city hall. The city council met that day at the home of the mayor, but rejected a proposal that they return to city hall. Though the communards managed to accumulate a large storage of arms at city hall, demoralization quickly set in after the death of the prefect and news of the arrival of troop reinforcements on March 27. Several communard leaders abandoned their posts. By the morning of March 28, only a small contingent of approximately sixty insurgents remained at city hall. Étienne Faure, one of the working-class leaders of the commune, later denounced both Durbize and Jolivalt as bourgeois "traitors to our cause."[59] Soldiers surrounded the building and the outnumbered communards surrendered without firing a shot. Several communard leaders, including Jolivalt and Durbize, escaped and fled across the border into Switzerland, but fifty-six suspected leaders were later tried for their role in the insurrection. In December, twenty-one of them were sentenced to prison terms of varying length.

Although the communards were defeated by the end of March, radical Republicans retained control of the city council, and the National Guard was not yet disarmed. Radicals distanced themselves from the recent insurrection, but blamed it on the failure of the central government to make a firm commitment to the republic and on the provocations of reactionaries.[60] The new conservative prefect, Joseph Ducros, arrived on April 8. He refused the mayor's request to allow the National Guard to assume its post at city hall, and banned public meetings planned to prepare electoral lists for the municipal election of April 30.[61] Socialists did not run their own candidates in this election but backed the "Radical Democracy" slate of candidates supported by *L'Éclaireur*. This slate, which included several communard supporters, won thirty-one seats, while the conservative list (*Electeurs réunis*), supported by liberal Republicans of *Le Mémorial* and the conservative *Le Defenseur*, won only five seats.

The radical city council soon confronted the conservative prefect and the government of Versailles. On May 16, the city council sent a letter to the

National Assembly requesting the cessation of all hostilities against Paris, and the dissolution of the National Assembly now that it had fulfilled its mandate with the signing of a peace treaty.[62] The prefect annulled this city council session and dismissed the mayor, who had refused to provide him with National Guard registers, and to order the Guard to return its drums, bugles, and trumpets. The mayor claimed that this amounted to a first step in the disarmament of the National Guard, which had not yet been decreed. After police discovered a cache of weapons at city hall, the prefect requested that the attorney general arrest ex-mayor Pierre Boudarel, who had denied the existence of these weapons. On June 22, the central government suspended Saint-Étienne's city council and replaced it with a municipal commission whose members were selected by the prefect. In October, police raided a meeting of the *Alliance républicaine* and brought a group of the city's most prominent radical Republicans to trial for their alleged role in the commune. Most of the defendants, who insisted they had no sympathy for the communards, were acquitted.

WAR AND REVOLUTION IN ROUEN

News of the proclamation of the Third Republic prompted Rouen's Republicans to take to the streets to celebrate, but it did not produce the riots that conservative city council members feared. The change of regime was marked by conflicts between liberal and radical Republicans over positions of power within the new government. The city's radicals were disappointed when liberal party leader Desseaux was appointed the new prefect. Desseaux tried to pacify them by appointing radical lawyer Auguste Leplieux as secretary general of the prefecture. But he angered radicals by failing to remove Bonapartist police and judicial officials from office. The radical *Comité démocratique* sent two of its leading members—Charles Cord'homme and Duvivier—on a mission to Tours to urge the government to replace Desseaux. Minister of Justice Adolphe-Isaac Cremieux refused to appoint a new prefect, but allowed Cord'homme to replace Bonapartist judicial officials, and named radical leader Georges Letellier as attorney general. Long-time liberal republican leader Senard then intervened, persuading the government to remove Letellier from office. Cord'homme returned once again to Tours and convinced Cremieux to reinstate Letellier.[63] This initial skirmish among Republicans gave radicals control of several positions within the judiciary, but liberal Republicans remained in control of the prefecture.

Control over the prefecture gave liberal Republicans a decisive advantage in the ensuing struggle. It prevented radicals and socialists from capturing the city council and National Guard, both of which remained controlled by conservative Orleanists and Bonapartists. Rouen's radicals demanded the immediate dissolution of the conservative city council elected in August, and appointment of a provisional republican municipal government. The city council considered calling on the National Guard, commanded by the former orleanist deputy Louis Estancelin, to prevent their replacement by an appointed municipal commission.[64] Fearful of violence, and afraid that local business leaders might sabotage his efforts to raise money for the war effort, Desseaux agreed to allow the city council to remain in office. He strongly objected to the central government's plan to dissolve city councils and hold new municipal elections on September 25, contending that it would make it difficult to secure loans for the war effort.[65] The central government's decision to abandon plans for municipal elections enabled royalists and Bonapartists to retain municipal power in Rouen.

The deteriorating military situation made the organization of the defense effort top priority for the new government. On September 10, Desseaux appointed an eighteen-member departmental committee of defense. It included radical republican leaders Cord'homme, Berthelot, and Le Barbier, but the majority of members were royalists and liberal Republicans intent on preventing radicals and socialists from using the military crisis to arm workers for insurrection. Conservatives like Raoul Duval, though hesitant to lend their support to republican defense efforts, agreed to serve on the committee because of the need to "keep watch over certain elements who will succeed in organizing an insurrection if we stand aside. . . ."[66]

Radicals and socialists repeatedly called on the city council to arm workers to confront approaching Prussian troops. The radical *Comité central démocratique*, led by Cord'homme and Leplieux, as well as the radical newspaper *La Liberté de Rouen*, urged the government to open the ranks of the National Guard to all citizens and reorganize the municipal police force. *La Liberté de Rouen* complained about the case of several workers from the factory district of Saint-Sever who were denied arms.[67] U. Guillemard, the radical mayor of Le Havre, complained to the Minister of Justice about Desseaux's failure to organize the defense effort, and urged the government to move the prefecture from Rouen to Le Havre.[68] The socialist *Fédération ouvrière*, led by Émile Aubry, accused Bonapartists and Orleanists of sabotaging the defense effort. "The enemy is at our doors," wrote Aubry on September 25, 1870, "and nothing is yet seriously organized to repel them or stop their march. The fear of entrusting arms to the working class is one of the principal causes of this forbearance. Remember 92 and we will win!"[69] Desseaux, fearful of armed insurrection if weapons fell into the hands of socialist workers, allowed royalists to retain control of the local militia.

The advent of the republic stimulated renewed efforts by socialists to mobilize factory workers via the *Fédération ouvrière*, led by members of the local branch of the First International. During the period from September 22 to November 10, the *Fédération* organized thirteen public meetings, attended by radical republican leaders and socialist workers. Participants discussed defense issues and repeatedly called for an intensification of the war effort. At the September 22 meeting, attended by fifteen hundred people, participants created a *Committee of Vigilance*, a popular defense committee charged with coordinating grassroots defense efforts with official government activities. The gathering was followed by a public demonstration against any peace treaty that did not include the removal of all Prussian troops from French soil. At a subsequent meeting of approximately twelve hundred people on September 27, participants called for the dissolution of the city council, appointment of a provisional municipal committee, and dismissal of National Guard commander Louis Estancelin.[70] The gathering also expressed support for a number of social reforms, including abolition of convent workshops, higher wages for prison labor, and daily rather than hourly wages for those employed in municipal workshops.

The city council responded to these socialist initiatives with a protest to the prefect, announcing that it would not cede to intimidation by revolutionaries. Desseaux declared that he would not tolerate demonstrations that threatened public order and directed local police to keep watch over public meetings. The commander of the National Guard, Estancelin, denounced the efforts of club members to usurp public authority. He ordered detachments of National Guardsmen stationed at the prefecture and city hall.

While threatening repression, liberal republican authorities made efforts to co-opt socialist defense initiatives. At the end of September, Desseaux negotiated a compromise with socialist and radical delegates of the *Committee of Vigilance*. The settlement denied the committee the status of a legitimate public authority, but agreed to allow several key committee leaders to serve on existing government defense organizations. The *Committee of Vigilance* delegates acknowledged the status of their organization by changing its title to the *Committee of Initiative*, which implied a private advisory, rather than public surveillance, role. In return, Desseaux added seven radical and socialist members to the official departmental defense committee, including three members of Rouen's *Committee of Vigilance*, one of whom was the leader of the *Fédération ouvrière*, Ernest Vaughan. Desseaux portrayed the compromise as a decisive triumph over socialist agitators: "I encountered opposition from the socialist party, whose projects I thwarted when they tried to introduce in Rouen, as in Lyon and Marseille, the regime of the authoritarian Commune; in addition, I had to fight against several hot-headed democrats whose repeated demand to replace the city council of Rouen with a provisional commission I refused."[71]

As Prussian troops moved closer to Rouen, Republicans intensified their demands for arming the local population. Socialist militants organized a demonstration against the orleanist leader of the National Guard, Estancelin, and urged Léon Gambetta, during his visit to the city on October 7, to replace him. Subsequent protests took place on October 9, after Estancelin refused to arm a corps of about fifty republican volunteers, *La Guérilla rouennaise*.[72] News of the defeat in Metz at the end of October evoked accusations of treason and renewed demands for revolutionizing the war effort. On November 1, several thousand Republicans gathered at the Palais de Justice, at a meeting presided over by Ernest Vaughan, to demand a *levée en masse*, forced loans to finance the war effort, civilian control of the military, and a purge of the officer corps. The gathering also urged the city council to organize the production of weapons and construct defensive barricades.[73] No such measures were undertaken by the time forty to forty-five thousand Prussian troops began their march on Rouen at the beginning of December.

The key issue facing Rouen's authorities was whether to arm local workers against approaching Prussian troops. The departmental defense committee, which met at the prefecture on December 4, urged the population to arm itself against the invaders and called for arming the workers of the faubourgs. General Briand, though wary of defending a city surrounded by hills, approved plans to construct barricades within the city, and to sound the general alarm *(tocsin)* to call the people to arms. Desseaux and the city council rejected the idea of arming local workers for street fighting. On December 4, in a meeting with General Briand, city councilors, though fearful of socialist barricades and Prussian bombardment, expressed a reluctance to abandon Rouen without a fight. The council accepted a proposal for the mobilization of the National Guard but refused Briand's request to sound the general alarm. The *tocsin*, observed city councilor Cordier, means insurrection. The mayor, Étienne-Benoît Netien, expressed the fear that the council's refusal to sound the *tocsin* might serve as a pretext for military authorities to abandon the city. A resolution was unanimously adopted, which claimed that "to speak to the National Guard is to speak to all citizens, because they are all henceforth summoned into its ranks."[74] Neighborhood defense committees met with municipal and military officials on the evening of December 4 and announced their intention to construct barricades to prevent the entry of the Prussians into the city.[75] Finding the streets of Rouen deserted, and faced with a municipality unwilling to arm the population, military officials decided to retreat to Le Havre during the early morning hours, thus allowing the Prussians to occupy Rouen without resistance.

On the morning of December 5, National Guardsmen who had assembled to fight the Prussians were ordered to disperse. A number of guardsmen who had gathered in front of city hall angrily fired shots into the air, threw down their weapons, and threatened city councilors who began to arrive for an emergency meeting. Several angry members of the large crowd gathered in front of city hall grabbed the abandoned weapons and fired shots at city hall, breaking a number of windows.[76] The city council, surrounded by a hostile crowd and fearful of an attack upon the building, issued a proclamation blaming General Briand for the evacuation of Rouen. Rumors spread throughout the city, attributing the troop withdrawal to a secret deal between the city council and Prussian authorities.[77] Radical republican leader Auguste Leplieux angrily denounced the city councilors as traitors who merited execution.

After the fall and occupation of Rouen, Republicans who found refuge at Le Havre used that city's newspapers to denounce those responsible for the absence of resistance. Radicals blamed the lack of resistance on the city council, which had failed to pursue the war effort actively, out of fear of arming the city's workers.[78] National Guard commander Estancelin blamed the republican central government for refusing him permission to purchase weapons from England, and for ordering the withdrawal of troops from Rouen.[79] Commanding general Briand attributed the fall of Rouen to the unwillingness of the municipal government to mobilize the population for the defense effort.[80] Anger over the failure to defend Rouen prompted the radical republican mayor of Le Havre, U. Guillemard, to deny refuge to liberal republican leader Desseaux, whose presence, he argued, might provoke popular disorders.[81]

The occupation of Rouen by Prussian troops intensified the economic crisis. Commerce came to a standstill, with the blockade of the Seine by French naval vessels and the cessation of rail traffic between Rouen, Paris, and Le Havre. Cut off from supplies of coal and raw cotton, Rouen's textile factories shut down, leaving tens of thousands of workers unemployed. The city council implemented traditional measures of poor relief, including public works projects for the unemployed, bread coupons, and soup kitchens, all of which had aided an estimated thirty thousand indigent workers by the end of the year. Although hopeful that such measures would appease workers, many of whom attributed the fall of Rouen to the treason of the city's bourgeoisie, city councilors still feared insurrection. In early December, they asked Prussian authorities to allow National Guardsmen to keep their weapons in order to maintain public order.[82] Cardinal Bonnechose met with the Prussian general de Manteuffel and warned of the threat of a working-class insurrection after the withdrawal of Prussian troops. He secured a promise from occupying authorities that they would allow rearmament of the National Guard after troop withdrawal.[83]

Prussian authorities were also fearful of working-class rebellion. Afraid of working-class attacks on their troops, the military commander in Rouen demanded a ransom of 500,000 francs, to be confiscated in the event of public disorders or popular reprisals against his troops. Prussian authorities demanded an additional 500,000 francs to be placed at the disposition of the new prefect Cramer. The city council, though willing to provide a 250,000 franc indemnity payment, refused the demand for a ransom payment. Instead, they offered to provide several council members as hostages as a guarantee for the safety of occupying troops.[84]

The National Assembly election of February 8, 1871 took place under conditions of economic crisis and military occupation. Local newspapers, including the liberal *Journal de Rouen* and radical *La Liberté*, reappeared only a few days before the election. Conservatives united under a single party of order slate, that included Orleanists, Bonapartists, Legitimists, and a few liberal Republicans. Republicans remained divided on six different electoral lists, including two liberal and four radical slates. Each list reflected different patterns of cooperation and conflict among liberal, radical, and socialist Republicans, as well as differences in the representation of Republicans from Le Havre and Rouen.[85] Conservative candidates emerged victorious, winning a large majority of the votes from a war-weary population anxious for an end to the economic crisis. The conservative list, headed by Adolphe Thiers, captured 74 percent of the votes, compared to only 11 percent for the liberal republican lists and 9 percent for the radical lists. Republicans fared better in the city of Rouen and its surrounding area than in the department. Within the city, the largest liberal republican slate captured 27 percent of the vote, the most successful radical list 13 percent, and conservatives 50 percent. As was the case in previous elections, Republicans did best in the predominantly working-class neighborhoods of Rouen, the 4th and 6th cantons.[86]

The issue of whether Paris or Versailles would govern France dominated the political agenda from mid-March until late May. Leaders of the Rouen branch of the First International, Aubry and Vaughan, were both visiting Paris on March 18, when the confrontation at Montmartre took place that sparked the commune. At the beginning of April, the Paris Commune named Aubry director of postal services. He remained in Paris but regularly corresponded with Rouen's socialists, who organized numerous meetings in support of the commune. These meetings were relatively small, private gatherings of twenty to forty socialist militants. Among the most active participants were the textile factory weavers Creigot, Louis Fossard, and Frechel, the Darnétal factory director Nauglan, the typographer Rondet, and the carpenter François Boulanger.[87] According to government reports of March and April, Rouen's socialists eagerly awaited the departure of Prussian troops so they could declare their own revolutionary commune.[88] They were especially active in the left-bank neighborhoods of Saint-Sever and Sotteville, inhabited by large numbers of textile factory workers and evacuated by Prussian troops after the armistice. Vaughan returned to Rouen from Paris in the hope of mobilizing support for a revolutionary commune. As the military situation facing Paris deteriorated in late April, he supported radical efforts for a negotiated settlement. Liberal Republicans of the *Journal de Rouen* supported the "legitimate" government at Versailles, expressed doubts that a compromise could be reached with revolutionaries, and soon called for prompt repression of the insurrection.[89]

The municipal election of April 30 once again revealed deep divisions among Republicans. Liberal Republicans could not reach an accord with radicals over a list of candidates after liberals refused to accept anyone who supported the Paris commune. The conservative party of order alliance urged "sincere Republicans and convinced monarchists not to hesitate to join forces on the terrain of true social principles. . . ."[90] The *Journal de Rouen* did not openly support the conservative slate but failed to put forth a liberal republican alternative and expressed support for national unity in the face of revolutionary disorder. Prior to the election, radicals and socialists negotiated an alliance. In a series of meetings on April 22, 23, and 24, leaders of the *Comité radical* met with socialist representatives of the *Fédération ouvrière* to discuss the upcoming municipal election and the Paris commune. The group decided in favor of electoral abstention, given limited time, inadequate organization, and the Prussian occupation. Radicals supported a blank ballot, which they argued was less dangerous for employees, while socialist leaders favored complete abstention, which they regarded as a more complete rejection of the legitimacy of the Versailles government. At the meeting of April 24, attended by around 250 activists, a petition in support of the Paris commune was circulated. Several participants expressed hesitations, noting that this would only lead to their arrest.[91] Radical spokesmen were more supportive of the Paris commune than working-class socialist leaders, who were wary of a movement that was not directed by workers and had implemented few economic reforms.[92] Participants rejected proposals by the socialist typographer Jean-Louis Lécureuil, calling for the proclamation of a commune in Rouen and the use of armed force if those who signed the petition were arrested.[93] Following these meetings, which had been infiltrated by police spies, local authorities ordered the arrest of leaders of both the *Comité radical* and the *Fédération ouvrière*.[94] With the city's most influential radical and socialist leaders behind bars, and the municipal government under the control of conservative royalists, Rouen remained quiet during the violent repression that crushed the Paris commune.

FAILED REVOLUTIONS AND THE LEGACIES OF
REPUBLICAN PARTY FORMATION

Local legacies of Republican party formation shaped the unfolding of political events at the beginning of the Third Republic. Republican prefects—Duportal in Toulouse, Bertholon in Saint-Étienne, and Desseaux in

Rouen—displayed different levels of willingness to cooperate with, or confront, advocates of a revolutionary commune. These dispositions were not simply a product of idiosyncratic individuals; they were consistent with local patterns of cooperation and conflict among liberal, radical, and socialist Republicans that preceded the new republican regime.

In Toulouse, radicals maintained cooperative ties with socialist workers throughout the final years of the Second Empire. Socialist workers did not run their own independent candidates in the election of 1869. They supported radical Republican Armand Duportal, who had close ties to his party's socialist wing but an antagonistic relationship with liberal Republicans, who tried unsuccessfully to remove him from the editorship of *Émancipation*. This legacy was evident during the early days of the Third Republic, in Duportal's willingness to appoint socialists to positions of municipal power, to open the ranks of the National Guard to socialist workers, and to rely on socialist club militants to resist central government efforts to remove him from office.

In Saint-Étienne, a very different pattern of conflict and cooperation among Republicans during the early months of the Third Republic reflected a distinctive history of Republican party formation. During the late 1860s, Saint-Étienne's socialist workers broke ranks with radical Republicans. They launched their own newspaper, *La Sentinelle populaire*, created their own independent political organization, the *Société populaire*, and ran their own candidate in the 1869 election. Although socialists and radicals were reconciled after 1869, the relationship was much more strained than in Toulouse. This political legacy was reflected in the events of 1870–71. Although Bertholon opened the ranks of the National Guard to socialist workers and appointed some socialist leaders to positions of power in the fall of 1870, by the beginning of 1871 he was urging the central government to ban socialist clubs and shut down the local socialist newspaper *La Commune*. By that time, radicals and socialists had parted company, publishing their own newspapers and organizing their followers into different organizations. During the spring of 1871, radical Republicans refused to cooperate with socialist supporters of the revolutionary commune, although a period of renewed cooperation followed the defeat of the commune.

The pattern of cooperation and conflict among Republicans in Rouen during the early Third Republic also reflected a distinctive history of local party formation. The weak position of radicals vis-à-vis liberals during the final years of the Second Empire was largely due to the failure of the Republican party to successfully incorporate socialist workers. In contrast to their counterparts in Toulouse and Saint-Étienne, Rouen's most prominent working-class socialist militants became active in the First International, not the Republican party. The willingness of liberal party leader Desseaux to cooperate with conservative royalists during the fall of 1870 reflected a legacy of liberal republican distrust of radicals as well as liberal fear of revolutionary socialist workers, rooted in a history of class antagonisms that included memories of the barricades of 1848.

The legacy of the Second Empire was evident in the very different local political situations facing Republicans following the triumph of the republic. The advent of the republic in Toulouse occurred in a situation in which Republicans already dominated municipal politics, having captured a large majority of votes in the August 1870 municipal election. In Saint-Étienne, radical Republicans had also won the municipal election in 1870, after coaxing recalcitrant socialists back into the fold following a divisive squabble during the 1869 election. In Rouen, the new republic was inaugurated in a less hospitable political context, which included a recently elected conservative city council and a Republican party that had been soundly defeated in the municipal election of August 1870. In Toulouse this political legacy meant opportunities for socialist workers and their radical allies to capture control of municipal institutions, like the National Guard and city council, that provided organizational capacities for insurrectionary action. Radical control of municipal government in Saint-Étienne offered socialist workers less of an opportunity, given that the city's radical republican leaders treated socialist workers less as allies than as dangerous threats. In contrast to their counterparts in Toulouse and Saint-Étienne, Rouen's Republicans had failed to capture municipal power during the final days of the Second Empire. Their relatively weak position, and the dominance of liberals within the new republican government, ensured continuing conservative control of the municipal institutions that elsewhere provided socialist workers with the organizational capacities to launch insurrections.

Local patterns of conflict and cooperation among Republicans of the late Second Empire were evident during the early Third Republic. The emergence of a revolutionary commune in Toulouse was the result of a continuing but tenuous alliance between radical and socialist Republicans during a period of intense crisis. Although this alliance had been forged many years earlier, in the context of the electoral struggles of the late 1860s, it remained relatively unstable due to handicraft artisans' strong propensity for autonomous political action and radical Republicans' hesitancy to embrace revolution under a republican regime. The nationwide election of a National Assembly in February 1871 made radicals hesitant to confront a government that had acquired the legitimacy conferred by elections under conditions of universal male suffrage. The continuing threat to the republic posed by a monarchist-dominated National Assembly encouraged some radical leaders to join the communards, but most radicals were ambivalent toward the Paris commune and hopeful that a negotiated settlement would prevent bloodshed. Duportal proclaimed his support for the government in

Versailles, yet was forced by communard leaders to serve as a reluctant figurehead for the insurrection. He had been willing to ally himself with socialist revolutionaries in the fall of 1870 to confront the Government of National Defense, when fear of monarchist restoration convinced him of the need for drastic action. But Duportal hesitated when socialists asked him to lead the commune and confront the Versailles government. The nonviolent resolution of the insurrection in Toulouse was due in large part to the role of liberal Republicans, who refused to take up arms alongside royalists to combat the revolutionary threat.

In Saint-Étienne, the legacy of conflict between radical and socialist Republicans that had marked the late Second Empire was evident during the early months of the new republic. The split between radicals and socialists that had erupted in 1869 reemerged during the winter of 1870–71, as socialists abandoned cooperation with radicals and created their own newspaper and as radical party leaders distanced themselves from the advocates of a revolutionary commune. During the spring of 1871, most radical leaders staunchly opposed the revolutionary commune. The marginalization of liberal Republicans, evident during the final years of the Second Empire, and their willingness to join royalists to contain the revolutionary threat, made the prospect of a negotiated settlement of the insurrection less likely. The accidental shooting of the prefect by socialist workers further reinforced radical republican hostility toward the commune, the defeat of which did not eliminate radical republican control of municipal institutions. Radical Republicans were much less compromised by the insurrection than their counterparts in Toulouse, despite the efforts of conservatives to portray them as supporters of violence and disorder.

The republican legacy of the Second Empire in Rouen included a weak party that had excluded working-class socialists but temporarily united radical and liberal Republicans behind a liberal republican agenda. Liberal dominance after the advent of the new republic meant that conservative royalist control of municipal institutions was never seriously challenged. The relative exclusion of radicals and socialists from positions of power in the new government encouraged greater cooperation between radicals and socialists during the fall of 1870. Though unwilling to join forces with socialists during the final years of the Second Empire, radical Republicans were angered by the liberal republican prefect's failure to challenge royalist control over the city council and National Guard and to arm workers for the war effort. Despite shared anger over the occupation of Rouen and hostility toward the armistice, radicals and socialists ran their own separate slates in the February 1870 election. It wasn't until the spring of 1871 that radicals finally joined forces with socialist workers, but they did so belatedly and under conditions of relative political weakness. Despite widespread fear of working-class rebellion among the city's bourgeoisie, a revolutionary commune never emerged, for liberals and royalists retained firm control of municipal institutions.

Although conflicts among liberal, radical, and socialist Republicans marked republican politics before and after the establishment of the Third Republic, the stakes were very different after September of 1870. After the establishment of the republican regime, the struggle shifted from an internal party dispute over candidate selection and control of the local newspaper to a struggle over who would control institutions of state power, including the prefecture, city hall, National Guard, police, and judiciary. The communards inaugurated situations of multiple sovereignty by creating new nongovernmental institutions, including revolutionary clubs, vigilance committees, and regional Leagues. They also challenged the government's monopoly over the organized means of coercion by temporarily capturing control over city councils and citizens' militias.

Radical republican prefects and city councils played a key role in creating space for revolutionary forces. Radical prefects willing to make concessions to republican socialists, in order to mobilize popular support for the war effort, allowed the communards to gain footholds in the National Guard and municipal administration. Some prefects, like Duportal, were willing to use the power at their disposal to empower revolutionary workers. Liberal republican leaders, like Desseaux, used state power to resist challenges to the government's monopoly over the organized means of coercion. Radical republican municipal governments in Toulouse and Saint-Étienne fostered a situation of multiple sovereignty by encouraging socialist workers to join local militias. In Saint-Étienne, the ability of radical city councilors to persuade the prefect to remove troops from the city hall square, in the face of an insurrectionary challenge, made the commune possible. In Rouen the city council and National Guard remained firmly under the control of liberal republican leaders and their conservative allies, who strongly resisted efforts to arm workers for the war effort. Only in Toulouse, where an alliance of socialists and radicals captured both city hall and the National Guard, did the conflict expand to encompass control over central state institutions, including the arsenal and military command.

The failure of the revolutionary communes in Toulouse and Saint-Étienne was due, in part, to the unwillingness of most radical Republicans who had worked closely with militant socialist workers during the 1860s, like Armand Duportal, to support the uprisings. The instability of the alliance between radical and socialist Republicans was rooted in radicals' reluctance to embrace revolutionary action under a republican form of government, after elections had provided legitimacy to the Versailles regime. More generally, this suggests that efforts at relegitimation of a political regime via elections can contribute to the destruction of revolutionary coalitions.

In all three cities, revolutionaries focused their attention on the city council and the National Guard. These institutions had been sites of republican electoral politics since the July Monarchy, when Republicans captured city councils and won National Guard elections despite a highly restricted suffrage. The judiciary, prefecture, and local police were also objects of contention, but these were appointed not elected positions of power. The focus on controlling the city council was also fostered by the ideology of federalism, which gave the notion of autonomous municipal government a status among republican socialists akin to that enjoyed by associations during the 1830s and universal male suffrage during the 1840s. It was also abetted by a long history of republican success in urban municipal, but not departmentwide, elections. The wartime situation, as well as the neighborhood-based character of National Guard units, also encouraged republican militants to focus their energies on gaining control of this local militia. Recruitment of the revolutionary battalions of the National Guard was based on the same informal residential networks of working-class republican strongholds that had provided sanctuaries during the repression of the 1850s.

The absence of a revolutionary challenge in Rouen was a result of the failure of radicals and socialists to capture key established institutions of municipal power and their inability to sustain alternative institutions, such as the vigilance committees. The city council and police remained under the control of conservative Orleanists and Bonapartists. In contrast to the situation in Toulouse and Saint-Étienne, the city council made little effort to arm the population for the war effort, excluding workers from the ranks of the National Guard. The only newly emergent alternative institution that threatened to challenge the government was the vigilance committees organized by socialist militants of the *Fédération ouvrière* and their radical allies. But the leaders of this popular initiative were coopted by the liberal republican prefect, who successfully appealed to their patriotism in the face of an approaching enemy. Rouen's socialists and radicals negotiated a compromise that transformed their vigilance committee from an alternative, into an accessory, to state power.

Can the absence of a revolutionary commune in Rouen be attributed to the relatively weak class capacities of Rouen's factory laborers, compared to the handicraft and household artisans of Toulouse and Saint-Étienne? During the Second Empire, the lack of a rich associational life among textile factory workers was reflected in the relative paucity of cooperative ventures and strikes and the small percentage of workers who joined the *Fédération ouvrière*. But relatively limited associational ties did not prevent Rouen's factory workers from taking to the barricades in 1848, when their radical political patron lost the election, thereby endangering the social reforms he had inaugurated. Rouen's workers created one of the largest

French branches of the First International during the 1860s, led by class-conscious workers who elaborated a program similar to that of revolutionary communards in other cities. The events of the fall of 1870 suggest that the same revolutionary forces that led the commune in other cities were present in Rouen. In October, local authorities feared that these forces would attempt to seize city hall. The key difference, which helps to explain the weakness of revolutionary forces in Rouen, was the balance of power within the Republican party and radicals and socialists' consequent lack of institutional leverage within either the city council or prefecture.

Socialist advocates of a revolutionary commune in Rouen confronted a different local political opportunity structure than their counterparts in other cities. Radicals, who had joined forces with socialists in Toulouse and allowed socialists to enter the National Guard in Saint-Étienne, were more excluded from local state power in Rouen. The absence of a commune during the spring of 1871 was a product of the Prussian occupation and of a local political situation which placed municipal power in the hands of royalists and liberal Republicans, who made sure that weapons did not fall into the hands of socialist workers. Rather than producing a revolutionary uprising, intense class antagonisms in Rouen encouraged bourgeois class solidarity, made city officials more wary of arming workers, and made liberal republican officials more willing to ally with royalists and Bonapartists, rather than radical members of their own party, to confront the threat posed by working-class socialists.

FAILED REVOLUTIONS: CONTINUITIES AND DISCONTINUITIES

The term revolution suggests an abrupt break with preceding social and political arrangements. This emphasis on discontinuity is consistent with most sociological discussions of violence and revolution. "The inclination of most analysts," writes Craig Jenkins, "has been to emphasize the disjuncture between violent and nonviolent actions, frequently categorizing nonviolent protest actions as persuasive rather than as congruent with coercive or bargaining strategies."[95] Other analysts have emphasized continuity, suggesting that the boundaries between routine politics and revolution are much more fluid. Charles Tilly's research on collective violence, for example, documents the way in which violent protests are often accompaniments and extensions of organized nonviolent efforts to achieve collective political goals. In this view, the conditions that generate violent protest and revolution are the same as those that produce nonviolent and nonrevolutionary types of collective political action.[96] The preceding account suggests that important elements of continuity contributed to creation of a revolutionary situation in 1870–71, evidenced in patterns of participation, organization, and ideology.

Many of the revolutionaries of late 1870 and early 1871 had previously participated in electoral politics at the end of the Second Empire. Given the altered circumstances created by war defeat, invasion, and the election of a monarchist-dominated National Assembly, the same workers who supported republican electoral efforts in 1868–70 and voted en masse for republican candidates in the municipal elections of 1870 took up weapons, seized city halls, and built barricades after September of 1870. The opening of the National Guard to workers put weapons into the hands of many socialists who had previously been excluded from local citizens' militias, thus giving them the capacity to engage in revolutionary politics. The same neighborhoods that were centers of revolutionary activity in 1870–71—Saint-Cyprien in Toulouse, the silk weavers' neighborhoods of Montaud and Valbenoîte in Saint-Étienne, and the factory districts of Saint-Sever and Sotteville in Rouen—had been radical and socialist republican electoral strongholds during the final years of the Second Empire. Republican socialist workers did not suddenly renounce their reformist past and embrace a revolutionary class consciousness. A crisis situation, namely, the threat posed to the new republic by Prussian troops and French monarchists, gave a revolutionary character to previously reformist republican activities.

Continuity between the revolutionary communes and nonrevolutionary republican politics of the late Second Empire is also evident in the biographies of communard leaders, many of whom had been involved in republican electoral politics during the late Second Empire. Saint-Étienne's communard leaders, Adrien Duvand, Félix Bouzols, Antoine Chastel, and Barthélémy Durbize, organized a public lecture for Jules Simon in 1869, and actively participated in the successful republican campaign during the May 1870 plebiscite. The biographies of revolutionary leaders in Toulouse and Rouen also suggest continuity with the republican movement of the Second Empire, moreso for bourgeois radicals than for working-class socialists. Many of the working-class supporters of the commune, including Émile Aubry and Ernest Vaughan in Rouen, Léopold Cros and Jean Jacob in Toulouse, and Johanès Caton and Étienne Faure in Saint-Étienne, had been active in the First International, which kept its distance from republican politics. But radical supporters of the revolutionary communes, including Antoine Calvet and Edmond Valette in Toulouse, Adrien Duvand and Barthélémy Durbize in Saint-Étienne, and Charles Cord'homme and Auguste Leplieux in Rouen, shared a history of republican electoral activism.

The organizational context of the revolutionary upheaval of 1870–71 also suggests that a certain degree of continuity contributed to the revolutionary situation. In 1870–71, as in 1848, political clubs played a key role in mobilizing socialist workers. Units of the National Guard from working-class neighborhoods also emerged as centers of revolutionary organization during both periods. Republican party newspapers, such as *Émancipation*, which had served as vehicles of electoral organization during the late Second Empire, gave voice to the revolutionary aspirations of socialist workers in 1870 and 1871. The connection between the republicanism of the Second Empire and the revolutionary struggles of 1870–71 is also evident in the persisting pattern of conflict among Republicans over the meaning of the republic. The same struggle among liberal, radical, and socialist Republicans that animated the electoral battles of 1869 and 1870 continued to dominate republican politics after the establishment of a republic in September of 1870. The electoral program advocated by republican socialists during the final years of the Empire was similar in most respects to the program espoused by the regional Leagues and by the revolutionary communards of 1870–71.

The continuity of republican electoral politics of the Second Empire with the revolutionary agitation of 1870–71 is also suggested by the statistics in table 2.[97] Revolutionary communes occurred in Toulouse and Saint-Étienne in 1871, where Republicans had captured municipal power five years prior to the downfall of the Empire. In Rouen, where Republicans failed to win municipal power via the ballot box in 1865 and 1870, there was not a revolutionary commune. This suggests continuity between electoral and revolutionary politics, rooted in the ability of Republicans to use institutions of municipal power captured via electoral means for revolutionary purposes. In legislative elections of the 1850s and 1860s, growing republican and opposition electoral strength was connected to declines in abstentions in Toulouse and Rouen, but Saint-Étienne witnessed persistently high levels of electoral abstention alongside a republican electoral resurgence. The return to the ballot box did not inevitably result in a rejection of socialist or radical doctrines in favor of liberalism nor did high levels of abstention in Saint-Étienne prevent republican victories. The consequences of electoral participation depended on the balance of power within local Republican parties, which was also a decisive factor in the emergence of revolutionary communes.

Organizational continuity is also evident in the role played by the First International, which appeared on the scene during the late Second Empire. Working-class socialists of the First International played a role in communard activities in all three cities. Local branches of the First International did not organize the communes, but they did serve as important training grounds for revolutionary leaders. The other organizations that played a central role in mobilizing revolutionary action, the clubs and National Guard units, had disappeared during the late Second Empire, but they were an important part of the republican political legacy. As in 1830 and 1848,

TABLE 2
Republican Electoral Strength—Second Empire

	Toulouse	Saint-Étienne	Rouen
I. Plebiscites			
Dec. 1851:			
% No votes	35%	41%	18%
% Abstentions	36%	28%	22%
Nov. 1852:			
% No votes	8%	7%	12%
% Abstentions	36%	54%	32%
May 1870:			
% No votes	57%	77%	48%
% Abstentions	28%	26%	14%
II. Legislative Elections			
1852:			
% Abstentions	46%	66%	50%
% Republican	0%	50%	26%
% Opposition	7%	66%	26%
1857:			
% Abstentions	42%	45%	57%
% Republican	54%	61%	30%
% Opposition	54%	61%	46%
1863:			
% Abstentions	37.5%	60%	28%
% Republican	36%	82%	43%
% Opposition	55%	82%	50%
1869:			
% Abstentions	32%	44%	17%
% Republican	49%	75%	52%
% Opposition	72%	75%	52%
III. Municipal Elections			
1865 City Council			
# Republican Seats	32	31	2
(36 total)			
1870 City Council			
# Republican Seats	36	34	0
(36 total)			

Sources: Armanieu, "Elections Legislatives"; Armengaud, *Les populations*, pp. 393, 402, 404, 407, 441; Brossard, *Les Elections*, pp. 64–69; Martourey, *Formation et Gestion*, pp. 816, 846; Merly, "Les Elections," pp. 73, 85–92; Boivin, *Le mouvement ouvrier*, pp. 101–3, 111, 149, 163, 175, 298–99, 386, 399.

these organizations emerged during the crisis of 1870–71 to provide Republicans with vehicles for popular mobilization.

Continuity between the parliamentary politics of the 1860s and the revolutionary upheavals of 1870–71 is evident in the communards' ideology, especially in their respect for the rule of law. Communards in Toulouse and Saint-Étienne followed up their seizures of local state power with proclamations that expressed a strong commitment to the rule of law. They justified their rejection of the Versailles government in legal terms. The National Assembly, they argued, had gone beyond its legal mandate, which was simply to negotiate an end to the war. Saint-Étienne's communard leader, Étienne Faure, the thirty-three-year-old anarcho-socialist shoemaker who became police commissioner for three days, argued that the communards were merely carrying out the democratic mandate of the officers of the National Guard, who were elected to act as agents responsible for "transmitting the popular will to local authorities."[98]

Saint-Étienne's communards repeatedly demanded new municipal elections, hoping to create a revolutionary commune via the ballot box. They negotiated this demand with established elected and appointed authorities. Only after several failures to secure municipal elections did they illegally seize municipal power. After doing so, they maintained great respect for the rule of law, as evidenced by the proceedings of their revolutionary tribunal and by their eagerness to quickly call elections to legitimate their seizure of power. The revolutionary tribunal established by the communards in Saint-Étienne, though headed by a professional soldier, Jean Jolivalt, acted as a grand jury rather than military court, reviewing each case with the intention of passing it along to the established judiciary if there was sufficient evidence of criminal behavior. The communards did not simply seize ammunition from the powder factory. They provided the guard on duty with receipts, in the form of vouchers from the central committee of the National Guard. In Toulouse, the communards also tried to convey an image of legality to the population, making great efforts to secure the support of elected municipal officials and to persuade the prefect to join their cause.

The revolutionaries of 1871 rejected conservative criticisms that they lacked respect for law and order. After the killing of the prefect, Saint-Étienne's newspaper *La Commune* reassured its readers, in its last issue of March 26, that the commune was committed to legality and order: "Friends of Order. Don't hesitate any longer to call municipal elections. Install your Commune. . . . Not with violence but with firmness of purpose. In the name of order and public tranquility, workers, act together publicly and peacefully." Years of republican activism had imbued the revolutionaries of 1870–71 with a respect for the rule of law and elections. This respect was fostered by the presence of lawyers in the ranks of the republican leadership and by the repression of the 1850s, in which the arbitrary power of state officials made life difficult for Republicans, especially republican socialists.

The revolutionary language of republicanism in 1848 and 1870 suggests continuity not only across these two revolutions but also with the more distant past. The revolutionaries of 1848 and 1870–71 constantly looked back to 1793, adopting the slogans and imagery of the French Revolution. Following in the footsteps of their predecessors, republican socialists of 1870 raised the alarm of "la patrie en danger," established local Committees of Public Safety, and denounced supporters of the Versailles government as "Vendéens," harkening back to the counterrevolutionaries of 1793. In adopting the term "commune" to describe their revolutionary project, the insurrectionaries also looked back to the French revolution. The term referred not only to the smallest unit of local government in France but also to the first Paris Commune of 1792, which marked the advent of the most radical phase of the Revolution and establishment of a revolutionary tradition of direct democracy.

Another element of continuity that contributed to the emergence of a revolutionary situation is evident in the intense anticlericalism that informed republican ideology. The anticlerical issues that were raised by republican candidates during the electoral contest of 1869 found expression both in the proclamations of the Leagues and programs of the communards and in the actions taken by republican city councils in 1870–71. Although the war dominated the public agenda, drawing attention away from social issues, the rhetoric of a threatened monarchist restoration, which unified diverse republican elements, contributed to anticlerical passions, given the close identification of the clergy with monarchy. Since schooling was traditionally a responsibility of municipal government, and since clerical power over education had been a target of republican attacks throughout the 1860s, radical republican efforts to secularize education during the fall of 1870 are not surprising. Efforts to seize control over municipal institutions, such as schools, were legitimated by appeals to anticlerical passions that had played an important role in mobilizing republican support during the 1860s.

The ideology of republicanism in 1870–71 reveals both continuities and discontinuities. Unlike their predecessors of 1848, republican socialists of the early Third Republic expressed, in both words and deeds, a commitment to federalism and decentralism rather than to one indivisible republic. Whereas republican revolutionaries of 1848 waved tricolor flags, planted liberty trees, and urged class conciliation, the revolutionaries of 1870–71 unfurled red flags, emphasized equality more than liberty, and more readily adopted a rhetoric of class antagonism. Fear of monarchist restoration, and a desire to establish the republic on firm institutional grounds, characterized revolutionaries of both periods. But the social and political texture of the republicanism of 1870–71 reflected changes in state power and class relations that had taken place during the Second Empire.

In all three cities, republican ideology of 1870–71 was informed by nationalist sentiments, expressed as patriotism. This played an important role in mobilizing workers for the war against Prussia in 1870 and in generating opposition to the policies of the liberal republican Government of National Defense. But, as was the case during the 1840s, this was a nationalism embedded in an egalitarian vision of the social republic. As the attorney general in Toulouse noted in a report of August 31, 1870, after the government decided to call up married men aged twenty-five to thirty-five who had previously done military service: "Though beneficial for national defense, [this policy] has offended egalitarian instincts that are part of the national character." "National sentiments," he lamented, "are not developed here" because "the enemy is too far away. . . ."[99] In Toulouse, the most ardent working-class supporters of an all-out war effort after September 1870 were the same socialist workers who had joined the conscription riots of 1868 and demonstrated against the war in early August 1870, amid shouts of "Long Live the Republic!" and "Long Live Prussia!" The war did not prompt socialist workers to abandon class identities and concerns in favor of civic identities that inspired nationalism; rather, workers temporarily put aside their struggles against employers so as to defend the new republic against occupying Prussian forces. In Rouen, where nationalist sentiments were relatively strong, workers voted overwhelmingly in 1869 for two candidates, Pouyer-Quertier and Desseaux, who campaigned on platforms opposing foreign military interventionism and favoring reductions in the military budget. In October 1870, Émile Auby's call to arms appealed to both national and class identities, urging the city's workers to "Arm yourselves initially to repell the enemy, then turn your weapons against the bourgeoisie."[100]

In the provinces, communard activities were imbued with a strong commitment to decentralism and federalism, which was also evident in republican rhetoric of the late Second Empire. In contrast to Paris, where Jacobin and Blanquist revolutionaries played a central role, in the provinces advocates of a decentralized federalist vision of socialism dominated working-class politics. Socialist workers, despite their willingness to embrace the legacy of the French Revolution by creating committees of public safety, envisioned a social republic based on principles of federalism. Whereas Jacobin socialism was ascendent in 1848, by the time of the revolutionary communes, a decade of central state repression made decentralism and federalism a more dominant strain in provincial socialist thought and practice. To the extent that a revolutionary vision of Jacobin centralism found expression during the communes, it was voiced by radical republican prefects, like Duportal and Bertholon, both of whom urged

Gambetta to institute a Jacobin dictatorship in response to the wartime crisis.[101]

The decentralist impulses motivating the revolutionary communes have led some historians to portray these municipal insurgencies as continuations of the age-old struggle of cities and regions against central state power.[102] This emphasis on the continuity of the communes with earlier municipal struggles ignores key discontinuities with prior movements for communal liberty. Although nineteen years of Bonapartist centralization helped popularize antistate political ideologies, like Proudhonian socialism, as well as revolutionary demands for communal liberties and federalism, the revolutionary communes of 1870–71 were much more than struggles against overly centralized state power. The revolutionary communards' quest for communal liberties differed from earlier struggles in that regional and local resistance to the central state came to embody issues of national defense and working-class social and political aspirations. The revolutionaries did not regard the communes simply as vehicles for achieving municipal liberties. The communes were also a way in which to rally popular support for the war effort and create an alternative form of government, a radical social and democratic republic that would redress existing inequalities of wealth and power. Parisian communards, like their counterparts in the provinces, took actions to deal with longstanding working-class and shopkeepers' grievances, via moratoriums on debt repayment, rent cancellations, and the return of pawned goods. Although they made no attempt to nationalize the Bank of France or other industries, they did turn over the factories of employers who had fled Paris to workers' cooperatives. The communards also briefly implemented the republican socialist vision of direct democracy, by instituting popular control of the citizens' militia, demanding a democratic reorganization of army and police bureaucracies, and encouraging club activities that provided forums for popular participation. The program of the League of the Southwest, quite similar to that subsequently elaborated by the Parisian communards, proclaimed a commitment to "dealing with and resolving social questions in the best interest of the working class."[103] These actions and words suggest that the communes, though reflecting local legacies of Republican party formation, were not simply continuations of age-old municipal expressions of hostility to central state power.

Revolutions are moments of both continuity and disjuncture. They provide intense learning experiences in which participants create new political strategies, cultural forms, and repertoires of collective action.[104] But when revolutions fail and are short-lived, as in the case of the provincial communes of 1871, revolutionaries have a limited opportunity to encounter the creative, hot-house experience of revolution. As a result, failed revolutions appear to exhibit pronounced elements of continuity with local prerevolutionary political histories.

CHAPTER EIGHT

Conclusion: Political Change, Class Analysis, and Republicanism

DURING THE MIDDLE DECADES of the nineteenth century, Republican party formation lead to the victory of an alliance of radical and socialist Republicans in Toulouse, the triumph of radical republicanism in Saint-Étienne, and the triumph of socially conservative liberalism in Rouen. These different patterns of change produced varied local responses to the crisis of 1870–71, generating revolutionary communes in Toulouse and Saint-Étienne but not in Rouen. The preceding narratives suggest that the political outcomes of 1871 were the culmination of a long-term process of Republican party formation, which varied across cities due to the impact of the timing of economic and political change on the shifting balance of power among liberal, radical, and socialist Republicans.

The timing, not just the content, of local economic development vis-à-vis the process of Republican party formation and the shifting national political opportunity structure helps to account for the balance of power within local Republican parties.[1] First, because the class conflicts generated by distinctive local patterns of early capitalist industrialization took place at different times vis-à-vis the process of Republican party formation, they had very different political consequences. Second, autonomous political activity by workers also had varied consequences across cities. These consequences depended on the timing of its emergence vis-à-vis local Republican party formation. Third, the national political repression of the 1850s had different consequences across cities because it intersected in varied ways with local patterns of economic development and class formation. Fourth, the timing of the rise to political power of the industrial bourgeoisie vis-à-vis the extension of universal male suffrage and the development of working-class politics helps to explain different patterns of Republican party formation.

The shifting balance of power among liberal, radical, and socialist Republicans helps to explain the origins and consequences of suffrage reform. Prior to 1848, the outcome of conflicts among Republicans produced different positions by local parties on the question of universal male suffrage and different relations between workers and Republicans. The long-term consequences of working-class participation in parliamentary politics also varied across cities, depending on the balance of power among Republicans. This shifting balance also shaped the disposition of workers to turn to the barricades rather than the ballot box and the willingness of workers to accept bourgeois political leadership.

THE TIMING OF ECONOMIC AND POLITICAL CHANGE

A comparison of early Republican party formation in Toulouse, Saint-Étienne, and Rouen suggests the importance of the timing of working-class struggles in the process. In each city, specific class struggles marked key turning points in the development of local Republican parties. Class struggles decisively shaped Republican party formation not because they led to working-class control of local parties but because they defined key conjunctures, points at which republican leaders were forced to make choices that had enduring consequences for subsequent paths of development, channeling the direction of subsequent events along a particular path and delimiting future options. It was not simply the intensity of the class struggles generated by early capitalist development, but the way in which these struggles intersected with the process of local Republican party formation, that produced different balances of power among liberals, radicals, and socialists.

In Toulouse, the transformation of consumer goods handicraft industries during the 1830s, especially the growth of "sweated" shoe making and tailoring, generated pressures for uniform industrywide piece rates, which found expression in the strikes of 1841. By forcing Republicans to take the side of small employers in order to gain votes and win the municipal election, these struggles stimulated the growth of autonomous working-class politics, which initially took the form of a strong Icarian communist movement but then developed into a working-class socialist movement that enabled workers to gain influence within republican politics. This early development of autonomous working-class politics shaped subsequent internal party conflicts, ensuring an important role for militant socialist workers within the city's Republican party. The key local class struggle in Toulouse, which took place in handicraft industry, occurred after liberal republican leaders had forged an alliance with Legitimists, embarked on an electoral road to power, and displayed little if any concern with the "social question."

In Saint-Étienne, a decisive class struggle occurred earlier, in 1833–34, before Republicans became committed to an electoral strategy for change and in the context of political crisis and social upheaval. By 1834, much of the initial enthusiasm for liberal principles that had rallied republican support for the orleanist regime had waned and a republican socialist movement had already taken hold, which attempted to meld liberal republican principles with the cooperative associationalist themes of a nascent labor movement. The silk weavers' struggle against merchant capitalists, rooted in changes in production relations within household industry, began as an economic confrontation but rapidly became politicized. It culminated in barricades and insurrection in 1834, which radicalized bourgeois party leaders and secured the loyalties of the largest segment of the city's working-class for the Republican party at a very early date. This created an enduring legacy for republicanism, making socialist household silk weavers and radical bourgeois Republicans central actors in the subsequent history of local party formation.

The violent rebellions of textile factory workers in Rouen in 1830 also marked a decisive turning point in the process of local Republican party formation. This violent conflict took place relatively early in the formation of the Republican party, in a very different political context than the Toulouse handicraft artisan strikes of the early 1840s or the silk weavers' insurrection of 1834 in Saint-Étienne. The class struggles of Rouen's factory workers occurred when a new liberal regime had just replaced the Bourbon monarchy and when republicanism largely meant the triumph of liberal over monarchist political principles, prior to the development of a republican socialist movement. By generating widespread fear among property holders, the class struggles of 1830 polarized class relations and subsequently made bourgeois republican leaders more amenable to liberalism and more wary of collaborating with socialist workers, thus setting the stage for an enduring and bitter division within the party between socially conservative liberal leaders and their radical and socialist counterparts. The class struggles of Rouen's factory workers in 1830 did not mean a stronger political presence for workers or a more prominent place for socialist ideas and practices on the local political agenda. They helped foster liberalism among the city's republican leaders, rather than the radicalism that characterized bourgeois party leadership in Saint-Étienne.

During the middle decades of the nineteenth century, French workers began to organize independent political initiatives, creating their own newspapers and electoral organizations and running working-class candidates for office. The timing of these activities varied across cities. In Toulouse, militant artisans organized demonstrations led by Icarian communist militants in 1842, refused legal aid from bourgeois republican leaders in 1843, boycotted republican demonstrations in 1844, started their own independent working-class newspaper in 1847, and created a working-class electoral association in 1848. In contrast, prior to 1848, the militant socialist ribbon weavers of Saint-Étienne accepted bourgeois leadership and looked to radical republican leaders to publish newspapers that spoke to working-class interests, to defend workers arrested for illegal associational and strike activity, and to run for office as candidates who would address the grievances of workers. Socialist workers found a home in the Republican party at a very early date, and continued to press their demands within a party whose leadership was dominated by bourgeois radicals. In Rouen, local textile workers also sought leadership from radical bourgeois Republicans who supported their right to the suffrage prior to 1848 and who rapidly implemented numerous workplace reforms in early 1848. Independent political organizing by textile workers did not appear until the 1860s, when, under the guidance of the local branch of the First International, socialist workers organized independent electoral activities. Although effective indigenous working-class leadership emerged in strikes and economic struggles at the workplace, given limited literacy, lengthy hours of work, and very limited discretionary financial resources, textile factory workers looked to the radical bourgeoisie to provide leadership in the political arena.

A comparison of the consequences of autonomous working-class political efforts suggests that the willingness of workers to accept bourgeois leadership did not inevitably lead to co-optation and a shift from revolutionary socialist to radical reformist politics. In Toulouse, radical bourgeois leaders played an important role in the development of the revolutionary movement of 1870–71. They exercised their leadership in the context of strong autonomous working-class politics, and their alliance with working-class socialists helped place working-class grievances on the agenda of local politics. In Saint-Étienne, radical bourgeois republican leaders mobilized working-class support throughout the mid-century, but, after the Second Republic, gradually distanced themselves from socialism, thus facilitating the incorporation of workers under the banner of a radical vision of the republic. In Rouen, radical bourgeois leaders played a central role in mobilizing working-class activists and in placing working-class grievances at the center of the political agenda in 1848. But during the 1860s, the willingness of radical bourgeois leaders to join forces with liberals, rather than provide leadership for socialist militants, led to the growth of the First International as well as to a marginalization of working-class interests and grievances in the local political arena. These varying outcomes of working-class reliance on bourgeois political leadership suggest that there was no inevitable consequence of accepting bourgeois leadership.

The consequences of working-class reliance on bourgeois leadership depended on the circumstances in which this leadership was provided, especially the timing of the emergence of autonomous working-class political organization vis-à-vis the process of local Republican party formation. Early efforts to create autonomous working-class political activity in Toulouse paved the way for a strong republican socialist movement and a strong position for socialist workers within the Republican party. Subsequent decisions by Toulouse's working-class leaders to continue working within the Republican party during the 1860s insured a strong presence within the party during the volatile early days of the Third Republic and a measure of institutional power that provided room for revolutionary agitation in 1870–71. The autonomous working-class political activities of the 1860s in Rouen and Saint-Étienne, which included independent socialist candidates in the elections of 1869, had very different consequences. They took place at a time when local Republican parties, despite many years of repression, had consolidated their organization and established an electoral presence. This autonomous activity strained relations between radical Republicans and socialists. Given the very weak electoral showing of independent socialist candidates, it also marginalized socialist militants, and weakened the position of socialists within local Republican parties. When these parties seized power in 1870, socialists were in a much weaker position than their counterparts in Toulouse, who used their institutional footholds in municipal government to arm workers and organize revolutionary actions.

The importance of the timing of economic and political change is also evident in the divergent local consequences of the political repression of the 1850s. Repression severely weakened Republican party leadership in all three cities. Whether this created an opportunity for radical bourgeois industrialists, as in Saint-Étienne, or militant socialist workers, as in Toulouse, to take advantage of the situation and offer new leadership depended on the way in which central state policies intersected with distinctive local patterns of class formation. Political repression altered the opportunities available to Republicans, but the actors who were capable of taking advantage of these opportunities varied across cities depending on the timing of socioeconomic changes and attendant processes of class formation.

A comparison of the political role of the industrial bourgeoisie in Saint-Étienne and Rouen suggests that the timing of the rise to political power of the industrial bourgeoisie vis-à-vis the extension of the suffrage and the development of working-class politics helps to explain different patterns of Republican party formation. In Rouen, the industrial bourgeoisie, which acquired political power prior to the formation of a politically active working class and the extension of the suffrage, was less likely to embrace a radical republican vision. In contrast, in Saint-Étienne, where the rise to political power of the industrial bourgeoisie was both blocked by merchant capitalists and occurred after working-class political incorporation, radical republicanism emerged among the ranks of industrialists led by Frédéric Dorian. In Toulouse, where there was no industrial bourgeoisie to speak of, early bourgeois political activism was motivated in part by competition with the aristocracy. An entrenched aristocracy, alongside a militant working-class with a strong tradition of political autonomy, placed republican socialism at the center of the political agenda.

THE ORIGINS AND CONSEQUENCES OF SUFFRAGE REFORM

The connection between democratization and industrialization in mid-nineteenth-century France can be found in the way in which industrialization fostered a growing role for radicals and socialists within a nascent Republican party, which inaugurated universal male suffrage in February 1848. Industrialization strengthened the political role of workers and bourgeois, but the former did not express an inevitable inclination for democracy, nor did the latter display a uniform preference for liberalism. Although handicraft and household production fostered cooperative and communal values that made an affinity with democracy likely, wage laborers experienced a diversity of work settings and embraced a variety of political ideologies, including the authoritarian populism of Louis Napoleon Bonaparte. The struggle for universal male suffrage was led by a multiclass party that incorporated both workers and bourgeois, and mobilized them around a variety of different class and cross-class issues, including but not limited to suffrage reform. An adequate understanding of the struggle for suffrage reform requires an analysis of the way in which grievances and aspirations generated by economic development were mobilized by cross-class organizations around political projects that promised remedies for diverse groups.

The struggle for suffrage rights embraced lawyers, doctors, and professors denied full political rights; handicraft artisans threatened by capitalist development; household weavers aspiring for a sympathetic state that would support their cooperative ventures; and proletarianized textile factory workers and miners who believed that universal male suffrage would mean a government more sympathetic to their workplace grievances. The strongest movement for universal male suffrage developed in Toulouse, where liberals, radicals, and socialists united around this goal. In the other two cities, the issue divided liberal Republicans, who favored lower property requirements on voting rights, from radicals and socialists. Radical and socialist Republicans, a socially heterogeneous group, favored universal male suffrage because they believed it would inaugurate a social republic. The consequences of the extension of suffrage rights, however, failed to confirm either the fears of liberals and conservatives or the hopes of radicals and socialists.

After the extension of universal male suffrage in 1848, French workers increasingly pursued their goals in the electoral arena. This does not, at least initially, appear to have reduced the political saliency of class identities. The extension of civil liberties and universal male suffrage in 1848 did not diminish the importance of class-based issues due to republican appeals to fraternity and national unity. In each city, the class character of the issues that dominated local political agendas during the early days of the Second

Republic was evident in struggles over the reorganization of the National Guard, in conflicts concerning municipal workshops for the unemployed, in battles over electoral lists, and in official responses to strikes and club agitation. In Rouen and Saint-Étienne, where radicals and socialists played a central role in the new government, Republicans appealed directly to working-class interests and grievances, sometimes enacting measures that cost them large numbers of votes, like new taxes to support unemployed workers. Even in Toulouse, where liberals dominated the new government, class issues remained salient, as liberal Republicans joined radicals and socialists in professing concern for the plight of the working class. This suggests that electoral politics promoted *both* working-class solidarities and class collaboration. Republican electoral campaigns helped to politicize workers' economic grievances at the same time it channeled these grievances into a parliamentary terrain on which workers, lacking financial and other resources, were disadvantaged and dependent on the leadership of sympathetic bourgeois radicals and socialists.

The electoral defeats of 1848, and the consequent search for allies and electoral majorities, did not encourage Republicans to downplay class antagonisms. The Mountain campaigns of 1849–51 mobilized support around a socialist ideology that attacked large concentrations of wealth and property and appealed to small property owners by elaborating a cooperative vision that suggested resistance to, rather than glorification of, proletarianization. While attracting peasant smallholders, radical and socialist Republicans simultaneously helped to create working-class solidarities, by forging bonds among workers across occupational lines and creating an ideology that identified the interests of workers with the interests of the nation.

A functionalist view of parliamentary parties as necessarily vehicles of working-class integration and demobilization ignores the historical variability of the role of political parties at different points in the process of working-class formation and in different localities. Although the immediate consequence of suffrage reform was to unleash working-class protests and stimulate working-class capacities for collective action, the longer-run consequences varied across localities, depending on the character of local Republican parties. These parties contained competing voices that, on the one hand, appealed to class solidarities and antagonisms and called for socialist solutions to the problems facing workers, and, on the other hand, appealed to class conciliation, the duties and shared interests of all French citizens, and the need for social order and political stability. The ideological and organizational consequences of parliamentary institutions for the French working-class were not given by the nature of the institutions themselves; they were varied and contradictory, depending upon the strategies pursued and alternatives offered in the electoral arena by local Republican parties. These strategies and alternatives depended, in turn, on the balance of power among liberal, radical, and socialist Republicans.

BALLOTS AND BARRICADES

The turn toward the ballot box after 1848 did not mean an abandonment by workers of the French revolutionary tradition. In all three cities, the revolutionary tradition survived alongside electoral politics, although after 1848 it took on a more defensive cast. Workers showed up at the polls in massive numbers in 1848, convinced that the ballot box was an avenue for social justice. At the same time, however, they did not abandon the revolutionary tradition, in large part because of the fragility of their victory, which became evident in the first national election of 1848. As long as royalists, sometimes in alliance with liberal Republicans, were capable of winning elections, the future of the social republic remained in doubt. Given this political context, many workers viewed elections not simply as contests between powerful elites over the distribution of scarce resources but as decisive battles over the form of the state. Electoral defeat thus meant a regime committed to preserving class inequalities, rather than a social republic that would aggressively pursue greater socioeconomic equality. In early 1848, Rouen's workers combined revolutionary violence with a willingness to petition sympathetic radical republican government officials. Their revolutionary actions were a response to the electoral defeat of a radical republican official who had granted them numerous important concessions over a very short period of time. They took to the barricades after the electoral defeat of Deschamps in 1848 because they regarded the electoral outcome as a defeat of the social republic, evidenced by the continuing power of the royalist-dominated National Guard.

The electoral defeats of April and December 1848 did not prompt Republicans to abandon the ballot box in favor of the barricades. It led to the triumph of a Mountain alliance of radicals and socialists that reformulated republican programs so as to appeal to rural voters. The defeats of 1848 prompted Republicans to craft a Mountain ideology that spoke to the class interests and identities of both wage laborers and small property holders. Suffrage extension did not eliminate the revolutionary tradition, but it made workers more wary of taking to the barricades, especially after Mountain electoral victories in 1849 and 1850. Only after these successes prompted restrictions on suffrage rights in 1850 did strong divisions among Republicans over revolutionary versus electoral strategies reemerge.

The new electoral law of 1850 inspired the creation of extraparliamentary secret societies and a revival of underground revolutionary activity in all three cities. In Toulouse, radicals joined socialists in creating a secret revolutionary militia, which was plagued by the class divisions that stamped the city's republican movement. But radical and socialist Republicans continued to place their faith in the suffrage, awaiting the election of 1852 with hope of victory. This was also the case in Rouen, where radicals and socialists did not abandon their efforts to mobilize rural electoral support, in the hope that the next election would bring victory. Radicals and socialists in Saint-Étienne appear to have been much more ambivalent about electoral politics, despite their greater success in the electoral arena.[2] They boycotted municipal elections following the implementation of the new electoral law and turned to revolutionary politics, despite repeated pleas from bourgeois republican leaders to keep their faith in the ballot box. In all three cities, workers' willingness to turn to the barricades rather than elections was a product of both the persistence of a revolutionary tradition as well as a pragmatic response to, and assessment of, changing political circumstances and possibilities.

THE RELATIONSHIP BETWEEN WORKERS AND BOURGEOIS REPUBLICANS

Bourgeois leadership had different consequences for working-class politics depending on whether it was provided by liberal, radical, or socialist Republicans. This was evident during the early days of the Second Republic, when bourgeois republican leaders altered local political opportunity structures and thereby shaped working-class collective political actions. In all three cities, opportunities for collective action provided by newly won freedoms of association, assembly, and the press unleashed class struggles and generated the mass mobilization of workers. Since this mobilization was not confined to the electoral arena, bourgeois republican officials were forced to consider using police and troops against rebellious workers who were strong supporters of republicanism. Local republican power-holders faced the dilemma of having to legitimate the new government to an increasingly mobilized and politicized working class and simultaneously placate segments of the bourgeoisie whose fear of socialism plunged their cities, and the nation, into economic crisis during the early months of 1848. In attempting to meet these contradictory demands, liberal and radical republican officials exhibited different levels of willingness to employ repression against rebellious workers. Faced with strikes and violent working-class collective actions, republican officials responded to growing liberal and conservative demands for repression in different ways. In Saint-Étienne and Rouen, where radical and socialist leaders gained control, a hesitancy to repress popular protest encouraged workers to use nonelectoral means to collectively express their grievances.

The willingness and ability of workers to challenge bourgeois political leadership by launching autonomous working-class political initiatives was not simply a reflection of their level of class consciousness. The independent socialist candidacy of Émile Aubry in Rouen, which contrasted with socialist workers' support for the candidacy of radical bourgeois republican leader Armand Duportal in Toulouse, did not reflect a higher level of class consciousness or greater political militancy on the part of Rouen's factory workers. On the contrary, it reflected these workers' relative political weakness and their marginalization from Republican party inner circles. The failure of bourgeois radicals in Rouen to provide the political leadership that their counterparts in Toulouse offered to socialist workers severely weakened the Republican party, making Rouen the only one of the three cities in which Republicans did not attain municipal power prior to the fall of the Empire. In contrast, although socialist workers in Saint-Étienne and Toulouse also created branches of the First International, most socialist workers in these cities were incorporated into republican politics and workers did not run their own independent candidates in the 1870 municipal election. This incorporation subsequently provided working-class socialists with a strong organizational base from which to launch revolutionary communes in 1871. It strengthened the political position of socialists in both cities, especially in Toulouse where incorporation took place on more favorable terms. The absence of autonomous working-class electoral activity in Toulouse reflected workers' greater voice within the Republican party and the availability of alternative political means by which workers could seek to remedy their grievances, not workers' inability to organize independently. In short, the meaning of autonomous working-class political organization can only be understood in terms of the larger political context within which it occurs or fails to occur.

During the final decades of the nineteenth century, the triumph of radical republicanism in Saint-Étienne was replicated at the national level, by a party and leadership that adopted a rhetoric and strategy that had proven so successful at the local level. This triumph fostered the subsequent development of more autonomous working-class political projects during the late nineteenth century. It led to the divorce of socialists from the Republican party, but not from the institutions of the republic, and to the emergence of more distinctly class-based socialist parties. Late nineteenth-century socialist party leaders retained a republican commitment to parliamentary politics, which in turn helped foster a strong revolutionary syndicalist movement. In short, the mid-century experience of workers and socialists with republican politics helped create a tradition of electoral socialism that remained heavily reliant on bourgeois political leadership, as well as a legacy of autonomous working-class politics.

LESSONS FROM THE PAST?: THE LIMITS AND CONTRIBUTIONS
OF REPUBLICANISM

The successes and failures of mid-nineteenth-century French republicanism can be understood in terms of a relatively fluid ideology and practice
that combined the ability to integrate diverse, and sometimes divergent,
elements from various political traditions with an unwillingness to acknowledge citizenship rights for women. The capacity of French republicanism to incorporate liberal and socialist themes enabled Republicans to
mobilize support across class boundaries and to combine a civic vision that
spoke to issues of common existence with attention to the interests of oppressed groups. Yet the fraternal ideology and organization of republicanism presented a key obstacle to republican efforts to mobilize broad-based
popular support.

The limitations of mid-nineteenth-century republicanism are evident in
its gendered ideology and practice. In none of the three cities did Republicans' demand for suffrage rights extend to female workers, despite the important role played by women in the major collective protests of the July
Monarchy. Women were active in the political charivaris of the early 1830s
and in the census riot of 1841 in Toulouse. Their presence was noted by
government officials during the silk weavers' insurrection of 1834 and the
coal miners' strike of 1846 in Saint-Étienne. Women also played a prominent role in the 1830 protests of Rouen's factory spinners, and radical republican leaders intervened in support of striking female textile workers
during the final years of the July Monarchy. Despite the growth of female-
dominated shoe making and tailoring household production in Toulouse,
the central role played by women in silk ribbon weaving in Saint-Étienne,
and the feminization of factory spinning in Rouen, Republicans made no
effort to mobilize political support among women. The campaign for suffrage reform, even when radicals and socialists played a central role, as in
Toulouse, never raised the issue of women's political rights. Despite very
different gender divisions of labor, republicanism retained its fraternalist
character in all three cities.

The exclusion of women from republican electoral politics did not prevent them from playing an active role in the revolutionary agitation of
1848. Although largely absent from the 1848 protests in Toulouse, women
led the convent workshop riots in Saint-Étienne. Women signed petitions,
took to the streets, and joined men on the barricades during the early days
of the Second Republic in Rouen.[3] Though excluded from handicraft production, or relegated to an auxiliary role, women were central to household
production in Saint-Étienne and textile factory production in Rouen. The
protests of 1848 in these two cities centered around the workplace grievances of key occupational groups—household weavers and textile factory

workers—that included large numbers of women. In contrast, the protests of 1848 in Toulouse focused on the exclusion of male workers from the citizens' militia and the grievances of the male-dominated baking trade. During the political upheavals of 1870–71, however, women were much less visible. Their absence from the scene may be, in part, an artifact of the incomplete historical record. However, it may also reflect the centrality of the male National Guard in the uprisings of 1871 and the increased focus of republican politics on an electoral arena that excluded women and remained dominated by fraternalist organizations and ideology.

Does the study of mid-nineteenth-century French politics have anything relevant to say to late twentieth-century democratic socialist activists? Given the vast economic, political, cultural, and social changes that have marked the past century, one might reasonably entertain a negative answer to this question. Twentieth-century transformations in class structures, political institutions, and political cultures have dramatically altered the strategic opportunities facing working-class movements. In an age of mass-media politics and multi-million-dollar sound-bites, the resources needed for attaining political office and exercising political power are very different, as are the institutions that organize political socialization and communication. Whereas artisanal work experiences fostered democratic aspirations and made possible close connections between work, community, and politics, the current context features routinized, often deskilled, workplaces; a mass media owned by a small number of large corporations; bureaucratized political parties and labor unions; and a welfare state that turns citizens into passive clients and spectators.

"The main value of studying history," argues Herbert Gutman, "is that it allows us to treat the given in our lives, the world we live in, as conditional, that is to say, not as something that we need to take for granted, not as something which, just because it exists has existed forever."[4] The study of early French republicanism should facilitate this ability to view the present as conditional by reminding us that republicanism is a rich and varied tradition with a variety of different visions rooted in diverse relations with liberalism, socialism, and participatory democracy. The historical record suggests that liberalism and socialism were not monolithic entities. They were complex ideologies and practices, strands of which were incorporated into republicanism in different ways in different times and places. Mid-nineteenth-century French republicanism was a robust ideology, capable of assimilating diverse and contradictory messages and practices, including respect for liberal principles of civil liberties and the rule of law, a socialist understanding of how the class inequalities of capitalism undermined democracy, and a democratic commitment to popular participation in politics that is alien to liberal theory and practice. The radical republican synthesis combined elements of both traditions, fusing a respect for parliamentary institutions and hostility to arbitrary power with a vision of democracy in which popular participation remained central.

The dialogue between liberalism and socialism that characterized mid-nineteenth-century French republicanism was interrupted, but not eliminated, by the Bolshevik revolution of 1917 and its aftermath. It has been reinvigorated by the late twentieth-century crisis and downfall of communist regimes. By situating the death of communism within the long-term historical development of socialism, we are reminded that what has recently disappeared is a particular twentieth-century version of socialism, which became dominant within the socialist movement only after 1917, with the triumph of Leninism. This socialist project, in contrast to many of its nineteenth-century counterparts, was state-centered, workerist, and centralist in character. Faced with circumstances not at all conducive to democratic politics, it rapidly degenerated into authoritarian regimes characterized by bureaucratic rigidity, arbitrary exercises of power, and rule by the few.[5]

The downfall of communist regimes has opened new possibilities for change and stimulated renewed debate about the relationship between socialism, liberalism, and democracy. The nineteenth-century French republican experience can contribute to this debate, if only by making us more aware of the richness of the socialist tradition and of its suppressed cooperative, participatory democratic, and decentralist elements.[6] The history of socialism reveals democratic as well as antidemocratic themes. The centralist elements of the Blanquist and Leninist visions existed alongside the communitarianism of early "utopian" socialists and the federalism of the communards. Elitist visions of socialism, which privileged either a revolutionary vanguard or certain groups of male industrial workers, coexisted alongside a republican socialist tradition committed to the arduous task of slowly building a multiclass majority committed to egalitarian and democratic values. Contemporary democratic socialists need to reappropriate the decentralist and democratic elements of the early socialist tradition, reject the fraternalism and patriarchy that informed this tradition, and radicalize, rather then reject, the democratic contributions of liberalism.

Despite the triumphalist cries of apologists for capitalism, the demise of communism may herald a revitalization of the socialist project via a creative synthesis of socialism, feminism, liberalism, and republicanism. Such a synthesis would combine the participatory and egalitarian themes of the socialist and feminist traditions, the respect for parliamentary institutions, civil liberties, and minority rights bequeathed by liberalism, and the republican commitment to a civic vision that can invigorate public life. The synthesis would take mid-nineteenth-century socialist efforts to extend democratic principles beyond the polity to the economy even further, into the realms of family, schools, and the mass media. The egalitarian values of the socialist tradition are a necessary ingredient in the revitalization of democracy, because the persistence of extensive class inequalities continues to drain republican institutions of substantive democratic meaning and make life miserable for millions around the globe. A revitalized democratic vision would take from feminism a recognition of the need for a radically different understanding of the public sphere, based on a redrawing, not a dissolution, of the boundaries separating transformed private and public spheres.[7]

The republican tradition would add to a revitalized democratic vision the universalism of its civic vision. The republican civic vision is based on universal values while the socialist and feminist traditions recognize the need to acknowledge class and gender differences in order to empower oppressed groups who can create a world in which universal bonds of humanity can become meaningful. In the mid-nineteenth century, the contradiction between universalism and particularism was evident in the tension between working-class autonomy and republican solidarity. Working-class republican militants tempered their pursuit of the class interests of the oppressed with a recognition of the need to build a civic community that transcended the particularistic interests of workers. In the global economy of the twentieth century, multicultural societies divided by bonds of class, gender, race, and ethnicity embody a different form of the same contradiction.[8] The struggle for social justice must begin with an acceptance of separate identities and assertion of group interests, so as to empower marginalized groups and give them the capacity to formulate their own agendas and hold party and movement leaders accountable. In the long run, however, we need to move beyond sectional interests to a civic republicanism that understands democratic politics as more than the pursuit of private or parochial interests. A socialist feminist vision that champions the interests of the oppressed without losing sight of a broader civic vision offers the prospect of a renewed public life. It offers hope to late twentieth-century democrats, who will find both inspiration and despair in the ambiguous legacy of early French republicanism.

Abbreviations Used in the Notes and Bibliography

A.D.H.G.	Archives départmentales de la Haute-Garonne (Departmental Archives of the Haute-Garonne)
A.D.L.	Archives départmentales de la Loire (Departmental Archives of the Loire)
A.D.S.M.	Archives départmentales de la Seine-Maritime (Departmental Archives of the Seine-Maritime)
A.M.R.	Archives municipales de Rouen (Municipal Archives of Rouen)
A.M.S.E.	Archives municipales de Saint-Étienne (Municipal Archives of Saint-Étienne)
A.M.T	Archives municipales de Toulouse (Municipal Archives of Toulouse)
A.N.	Archives nationales de la France (National Archives of France)
B.M.R.	Bibliothèque municipale de Rouen (Municipal Library of Rouen)
B.M.S.E.	Bibliothèque municipale de Saint-Étienne (Municipal Library of Saint-Étienne)
B.N.	Bibliothèque nationale de France (National Library of France)

Notes

CHAPTER ONE
THE POLITICAL CONSEQUENCES OF EARLY INDUSTRIALIZATION

1. "The distinctive categories and concepts of the discipline," argues Abrams, "its critical problems and theories, are all coloured by the underlying assumption that industrialization is the general historical process we most need to understand." *Historical Sociology*, p. 18.

2. Marx and Engels, "Manifesto of the Communist Party" in *Karl Marx & Frederick Engels: Selected Works*, p. 46.

3. See, for example, Alford, *Party and Society: The Anglo-American Democracies*.

4. Lipset, *The First New Nation*, p. 288.

5. See, for example, the work of Erik Olin Wright, including *Class, Crisis, and the State*; *Classes*; and *The Debate on Classes*.

6. A.D.H.G.: 4M 63.

7. Traugott, *Armies of the Poor*, pp. 184–86.

8. Sewell, Jr., "Uneven Development," pp. 604–37.

9. Judt, *Marxism and the French Left*, p. 112.

10. Reddy, *Money and Liberty*, pp. xi, 71.

11. Furet, *Penser la Révolution française*, pp. 71–72.

12. Scott, *Gender and the Politics of History*.

13. For a discussion of the concept of contradictory class locations, see Wright, *Classes* and *Class, Crisis, and the State*.

14. See the discussion of the concept of "mediated class location" in Wright, "Rethinking, Once Again, the Concept of Class Structure," pp. 325–29.

15. Cottereau, "The Distinctiveness of Working-Class Cultures in France," p. 142.

16. A.D.S.M.: 3M 236, Corps législatif. Second tour de scrutin. Elections des 6 et 7 Juin 1869.

17. B.M.R: Ng 144. Décision des comités corporatifs réunis en assemblée général le 25 April 1869.

18. For analyses emphasizing the narrative constitution of social identities, see Somers, "Narrativity, Narrative Identity, and Social Action," and Hart, "Cracking the Code."

19. "To attempt to persuade someone that one course of action, rather than another is in their interests," writes T. Benton, "is to play a part in the social constitution and/or reconstitution of their social and personal identity. Ideological struggles are, in general, struggles over the constitution and incorporation of individuals into opposed patterns of social identity, loyalty, and commitment, together with the interests these carry." "'Objective' Interests and the Sociology of Power," pp. 181–82. See also Hindess, "Power, Interests and the Outcomes of Struggles."

20. In pinpointing the limits of a structuralist analysis of politics, Craig Jenkins writes: "At most, a structural theory can account for the type of groups that are likely to be in contention in a particular social context, what relative powers and vulnerabilities the contending parties will possess by virtue of their structural positions, and the range of issues that are likely to come under contention. The questions of exactly when they will go into battle, what stratagems will be deployed to mobilize resources or to undermine the opposition, and what the outcome of conflict is likely to be require an analysis of the dynamics of mobilization, the contingencies shaping the selection of strategy and tactics, and the dynamics of conflict itself." "Sociopolitical Movements," p. 114.

21. For a discussion of the concept "political opportunity structure," which emphasizes the openness/closure of the political system, the stability/instability of alignments among contenders for power, the availability and strategic posture of potential political allies, and divisions within elites, see Tarrow, *Struggling to Reform*, pp. 26–34 and *Struggle, Politics, and Reform*, pp. 32–39. Several studies have explained variations in the structures, strategies, and outcomes of social movements with similar goals in terms of different national political opportunity structures. See, for example, Kitschelt's study of the anti-nuclear movement, "Political Opportunity Structures and Political Protest," pp. 47–85.

22. Judt, *Marxism and the French Left*.

23. The term artisan refers to skilled workers who exercised substantial control over recruitment into their trades and training, not to all skilled workers, or to a particular form of production, or to a distinctive set of class relations. Nineteenth-century French artisans worked in diverse settings, ranging from nonmechanized factories to households to small workshops, each of which was characterized by different class relations.

24. Woloch argues that the years from 1795 to 1799 witnessed the initial but short-lived emergence of political parties. *Jacobin Legacy*. Hunt, Lansky, and Hanson identify the final years of the eighteenth century as giving birth to political parties. "The Failure of the Liberal Republic," p. 755. Artz locates the birth of the first modern parties in the early nineteenth century, during the years of the Bourbon constitutional monarchy. "Les débuts des partis modernes," p. 275. Berenson cites 1848, with the formation of Republican Solidarity, as the key date. *Populist Religion*. Huard sees the middle decades of the nineteenth century as a period of the "prehistory" of parties, suggesting that real parties did not emerge until the final decades of the century. *Le mouvement républicain*.

25. Epstein, for example, defines a party as "any group, however loosely organized, seeking to elect government officeholders under a given label." *Political Parties in Western Democracies*, p. 9. Sartori defines a party as "any political group identified by an official label that presents at elections, and is capable of placing through elections (free or nonfree) candidates for public office." *Parties and Party Systems*, p. 63.

26. Dubois, *Le vocabulaire politique et social en France*, pp. 31–35.

27. Sartori, "From the Sociology of Politics to Political Sociology," pp. 86–87.

28. Przeworski and Sprague, *Paper Stones*, pp. 7–8.

29. Burawoy, "Marxism Without Micro-Foundations."

30. Pinkney characterizes the period from 1840 to 1847 in France as one of rapid change that produced "a crisis of identity" and prompted a search for new identities. *Decisive Years in France*, pp. 70–91.

31. On the relationship between liberalism and democracy in Germany and England, see Blackbourn and Eley, *The Peculiarities of German History*.

32. *L'Avenir républicain*, May 10, 1850.

33. Writing in 1871, M. Sempé noted that "the different parties, which are at war and aspire to power, are composed of a multitude of heterogeneous elements, without cohesion, without ties, without unity. . . ." Dubois, *Le vocabulaire politique et social en France*, pp. 366–67.

34. "Constitutions," writes Said Arjomand, "are monuments around which institutions can crystallize. They can thus create a new constellation of institutional interests, and thereby, new agenda for politics." "Constitutions and the Struggle for Political Order," p. 40.

35. Moore's definition also includes "a share for the underlying population in the making of rules" but the struggles for suffrage extension that made this possible are not part of his analysis. *Social Origins*, p. 414.

36. For an elaboration and modification of Moore's thesis, based on a much larger number of Western European cases, see Stephens, "Democratic Transition and Breakdown in Western Europe." See also Rueschemeyer, Huber Stephens, and Stephens, *Capitalist Development and Democracy*.

37. See, for example, Bollen, "Political Democracy and the Timing of Development" and Bollen and Jackman, "Economic and Noneconomic Determinants of Political Democracy in the 1960s."

38. Lipset, *Political Man*, p. 61.

39. Stephens, "Democratic Transition and Breakdown," p. 1035.

40. Therborn, "The Rule of Capital and the Rise of Democracy," p. 24.

41. Bendix, *Nation Building and Citizenship*.

42. For a critique of the notion that the bourgeoisie naturally embraces liberalism and that the weakness of liberalism in Germany can therefore be explained in terms of an underdeveloped bourgeoisie, see Blackbourn and Eley, *The Peculiarities of German History*.

43. For an excellent review of pluralist and elitist perspectives on politics, see Alford and Friedland, *Powers of Theory*.

44. For examples of each of these arguments see San Francisco Bay Area Kapitalistate Group, "Political Parties and Capitalist State Development," p. 8; Wright, *Class, Crisis, and the State*, p. 103; Poulantzas, *Political Power and Social Classes*; and Przeworski, "Material Interests, Class Compromise, and the Transition to Socialism," p. 29.

45. For a discussion of Marx's emphasis on the importance of limiting executive power, see Draper, "Marx on Democratic Forms of Government."

46. In the election of 1846, for example, three-fourths of the electoral districts had under six hundred eligible voters. One-third of all deputies were elected by less than two hundred votes and the majority (84%) of deputies were elected with fewer than four hundred votes. Tudesq, "Les comportements électoraux," p. 108.

47. Agnew, *Place and Politics*, pp. 2–3.

48. Elwitt, *The Making of the Third Republic*, pp. 19–102.

49. For a discussion of the problems of comparability in cross-national research, see Smelser, "The Methodology of Comparative Analysis"; Nowak, "Meaning and Measurement in Comparative Studies"; and Armer, "Methodological Problems and Possibilities in Comparative Research."

50. See Hunt, *Politics, Culture, and Class* for a discussion of these shared political symbols and rituals, and Tilly, *The Contentious French* for a discussion of shared repertoires of collective political action.

51. "With rare exceptions," notes William Sewell, Jr., "attempts to assure equivalence in historical cases will actually result in decreasing the independence between cases—and vice versa." "Three Temporalities: Toward an Evenemental Sociology," p. 25.

52. "Its silences," writes Philip Abrams, "make narrative a superficially effective means of making theoretical points but one that is ultimately fraudulent. So does its tolerance of irrelevant noise. A clever narrator will interject or weave into the texture of a story a good deal of interpretative and analytic matter which is not properly part of the story at all although vital for its persuasive allure . . . an essential feature of narrative would seem to be its ability both to carry analysis and to protect analysis from the sorts of critical reading appropriate to it. . . ." *Historical Sociology*, pp. 308–9.

53. For a discussion of the strengths and weaknesses of narrative in historical explanations, see Griffin, "Narrative, Event-Structure Analysis, and Causal Interpretations."

CHAPTER TWO
MID-NINETEENTH-CENTURY FRENCH REPUBLICANISM:
ORGANIZATION, IDEOLOGY, AND OPPORTUNITIES

1. For documentation of this negative ambivalence, see Howorth, "From the Bourgeois Republic to the Social Republic."

2. My categorization of Republicans into liberal, radical, and socialist camps is not shared by all French political historians. Claude Nicolet offers an alternative classification of the nineteenth-century French left, which utilizes vaguer, more philosophical, criteria, emphasizing the romanticism and "rousseauist" leanings of Ledru-Rollin, Louis Blanc, Edgar Quinet, Jules Michelet, and Victor Hugo; the liberalism of Étienne Vacherot and Jules Simon; the positivism and juridicism of Emile Littré, Leon Gambetta, and Jules Ferry; and the revolutionary aspirations of men like Auguste Blanqui and Louis-Charles Delescluze. *L'idée républicaine en France*, pp. 152–57. For another categorization, which emphasizes means and moral themes as well as goals as the criteria for distinguishing divisions within the mid-nineteenth-century French left, see Rials, "Néo-Jacobinisme et néo-hébertisme au milieu du XIXe siècle," pp. 284–300.

3. For histories of these associations, see Weill, *Histoire du parti républicain en France* and Moss, "Parisian Workers and the Origins of Republican Socialism."

4. Kent, *Electoral Procedure under Louis Philippe*, pp. 143–49.

5. Agulhon, *The Republican Experiment*, p. 16.

6. The *scrutin uninominal d'arrondissement* was reinstituted by the Second Empire to inhibit the role of political parties and encourage patronage politics. After a brief experiment with the *scrutin de liste* in 1871 and 1873, the conservative majority of the National Assembly reestablished the old system in 1875.

7. Berenson, *Populist Religion and Left-Wing Politics*, pp. 89, 93. The statutes of Republican Solidarity and a list of the sixty-four members of its general council are reprinted in Latta, *Un républicain méconnu*, pp. 279–304.

8. "Social and political debate took place in the established locations and institutions of working-class sociability," writes Agulhon, "because this was convenient, because it was discreet (at least anywhere but in the tavern) and also to exploit a trait. . . : these simple men who looked upon each other as brothers were prone to group reactions and once an idea took hold it was not long before it was accepted by all." "Working Class and Sociability in France before 1848," p. 57.

9. Oberschall, *Social Conflict and Social Movements*, pp. 123–24.

10. The republican activities of 1849–51 built upon and transformed what Maurice Agulhon has referred to as the "global traditionalism" of rural France, which included suspicion of tax collectors and military recruiters as well as of urban bourgeois reformers scornful of popular traditions. *La vie sociale en Provence intérieure*, p. 474. See also *La République au village*.

11. Huard, "La genèse des partis démocratiques modernes en France," p. 115. Huard characterizes the mid-century Republican party as a "transitional political structure" lacking a "stable, solid, unitary organizational form." *Le mouvement républicain*, p. 22.

12. Huard, *Le mouvement républicain*, p. 86.

13. For a feminist critique of the orthodox historiography of the Republic, see Reynolds, "Marianne's Citizens?"

14. This account relies heavily on the work of Mary Ann Clawson, who identifies four elements that define fraternalism as a unique social form: corporatism, ritual, masculinity, and proprietorship. "A corporatist impulse, a fascination with dramatic ritual, and an attachment to the inter-connected identities of proprietorship and masculinity characterize early modern fraternalism and its nineteenth century counterparts." *Constructing Brotherhood*, pp. 51–52.

15. On the political activities of women during the French Revolution, see Racz, "The Women's Rights Movement in the French Revolution"; Hufton, "Women in the Revolution"; Graham, "Loaves and Liberty"; and Landes, *Women and the Public Sphere*.

16. Landes, *Women and the Public Sphere*, pp. 66–89.

17. "Not even the fiercest republicans," notes Reynolds, "seriously suggested depriving churchgoers of their vote. It was because women had originally been excluded from the Republic that it was easy to convert an argument about rights into an argument about the putative result of giving women the vote." "Marianne's Citizens?" p. 113.

18. Landes, *Women and the Public Sphere*, pp. 171–72.

19. *L'Ami du peuple*. March 26–April 29, 1848.

20. For an analysis of these networks in the city of Toulouse, see Aminzade, "Breaking the Chains of Dependency."

21. Although most historians, including Maurice Agulhon, John Merriman, and Philippe Vigier, have emphasized the ideological appeal of republicanism, Eugen Weber argues that French peasants of the Second Republic were motivated not by politics or ideological convictions but by traditional personal loyalties. Weber dismisses the role of ideology by wrongly equating politics with national politics and by adopting an overly narrow view of ideology as the highly structured formal system of abstract ideas espoused by a political party. In his account, republican mobilizations based on issues of debts and taxes, because they reflected long-standing peasant grievances, were not "ideological." Nor were they "political" because of their local orientation. "The Second Republic, Politics, and the Peasant." For a more reasonable view of popular ideology which acknowledges the fusion of "inherent" traditional elements and "derived" beliefs belonging to a more structured system of ideas, see Rudé, "The Ideology of Popular Protest."

22. *La Gazette du Languedoc*, August 2, 1847.

23. After acquiring state power in the 1870s, Republicans did turn to party patronage strategies of mobilization. This shift was due in part to the very different electoral base of support that the party had during the 1870s compared to 1848, due to a widening of its electoral appeal beyond the cities into the countryside. The political legacy of the Second Empire also played an important role. Napoleon III's failure to develop a patronage party, and his policies of enhancing the autonomy of state bureaucrats from politicians, meant that Republicans of the 1870s were not very hostile to party patronage but highly distrustful of autonomous bureaucratic power.

24. Bernard Moss describes the organization as "a working-class army commanded by young middle-class or déclassé generals." "Parisian Workers and the Origins of Republican Socialism," p. 214.

25. Latta, *Un républicain méconnu*, pp. 301–2.

26. Zévaès, "Les candidates ouvrières et révolutionnaires sous le Second Empire."

27. *Le Progrès de Rouen*, May 19, 1869.

28. Dubuc, *Les élections*, p. 331.

29. O'Boyle, "The Image of the Journalist."

30. Agulhon, *Marianne into Battle*, p. 182.

31. "No ideology is ever wholly logical or consistent," writes Stuart Hall. "All the great organic ideologies bring together discordant elements and have to struggle to make contradictory ideas fit the scheme. There are always loose ends, breaks in the logic, gaps between theory and practice, and internal contradictions in *any* current of thought. . . ." "Variants of Liberalism," p. 36.

32. These events are documented in the newspaper *L'Indépendant*, April 2, 1848; and in R. Aubé, *Bibliographie de la presse rouennaise (1762–1928)*, B.M.R.: Ms 233.

33. The classic work on French Republican party formation is Weill, *Histoire du parti républicain*. See also Tchernoff's three volumes: *Le parti républicain sous la Monarchie de Juillet*; *Associations et sociétés secrètes sous la Seconde République*; and *Le parti républicain au coup d'état*.

34. On Old Regime corporatism, see Sewell, Jr., *Work and Revolution*, pp. 16–39.

35. *Émancipation*, July 12, 1839.

36. Sheehan, *German Liberalism in the Nineteenth Century*, p. 274. See also Blackbourn and Eley, *The Peculiarities of German History*.

37. Baker, "Representation," p. 480. Baker traces the roots of this liberal view of representation to the theory of rational representation developed by royalist reformers during the final years of the Old Regime.

38. Birch, *Representation*, p. 46.

39. Bastid, *Les institutions politiques*, p. 219.

40. Moss, "Producers' Associations and the Origins of French Socialism."

41. Noiret, "Deuxième lettre aux travailleurs," p. 6.

42. Wuthnow observes that "the unity of the socialist movement owes more to the reconstructive efforts of subsequent leaders, and even of historians, than it does to any single unifying creed or philosophical consensus." *Communities of Discourse*, p. 362.

43. *La Sentinelle populaire*, July 19, 1848. A.N.: Jo 596.

44. Vincent, *Pierre-Joseph Proudhon*, pp. 144, 212. For a balanced assessment of the influence of Proudhon on the early French labor movement, see Fitzpatrick, "Proudhon and the French Labour Movement." "Proudhon's immense, diffuse, and contradictory writing," argues Fitzpatrick, "presents considerable difficulties for those seeking to distinguish a coherent socialist philosophy."

45. *La Commune*, December 29, 1870; February 15, 1871; February 26, 1871.

46. Jolivalt, *Renseignments utiles*, p. 80.

47. Sewell, Jr., "Artisans, Factory Workers, and the Formation of the French Working Class, 1789–1848," p. 62. See also *Work and Revolution*.

48. Moss, "Parisian Workers and the Origins of Republican Socialism." Loubère, "The Intellectual Origins of French Jacobin Socialism."

49. Bezucha, *The Lyon Uprising*; Rudé, *L'insurrection Lyonnaise*.

50. *Civilisation*, November 17, 1851.

51. See, for example, Charles Noiret's two pamphlets, published in 1840 and 1841, "Aux Travailleurs" and "Deuxième lettre aux travailleurs."

52. A.N.: CC 791. Procès contre Charavay et autres, 1841.

53. This principle dated back to the elections of the Estates General of the Old Regime. Delegates to this assembly were mandated not to deliberate on issues but to accurately present the wishes of their constituents, as expressed in the documents (*cahiers*) drawn up separately by each order in local and regional deliberative assemblies. Any attempt by delegates to usurp the power of their constituents by exercising initiative and going beyond the explicit mandate elaborated in the *cahiers* was punished by removal from office as well as judicial and financial penalties. See Soule, *Les États Généraux*, pp. 76–78 and "La notion historique de représentation politique," p. 19; Halevi, "Modalités, participation, et luttes électorales," p. 98.

54. Nicolet, *L'idée républicaine*, pp. 109–10.

55. Cottereau, "The Distinctiveness of Working-Class Cultures," pp. 146–47.

56. See Offe's discussion of the problematic nature of majority rule as a legitimating principle: "Legitimation Through Majority Rule?"

57. *La Sentinelle des travailleurs*, June 27, 1848.

58. Prior to 1848, Republicans of various political persuasions, including liberal

Republicans with socially conservative views, adopted the term radical because it was illegal to use the term republican. Despite this indiscriminate use of the term by Republicans prior to 1848, distinctions among liberal, radical, and socialist Republicans over the issues discussed in this chapter are evident before and after 1848.

59. Cottereau, "The Distinctiveness of Working-Class Cultures," pp. 150–51.

60. Proudhon was one of the few socialists who resisted this effort to separate these two issues, which accounts in part for his poor relations with members of the Mountain. Combined with Proudhon's repeated denunciations of Jacobinism and his reluctance to embrace a political solution to the social question, this made him an outcast on the left in 1849. Vincent, *Pierre-Joseph Proudhon*, p. 185.

61. *L'Éclaireur*, February 7, 14, 1869.

62. McPhee, "The Crisis of Radical Republicanism," p. 76.

63. Elwitt, *The Making of the Third Republic*, p. 178.

64. Friedman, "Capitalism, Republicanism, Socialism, and the State," pp. 155–56.

65. McPhee, "The Crisis of Radical Republicanism," p. 78.

66. Ibid., pp. 71–88.

67. Some radical leaders, including Jules Miot, Louis-Charles Delescluze, and Félix Pyat in Paris and Armand Duportal in Toulouse, supported the revolutionary communes with varying degrees of hesitation. The majority of radical Republicans, including Étienne Arago and Jules Favre in Paris, Alphonse Equiros in Marseilles, and César Bertholon in Saint-Étienne, viewed the communes as violations of majority rule and supported the Versailles government.

68. For an analysis of the shifting relationship between French Jacobinism and socialism during the first half of the nineteenth century, see Loubère, "The Intellectual Origins of French Jacobin Socialism."

69. Furet, *La gauche et la révolution*; Nicolet, *L'idée républicaine*, pp. 93–94; Weill, *Histoire du parti républicain*, p. 373.

70. Elwitt, *The Making of the Third Republic*, pp. 32–33.

71. Most Republicans, argues Agulhon, interpreted the Terror as a tragic product of special circumstances, not as a model that they wished to repeat. "The Heritage of the Revolution and Liberty in France," p. 414. The neo-Jacobin Peyrat, in his polemics with Ferry, insisted that reverence for the Jacobin tradition did not imply the need for a new Reign of Terror. "We honor the Jacobins as our masters," he wrote, "but thanks to them we don't have to study them as models. They did what they did so well that we no longer need to do it." *La révolution et le livre de M. Quinet*, p. 196.

72. Berenson, *Populist Religion and Left-Wing Politics*.

73. Singer, *Village Notables in Nineteenth-Century France*.

74. On the impact of positivism on French republicanism see Bertocci, "Positivism, French Republic and the Politics of Religion 1848–1883" and Nicolet, *L'idée républicaine*, pp. 187–277.

75. *L'Éclaireur*, January 1, 1869.

76. For a more detailed analysis of these associations, see Auspitz, *The Radical Bourgeoisie*. By the end of the 1860s, the adult education movement had created more then 31,000 classes for workers, serving an estimated 780,000 students. Elwitt, *The Third Republic Defended*, p. 248.

77. Auspitz, *The Radical Bourgeoisie*, p. 34.

78. Vigier, "Élections municipales et prise de conscience politique," p. 277.

79. Within the ranks of the Mountain, eighty-four deputies supported a nonviolent parliamentary strategy in response to the law but twenty-four, led by Michel de Bourges, created the New Mountain, which was unwilling to renounce revolutionary violence in the absence of universal male suffrage. It was the "New Mountain" that organized the revolutionary secret societies that proliferated in the provinces in 1850 and 1851. Weill, *Histoire du parti républicain*, p. 251; Huard, "La genèse des partis démocratiques," p. 109.

80. On the repressive policies of this period, see Payne, *The Police State of Louis Napoleon Bonaparte*; Merriman, *The Agony of the Republic*; and Price, "Techniques of Repression."

CHAPTER THREE
PATTERNS OF INDUSTRIALIZATION AND CLASS FORMATION

1. Samuel, "Workshop of the World," p. 8.

2. Jones, "The Mid-Century Crisis and the 1848 Revolutions." For an analysis of early European industrialization that emphasizes changes in the organization of labor, innovations in nonmechanical technologies, and the role of protoindustry, see Berg, Hudson, and Sonenscher, *Manufacture in Town and Country*.

3. O'Brien and Keyder, *Economic Growth in Britain and France*, pp. 164–67. See also Sabel and Zeitlin, who correctly insist upon the flexibility and technical dynamism of small-scale craft industries but misrepresent the social consequences of technical innovations, like the Jacquard loom, and the situation of small masters. "Historical Alternatives to Mass Production."

4. Roehl, "French Industrialization: A Reconsideration," pp. 241–42.

5. Markovitch, "Le revenu industriel et artisanal," pp. 79, 85, 87.

6. Markovitch, *L'industrie français*, vol. 7, pp. 78–79.

7. These factors are highlighted by O'Brien and Keydar, *Economic Growth* and by Sewell, Jr., "Artisans, Factory Workers, and the Formation of the French Working Class," pp. 45–50.

8. Social historians, however, have focused their attention on these internal transformations. See, for example, Hanagan, *Nascent Proletarians*.

9. For a comparison of the different incidence, form, targets, and content of industrial protest generated by handicraft, household, and factory production, see Aminzade, "Capitalist Industrialization and Patterns of Industrial Protest."

10. See, for example, the articles collected in Joyce, *The Historical Meanings of Work*.

11. On the issue of deskilling, see Lequin's documentation of the extensive technical knowledge required by workers in early textile mills, steelworks, and mines. The growth of factories, argues Lequin, did not destroy systems of apprenticeship but severed their tie to intragenerational mobility. "Apprenticeship in Nineteenth Century France," pp. 471, 474.

12. For a good survey of the debate on the labor aristocracy, see McLennan, *Marxism and the Methodologies of History*, pp. 206–32.

13. Hobsbawn, "The Labour Aristocracy," p. 208.

14. On the gender division of labor in mid-nineteenth-century French industry, see Tilly, "Paths of Proletarianization" and Scott, *Gender and the Politics of History*, pp. 93–163.

15. "Skill is a social product, a negotiated identity," writes Charles Tilly. "Although knowledge, experience, and cleverness all contribute to skill, ultimately skill lies not in characteristics of individual workers but in relations between workers and employers. . . ." "Solidary Logics," p. 453.

16. The following discussion is based upon the data presented in Daumard, *Les fortunes en France*, pp. 570–972.

17. Armengaud, "A propos des origines du sous-développement industriel."

18. A.M.T.: Recensements de 1830, 1872. These figures are based on a 10 percent systematic sample of these records.

19. Ibid.

20. Ibid.

21. The 1865 de Planet industrial survey lists 797 factories in Toulouse employing 8,587 workers, for an average of fewer than 11 workers per factory, as well as four government-owned factories employing 1,434 workers. There were only thirty-five establishments in the city that employed more than twenty workers, with a total of 2,401. *Statistique industrielle*.

22. Ibid.

23. Ibid.

24. A.D.H.G.: 12M 32.

25. A.M.T.: Annuaires de Toulouse, 1840, 1872.

26. For analysis of subcontracting in nineteenth-century France, see Mottez, *Systèmes de salaires*; Fraysse, "Le marchandage dans l'industrie du bâtiment"; and Bezucha, "The French Revolution of 1848 and the Social History of Work."

27. A.M.T.: 2F 5.

28. A.D.H.G.: 4M 60.

29. A.D.H.G.: M 196.

30. A.D.H.G.: 223U 10.

31. A.D.H.G.: wU 72.

32. Sewell, Jr., notes a similar division within the working-class of Marseille: "Proletarians were impoverished, oppressed, frequently illiterate, often without family ties, unorganized, nomadic, and, to judge from their high crime rate, often personally disoriented as well. Artisans, by contrast, were moderately well-paid, respectable, literate, organized, and rooted in the city, in their trade, and in a long-standing urban corporate tradition." "Social Change and the Rise of Working-Class Politics," p. 82.

33. A.D.H.G.: 12M 34, Salaires industriels dans la ville chef-lieu du département. Average daily wage figures for 1832, 1839, 1842, 1847, and 1853 reveal similar variations. A.D.H.G.: 10M 21, 10M 26, 12M 32, 12M 34.

34. A.M.T.: Secretariat général 3D 137.

35. In 1830, 72 percent of all artisans who married in Toulouse were able to sign their names, compared to only 50 percent of proletarian manufactory workers and 31 percent of workers not employed as artisans or in manufactories. By 1872 the overall literacy rate of the city's population, as measured by the ability to sign one's name on a marriage record, had increased from 69 to 87 percent. The vast majority

of artisans who married in that year (88%) were able to sign their names, while the percentage of factory workers (65%) and of all other workers (75%) had also risen, but remained below the figure for artisans. These figures are based upon the *Actes de mariages* of 1830 and 1872, located in the municipal archives of Toulouse.

36. The percent of native-born residents in each group was comparable in 1872, when only 39 percent of artisans and 35 percent of proletarians were born in Toulouse. A.M.T.: Recensements de 1830, 1872.

37. Ibid.

38. A.D.H.G.: 223U 10.

39. A.M.T.: Recensement de 1830.

40. A.M.T.: Archives modernes, epi 43, tr. 4, Rapports du commissaire centrale du police.

41. Delaye, *Rapport sur les sociétés de secours mutuels d'ouvriers*; A.N.: BB30 388.

42. In 1842–1843, most of this association's members were artisans, but membership included eight factory artisans—seven of whom were metalworkers—as well as two workers from the local tobacco factory. A.M.T.: 2Q 6.

43. A.D.H.G.: 4M 55.

44. *Journal de Toulouse,* April, 1848.

45. A.D.H.G.: 4M 66.

46. This strike is documented in A.D.H.G.: 4M 87; A.N.: F12 4503, Flc III 14; A.M.T.: epi 43.

47. The figure for the beginning of the century includes the four adjacent suburban communes of Valbenoîte, Outre-Furens, Montaud, and Beaubrun, which were annexed by the city in 1855. The city itself had only 16,259 inhabitants in 1801. Fournial, *Saint-Étienne*, p. 232.

48. Gordon, "Industrialization and Republican Politics."

49. For an analysis of the distribution of wealth in Saint-Étienne, see Gordon, *Merchants and Capitalists*, pp. 77–78, 175–76, 187.

50. Silk workers remained the largest segment of the region's working class up to 1872, numbering 40,000 to 45,000 individuals, compared with 3,000 hardware producers, 4,900 artisanal arms producers, 5,000 workers in the government arms factory, 16,700 coal miners, and 12,000 workers in heavy metallurgy. Silk ribbon weavers in the city of Saint-Étienne and adjacent suburbs numbered approximately 12,500 in 1825–27 and nearly 20,000 by 1851. Gonnard estimates their number at only 8,000 in 1833–34. These different estimates are explicable in terms of whether the authors included the four suburban communes in their calculations and the sharp yearly fluctuations in the ribbon industry, which experienced boom and bust years. Workers in the city's four other major industries—hardware, armaments, mining, and steel—numbered approximately 7,400 in 1828 and 13,716 by 1848–51. Lequin, *Les ouvriers*, vol. 1, pp. 33, 36–37, 40–41; Fournial, *Saint-Étienne*, pp. 198–204; Gras, *Histoire économique de la métallurgie*, p. 232; Schnetzler, *Les industries et les hommes*, p. 78; Gonnard, "Les passementiers," p. 2; Martourey, *Formation et gestion*, p. 103.

51. The master's wife or daughter typically wound thread on spools while a skilled journeyman threaded the warp. The master, along with another worker or

family member, wove the silk. Gonnard estimates an average of four workers per ribbon master in Saint-Étienne in 1832–33. "Les passementiers," p. 2.

52. Bonnefous, *Histoire de Saint-Étienne*, pp. 400, 428. In 1849, the majority (56%) of the 21,000 ribbon workers employed within the city and adjacent communes were women (51%) and children (5%). A.D.L.: 87M 7. October 20, 1849.

53. Local ribbon merchants persistently complained about the theft of thread (*piquage d'once*) and the artificial weighing and stretching of thread by weavers. Raw materials were very expensive, accounting for approximately two-thirds of the cost of production. There was a large underground market in stolen thread in Saint-Étienne despite harsh penalties. Gras, *Histoire de la rubanerie*, p. 144. Merchants also complained about the unwillingness of household producers to work longer hours during periods of peak demand. In October 1849 Saint-Étienne's police commissioner informed the prefect that although the ribbon industry was very active, merchants were refusing many orders because "the workers refuse to allow anyone to work past 7:00 P.M.," even though "the prices paid to them for their ribbons are more than double what they received one year ago." A.D.L.: 10M 31.

54. The convent workshops were a constant source of complaints and rumors concerning poor diets, dungeons, oppressive working conditions, and sexual perversion. In the industrial survey of 1848, ribbon weavers denounced the workshops as submitting adolescent women to "the tortures of the Inquisition" and to the "most humiliating practices." Vanoli, "Les couvents soyeux"; Guillaume, "La situation économique et sociale," p. 19.

55. Productivity gains are evidenced by the following figures: from 1815 to 1825, the number of weavers declined 21.9 percent and the number of looms 2.9 percent, while production rose 71 percent. Martourey, *Formation et gestion*, p. 42.

56. The commercial sector employed 65 percent of the region's 4,600 arms workers in 1847, but by 1872 it employed 49 percent of the industry's 9,900 arms workers. The state arms factory expanded its labor force from 628 workers in 1839 to 5,000 by 1872. Schnetzler, *Les industries*, p. 78. These figures refer to the number of permanent workers (*ouvriers engagés*) who signed six-year contracts and were prohibited from working in the commercial sector, not to the numerous workers (*ouvriers libres*) who were employed irregularly by the state factory, moving back and forth between the factory and household workshops. They need to be interpreted cautiously, since the number of workers employed in the factory fluctuated greatly from year to year.

57. In 1833, the first steam engine was installed in the factory. During the next fifteen years, a number of technical changes were introduced to speed up work and increase production, including a new method of forging barrels, the use of rollers rather than forges, a new turning machine to cut spiral grooves in the barrels of guns, new processes to dry wood by steam, the repositioning of workers alongside rather than above grindstones, and the use of steam power in sharpening, drilling, laminating, and polishing. A new factory, opened in April 1866, mechanized all aspects of production to produce interchangeable parts of the new breech-loading rifles. Bonnefous, *Histoire de Saint-Étienne*, pp. 450–52.

58. The preceding account is based on the attorney general's report of May 30, 1844. A.N.: BB18 1420.

59. Bonnefous, *Histoire de Saint-Étienne*, pp. 403–5. Guillaume, *La compagnie des mines*, p. 42.

60. Guillaume, *La compagnie des mines*, p. 137. During the industrial expansion of the Second Empire, the number of miners in Saint-Étienne grew rapidly, from 2,946 in 1851 to 5,000 by 1868.

61. Ibid., p. 121.

62. Ibid., pp. 144–45.

63. A.N.: BB18 1420.

64. A.D.L.: 84M 7. These figures were provided by representatives of the miners. Other sources provide different figures but also suggest a lengthening of the workday.

65. A.N.: C 956.

66. Schnetzler, *Les industries*, p. 67.

67. Gaussin, *Saint-Étienne et son agglomeration*, p. 19.

68. The 1848 industrial survey (*enquête*) lists 1,156 workers employed in heavy metallurgy in the two cantons of Saint-Étienne: 770 in blast furnaces, 80 in steelworks, 251 in scythe and file factories, and 55 foundry workers. Industrial statistics for 1859 enumerate 173 local workers employed at the blast furnaces of Terre-Noire, 767 iron foundry workers, and 130 steel workers, for a total of 1,070 workers. The figures for both these surveys are from Gras, *Histoire èconomique de la métallurgie*, pp. 231–32, 236.

69. Gras, *Histoire économique de la métallurgie*, pp. 45–46.

70. Reybaud, *Le fer et la houille*, pp. 144–47. For a discussion of the decline of this system in the Stéphanois valley during the latter decades of the nineteenth century, see Hanagan, *The Logic of Solidarity*, pp. 62–68.

71. Average daily wage figures for 1841, 1856, and 1865 are provided in A.D.L.:85M 2. Miners earned an average daily wage of 2.65 francs in 1847, 2.88 francs in 1848, 2.84 francs in 1849, 2.6 francs in 1850, 2.85 francs in 1851, 2.73 francs in 1852, and 2.87 francs in 1853. These averages are poor indicators of material well-being given differences among workers' needs due to family status, piece-rate systems that made age and health an important determinant of income, and fluctuations across pits and over time in the number of hours and days worked. Miners were a workforce divided into cutters, timbermen, and carters, each of whom received different wage rates.

72. The harsh working conditions in local coal mines are documented in A.D.L.: 84 M7, Tableau 1830–1833 dressée par un délégue mineur en réponse aux questions de l'enquête industrielle et commerciale du 25 mai 1848. Baret lists 419 deaths in the Saint-Étienne basin for the seven years from 1836 to 1843, from floods, cave-ins, explosions, asphyxiation, and injuries from machinery. *Histoire locale du travail*, p. 122.

73. These figures are from Guillaume, *La compagnie des mines*, pp. 138–43.

74. Bonnefous, *Histoire de Saint-Étienne*, pp. 414, 443.

75. The 1848 *enquête* lists workers in large-scale metallurgy as earning average wages ranging from 3.75 francs per day for men working in blast furnaces and steel mills to 2.5 francs per day for those employed in scythe factories and foundries. Gras, *Histoire économique de la métallurgie*, p. 232. The average daily wage figures

provided in the wage surveys of 1841, 1856, and 1865 also reveal the relatively privileged position of factory workers in heavy metallurgy. A.D.L.: 85M 2.

76. Bonnefous, *Histoire de Saint-Étienne*, pp. 450–52. Those skilled arms factory workers who were hired as permanent (*engagés*) rather than temporary (*ouvriers libres*) workers received six-year contracts. Abrogast, *L'industrie des armes*, p. 39.

77. A.D.L.: 85M 2.

78. Gordon, *Merchants and Capitalists*, pp. 98–99.

79. In 1848, Antoine Limousin calculated the annual income of a master weaver who owned two looms at only 866 francs, far below the 1,323 francs he estimated as necessary to decently support a family of four. *Enquête industrielle et sociale*, pp. 15–18.

80. This is well documented by Lequin, *Les ouvriers*, vol. l, pp. 208, 215–17. See also Tenand, *Les origines de la classe ouvrière stéphanoise*, pp. 86–134 and Merley, "La contribution de la Haute-Loire," pp. 165–80.

81. In 1851 and 1869 most of the sons of ribbon weavers (89% and 68%, respectively) exercised this occupation. The figures were quite similar for the sons of arms makers, with 82 percent and 68 percent of arms makers' sons taking up the same occupation as their fathers. In contrast, only 40 percent of the sons of miners listed in the marriage records of 1869 inherited their fathers' occupations. Martourey, "Mécanismes d'urbanisation," pp. 64–65. Fifty-four percent of ribbon weavers and 57 percent of arms producers were born in the Stéphanois basin in 1850–51, compared to only 32 percent of miners and 25 percent of metalworkers. Lequin, *Les ouvriers*, vol. l, pp. 224, 423, 469.

82. In August 1845, the *procureur général* observed that most of the city's seventy carpenters regularly returned to their rural communities during the winter. A.N.:BB18 1435, August 27, 1845. Masons, stonecutters, and bricklayers, observed the police commissioner of Montaud in April 1841, constituted a "floating population" because "they remain in town for only six to nine months each year, depending on the weather." A.D.L.: 85M 2.

83. Conflicts over the use of urban space and the efforts of ribbon merchants to implement an early form of zoning are documented in Vant, *Imagerie et urbanisation*, pp. 48–70.

84. The blowgun was a very popular sport among Saint-Étienne's weavers, as evidenced by the twenty-five blowgun clubs in the city in 1851. There were yearly competitions (*papegai*) in which the winner presided over dances and festivities. Bonnefous, *Histoire de Saint-Étienne*, p. 433.

85. "A clandestine organization of presidents exists. . . ." wrote the attorney general in June 1848. "For the miners these presidents are the only legitimate authority." A.N.: BB18 1461.

86. Arms makers formed a mutual aid society in June 1848 but this association attracted only one hundred workers, in contrast to the weavers' mutual aid society which had over eight thousand members grouped into two hundred sections by the end of 1848. A.D.L.: 94M 2.

87. The organization did not keep any written records. To avoid repression, weavers used a secret system of communication involving a shuttle covered with

pieces of colored cloth. Festy, *Le mouvement ouvrier*, p. 188; Gonnard, "Les passe-mentiers," p. 8.

88. This effort to create a production cooperation, and its close ties to the local republican movement, are extensively documented in A.N.: BB18 1390.

89. Audiganne, *Les populations ourvrières*, p. 124.

90. In 1855, ribbon weavers founded a consumer cooperative which, by 1865, operated a bakery that sold seven hundred kilograms of bread daily. Office du Travail, *Les Associations professionelles ouvrières*, p. 347. In 1863, over eleven hundred weavers formed a commercial cooperative whose members owned over three thousand looms. In 1866, the cooperative did over one hundred thousand francs' worth of business but the crisis within the industry took its toll and the association was dissolved in 1867, after republican activists made an unsuccessful attempt to create a fund to aid the troubled cooperative. A.N.: BB30 379. The velvet ribbon weavers tried to create a production cooperative after their unsuccessful strike of 1865. After raising sixty thousand francs in 1866, the cooperative disbanded in 1867 before starting operations. Gras, *Histoire de la rubanerie*, p. 622; A.D.L.: 10M 60.

91. Durousset, *La vie ouvrière dans la région stéphanoise*, p. 121.

92. Guillaume, "Grèves et organisations," p. 10.

93. Martourey, *Formation et gestion*, p. 765.

94. On the distribution of wealth at Rouen, see Chaline, *Les bourgeois de Rouen*, pp. 127–60, 468–69.

95. A.D.S.M: 10 MP 1614.

96. Reddy, *The Rise of Market Culture*, p. 119.

97. Ibid., p. 207.

98. Ibid., pp. 206–9.

99. A.D.S.M.: 10MP 1614.

100. Suzuki, *L'évolution*, p. 22.

101. Levainville, *Rouen*, p. 216.

102. Suzuki, *L'évolution*, p. 147.

103. Noiret, *Mémoires d'un ouvrier rouennais*, pp. 19–20.

104. Suzuki, *L'évolution*, p. 200.

105. A.D.S.M.: F 359.

106. Suzuki, *L'évolution*, p. 200.

107. A.D.S.M.: 10MP 1614.

108. Whereas there were sixty to seventy factories in the Rouen area employing eleven thousand cotton print workers in 1834, by 1847 the industry employed only seven thousand cotton print workers in only forty-three factories. Fohlen, *L'industrie textile*, pp. 201–2.

109. Suzuki, *L'évolution*, p. 161.

110. Ibid., p. 158.

111. The number of cotton print workers in the department dropped from seven thousand in 1847 to five thousand in 1869 and the number of factories declined from forty-three in 1859 to twenty-one in 1869. Suzuki, *L'évolution*, p. 200; Mollat, *L'histoire de Rouen*, p. 338.

112. Suzuki, *L'évolution*, p. 154.

113. Noiret, *Mémoires*, p. 7.

114. In November of 1860 the police spy Philippon reported to the prefect that employers had greatly increased workloads after the introduction of new chemical procedures. Whereas workers had previously been required to wash and dye sixty kilos of cotton for their daily wage of 2–2.25 francs, the new workload was one hundred kilos per day for a wage of 2.5–2.75 francs. Employers justified the increase by arguing that the new chemicals meant that the cotton did not have to remain in vats as long, but workers responded that the time thus saved was more than compensated for by the lengthier preparatory work that was required. A.D.S.M.: 4MP 4279.

115. Reddy, *The Rise of Market Culture*, p. 163.

116. Reddy, "Family and Factory," p. 104; "The Textile Trade and the Language of the Crowd," p. 78; *The Rise of Market Culture*, pp. 162–63.

117. At the end of November 1855, for example, workers at several spinning factories at Darnétal and St. Léger faced unemployment and lower wages because of insufficient water power to run the machinery in their factories. Those employed in steam-powered factories continued to work. A.D.S.M.: 4MP 4279; rapport d'Antoine Philippon au préfet, December 3, 1855.

118. For example, at the Crepet factory in 1848, the foreman earned 4 francs per day, the steam-engine fireman 3.5–4.25 francs, the spinners and *rattacheurs* 2.2–2.5 francs, and the day laborers only 2 francs. Démier, "Les ouvriers," p. 14.

119. Reddy points out that spinners in early cotton mills were independent operators who did not receive wages but a price for the thread they produced. "Skeins, Scales, Discounts, Steam, and other Objects of Crowd Justice," pp. 204–13. He notes a variety of factors which determined an individual factory spinners's pay level, including age and experience, the grade of yarn to be produced, the state of the machinery and raw materials, the mill owner's readiness to pass on fluctuations in yarn prices by altering rates, and the state of the cotton trade in general. *The Rise of Market Culture*, p. 161.

120. B.N.: Le77 2614.

121. A.D.S.M.: 4MP 4279, rapport du Philippon, December 26, 1859.

122. Ibid. Mollat's study of rent levels and indigence also documents a division between textile factory workers and better-off handicraft artisans and skilled metal factory workers. *L'histoire de Rouen*, p. 350.

123. These observations were made by the city's weavers in the 1848 *enquête* as well as by a number of prominent bourgeois reformers, including Louis Villermé and Adolphe Blanqui. For an analysis of the discourse of these bourgeois observers, see Reddy, *The Rise of Market Culture*, pp. 150–84. Even well-informed government sympathizers could not ignore the abject misery of many local workers. In October 1851, Philippon reported that the city's fifteen hundred dyers "face a situation that is difficult to describe, worsened by the family burdens that many of them have . . . the approach of winter inspires terror among these poor men, who will not be able to afford even the most basic necessities. . . ." A.D.S.M.: 4MP 4279, Rapports d'Antoine Philippon au préfet, October 23, 1855.

124. Mollat concludes, from his study of tax assessments, inheritance records, and rent levels that income and wealth distribution in Rouen resembled a pyramid, "with a very large base of poverty and a small minority of opulent families at the summit." *L'histoire de Rouen*, p. 345.

125. Data on alcohol consumption, infant mortality, consumption, and mortality are provided by Levainville, *Rouen*, pp. 352–61. Cholera epidemics and consumption, aggravated by cotton dust, took a severe toll among the city's workers. During the years from 1861 to 1881, the mortality rate in Rouen was 32.74 per 1,000 compared to 24.29 at Paris. For a discussion of demographic patterns during this period see Mollat, *L'histoire de Rouen*, pp. 319–28.

126. Maitron, *Dictionnaire biographique*, vol. 3, p. 245.

127. A.D.S.M.: 10MP 2002.

128. A.D.S.M.: 4MP 4279, Rapports de Philippon, May 24, 1857; May 10, 1858.

129. Levainville, *Rouen*, p. 365.

130. Démier, "Les ouvriers," p. 11.

131. Patterns of residential settlement and population growth by canton are documented in Levainville, *Rouen*, pp. 341–43.

132. Noiret, *Mémoires*, pp. 42–43.

133. Audiganne, writing in 1860, commented that Rouen's mutual aid societies "have always remained within their proper sphere. None of them have dreamed of becoming involved in politics or allowed access to old socialist influences." *Les populations ouvrières*, p. 77. The largest mutual aid society in 1860, the *Société d'émulation chrétienne*, retained close ties with the Catholic church. Its leadership preached respect for social order to its three thousand members, one-third of whom were women.

134. A.D.S.M.: 10MP 1614. Enquête sur les conditions du travail, 1872.

135. In September 1848, after the republican government allocated funds to sponsor workers' cooperatives, two groups of spinners and one group of weavers sent applications to government officials requesting funds to finance cooperatively owned workshops, but nothing came of these requests. A.D.S.M.: 10MP 1467.

136. In November 1848, led by republican socialist activists, workers in the Saint-Sever factory district created a consumer cooperative that provided meat and bread to workers at lower prices. By January 1849, the cooperative had recruited two hundred subscribers, each of whom contributed five francs, and had established branches at Rouen and Déville. In May 1850, political activists, including the future leader of the First International Emile Aubry, made plans to create a cooperative restaurant for workers. Maitron, *Dictionnaire biographique*, vol. 1, pp. 119, 480, 458; vol. 2, p. 509; vol. 3, p. 83.

137. A.D.S.M.: 10MP 1614. Enquête sur les conditions du travail, 1872.

138. A.D.S.M.: F359. *Enquête de 1848 sur les tisserands de Rouen*, p. 14.

139. A.D.S.M.: 4MP 4279.

140. This estimate is provided by the city's central police commissioner in the industrial survey of 1872. A.D.S.M.: 10MP 1614.

141. Audiganne, *Les populations*, p. 79.

142. These activities are documented by Reddy, *The Rise of Market Culture*, pp. 119–25.

143. For accounts of these actions see Aguet, *Les grèves sous la Monarchie de Juillet*, pp. 38–42; Reddy, "The Textile Trade and the Language of the Crowd," pp. 74–81.

144. Chaline, *Rouen sous la Monarchie de Juillet*, p. 23.

145. A.N.: C940.

146. In 1869 the *Fédération ouvrière rouennaise* included trade organizations of wool spinners, cotton spinners, weavers, tanners, and printers while the Darnétal section included cotton print workers, dyers, carpenters, mechanics, steam-engine stokers, and plumbers. Documentation on this organization is provided in ADSM: 4MP 4235, January 10, 1872, and in Boivin, "La Fédération ouvrière rouennaise," pp. 322–42.

147. Rougerie, "Les sections françaises de l'association internationale des travailleurs," pp. 93–127.

148. A.D.S.M.: 10MP 1614.

149. Sewell, Jr., "Artisans, Factory Workers, and the Formation of the French Working Class," p. 53.

150. For an analysis which highlights the importance of communal ties in the collective actions of nineteenth-century workers, see Calhoun, *The Question of Class Struggle* and "The Radicalism of Tradition."

CHAPTER FOUR
TOULOUSE: FROM LIBERAL REPUBLICANISM TO AN ALLIANCE
OF RADICALS AND SOCIALISTS

1. A.D.H.G.: 4M 59.

2. A.D.H.G.: 4M 56.

3. *Journal de Toulouse*, March 8 & 9, 1848.

4. These events are documented in A.N.: BB 18 1766, BB 30 390, and Jean Casevitz, *Une loi manquée*.

5. *Émancipation*, May 22, 1869.

6. Maitron, *Dictionnaire biographique*, p. 426.

7. A.D.H.G.: 4M 48.

8. The street demonstrations of the early 1830s are documented in A.D.H.G.: 4M 48, 4M 72, 4M 49; and A.N.: BB18 1215.

9. A.N.: BB18 1354 B.

10. A.D.H.G.: 4M 51.

11. A.N.: BB18 1360.

12. A.M.T.: S.G.3D 137.

13. A.D.H.G.: 12M 32.

14. A.N.: BB30 167.

15. Burney, "La Faculté des Lettres de Toulouse," pp. 289–90.

16. A.N.: BB18 1388.

17. The census riots of 1841 are documented in A.N.: BB18 1386, 1395C; Archives du Ministère de Guerre: E5 150; A.D.H.G.: 4M 55; A.M.T.: S.G. 7D 483, 2I 1, 59, 63. See also Hermet, "A Toulouse en 1841 et 1842" and Paul, "L'agitation républicaine à Toulouse."

18. The term Icarian communist refers to the title of Étienne Cabet's book, *Vogage to Icaria*, in which he elaborated the vision of socialism that inspired the movement.

19. Johnson uses the number of subscribers to Cabet's newspaper *Le Populaire* as an indicator of the varying local strength of the Icarian movement. Only Paris and Lyon led Toulouse in the number of subscriptions. *Utopian Communism in France*.

20. A.D.H.G.: 4M 55.

21. A.D.H.G.: 4M 76.

22. Droulers, *Action pastorale et problèmes sociaux*, p. 67.

23. A.D.H.G.: 4M 55.

24. A.D.H.G.: 4M 56.

25. After 1844, observes Johnson, Cabet developed a policy of greater exclusivism that emphasized his leadership. *Utopian Communism*, p. 136. This may have been a factor in the conversion of some working-class Icarians to republican socialism.

26. A.D.H.G.: 4M 56.

27. *La Voix du peuple*, February 1847.

28. A.D.H.G.: 4M 58.

29. *La Gazette du Languedoc*, August 2, 1847.

30. On the banquet campaign in Toulouse, see Henry, "La Campagne des banquets à Toulouse."

31. *Émancipation*, January 7, 1848.

32. Ibid., December 29, 1847.

33. Henry, "La campagne des banquets," p. 62.

34. For a more detailed account of the occupational distribution of republican militants at Toulouse during the July Monarchy, see Aminzade, *Class, Politics, and Early Industrial Capitalism*, pp. 136–40.

35. *Journal de Toulouse*, March 10, 1848.

36. A.D.H.G.: 4M 62. Letter from the chef du 13e légion de gendarmes to Joly, April 1, 1848.

37. A.D.H.G.: 4M 62.

38. A.D.H.G.: 4M 60.

39. A.D.H.G.: 54Y 42.

40. *Journal de Toulouse*, April 17, 1848.

41. Radical Jean-Pierre Soulès placed 19th with 29,808 votes, and radical leader Marcel Lucet came in 32d with 9,633.

42. *Journal de Toulouse*, May 1, 1848.

43. A.M.T.: 1I 71.

44. A.D.H.G.: 4M 60.

45. A.D.H.G.: 4M 62.

46. A.D.H.G.: 4M 72.

47. Police spy reports on these meetings are contained in A.D.H.G.: 4M 64.

48. A.N.: BB30 365. *Procureur général*, March 29, 1849.

49. A.N.: BB 30 388.

50. A.D.H.G.: 4 M63.

51. A.D.H.G.: 4M 67.

52. A.D.H.G.: 4M 66, 67.

53. A.D.H.G.: 4M 66.

54. A.D.H.G.: 4M 69.

55. Ibid.

56. A.N.: BB30 394.

57. A.D.H.G.: 4M 74.

58. A.N.: F1c III 7.

59. A.N.: BB30 389. January 27, 1855.

60. A.D.H.G.: 4M 82.

61. A.N.: BB30 389.

62. The repression appears to have had a similar impact on the Republican party of the Gard. By eliminating bourgeois republican leaders from the scene, argues Raymond Huard, it "accentuated the popular character of resistance to the regime during the early years of the Empire" and reinforced "the autonomy of the popular wing within the Republican party." *Le mouvement républicain*, p. 102.

63. A.N.: BB30 389.

64. Aminzade, *Class, Politics, and Early Industrial Capitalism*, pp. 211–13.

65. Bremond, *Histoire de l'élection municipale de 1865*.

66. Ibid.

67. A.D.H.G.: 4M 87.

68. Ibid.

69. A.N.: BB18 1766; A.D.H.G.: 223U 25; A.M.T.: epi 43 tr 4.

70. This gathering is documented in A.N.: F1c III 4, 14 and BB30 390.

71. Massip, *Procès de l'Internationale*; Rouja, *L'Opinion toulousaine en face de la première Internationale*.

72. A.N.: C 2884, Enquête Carol.

73. *Émancipation*, August 1868.

74. A.D.H.G.: 4M 86, April 6, 1866.

75. A.N.: BB18 1795.

76. Armanieu, "Élections législatives et plébiscites à Toulouse."

CHAPTER FIVE
SAINT-ÉTIENNE: THE TRANSFORMATION AND TRIUMPH
OF RADICAL REPUBLICANISM

1. Latta, *Un républicain méconnu*, pp. 25–27.

2. The following account is based upon Latta, *Un républicain méconnu*.

3. These events are documented in Bossakiewicz, *Histoire générale de Saint-Étienne*, pp. 148–50; Faure, *Histoire du mouvement ouvrier*, pp. 109–10; and Festy, *Le mouvement ouvrier*, p. 183.

4. A.D.L.: 10M21, April 7, 1831.

5. Ibid., July 3, 1832.

6. Ibid., *sous-préfet de Saint-Étienne*, July 3, 1832.

7. Martourey estimates that small property holders ("le petit peuple") composed almost half the municipal electorate in Saint-Étienne and the majority in the adjacent communes that were later annexed by the city. *Formation et gestion*, pp. 716–19.

8. Ibid., p. 737.

9. A.D.L.: 92M 2.

10. Gonnard, "Les passementiers," p. 7.

11. A.D.L: 92 M2.

12. Festy, *Le mouvement ouvrier*, p. 320.

13. A.N.: BB18 1215.

14. Mourier, "La presse de Saint-Étienne."

15. *Le Mercure ségusien*, March 27, 1834.

16. Ibid., April 24, 1834.

17. Mourier, "La presse de Saint-Étienne," pp. 101–6.

18. A.D.L.: 92M 3, August 7, 1840.

19. Gourvitch, "Le mouvement pour la réforme électorale."

20. Ibid., p. 184.

21. Tristan, *Le Tour de France*, p. 134.

22. A.N.: BB18 1390.

23. Ibid.

24. Guillaume, *La compagnie*, p. 102.

25. Ibid., p. 68.

26. A.D.L.: 84M 7, February 1846.

27. A.D.L.: BCh 2099. "Rapports de commissions et déliberations du conseil municipal de Saint-Étienne relativement à la coalition des mines de houille du bassin de la Loire."

28. A.N.: BB18 1420.

29. A.N.: BB18 1421, Procureur royal, May 1, 1844.

30. A.N.: BB18 1450.

31. Aguet, *Les grèves sous la Monarchie de Juillet*, p. 348.

32. Gras, *Histoire économique générale des mines*, p. 317.

33. A.N.: BB18 1437, April 5, 1846.

34. B.N.: Le54 1921. August 3, 1846.

35. Brossard, *Les élections*.

36. The following is based on newspaper accounts provided in *Le Mercure ségusien* of January 23, February 9, and February 20, 1848.

37. The following narrative of events in Saint-Étienne is based on: Durousset, *La vie ouvrière*, pp. 205–27; Bossakiewicz, *Histoire générale*, pp. 245–53; Guillaume, *La compagnie*, pp. 199–208; A.D.L.: 10M 20, 28; A.N.: BB18 1461; BB30 361, 366; and accounts in *Le Mercure ségusien* and *L'Avenir républicain*.

38. B.M.S.E.: F1649, *Société populaire de Saint-Étienne*, Recueil factice de tracts électoraux du XIXe siècle; *Le Mercure ségusien*, March 26, 1848.

39. A.M.S.E.: 1D 28.

40. A.N.: BB18 1461.

41. Guillaume, *La compagnie*, p. 139.

42. Available documents identify the occupations of 134 persons who were arrested. Among them were 36 weavers, 29 miners, 19 hardware workers, 16 arms makers, 13 day laborers, and 21 construction artisans. Durousset, *La vie ouvrière*, p. 222.

43. *La Voix du peuple*, April 14, 15, 1848. B.M.S.E.: J 006.

44. A.D.L.: 10M 37.

45. A.N.: C 939. Rapport de Le Bosse, April 17, 1848.

46. *L'Avenir républicain*, March 28 and May 10, 1848.

47. A.D.L.: Bibliothèque Chaleyer 2127. *Comités unis de l'Association républicaine de Saint-Étienne*, April 17, 1848.

48. *Le Mercure* responded on April 14 that the temporary alliance of Republicans and Icarians was based upon a shared desire to achieve democracy. *L'Avenir* retorted on March 22 that Callet's brief association with Legitimists during the late 1840s was based upon a common commitment to suffrage reform.

49. A.D.L.: 3M 5.

50. A.D.L.: 10M 28.

51. Guillaume, *La compagnie*, p. 201.

52. A.N.: BB30 361.

53. The republican socialist ideology of the *La Sentinelle populaire* was elabo-rated in a series of articles published between July and December of 1848. The clearest statement of the newspaper's political position is provided in an August 6, 1848 article entitled "How We are Socialists."

54. A.D.L.: 10M 30, Rapport du commissaire central de police, January 20, 1849.

55. *La Sentinelle populaire*, November 22, 1848.

56. A.D.L.: 10M 30.

57. Ibid., January 20, 1849.

58. *L'Avenir républicain*, March 7, 1849.

59. The newspaper contended, however, that this did not reflect the growing strength of socialism but the failure of the party of order to choose stronger candi-dates and the intimidation and lies of revolutionary agents. *L'Avenir républicain*, May 20 and June 1, 1849.

60. A.D.L.: 10M 30. June 4, 1849.

61. These events are documented in A.D.L.: 10M 30, Rapport addressé au pro-cureur général, evénements de Saint-Étienne et Rive-de-Gier pendant les journées de 15 et 16 Juin 1849.

62. A.D.L.: 10M 37.

63. Ibid.

64. See especially *L'Avenir républicain*, July 22, 1849.

65. A.D.L.: 3M 8; *L'Avenir républicain*, March 15, 1850.

66. These figures are based on prefectoral reports, but Martourey estimates the percentage of voters excluded from suffrage rights even higher, at 81.5 percent. His estimates are based on a comparison of registration lists for June 1848 and Septem-ber 1850. *Formation et gestion*, pp. 802–3.

67. *L'Avenir républicain*, October 1, 1850.

68. A.N.: BB30 379, August 20, 1850.

69. A.N.: BB30 379.

70. A.D.L.: 10M 34.

71. A.N.: BB30 379. November 12, 1851.

72. A.D.L.: 10M 36, 37. Commissaire central de Saint-Étienne, December 10, 11, 1851.

73. A.D.L.: 10M 37, 39; Fournial, *Saint-Étienne*, p. 247; Lequin, *Les ouvriers*, vol. 2, p. 166.

74. A.D.L.: 10M 39; A.N. BB30 379. Procureur général, March 8, 1852; Bros-sard, *Les élections*, p. 65.

75. A.D.L.: 6M 15.

76. A.D.L.: 6M 1. September 6, 1852.

77. A.N.: BB30 379, July 1857.

78. Gordon's analysis of death records reveals a relative decline in the wealth of notables with interests in the traditional household sectors of the economy, includ-ing ribbon merchants. *Merchants and Capitalists*, p. 78.

79. Government railroad policy protected the position of the six giant companies, which took advantage of their positions to charge high rates, discriminate against smaller customers, and drive competing canal companies out of business. For a discussion of the opposition this generated among small producers, see Gaillard, "Notes sur l'opposition au monopôle des compagnies de chemins de fer."

80. Guillaume, *La compagnie*, pp. 54, 88.

81. On the practice of industrial paternalism in nineteenth-century France, see Reid, "Industrial Paternalism: Discourse and Practice."

82. In October 1866 the attorney general reported that, despite repeated republican efforts to gain their sympathies, the 1,180 workers employed at the Terrenoire steel works voted overwhelmingly for their factory director de Bouchaud when he ran for office in the *conseil général* election of 1864. A.N. BB30 379. October 22, 1866. After Terrenoire's directors abandoned the regime and lent their support to the legitimist opposition, their workers continued to provide them with electoral support. Other industrialists with close ties to the regime, including Verdié, the director of the Firminy steel mills, mobilized their workers to support Imperial candidates.

83. A.D.L.: 3M 11. Brossard, *Les élections*, p. 68.

84. A.N.: BB30 379.

85. Terme, *Des élections municipales.*

86. A.N.: BB30 379. July 3, 1864, Procureur Imperial.

87. Ibid.

88. Ibid., December 22, 1866.

89. Martin responded to the accusations in a brochure entitled *Antide Martin et ses détracteurs*, in A.D.L.: Bibliothèque Chaleyer 2676. The attacks on Martin, and his responses, were reprinted as campaign brochures, which are collected in B.M.S.E.: F 1649. *Recueil factice de tracts électoraux du XIXe siècle.*

90. Comité électoral de l'Union démocratique, *Aux Démocrates de Saint-Étienne.* A.D.L.: Bibliothèque Chaleyer 2128.

91. A.M.S.E.: 7K 1. Commissaire central au maire, May 9, 1869.

92. Ibid., May 16, 18, 1869. For a discussion of the centrality of anticlerical educational themes among Saint-Étienne's Republicans during the late Second Empire, see Hanagan, *Nascent Proletarians.*

93. A.M.S.E.: 7 K1. Commissaire central de police, May 16, 18, 1869.

94. During the campaign, republican silk weavers at Montaud shouted down the Legitimist candidate Rochetaillée when he appeared in their neighborhood on May 6 and workers in Saint-Étienne disrupted an electoral gathering of legitimist supporters. This prompted the legitimist candidate to cancel a subsequent electoral meeting so as to avoid a violent confrontation. A.M.S.E.: 7K1. Commissaire central de police.

95. Merley, *Les élections de 1869*, pp. 89–90.

96. On the earlier efforts of Napoleonic officials to win the political support of miners, see Delabre, "La grève de 1869"; Guillaume, *La compagnie*; Hanagan, "Agriculture and Industry"; and A.N.: BB30 379, procureur général, March 27, 1866.

97. The best account of the strike is provided by Delabre, "La grève de 1869."

98. A.D.L.: 6M 3. Prefect to Minister of Interior, June 21, 1869.

99. Maitron, *Dictionnaire biographique*; A.D.L.: 10M 37, 63, 66, 75, 80.

100. A.D.L.: 10M 62.
101. A.M.S.E.: 5 K1. Commissaire central de police au maire, April 29, 1870.
102. Ibid.
103. A.D.L.: 5M 79.
104. A.D.L.: 10 M 62. January 24, 1869.

CHAPTER SIX
ROUEN: THE TRANSFORMATION OF RADICALISM
AND TRIUMPH OF LIBERALISM

1. A.D.S.M.: 1MP 3196.
2. *Le Progrès de Rouen*, January 27, 1869.
3. Maitron, *Dictionnaire biographique*, vol. 2, p. 72.
4. These events are documented in Marec, "Lendemains de révolution."
5. A.D.S.M.: 1MP 3196, 4MP 4706.
6. This account of the Rouen branch of the association is based on documents catalogued in A.D.S.M.: 4MP 4245, 1MP 3196, and A.N.: BB18 1224.
7. A.N.: BB18 1224. July 7, 1834, procureur du roi.
8. A.D.S.M.: 4MP 4234. January 22, 1834, maire de Rouen.
9. A.N.: F 1C III Seine-Inférieure 6, préfet, December 5, 1833.
10. Although there were a number of extremely wealthy voters in Rouen, those paying less than five hundred francs in taxes comprised two-thirds of the local electorate. In 1836 there were only 2,370 qualified voters, who constituted only 2.5 percent of a population of 92,083. Chaline, *Rouen sous la Monarchie de Juillet* p. 13 and *L'affaire Noiret*, p. 15.
11. On the debate over the cost of credit in Rouen, see Chaline, "La banque à Rouen au XIXe siècle."
12. A.D.S.M.: 1MP 3446. October 20, 1834.
13. Chaline, *L'affaire Noiret*, p. 20. *Les bourgeois de Rouen*, p. 355.
14. A.D.S.M.: 1MP 3446. Rapports confidentielles, September 19, 23, 24, 1834.
15. Weill, *Histoire du parti républicain*, pp. 123–24.
16. A.D.S.M.: 1M 3446. February 19, 1839.
17. Gourvitch, "Le mouvement pour la réforme électorale," pp. 176–77.
18. A.N.: CC 772.
19. A.D.S.M.: 4MP 4706. Commissaire central de police, December 26, 30, 1843.
20. A.N.: BB18 1421. Procureur royale, April 23, 28, 1844.
21. A.N.: BB18 1428. Procureur royale, December 30, 1844.
22. After a speech by Ledru-Rollin denouncing communism, Cabet attacked *La Réforme* as "an organ of the bourgeoisie" and warned workers of the dangers of collaborating with bourgeois Republicans. Johnson, *Utopian Communism*, pp. 223–26.
23. The newspaper had to pay a twelve thousand franc security deposit in Rouen, compared to fifty thousand francs in Paris.
24. A.D.S.M.: 4MP 4706. Commissariat central de police, December 8, 16, 1846.

25. For a more detailed account of this conflict, see Blondel, *La crise du milieu du XIXième siècle*, pp. 138–41.

26. B.N.: Le 2109. "Élections de Rouen. Le Comité radical aux électeurs."

27. Jean-Pierre Chaline, by ignoring working-class politics and the rapid growth of a radical and socialist opposition during the final years of the July Monarchy, misconstrues the local political climate and misrepresents the advent of the Second Republic as a complete rupture with preceding political developments. He mistakenly contends that "the only significant opposition came from a moderate left respectful of [existing] institutions and claiming only reforms. . . ." He also equates a dominant tendency within the city's bourgeoisie—a preoccupation with order and liberty and an indifference to the form of government—with a distinctive "local political temperament." "Rouen au milieu du XIXième siècle."

28. A.N.: BB18 1456. October 6, 1847.

29. Blondel, *La crise du milieu du XIXième siècle*, pp. 155–58.

30. A.D.S.M.: 3 MP 866. Liste confidentielle des membres du conseil municipal; A.D.S.M.: 3M 580.

31. *Journal de Rouen*, April 4, 1845; April 30–May 1, 1846; December 19, 1847.

32. These events are documented in A.D.S.M.: 3M 1250 and in the *Journal de Rouen*, July 3, 1847.

33. Marec, *1848 à Rouen*, p. 50.

34. Charles Cord'homme, in a memoir written in 1894, observed that during the 1847 campaign for suffrage reform, Rouen's Republicans and communists marched alongside one another, united in the struggle for universal male suffrage. Marec, *1848 à Rouen*, p. 49.

35. B.N.: Lb51 4398. *Les démocrats de Rouen*. 1847.

36. A.D.S.M.: 1MP 3446. *Proclamation de la République, Rouen*. February 25, 1848.

37. These early conflicts over control of the new republican municipality are documented in Toutain, *La révolution de 1848*, pp. 49–50; Dubuc, "Les émeutes de Rouen et d'Elbeuf," p. 249; and Blondel, *La Crise du milieu du XIXième siècle*, pp. 197–98.

38. A.N.: BB30 323. Lettres de Senard, April 20, 1848.

39. Leblanc, "Mémoires de l'ouvrier François Leblanc," p. 30.

40. The republican political impetus for the attacks on the railroad bridges is evidenced by the participation of workers from various trades, with very few dockers and boatsmen involved in these incidents. A.N.: BB 30 288. Lettre de Senard, March 2, 1848.

41. Blondel, *La crise du milieu du XIXième siècle*, p. 196.

42. Delale, "Rouen 1848: La Saint-Barthelemy rouge," pp. 71–72. The workers' demonstrations of early 1848 are also documented in A.N.: BB18 1461.

43. A.N. BB30 387. Procureur général, January 10, 1850.

44. The departmental archives contain petitions drawn up by various artisanal trades (cabinetmakers, masons, joiners, plasterers, handloom weavers, bakers, tailors, belt makers) as well as by textile factory workers (spinners, weavers, calico printers, dyers), semiskilled and unskilled laborers (sawmill workers, dockers, grain

haulers), and unemployed workers. The grievances documented were varied, ranging from substandard wages and dangerous working conditions to the lack of sympathy shown by clerical authorities for the plight of the poor to unemployment caused by mechanization and competition from prison workshops. A.D.S.M.: 10MP 2001.

45. Reddy argues that Deschamps, unfamiliar with the piece-rate system, was unaware of the important implications of this decree, which resolved a confrontation over the distribution of the benefits of new technologies in favor of factory workers. *The Rise of Market Culture*, pp. 206–8.

46. For further discussion of the reforms introduced by Deschamps during this period, see Dubuc, "Frédéric Deschamps, commissaire de la République."

47. Marec, *1848 à Rouen*, pp. 67–68.

48. A.N.: C 940.

49. *La Tribune du peuple*. April 1848.

50. A.N.: BB30 365.

51. *L'Ami du peuple. Journal des véritables intérêts des travailleurs*, March 29, 31, 1848.

52. A.N.: BB18 1461. Letter of April 4, 1848.

53. The events at Lillebonne are documented in greater detail in Senard's letters to the Minister of Justice, dated April 1, 2, 4, and 7, 1848. A.N.: BB18 1461. In a letter of April 7, 1848, Senard criticized Deschamps's failure to take action against the *Comité démocratique*'s interference in Rouen's municipal affairs but praised his handling of the Lillebonne affair. A.N.: BB30 366.

54. According to Dahubert, a delegate from the Parisian Club of Clubs, Deschamps failed to challenge the exclusion of workers in order "to avoid troubles that would benefit our enemies." A.N.: C 940.

55. Dubuc, "Frédéric Deschamps," pp. 386–87.

56. B.N.: Lb54 1648. *Procès des insurgés de Rouen*, Cour d'Assises du Calvados, p. 2.

57. *La Tribune du peuple*, April 22, 1848.

58. Ibid., April 8, 1848.

59. The liberal republican slate included four workers: a mechanic, a barrel maker, a weaver, and the working-class poet and former calico print worker Lebreton. This list included Deschamps, even though the radical list rejected all of those on the liberal republican slate. The royalist slate was also headed by Lamartine and included two workers—the weaver Dobremel and working-class poet Lebreton—but it was headed by several former orleanist deputies and excluded Senard. There were nine workers on the radical slate, including two weavers, a dyer, a spinner, a foundry worker, a shoemaker, an ivory carver, a tailor, and a caulker. B.M.R.: Ng 144; A.D.S.M.: 4MP 4237. During the months of March and April, the liberal republican newspaper *L'Ami du peuple* appealed to local workers, proclaiming itself to be the "newspaper of the true interests of workers."

60. The insurrection in Rouen is documented in Dubuc, "Les émeutes de Rouen et d'Elbeuf"; Toutain, *La révolution de 1848 à Rouen*; Bouteillier, *Histoire des milices bourgeoises*; Blondel, *La crise du milieu du XIXième siècle* and Merriman, *The Agony of the Republic*.

61. Zévaès asserts that the unprovoked murder of a man named Quesnel by the commander of the National Guard unit surrounding city hall was the spark which ignited the insurrection, after numerous previous provocations by National Guardsmen intent on provoking a bloody confrontation. "La lutte des classes à Rouen," pp. 214–15. Senard provides a very different account of the confrontations that sparked the uprising, attributing the provocations to the demonstrators. A.N. BB30 365. Letter of May 5, 1848. For a balanced account, see Blondel, *La crise du milieu du XIXième siècle*, pp. 248–51.

62. Figures on the number of insurgents killed vary, due in part to a number who later died of their wounds. Desseaux estimated the number of deaths at thirty-nine in a report to the Minister of Justice dated July 25, 1848. Although contemporary observers, and subsequent historians, regarded the absence of deaths among National Guardsmen and soldiers as evidence that the insurgents were unarmed, Desseaux contended, in a report of May 5, 1848, that the rebels' rifles simply misfired, spraying bullets over the heads of onrushing troops. A.N.: BB30 365.

63. "Documents officiels sur l'émeute de Rouen (27 et 28 avril 1848)," p. 105.

64. A.N.: BB30 365. Undated letter, written sometime in April or May 1848.

65. *Supplément au Journal de Rouen*. November 14, 1848.

66. *La Sentinelle des travailleurs*, May 28, 1848.

67. B.N.: Lb54 1684 *Procès des insurgés de Rouen*.

68. B.M.R.: Ng 144.

69. *Journal de Rouen*, July 20, 1848.

70. Ibid., December 12, 1848.

71. The police commissioner Leon Bertran compiled detailed surveillance reports on the club's meetings from October 5, 1848 to May 12, 1849. These are collected in A.M.R.: 2I 11, *Registre des procès-verbaux de police judiciaire concernant le club Nitrière* (1848–49).

72. *Le Républicain de Rouen*. May 12, 1848.

73. See, for example, the electoral proclamation of May 12, 1849 published by *Le Républicain de Rouen*.

74. Blondel, *La crise*, p. 327; Marec, *1848 à Rouen*, p. 15.

75. *Le Républicain de Rouen*. July 7, 1849.

76. A.N.: BB30 387.

77. An account of unsuccessful republican efforts to organize resistance to the coup is provided by Charles Cord'homme in Marec, *1848 à Rouen*, pp. 156–62. See also Blondel, *La vie politique*.

78. A.N.: BB30 397. Travaux de la commission mixte.

79. Ten percent of the ballots were declared invalid. Marec, *1848 à Rouen*, p. 170.

80. A.N.: BB30 387. July 2, 1852.

81. A.D.S.M.: BB30 387. July 1 and August 14, 1855.

82. A.D.S.M.: 4MP 4279. This paragraph is based on the following reports by Philippon: October 7, 9, and 23, November 19, and December, 6, 1855; December 14, 1858; and September 23 and December 26, 1859.

83. The factory spinner Perier was fired from his job for distributing republican

ballots during the 1857 election. Unable to find work in any other factory, he was forced to migrate. A.D.S.M.: 4MP 4279. Rapport du Philippon, November 8, 1857.

84. A.D.S.M.: 4MP 4279. Rapports du Philippon, December 19, 1856; March 15, 1858; December 14, 1858; February 13, 1858; June 7, 1858.

85. A.N.: BB30 387.

86. The 1862 reports of Philippon document widespread unemployment, the dismissal of textile workers unwilling to accept wage cuts, and public works projects for the unemployed that featured "a brutality that discourages the majority and disgusts many." In the face of the economic crisis, he noted, "the demogogues continue to exhibit great cautiousness." A.D.S.M.: 4MP 4279.

87. A.D.S.M.: 3M 228. Electoral brochure of May 19, 1863.

88. Ibid., Élections législatives de 1863.

89. Dubuc, Les élections au Corps législatif, pp. 314–15.

90. A.N.: BB30 387. January 12, 1867.

91. Boivin, Le mouvement ouvrier, p. 163.

92. Elwitt, The Making of the Third Republic, p. 43.

93. Boivin, "Les origines de la ligue," p. 226; B.N.: Rp 10397. Rapport sur les travaux et la marche du cercle depuis le 23 août 1868. Publication du cercle d'études économiques de l'arrondissement de Rouen. In other cities, such as Marseille, where bourgeois radicals like Alphonse Esquiros were more open to cooperating with socialists, local leaders of the First International, such as André Bastelica, participated in the Ligue de l'enseignement. Duveau, La pensée ouvrière, p. 41.

94. Boivin, "La Fédération ouvrière rouennaise," p. 332.

95. Official reports on these strikes never mention republican activists nor raise the fear that the economic grievances raised by workers will become politicized. A.N.: F 1c III 17.

96. The following account is based on Boivin, "La Fédération ouvrière rouennaise," pp. 322–42, 524–48 and A.D.S.M.: 4MP 4235, Rapport sur les causes de l'insurrection du 18 mars et ses ramifications dans le département de la Seine-Inférieure, July 26, 1871.

97. For a more detailed discussion of this organization, see Boivin, Le mouvement ouvrier, pp. 201–38.

98. A.D.S.M.: 4MP 4235, Préfet au préfet du Rhone, January 10, 1872.

99. Electoral rallies organized by Aubry in early May 1869 admitted only members of workers' associations (corporations) and refused entry to several bourgeois radicals who were "well-known for the exaltation of their ideas." A.D.S.M.: 3MP 1027, Commissaire central au préfet, May 10, 1869.

100. A.D.S.M.: 3MP 1027.

101. Membership in the local branch of the association declined at the end of 1869 as a result of opposition by some of Rouen's members to centralized control of organizational dues and their absence of control over the allocation of strike support funds. By January 1870 there were only eleven hundred members. A.D.S.M.: 4MP 4235, Rapport sur les causes de l'insurrection.

102. A list of the founders of Le Progrès is provided by Charles Cord'homme in Marec, 1848 à Rouen, p. 205.

103. In December 1869, when Pouyer-Quertier and other textile industrialists led a petition campaign to protest tariff policies, the three thousand workers who belonged to the *Cercle d'études économiques* followed Aubry's advice and refused to associate with their employers despite shared opposition to the recent treaty of commerce with Britain.

104. Aubry's campaign posters are collected in A.D.S.M.: 3MP 1027, 3M 236. The eighteen-point program of the *cercle* is specified in Aubry's electoral brochures (B.M.R.: Ng144) and its statutes are contained in documents of December 1869. A.D.S.M.: 4MP 4235. The statutes denounce strikes as "an economic heresy" but acknowledge that under certain circumstances workers are forced to strike. They renounce "political and religious questions," stating that their central goal is the development of workers' production and consumer cooperatives, freed from "bankocratic influence" by the creation of cooperative credit institutions.

105. Boivin, *Le mouvement ouvrier*, p. 295.

106. B.N.: Le77 2613. Candidature de M. Pouyer-Quertier. A.D.S.M.: 3M236. "Un dernier mot sur la candidature de M. Pouyer-Quertier" and "M. Pouyer-Quertier, deputé sortant, candidat independent et libéral." A.N.: Le77 2656. "Votes et opinions de M. Pouyer-Quertier."

107. A.D.S.M.: 3M 236.

108. These visits prompted worker protests at the Valery machine construction factory in Saint-Sever, where republican supporters of Desseaux, joined by workers from nearby factories, prevented the candidate from speaking by repeatedly shouting "Down with Pouyer-Quertier!" A.D.S.M.: 3MP 1027. Gendarmerie commander to prefect, June 4, 1869.

109. B.N.: Le77 2614. Protestation des ouvriers de La Foudre. Dubuc, "Les élections de 1869," p. 334.

110. A.D.S.M.: 3MP 1027. Élections de 1869, Scrutin de ballottage, Candidature ouvrière Émile Aubry, May 30, 1869.

111. The ongoing debate between Varlin and Aubry on this issue is documented in Boivin, "La Fédération," pp. 322–42.

112. Boivin, *Le mouvement ouvrier*, p. 399.

CHAPTER SEVEN
FAILED REVOLUTIONS: THE COMMUNES OF 1870–1871

1. For example, see Skocpol, *States and Social Revolutions*. For excellent introductions to the sociological literature on revolution, see Goldstone, *Revolutions* and Kimmel, *Revolution*.

2. Most analyses of European state-building, notes Charles Tilly, focus on "the survivors of a ruthless competition in which most contenders lost." Comparing the histories of the winners in this process, he notes, weights the inquiry toward a certain kind of outcome that was quite rare. *The Formation of National States*, p. 15.

3. After the repression of the communes, French socialists began to increasingly question the assumption that the republic provided an advantageous framework for the triumph of socialism. This shift is evident in the writings of Karl Marx, who defended the republic as an ideal terrain for proletarian struggles in *The Class*

Struggles in France but subsequently changed his position in *The Civil War in France*.

4. Tilly, *From Mobilization to Revolution*, pp. 216–17 and "Revolutions and Collective Violence," pp. 483–555.

5. Edwards, *The Paris Commune*, p. 54.

6. A notable exception is Gaillard's *Communes de province*.

7. A.N.: BB30 390. Procureur impérial.

8. A.D.H.G.: 4M 94. Enquête Résseguier, August 1872.

9. A.N.: C 2884. Enquête Carol.

10. Ibid.

11. Ibid.

12. A.D.H.G.: 4M 94. Enquête Résseguier.

13. A.N.: C2884. Enquête Carol.

14. A.D.H.G.: 4M94. September 18, 1870.

15. A.D.H.G.: 4M94. Enquête Résseguier.

16. Ibid.

17. *Émancipation*. October 12, 1870.

18. A.D.H.G.: 4M 94.

19. Ibid.

20. A.D.H.G.: wU 3797; A.M.T.: Procès-verbaux. Police municipal.

21. *Émancipation*. January 30, 1871.

22. A.D.H.G.: 4M 94; *Émancipation*. February 9, 1870.

23. A.D.H.G.: 4M 95.

24. *Émancipation*. March 29, 1871; Duportal, *La Commune à Toulouse*, p. 41.

25. A.M.T.: Régistre de contrôle. Garde Nationale Sédentaire de Toulouse.

26. A.N.: C 2884. Enquête Carol.

27. *Association républicaine*.

28. de Puybusque, *La prise des armes*, p. 5.

29. A.D.L.: 10M 67. Rapport du commissaire central, August 8, 1870.

30. Ibid., August 14, 1870. The clergy were exempt from military service and the rich were able to buy replacements if drafted.

31. "Enquête sur les actes du gouvernement de la Défense national. *Annales de l'Assemblée Nationale*. Telegrams of September 4, 5, 1870, pp. 1094–95.

32. *L'Éclaireur*. September 8, 1870.

33. A.D.L.: 10M 64. September 7, 1870; Bertholon to Minister of the Interior. "Enquête sur les actes." *Annales de l'Assemblée Nationale*, p. 1096.

34. "Enquête sur les actes." *Annales de l'Assemblée Nationale*, p. 1096. Telegram of September 16, 1870.

35. *L'Éclaireur*. September 16, 1870.

36. Bossakiewicz, *Histoire générale de Saint-Étienne*, p. 264.

37. "Enquête sur les actes." *Annales de l'Assemblée Nationale*, p. 1099.

38. Ibid., p. 1100.

39. A.D.L.: 6M 3.

40. A.D.L.: BH 3163: *Procès des Alliances républicaines*, p. 196.

41. *L'Éclaireur*, October 31, 1870.

42. A.D.L.: 6M3. November 8, 1870.

43. A.D.L.: BH 3163: *Procès des Alliances républicaines*, p. 198. A.D.L.: 10M 67, undated, pièce 272.

44. *La Commune*. December 29, 1870.

45. Ibid.; February 15, 1871; February 26, 1871.

46. A.D.L.: BH 3163: *Procès des Alliances républicaines de Saint-Étienne, Terrenoire, et Roanne*. Testimony of Bertholon.

47. Lequin, *Les ouvriers*, vol. 1, p. 175.

48. "Enquête sur les actes." *Annales de l'Assemblée Nationale*, p. 1104. Telegram of January 28, 1871, to the Minister of the Interior at Bordeaux.

49. Ibid., p. 1105.

50. A.M.S.E.: 10D 47.

51. *La Commune*. February 8, 1871.

52. Ibid., March 24, 1871. The following account is based heavily on the March 27, 28, and 29 editions of *L'Éclaireur* and on Vidal, *La Commune de 1871*, available in A.M.S.E.: 6C 2, Vida. Vidal provides an excellent narrative of the events of March but a very incomplete account of the preceding events of the fall of 1870.

53. *L'Éclaireur* contended that the shooting that sparked the invasion of city hall was the work of reactionaries determined to provoke disorders that would benefit their cause. It offered no evidence to support this claim.

54. Jolivalt was an active member of the *la Vierge* club. His republican socialist views are elaborated in a book that includes reflections on the failure of the Second Republic, which he attributed to the moderation of its leaders and their failure to implement a program of radical democracy. *Renseignements utiles*.

55. A.N.: C2884. *Enquête parlementaire sur l'insurrection du 18 March 1871*, Déposition de M. Ducros, p. 388.

56. Vidal, *La Commune de 1871*, p. 119.

57. Cherrier, "Les ouvriers communalistes stéphanois (1870–1871)."

58. A.D.L.: 10M 69.

59. Faure, *La Commune en province*, p. 11.

60. *L'Éclaireur*. March 26, 27, 1870.

61. A.N.: C2884. *Enquête parlementaire sur l'insurrection du 18 mars 1871*, Déposition de M. Ducros, p. 388.

62. A.D.L.: 6M 3.

63. Marec, *1848 à Rouen*, pp. 181–82.

64. *Enquête parlementaire sur les actes du gouvernement de la Defense nationale*, vol. 4, p. 493.

65. "Enquête sur les actes." *Annales de l'Assemblée Nationale*, vol. 25, pp. 1355–56. Telegraph of October 1, 1870, to Minister of the Interior.

66. Boivin, *Le mouvement ouvrier*, pp. 414–15.

67. Ibid., p. 434.

68. "Enquête sur les actes." *Annales de l'Assemblée Nationale*, vol. 25, p. 1355. Telegraph of September 12, 1870, to Cremieux, Minister of Justice.

69. Boivin, *Le mouvement ouvrier*, p. 416.

70. Ibid., pp. 416–17; Estancelin, "La verité," p. 25.

71. Boivin, *Le mouvement ouvrier*, p. 435.

72. Estancelin portrayed this event as an effort by armed insurgents to seize control of the prefecture, which was thwarted by his willingness to threaten the use of force. "La verité," p. 28.

73. Boivin, *Le mouvement ouvrier*, p. 423.

74. A.D.S.M.: 4MP 2318; *Journal de Rouen*, special edition of December 6, 1870–February 5, 1871.

75. Boivin, *Le mouvement ouvrier*, p. 426.

76. Special edition of the *Journal de Rouen*, December 6, 1870–February 5, 1871. A.D.S.M.: 4MP 2318.

77. Radical leader Cord'homme later claimed that he had intervened in early November to prevent the arrest of prominent industrialist Pouyer-Quertier for holding secret talks with the Prussians. Marec, *1848 à Rouen*, pp. 187–90.

78. These accusations were published by Rouen's radical leaders in the *Journal du Havre* on December 9, 1870.

79. Estancelin, *La verité*.

80. *Journal du Havre*, January 4, 1871.

81. Boivin, *Le mouvement ouvrier*, p. 443.

82. B.N.: Lk18 1678. *Procès-verbaux du conseil municipal de la ville de Rouen*, December 7, 11, 1870.

83. Boivin, *Le mouvement ouvrier*, p. 447.

84. B.N.: Lk18 1660. Conseil municipal de la ville de Rouen.

85. The liberal republican list, organized by the *Comité départemental républicain* and supported by the *Journal de Rouen*, was headed by Senard and Deschamps but contained a number of radical Republicans, including Duvivier and Dautresme. A second liberal list included several nonrepublicans. The four radical lists included those drawn up by the *Comité central républicain*, which included Cord'homme, Vaughan, Regnier, and Manchon, the *Comités républicains réunis*, which included more candidates from the Havre region as well as the socialist Aubry, and lists of the *Patriots de Rouen* and the *Comité radical républicain*, which included a number of prominent Republicans from outside the region. Socialists of the First International were represented to varying degrees on all four radical lists.

86. Boivin, *Le mouvement ouvrier*, p. 451.

87. A.D.S.M.: 4MP4235. Prefect's report to Minister of the Interior.

88. The prefect made this claim in his April 26, 1871 and July 1871 reports on the causes of the insurrection. A.D.S.M.: 4MP 2318, 4235.

89. *Journal de Rouen*. March 20, April 10, 28, May 6, 12, 1871.

90. *Le Nouvelliste de Rouen*. April 29, 1871. Cited in Boivin, *Le mouvement ouvrier*, p. 456.

91. A.D.S.M.: 4MP 4235. Prefect, April 26, 1871.

92. Boivin, *Le mouvement ouvrier*, p. 464.

93. Ibid., p. 460.

94. In November 1871, they were convicted and sentenced to varying terms in prison, with the harshest sentences, two years behind bars, reserved for Cord'homme and Vaughan. A.D.S.M.: 4MP 4235.

95. Jenkins, "Sociopolitical Movements," p. 139.

96. Tilly, *From Mobilization to Revolution* and "Collective Violence in European Perspective."

97. Figures for opposition votes in this table refer to the percentage of votes received by republican, orleanist, and legitimist candidates. These figures were difficult to compile, given the changes made in Second Empire electoral boundaries, including the partitioning of urban republican strongholds like Toulouse, Saint-Étienne, and Rouen into several electoral districts. Whenever possible, the total number of votes cast for republican or opposition candidates in the different districts into which the city was divided are used. Thus, for example, the percentage of votes received by Republicans in Toulouse in 1869 includes the total number of votes cast by Toulouse residents for the three republican candidates—Mulé (1st district), Duportal (2d district), and Calès (3d district), i.e., 11,229 votes, divided by the total number of votes cast in the city, i.e., 22,860. Where percentages for districts, rather than the number of votes, were available, I used averages. Thus, for example, in 1863, the two republican candidates in Saint-Étienne won 46 percent of the votes in the first district and 52 percent in the second district, hence the figure of 49 percent in this table. Figures for Saint-Étienne include the adjacent communes of Beaubrun, Montaud, Outrefurens, and Valbenoîte, which were annexed by the city in March 1855.

98. Faure, *La Commune en province*, p. 13.

99. A.N.: BB30 390.

100. Maitron, *Dictionnaire biographique*, p.149.

101. In contrast to the programs of the Leagues of the South and East, the League of the Southwest rejected federalism as a system that would weaken the Republic in its pursuit of the war effort and affirmed its devotion to the "one and indivisible Republic." The Jacobin sympathies of Duportal prevailed in Toulouse, whereas the federalist leanings of republican socialists triumphed elsewhere.

102. See, for example, Greenberg, *Sisters of Liberty*.

103. A.M.T.: Affiche de la Ligue du Sud-Ouest.

104. See Hunt, *Politics, Culture, and Class*; Tilly, *The Contentious French*; and Tarrow, *Struggling to Reform*.

CHAPTER EIGHT
CONCLUSION: POLITICAL CHANGE, CLASS ANALYSIS, AND REPUBLICANISM

1. For a discussion of how historical sociologists incorporate time into their explanations, see Aminzade, "Historical Sociology and Time."

2. One plausible explanation of this anomaly, that is, the greatest ambivalence toward electoral politics in the city where Republicans had the greatest electoral strength, concerns the extremely high level of working-class disenfranchisement that resulted from the application of a three-year residency requirement in the 1850 electoral law, due to the highly mobile character of the city's and region's industrial labor force. Another relevant factor is the persistence of a revolutionary tradition among the city's silk weavers, who played a central role in working-class politics.

3. One of the leaders (*mandataires*) of the weaving factory workers who presented a petition to Deschamps in early 1848 was a woman named Rosée. Four women were arrested and tried for their role in the Rouen insurrection of 1848. Two of them were convicted and sentenced to five and twenty years of forced labor for helping to gather arms and munitions for the insurgents.

4. Rosenberg, "Herbert Gutman on American Labor History," p. 53.

5. Miliband, "Reflections on the Crisis of Communist Regimes."

6. For a lengthier discussion of these elements of the socialist tradition, see Eley, "Reviewing the Socialist Tradition."

7. For elaboration, see the essays in Calhoun, *Habermas and the Public Sphere*.

8. For discussions of the contemporary political debate on this issue, see Young, *Justice and the Politics of Difference*; Phillips, *Engendering Democracy*; Kauffman, "The Anti-Politics of Identity"; and Escoffier, "The Limits of Multiculturalism."

Bibliography

THIS is a selective list of sources that were directly utilized for this book. I have omitted a large number of manuscript sources, reference sources, articles, and books that have generally informed my research.

MANUSCRIPT SOURCES—NATIONAL ARCHIVES OF FRANCE

C 939, 940: Commission d'enquête sur les journées des 15 mai et 23 juin 1848.
C 956: Commission d'enquête sur le travail agricole et industriel, prescrite par décret du 25 mai 1848.
C 2884: Enquête parlementaire sur l'insurrection du 18 mars 1871.
C 2899 à 2991: Enquête parlementaire sur les actes du gouvernement de la Défense nationale.
CC 772, 791: Procès contre Charavay et autres. Pièces saisie à Rouen chez le Sr. Noiret.
F12 4503; F1c III: 4, 6, 7, 9, 14, 17.
BB18 (Criminal Division, Ministry of Justice): 1215, 1224, 1354B, 1360, 1386, 1388, 1390, 1395, 1395C, 1398, 1420, 1421, 1428, 1435, 1437, 1449, 1450, 1456, 1461, 1766, 1793, 1795.
BB30 (Affaires Politiques, Ministry of Justice): 167, 288, 323, 361, 365, 366, 379, 387–390, 394, 397, 415.

MANUSCRIPT SOURCES—ARCHIVES OF THE MINISTRY OF WAR

Vincennes

E5 150: Toulouse, census riots, 1841.

MANUSCRIPT SOURCES—DEPARTMENTAL ARCHIVES

Haute-Garonne

M196; 4M 47–53, 55, 56, 58–60, 62–67, 69–74, 76, 77, 81–84, 86, 87, 94, 95; 10M 21, 26; 12M 32, 34.
223U 10, 11, 14, 15, 17, 25; wU 72, 3797.
54Y 42.

Loire

3M 5, 8, 11; 5M 79; 6M 1, 3, 15; 10M 20, 21, 28, 30, 31, 34, 36, 37, 39, 60, 62–64, 66, 67, 69, 75, 80, 2001; 84M 7; 85M 2; 87M 7; 92M: 2, 3; 94M 2.
Bibliothèque Chaleyer: 2099, 2127, 2128, 2676.
BH 3163: *Procès des Alliances républicaines de Saint-Étienne, Terrenoire, et Roanne.*

Seine-Maritime

3M 228, 236, 580, 1250.
1MP 3196, 3446; 3MP 866, 1027; 4MP 2318, 4234, 4235, 4237, 4245, 4279, 4235, 4706; 10MP 1467, 1614, 2002.
F 359.

MANUSCRIPT SOURCES—MUNICIPAL ARCHIVES

Toulouse

Actes de mariages, 1830, 1872.
Affiche de la Ligue du Sud-Ouest, document non-classé.
Annuaires de Toulouse, 1840, 1872.
Archives Modernes, epi 43.
Procès verbaux. Police municipal.
Recensements manuscrits de 1830, 1872.
Régistre de contrôle. Garde Nationale Sédentaire de Toulouse.
Secretariat général: 126, 3D 137, 7D 483.
1I 71; 1K 21; 2I 1, 59, 63, 64.
2F 5.
2Q 6, 7.

Saint-Étienne

1D 28; 10D 47.
5K 1; 7K 1.

Rouen

2I 11—Registre des procès-verbaux de police judiciaire concernant le club Nitrière (1848–1849). *Normandie, révolution: Clubs politiques, surveillance.*

PRINTED PRIMARY SOURCES—NATIONAL LIBRARY OF FRANCE

Lb51 4398 "Les démocrats de Rouen"
Lb54 1684 "Procès des insurgés de Rouen. Cour d'Assises du Calvados"
Le54 1921 "Protestation de Camille Jacquemont"
Le77 2613 "Candidature de M. Pouyer-Quertier"
Le77 2614 "Protestation des ouvriers de La Foudre"
Le77 2656 "Votes et opinions de M. Pouyer-Quertier"
Le2109 "Elections de Rouen. Le Comité radical aux électeurs"
Lk18 1660 "Conseil municipal de la ville de Rouen. Extrait du registre des déliberations"
Lk18 1678 "Procès-verbaux du conseil municipal de la ville de Rouen. Compte-rendu des séances pendant l'occupation prussienne"
Rp 10397 "Rapport sur les travaux et la marche du cercle depuis le 23 août 1868. Publication du cercle d'études économique aux ouvriers de l'arrondissement de Rouen."

"Enquête sur les actes du gouvernement de la Défense nationale. Séance du 13 Novembre 1872." Vol. 25. *Annales de l'Assemblée Nationale.* Imprimerie du Journal Officiel. Paris, 1875.

PRINTED PRIMARY SOURCES—MUNICIPAL LIBRARIES

Saint-Étienne

F1649 Recueil factice de tracts électoraux du XIXe siècle.

Rouen

Ng 144 Affiches, proclamations, circulaires, professions de foi, listes d'électeurs concernant les élections de restauration et de 1848 à 1882 dans le département de Seine-Inférieure.

R. Aubé, *Bibliographie de la presse rouennaise (1762–1928)*, Ms 233.

PRINTED PRIMARY SOURCES—NEWSPAPERS

Toulouse

Association républicaine, 1870–1871. A.D.H.G.: Jour 37.
Civilisation, 1849–1851. B.N.: Jo 2889.
Émancipation, 1839, 1847, 1848, 1869–1871. B.N.:Jo 2856. A.D.H.G.: Per 63.
La Gazette du Languedoc, 1847. B.N.: Jo 124.
Journal de Toulouse, 1848–53. B.N.: Jo 2853.
La Voix du peuple, 1847. (Issue enclosed in the February 20, 1847 report of the attorney general, A.N.: BB18 1449).

Saint-Étienne

L'Avenir républicain, 1848–1852. B.N.: Jo 605.
La Commune, 1870–1871. A.M.S.E.: 2I 33.
L'Éclaireur, 1869–1871. B.M.S.E.
Le Mercure ségusien, 1834; 1844–1848. B.N.: Jo 2703. A.M.S.E.: 7C 21.
La Sentinelle populaire, 1848. B.N.: Jo 596.
La Voix du peuple, 1848. B.M.S.E.: J 006.

Rouen

L'Ami du peuple. Journal des véritables intérêts des travailleurs, 1848. B.N.: Jo 2665.
L'Indépendent. Journal du club national de Rouen, 1848. B.N.: Jo 3451.
Journal de Rouen, 1845–1847, 1848, 1870–1871. B.N.: Jo B17; A.D.S.M.:JPL3; A.M.R.: 2I11; B.M.R.: Norm 2605.
Journal du Havre, 1870–1871. B.N.: Jo 86205.
Le Progrès de Rouen, 1869. B.N.: Lc11 882 (11).
Le Républicain de Rouen, 1848–1849. B.N.: Jo 2689.
La Sentinelle des travailleurs, 1848. B.N.: Jo 2668.
La Tribune du peuple, Avril 1848. B.N.: Jo 4004.

BOOKS AND ARTICLES

Abrams, Philip. *Historical Sociology*. Ithaca, N.Y., 1982.

Abrogast, Marcel. *L'industrie des armes à Saint-Étienne*. Saint-Étienne, 1937.

Agnew, John A. *Place and Politics: The Geographical Mediation of State and Society*. Boston, 1987.

Aguet, Jean Pierre. *Les grèves sous la Monarchie de Juillet (1830–1847)*. Genève, 1954.

Agulhon, Maurice. *La vie sociale en Provence intérieure au lendemain de la Révolution*. Paris, 1970.

———. *La République au village: les populations du Var de la Révolution à la Second République*. Paris, 1970.

———. *Marianne into Battle: Republican Imagery and Symbolism in France, 1789–1880*. Translated by Janet Lloyd. Cambridge, 1981.

———. *The Republican Experiment, 1848–1852*. Cambridge, 1983.

———. "Working Class and Sociability in France before 1848." In *The Power of the Past: Essays for Eric Hobsbawn*, edited by Pat Thane, Geoffrey Crossick, and Roderick Floud. Cambridge, 1984.

———. "The Heritage of the Revolution and Liberty in France." *Review* 12, no.3 (1989), 405–22.

Alford, Robert R. *Party and Society: The Anglo-American Democracies*. Chicago, 1963.

Alford, Robert R., and Roger Friedland. *Powers of Theory: Capitalism, the State, and Democracy*. Cambridge, 1985.

Aminzade, Ronald. "Breaking the Chains of Dependency: From Patronage to Class Politics." *Journal of Urban History* 3, no. 4 (1977): 485–506.

———. *Class, Politics, and Early Industrial Capitalism: A Study of Mid-Nineteenth-Century Toulouse, France*. Albany, New York, 1981.

———. "Capitalist Industrialization and Patterns of Industrial Protest." *American Sociological Review* 49, no. 4 (1984): 437–53.

———. "Historical Sociology and Time." *Sociological Methods and Research* 20, no. 4 (1992): 456–80.

Arjomand, Said. "Constitutions and the Struggle for Political Order: A Study in the Modernization of Political Traditions." *European Journal of Sociology* 33 (1992): 39–82.

Armanieu, René. "Élections législatives et plébiscites à Toulouse sous le Second Empire." *Annales du Midi* 62 (1950): 151–80.

Armengaud, André. "A propos des origines du sous-dévelopment industriel dans le sud-ouest." *Annales du Midi* 72, no. 1 (1960): 73–81.

———. *Les populations de l'Est-Aquitain au début de l'époque contemporaine*. Paris, 1961.

Armer, Michael. "Methodological Problems and Possibilities in Comparative Research." In *Comparative Social Research: Methodological Problems and Strategies*, edited by Michael Armer and Allen D. Grimshaw. New York, 1973.

Artz, Frederic. "Les débuts des partis modernes en France." *Revue d'histoire moderne* 34 (1931): 275–89.

Audiganne, Armand. *Les populations ouvrières et les industries de la France*. Vol. 2. Paris, 1860.

Auspitz, Katherine. *The Radical Bourgeoisie: The Ligue de l'Enseignement and the Origins of the Third Republic, 1866–1885*. Cambridge, 1982.

Baker, Keith Michael. "Representation." In *The Political Culture of the Old Regime*, edited by Keith Michael Baker. Oxford, 1987.

Baret, H. *Histoire locale du travail*. Saint-Étienne, 1932.

Bastid, Paul. *Les institutions politiques de la monarchie parlementaire française (1814–1848)*. Paris, 1954.

Bendix, Reinhard. *Nation Building and Citizenship: Studies of Our Changing Social Order*. New York, 1969.

Benton, T. " 'Objective' Interests and the Sociology of Power." *Sociology* 15, no. 2 (1981): 161–84.

Berenson, Edward. *Populist Religion and Left-Wing Politics in France, 1830–1852*. Princeton, 1984.

Berg, Maxine, Pat Hudson, and Michael Sonenscher. *Manufacture in Town and Country Before the Factory*. Cambridge, 1983.

Bertocci, P. A. "Positivism, French Republic and the Politics of Religion, 1848–1883." *Third Republic/Troisième République* 2 (1976): 182–227.

Bezucha, Robert J. *The Lyon Uprising of 1834: Social and Political Conflict in the Early July Monarchy*. Cambridge, Mass., 1974.

————. "The French Revolution of 1848 and the Social History of Work." *Theory and Society* 12, no. 4 (1983): 469–83.

Birch, Anthony Harold. *Representation*. New York, 1972.

Blackbourn, David, and Geoff Eley. *The Peculiarities of German History: Bourgeois Society and Politics in Nineteenth-Century Germany*. Oxford, 1984.

Boivin, Marcel. "La Fédération ouvrière rouennaise et les évenements de 1870–1871." *Revue d'histoire économique et sociale* 40, nos. 3 & 4 (1962): 322–42, 524–48.

————. "Les origines de la ligue de l'enseignement en Scine-Inférieure, 1866–1871." *Revue d'histoire économique et sociale* 46, no. 2 (1968): 203–31.

————. *Le mouvement ouvrier dans la région de Rouen, 1851–1876*. 2 vols. Rouen, 1989.

Bollen, Kenneth. "Political Democracy and the Timing of Development." *American Sociological Review* 44, no. 4 (1979): 572–87.

Bollen, Kenneth A., and Robert Jackman. "Economic and Noneconomic Determinants of Political Democracy in the 1960s." In *Research in Political Sociology*, edited by Richard G. Braungart. Greenwich, Conn., 1985.

Bonnefous, Eugène. *Histoire de Saint-Étienne et ses environs*. Saint-Étienne, 1851.

Bossakiewicz, Stanislas. *Histoire générale de Saint-Étienne*. Saint-Étienne, 1905.

Bouteiller, H. *Histoire des milices bourgeoises et de la garde nationale de Rouen*. Rouen, 1850.

Bremond, Alphonse. *Histoire de l'élection municipale de 1865*. Toulouse, 1867.

Brossard, M. E. *Les élections et les réprésentants du département de la Loire aux Assemblés Législatives depuis un siécle (1789–1889)*. Saint-Étienne, 1889.

Burawoy, Michael. "Marxism Without Micro-Foundations." *Socialist Review* 19, no. 2 (1989): 53–86.

Burney, John. "La Faculté des Lettres de Toulouse de 1830 à 1875." *Annales du Midi* 94, no. 158 (1982): 277–99.

Cabet, Étienne. *Voyage en Icarie*. Paris, 1839.

Calhoun, Craig J. *The Question of Class Struggle: Social Foundations of Popular Radicalism during the Industrial Revolution*. Chicago, 1982.

―――. "The Radicalism of Tradition: Community Strength or Venerable Disguise and Borrowed Language?" *American Journal of Sociology* 88, no. 5 (1983): 886–914.

―――, ed. *Habermas and the Public Sphere*. Cambridge, Mass., 1992.

Casevitz, Jean. *Une loi manquée: la loi Niel (1866–1868)*. Paris, n.d.

Chaline, Jean-Pierre. *Rouen sous la Monarchie de Juillet*. Rouen, 1971.

―――. "La banque à Rouen au XIXe siècle." *Revue d'histoire économique et sociale* 52 (1974): 384–420.

―――. "Rouen au milieu du XIXième siècle: la révolution de 1848." *Connaître Rouen* 3 (1976): 1–16.

―――. *Les bourgeois de Rouen: une élite urbaine au XIXe siècle*. Paris, 1982.

―――. *L'affaire Noiret*. Rouen, 1986.

Cherrier, Claude. "Les ouvriers communalistes stéphanois (1870–1871)." *98e Congrés National des sociétés savantes, histoire moderne*. Vol. 2. Paris, 1975.

Clawson, Mary Ann. *Constructing Brotherhood: Class, Gender, and Fraternalism*. Princeton, N.J., 1989.

Cottereau, Alain. "The Distinctiveness of Working-Class Cultures in France." In *Working-Class Formation: Nineteenth-Century Patterns in Western Europe and the United States*, edited by Ira Katznelson and Aristide R. Zolberg. Princeton, N.J., 1986.

Daumard, Adeline. *Les fortunes en France au XIXe siècle*. Paris, 1973.

Delabre, Bernard. "La grève de 1869 dans le bassin minier stéphanois." *Études Foréziennes* (1971): 109–37.

Delale, Alain. "Rouen 1848: La Saint-Barthelemy rouge." *Luttes ouvrières* 1 (1977): 66–83.

Delaye, Jules. *Rapport sur les sociétés de secours mutuels d'ouvriers*. Toulouse, 1862.

Démier, Francis. "Les ouvriers de Rouen parlent à un économiste en juillet 1848." *Le mouvement social* (1981): 3–31.

de Planet, Edmond. *Statistique industrielle du département de la Haute-Garonne*. Toulouse, 1865.

de Puysbusque, Guillaume-Albert. *La prise d'armes contre la Commune à Toulouse, le 27 mars 1871*. Toulouse, 1921.

Documents Officiels. "Documents officiels sur l'émeute de Rouen (27 et 28 avril 1848)." *La révolution de 1848* 13 (1917–1918): 91–107.

Draper, Hal. "Marx on Democratic Forms of Government." In *Socialist Register*, edited by Ralph Miliband and John Saville. London, 1974.

Droulers, Paul. *Action pastorale et problèmes sociaux sous la Monarchie de Juillet chez Mgr. d'Astros*. Paris, 1954.

Dubois, Jean. *Le vocabulaire politique et social en France de 1869 à 1872.* Paris, 1961.

Dubuc, André. "Les émeutes de Rouen et d'Elbeuf." *Études d'histoires moderne* (1948): 242–75.

———. "Frédéric Deschamps, commissaire de la République en Seine-Inférieure (février–mai 1848)." *Actes du congrès historique du centenaire de la révolution de 1848* (1948): 381–95.

———. "Les élections au Corps législatif à Rouen en 1869." *Actes du 91e Congrès National des sociétés savantes.* Rennes, 1966.

Duportal, Armand. *La Commune à Toulouse, simple exposé des faits.* Toulouse, 1871.

Duveau, Georges. *La pensée ouvrière sur l'éducation pendant la Second République et le Second Empire.* Paris, 1948.

Edwards, Stewart. *The Paris Commune 1871.* New York, 1973.

Eley, Geoff. "Reviewing the Socialist Tradition." In *The Crisis of Socialism in Europe*, edited by Christiane Lemke and Gary Marks. Durham, North Carolina, 1992.

Elwitt, Sanford. *The Making of the Third Republic: Class and Politics in France, 1868–1884.* Baton Rouge, La., 1975.

———. *The Third Republic Defended: Bourgeois Reform in France, 1880–1914.* Baton Rouge, La., 1986.

Epstein, Leon D. *Political Parties in Western Democracies.* New York, 1967.

Escoffier, Jeffrey. "The Limits of Multiculturalism." *Socialist Review* 21, nos. 3–4 (1991): 61–73.

Estancelin, Louis. *La verité sur les évenements de Rouen.* Rouen, 1871.

Faure, Étienne. *La Commune en province: un condamné par la cour d'assises de Riom.* Genève, 1872.

Faure, Pétrus. *Histoire du mouvement ouvrier dans le département de la Loire.* Saint-Étienne, 1956.

Festy, Octave. *Le mouvement ouvrier au début de la Monarchie de Juillet (1830–1934).* Paris, 1908.

Fitzpatrick, Maria. "Proudhon and the French Labour Movement: The Problem of Proudhon's Prominence." *European History Quarterly* 15 (1985): 407–30.

Fohlen, Claude. *L'industrie textile au temps du Second Empire.* Paris, 1956.

Fournial, Étienne. *Saint-Étienne: histoire de la ville et de ses habitants.* Roanne, 1976.

Fraysse, Arthur. *Le marchandage dans l'industrie du bâtiment.* Paris, 1911.

Friedman. "Capitalism, Republicanism, Socialism, and the State: France, 1871–1914." *Social Science History* 14, no. 2 (1990): 151–74.

Furet, François. *Penser la Révolution française.* Paris, 1978.

———. *La gauche et la révolution au milieu du XIXe siècle: Edgar Quinet et la question du jacobinisme (1865–1870).* Paris, 1986.

Gaillard, Jeanne. "Notes sur l'opposition au monopôle des compagnies de chemins de fer entre 1850 et 1860." *1848* 42, no. 187 (1950): 233–49.

———. *Communes de province, Commune de Paris 1870–1871.* Paris, 1971.

Gaussin, Pierre-Roger. *Saint-Étienne et son agglomeration.* Colmar-Ingersheim, 1974.

Goldstone, Jack, ed. *Revolutions: Theoretical, Comparative, and Historical Studies*. San Diego, 1986.

Gonnard, Philippe. "Les passementiers de Saint-Étienne en 1833." *Revue d'histoire de Lyon* (1907): 1–16.

Gordon, David. "Industrialization and Republican Politics: The Bourgeoisie of Reims and Saint-Étienne under the Second Empire." In *French Cities in the Nineteenth Century*, edited by John M. Merriman. New York, 1981.

——. *Merchants and Capitalists*. University, Alabama, 1985.

Gourvitch, A. "Le mouvement pour la réforme électorale (1838–1841)." *Bulletin de la société d'histoire de la Révolution de 1848* 13 (1916–1917): 95–115, 173–92, 62–81.

Graham, Ruth. "Loaves and Liberty: Women in the French Revolution." In *Becoming Visible: Women in European History*, edited by Renate Bridenthal and Claudia Koonz. Boston, 1977.

Gras, Louis Joseph. *Histoire de la rubanerie et des industries de la soie à Saint-Étienne et dans la région stéphanoise*. Saint-Étienne, 1906.

——. *Histoire économique de la métallurgie de la Loire*. Saint-Étienne, 1908.

——. *Histoire économique générale des mines de la Loire*. 2 vols. Saint-Étienne, 1908.

Greenberg, Louis M. *Sisters of Liberty: Marseille, Lyon, Paris, and the Reaction to a Centralized State, 1868–1871*. Cambridge, Mass., 1971.

Griffin, Larry. "Narrative, Event-Structure Analysis, and Causal Interpretation." *American Journal of Sociology*, forthcoming.

Guillaume, Pierre. "La situation économique et sociale du département de la Loire d'après l'enquête sur le travail agricole et industriel du 25 mai 1848." *Revue d'histoire moderne et contemporaine* 10 (1963): 5–34.

——. "Grèves et organisations ouvrières chez les mineurs de la Loire au milieu du XIXe siècle." *Le mouvement social* 43 (1963): 5–18.

——. *La compagnie des mines de la Loire (1846–1854): essai sur l'apparition de la grande industrie capitaliste en France*. Paris, 1966.

Halevi, Ran. "Modalités, participation, et luttes électorales sous l'Ancien Régime." In *Explication du vote: un bilan des études électorales en France*, edited by Daniel Gaxie. Paris, 1985.

Hall, Stuart. "Variants of Liberalism." In *Politics and Ideology*, edited by James Donald and Stuart Hall. Philadelphia, 1986.

Hanagan, Michael. *The Logic of Solidarity: Artisans and Industrial Workers in Three French Towns, 1871–1914*. Urbana, Illinois, 1980.

——. "Agriculture and Industry in the Nineteenth-Century Stéphanois: Household Employment Patterns and the Rise of a Permanent Proletariat." In *Proletarians and Protest: The Roots of Class Formation in an Industrializing World*, edited by Michael and Charles Stephenson. New York, 1986.

——. *Nascent Proletarians: Class Formation in Post-Revolutionary France*. Oxford, 1989.

Hart, Janet. "Cracking the Code: Narratives and Political Mobilization in the Greek Resistance." *Social Science History* 16, no. 4 (1992):631–68.

Henry, Simone. "La campagne des banquets à Toulouse." In *La Révolution de 1848 à Toulouse et dans la Haute-Garonne*, edited by Jacques Godechot. Toulouse, 1848.

Hermet, André. "À Toulouse en 1841 et 1842: troubles du recensement . . . et comedie." *L'Auta* 533 (1988): 44–53.

Hindess, Barry. "Power, Interests and the Outcomes of Struggles." *Sociology* 16, no. 4 (1982): 498–511.

Hobsbawn, E. J. "The Labour Aristocracy in Nineteenth-Century Britain." In *Labouring Men: Studies in the History of Labour.* New York, 1965.

Howorth, Jolyon. "From the Bourgeois Republic to the Social Republic." In *Socialism in France: From Jaurès to Mitterand,* edited by Stuart Williams. New York, 1983.

Huard, Raymond. "La genèse des partis démocratiques modernes en France. L'expérience du XIXe siècle." *La pensée* 201 (1978): 96–119.

————. *Le mouvement républicain en Bas-Languedoc, 1848–1881.* Paris, 1982.

Hufton, Owen. "Women in the Revolution, 1789–1796." *Past and Present* 53 (1971): 90–108.

Hunt, Lynn Avery. *Politics, Culture, and Class in the French Revolution.* Berkeley, Calif., 1984.

Hunt, Lynn Avery, David Lansky, and Paul Hanson. "The Failure of the Liberal Republic in France, 1795–1799: The Road to Brumaire." *Journal of Modern History* 51 (1979): 734–59.

Jenkins, Craig. "Sociopolitical Movements." In *The Handbook of Political Behavior,* edited by Samuel Long. New York, 1981.

Johnson, Christopher. *Utopian Communism in France: Cabet and the Icarians, 1839–1851.* Ithaca, 1974.

Jolivalt, J. *Renseignements utiles.* Saint-Étienne, 1870.

Jones, Gareth Stedman. "The Mid-Century Crisis and the 1848 Revolutions." *Theory and Society* 12, no. 4 (1983): 505–19.

Joyce, Patrick. *The Historical Meanings of Work.* Cambridge, 1987.

Judt, Tony. *Marxism and the French Left: Studies in Labour and Politics in France, 1830–1981.* Oxford, 1986.

Kauffman, L. A. "The Anti-Politics of Identity." *Socialist Review* 20, no. 1 (1990): 67–80.

Kent, Sherman. *Electoral Procedure Under Louis Philippe.* New Haven, Conn., 1937.

Kimmel, Michael S. *Revolution: A Sociological Interpretation.* Philadelphia, 1990.

Kitschelt, Herbert. "Political Opportunity Structures and Political Protest: Anti-Nuclear Movements in Four Democracies." *British Journal of Political Science* 16 (1986): 47–85.

Landes, Joan B. *Women and the Public Sphere in the Age of the French Revolution.* Ithaca, 1988.

Latta, Claude. *Un républicain méconnu: Martin Bernard.* Saint-Étienne, 1980.

Leblanc, François. "Mémoires de l'ouvrier François Leblanc, adjoint au maire de Monville en 1848." Documents publiés par A. M. Gossez. *Bibliothèque de la révolution de 1848.* Vol. 2 (1907–1908): 1–67.

Lequin, Yves. *Les ouvriers de la région lyonnaise (1848–1914).* 2 vols. Lyon, 1977.

————. "Apprenticeship in Nineteenth Century France: A Continuing Tradition or a Break with the Past?" In *Work in France: Representations, Meaning, Organization, and Practice,* edited by Steven Laurence Kaplan and Cynthia J. Koepp. Ithaca, 1986.

Levainville, J. *Rouen: étude d'une agglomération urbaine*. Paris, 1913.

Limousin, Antoine. *Enquête industrielle et sociale des ouvriers et des chefs d'ateliers rubaniers*. Saint-Étienne, 1848.

Lipset, Seymour Martin. *The First New Nation: The United States in Historical and Comparative Perspective*. New York, 1979.

———. *Political Man: The Social Bases of Politics*. Baltimore, Md., 1981.

Loubère, Leo A. "The Intellectual Origins of French Jacobin Socialism." *International Review of Social History* 4 (1959): 415–31.

Maitron, Jean, ed. *Dictionnaire biographique du mouvement ouvrier français*. Pt. 1: 1789–1864. 3 vols. De la Révolution française à la fondation de la Première Internationale. Pt. 2: 1864–1871. 5 vols. De la fondation de la Première Internationale à la Commune. Pt. 3: 1871–1914. 6 vols. De la Commune à la Grande Guerre. Paris, 1964–1977.

Marec, Yannick. "Lendemains de révolution: l'agitation ouvrière dans la région rouennaise en 1830." *Études Normandes* 4 (1981): 47–56.

———. *1848 à Rouen: les mémoires du citoyen Cord'homme*. Rouen, 1988.

Markovitch, T. J. "L'industrie française de 1789 à 1964: conclusions générales." *Cahiers de l'institut de science économique appliquée*, series AF 7, no. 179. Paris, 1966.

———. "Le revenu industriel et artisanal sous la Monarchie de Juillet et le Second Empire." *Économies et sociétés*, series AF, 4 (1967).

Martourey, Albert. "Mécanismes d'urbanisation et modifications professionelles: example de Saint-Étienne au XIXe siècle." *Bulletin du centre d'histoire économique et sociale de la région lyonnaise* 4 (1974): 43–79.

Marty, Gabriel. *Étienne Cabet et le procès des communistes à Toulouse en 1843*. Toulouse, 1928.

Marx, Karl. *The Class Struggles in France, 1848–1850*. New York, 1964.

———. "The Civil War in France." In *Karl Marx & Frederick Engels: Selected Works*. New York, 1968.

Marx, Karl, and Frederick Engels. "Manifesto of the Communist Party." In *Karl Marx & Frederick Engels: Selected Works*. New York, 1968.

Massip, F. *Procès de l'Internationale, compte-rendu*. Toulouse, 1873.

McLennan, Gregor. *Marxism and the Methodologies of History*. London, 1981.

McPhee, Peter. "The Crisis of Radical Republicanism in the French Revolution of 1848." *Historical Studies* 16, no. 162 (1974): 71–88.

Merley, Jean. "Les élections de 1869 dans le département de la Loire." *Cahiers d'histoire* 6 (1961): 59–93.

———. "La contribution de la Haute-Loire à la formation de la population stéphanoise au milieu du XIXe siècle." *Cahiers de la Haute Loire* (1966): 165–80.

Merriman, John. *The Agony of the Republic: The Repression of the Left in Revolutionary France, 1848–1851*. New Haven, 1978.

Miliband, Ralph. "Reflections on the Crisis of Communist Regimes." *New Left Review* 177 (1989): 27–36.

Mollat, Michel, ed. *L'histoire de Rouen*. Toulouse, 1979.

Moore, Barrington. *Social Origins of Dictatorship and Democracy; Lord and Peasant in the Making of the Modern World*. Boston, 1966.

Moss, Bernard. "Parisian Workers and the Origins of Republican Socialism." In *1830 in France*, edited by John M. Merriman. New York, 1975.

——. "Producers' Associations and the Origins of French Socialism: Ideology From Below." *Journal of Modern History* 48, no.1 (1976): 69–89.

Mottez, Bernard. *Systèmes de salaires et politiques patronales*. Paris, 1966.

Nicolet, Claude. *L'idée républicaine en France (1789–1924): essai d'histoire critique*. Paris, 1982.

Noiret, Charles. *Mémoires d'un ouvrier rouennais*. Rouen, 1836.

——. "Aux Travailleurs." and "Deuxième lettre aux travailleurs." In *La parole ouvrière 1830–1851*, edited by Alain Faure and Jacques Rancière. Paris, 1976.

Nowak, Stefan. "Meaning and Measurement in Comparative Studies." In *Understanding and Prediction: Essays in the Methodology of Social and Behavioral Theories*, edited by Stefan Nowak. Dordrecht, Holland, 1976.

Oberschall, Anthony. *Social Conflict and Social Movements*. Englewood Cliffs, N.J., 1973.

O'Boyle, Lenore. "The Image of the Journalist in France, Germany, and England, 1815–1848." *Comparative Studies in Society and History* 10, no. 3 (1968): 290–317.

O'Brien, Patrick Karl, and Caglar Keyder. *Economic Growth in Britain and France, 1780–1914: Two Paths to the Twentieth Century*. London, 1978.

Offe, Claus. "Legitimation Through Majority Rule?" In *Disorganized Capitalism*, edited by John Keane. Cambridge, Mass., 1985.

Office du Travail. *Les associations professionelles ouvrières*. Vol. 1. Paris, 1899.

Paul, Pierre. "L'agitation républicaine à Toulouse et dans la Haute-Garonne de 1840 à 1848." In *La Révolution de 1848 à Toulouse et dans la Haute-Garonne*, edited by Jacques Godechot. Toulouse, 1848.

Payne, Howard C. *The Police State of Louis Napoleon Bonaparte, 1851–1860*. Seattle, 1966.

Peyrat, Alphonse. *La révolution et le livre de M. Quinet*. Paris, 1866.

Phillips, Anne. *Engendering Democracy*. University Park, Pa., 1991.

Pinkney, David H. *Decisive Years in France, 1840–1847*. Princeton, N.J., 1986.

Poulantzas, Nicos. *Political Power and Social Classes*. London, 1973.

Price, Roger. "Techniques of Repression: The Control of Popular Protest in Mid-Nineteenth-Century France." *The Historical Journal* 25, no. 4 (1982): 859–87.

Przeworski, Adam. "Material Interests, Class Compromise, and the Transition to Socialism." *Politics and Society* 10, no. 2 (1980): 125–53.

Przeworski, Adam, and John Sprague. *Paper Stones: A History of Electoral Socialism*. Chicago, 1986.

Racz, Elizabeth. "The Women's Rights Movement in the French Revolution." *Science and Society* 161 (1951–1952): 151–68.

Reddy, William M. "Family and Factory: French Linen Weavers in the Belle Epoque." *Journal of Social History* 8 (1975): 102–12.

——. "The Textile Trade and the Language of the Crowd at Rouen, 1752–1871." *Past and Present* 74 (1977): 62–89.

——. "Skeins, Scales, Discounts, Steam, and Other Objects of Crowd Justice in Early French Textile Mills." *Comparative Studies in Society and History* 21 (1979): 204–13.

Reddy, William M. *The Rise of Market Culture: The Textile Trade and French Society, 1750–1900*. Cambridge, 1984.

―――. *Money and Liberty in Modern Europe: A Critique of Historical Understanding*. Cambridge, 1987.

Reid, Donald. "Industrial Paternalism: Discourse and Practice in Nineteenth Century French Mining and Metallurgy." *Comparative Studies in Society and History* 27 (1985): 579–607.

Reybaud, Louis. *Le fer et la houille*. Paris, 1874.

Reynolds, Sian. "Marianne's Citizens? Women, the Republic, and Universal Suffrage in France." In *Women, State and Revolution: Essays on Power and Gender in Europe Since 1789*, edited by Sian Reynolds. Amherst, 1987.

Rials, Stéphane. "Néo-Jacobinisme et néo-hébertisme au milieu du XIXe siècle. Une contribution à la typologie des gauches." In *Révolution et contre-révolution au XIXe siècle*. Paris, 1987.

Roehl, Richard. "French Industrialization: A Reconsideration." *Explorations in Economic History* 13 (1976): 233–81.

Rosenberg, Mimi. "Herbert Gutman on American Labor History: An Interview with Mimi Rosenberg." *Socialism and Democracy* 10 (1990): 51–68.

Rougerie, Jacques. "Les sections françaises de l'association internationale des travailleurs." In *La Première Internationale. L'institution. L'implantation. Le rayonnement*. Colloque du 16–18 novembre 1964. Paris, 1968.

Rude, Fernand. *L'insurrection lyonnaise de novembre 1831: le mouvement ouvrier à Lyon de 1827 à 1832*. 2d edition. Paris, 1969.

Rudé, George. "The Ideology of Popular Protest." In *Ideology and Popular Protest*. New York, 1980.

Rueschemeyer, Dietrich, Evelyne Huber Stephens, and John D. Stephens. *Capitalist Development and Democracy*. Chicago, 1992.

Sabel, Charles, and Jonathan Zeitlin. "Historical Alternatives to Mass Production: Politics, Markets, and Technology in Nineteenth-Century Industrialization." *Past and Present* 108 (1985): 133–76.

Samuel, Raphael. "Workshop of the World: Steam Power and Hand Technology in Mid-Victorian Britain." *History Workshop* 3 (1977): 7–67.

San Francisco Bay Area Kapitalistate Group. "Political Parties and Capitalist State Development." *Kapitalistate* 6 (1977): 7–38.

Sartori, Giovanni. "From the Sociology of Politics to Political Sociology." In *Politics and the Social Sciences*, edited by Seymour Martin Lipset. New York, 1969.

―――. *Parties and Party Systems: A Framework for Analysis*. Cambridge, 1976.

Schnetzler, Jacques. *Les industries et les hommes dans la région de Saint-Étienne*. Saint-Étienne, 1975.

Scott, Joan Wallach. *Gender and the Politics of History*. New York, 1988.

Sewell, Jr., William H. "Social Change and the Rise of Working-Class Politics in Nineteenth-Century Marseille." *Past and Present* 65 (1974): 75–109.

―――. *Work and Revolution in France: The Language of Labor From the Old Regime to 1848*. Cambridge, 1980.

―――. "Artisans, Factory Workers, and the Formation of the French Working Class, 1789–1848." In *Working Class Formation*, edited by Ira Katznelson and Aristide Zolberg. Princeton, N.J., 1986.

————. "Uneven Development, the Autonomy of Politics, and the Dockworkers of Nineteenth-Century Marseille." *American Historical Review* 93, no. 3 (1988): 604–37.

————. "Three Temporalities: Toward an Evenemental Sociology." Forthcoming in *The Historic Turn in the Human Sciences*, edited by Terrence J. McDonald. Ann Arbor, Michigan.

Sheehan, James J. *German Liberalism in the Nineteenth Century*. Chicago, 1978.

Singer, Barnett. *Village Notables in Nineteenth Century France: Priests, Mayors, Schoolmasters*. Albany, N.Y., 1983.

Skocpol, Theda. *States and Social Revolutions: A Comparative Analysis of France, Russia, and China*. Cambridge, 1979.

Smelser, Neil. "The Methodology of Comparative Analysis of Economic Activity." In *Essays in Sociological Analysis*, Prentice Hall, 1968.

Somers, Margaret. "Narrativity, Narrative Identity, and Social Action: Rethinking English Working-Class Formation." *Social Science History* 16, no. 4 (1992): 591–630.

Soule, Claude. "La notion historique de représentation politique." *Politique* 6, no. 21–22 (1962): 17–32.

————. *Les États Généraux de France (1302–1789): étude historique, comparative et doctrinale*. Heule, UGA, 1968.

Stephens, John. "Democratic Transition and Breakdown in Western Europe, 1870–1939: A Test of the Moore Thesis." *American Journal of Sociology* 94, no. 5 (1989): 1019–77.

Tarrow, Sidney G. *Struggling to Reform: Social Movements and Policy Change During Cycles of Protest*. Ithaca, N.Y., 1983.

————. *Struggle, Politics, and Reform: Collective Action, Social Movements, and Cycles of Protest*. Ithaca, N.Y., 1989.

Tchernoff, I. *Le parti républicain sous la Monarchie de Juillet*. Paris, 1901.

————. *Associations et sociétés secrètes sous la Seconde République, 1848–1851, d'après des documents inédits*. Paris, 1905.

————. *Le parti républicain au coup d'état et sous le Second Empire*. Paris, 1906.

Terme, C. *Des élections municipales à Saint-Étienne en 1865*. Paris, 1865.

Therborn, Goran. "The Rule of Capital and the Rise of Democracy." *New Left Review* 103 (1977): 3–42.

Tilly, Charles. "Collective Violence in European Perspective." In *Violence in America*, edited by Hugh Graham and Ted Robert Gurr. Washington, D.C., 1969.

————. "Revolutions and Collective Violence." In *Handbook of Political Science*, edited by Fred I. Greenstein and Nelson W. Polsby. Reading, Mass., 1975.

————. *From Mobilization to Revolution*. Reading, Mass., 1978.

————. *The Contentious French*. Cambridge, Mass., 1986.

————. "Solidary Logics." *Theory and Society* 17 (1988): 451–58.

————, ed. *The Formation of National States in Western Europe*. Princeton, 1975.

Tilly, Louise. "Paths of Proletarianization: Organization of Production, Sexual Division of Labor, and Womens' Collective Action." *Signs* 7 (1981): 400–417.

Toutain, Jacques. *La révolution de 1848 à Rouen*. Paris, n.d.

Traugott, Mark. *Armies of the Poor: Determinants of Working-Class Participation in the Parisian Insurrection of June 1848*. Princeton, 1985.

Tristan, Flora. *Le Tour de France: journal inédit 1843–1844*. Paris, 1973.

Tudesq, André-Jean. "Les comportements électoraux sous le régime censitaire." In *Explication du vote: un bilan des études électorales en France*, edited by Daniel Gaxie. Paris, 1985.

Turgan, Julien. *Les grandes usines: études industrielles en France et à l'étranger*. Vol. 3. Paris, 1863.

Vanoli, Dominique. "Les couvents soyeux." *Révoltes logiques* 2 (1976): 19–39.

Vant, André. *Imagerie et urbanisation: recherches sur l'exemple stéphanois*. Saint-Étienne, 1981.

Vigier, Philippe. "Élections municipales et prise de conscience politique sous la Monarchie de Juillet." In *La France au XIXe siècle, études historiques*. Paris, 1973.

Vincent, K. Steven. *Pierre-Joseph Proudhon and the Rise of Republican Socialism*. New York, 1984.

Weber, Eugen. "The Second Republic, Politics, and the Peasant." *French Historical Studies* 11, no. 4 (1980): 521–50.

Weill, Georges. *Histoire du parti républicain en France 1814–1870*. Paris, 1928.

Woloch, Isser. *Jacobin Legacy: The Democratic Movement under the Directory*. Princeton, N.J., 1970.

Wright, Erik Olin. *Class, Crisis, and the State*. London, 1978.

———. *Classes*. London, 1985.

———. "Rethinking, Once Again, the Concept of Class Structure." In *The Debate on Classes*, edited by Erik Olin Wright. London, 1989.

Wuthnow, Robert. *Communities of Discourse: Ideology and Social Structure in the Reformation, the Enlightenment, and European Socialism*. Cambridge, Mass., 1989.

Young, Iris Marion. *Justice and the Politics of Difference*. Princeton, N.J., 1990.

Zévaès, Alexandre. "La lutte des classes à Rouen en avril 1848." *La révolution de 1848* 24 (1927–1928): 204–21.

———. "Les candidates ouvrières et révolutionnaires sous le Second Empire." *La révolution de 1848* 29 (1932): 132–54.

UNPUBLISHED DISSERTATIONS

Blondel, Eliane. *La crise du milieu du XIXième siècle en Seine-Inférieure (1845–1849)*. Thèse de 3ième cycle. Université de Rouen, 1978.

———. *La vie politique en Seine-Inférieure des élections de mai 1849 au Coup d'État du 2 décembre 1851*. Mémoire de maîtrisse. Université de Rouen, n.d.

Durousset, Maurice. *La vie ouvrière dans la région stéphanoise sous la Monarchie de Juillet et la Seconde République*. Diplôme d'Études Supérieures. Université de Lyon, 1958.

Martourey, Albert. *Formation et gestion d'une agglomération industrielle au XIXe siécle: Saint-Étienne de 1815 à 1870*. 5 vols. Thèse de Doctorat d'État, Université de Lyon 2, 1984.

Mourier, Jacqueline. "La presse de Saint-Étienne de 1825 à 1848." Mémoire de maîtrise. Université de Saint-Étienne, n.d.

Rouja, Nicole. *L'Opinion toulousaine en face de la Première Internationale.* Diplôme d'Études Supérieures. Université de Toulouse, 1965.

Suzuki, Hirmosa. *L'évolution de l'industrie cotonnière dans la région rouenaise au XIXe siècle.* Thèse de 3ième cycle. Université de Rouen, 1969.

Tenand, Daniel. *Les origines de la classe ouvrière stéphanoise.* Mémoire de maîtrise. Université de Lyon II, 1972.

Vidal, Jean-François. *La Commune de 1871 à Saint-Étienne.* Diplôme d'Études Supérieures, Université de Saint-Étienne, 1970.

Index

Abrams, Philip, 270n.52
Agnew, John, 23
Agulhon, Maurice, 37–38, 271nn.8, 10, 274n.71
anticlericalism, 50, 51, 167, 214, 219–20, 224, 249, 289n.92
Arjomand, Said, 269n.34
artisans: capitalist development and, 70; definition of, 268n.23; economic grievances of, 44; in factories, 67; role in republican politics, 35–36
Astima, Jean Baptiste, 75, 118–19, 125
Aubry, Émile, 8, 36, 98, 175, 199–202, 233, 237, 250, 261, 283n.135, 294n.99, 295n.104
Audiganne, Armand, 96, 283n.133

Baker, Keith Michael, 273n.37
Baune, Eugène, 139, 143, 151–52, 155
Bendix, Reinhard, 19
Benton, T., 267n.19
Bernard, Martin, 139–40, 158, 166
Bertholon, César, 167–68, 224–27
Blanc, Louis, 42, 43, 114, 181
Blanqui, Auguste, 43
bourgeois leadership, consequences of, 255, 260
Buchez, Pierre, 42–43
Buraway, Michael, 12–13

Cabet, Étienne, 42, 43, 112, 178, 284–85nn.18, 19, and 25, 290n.22. *See also* Icarian communism
Calhoun, Craig, 284n.150, 300n.7
capitalism, political consequences of, 3–4, 18
capitalist industrialization. *See also* industrialization
Caussidière, Louis Marc, 139, 141–143, 181
census riots of 1841, 110
Chaline, Jean-Pierre, 291n.27
citizenship, 19, 33. *See also* suffrage rights
class: antagonisms, 100–101; concept of, 6; identities, 8, 103; interests, 7–9; reductionism, 6, 9
class analysis, 4–11

class conflicts. *See also* class struggle, strikes
class relations, 4–13; complexity of, 7; as a determinant of politics, 4–6, 10; and party strategies, 12–13; and Republican party formation, 26
class solidarities, 72, 74–76, 87, 97–98, 101–3, 258
class structure: Rouen, 88, 206; Saint-Étienne, 76–77, 172; Toulouse, 65–66, 137
class structures, 4, 10, 13; effect of, 4, 10; party strategies and, 13
class struggles, 136, 171, 204–6, 253–54. *See also* strikes
Clawson, Mary Ann, 271n.14
clubs, political, 1848, 38–39, 117–19, 120, 122, 185, 191
clubs, political, 1870–71, 212, 216–17, 224–229, 234, 245
coal mining, 79–82
communal liberties, 109, 115
communal ties, 31, 32, 102–3, 284n.150
communes, revolutionary, 10–11, 43, 209–51; Rouen, absense of, 243–44; Saint-Étienne, 223–32, 297n.52–53; Toulouse, 216–23
Compagnie générale de la Loire, 80, 82, 145, 156
compagnonnages, 73–74, 85
comparison, strategies of, 24–26
conscription riots 1868, 106, 132–33
constitutions, 17, 45–46, 269n.34
contingency, 10
convent workshop riots, 87, 152–54, 166, 287n.42
convent workshops, 77–78, 152, 278n.54
cooperatives, commercial, 144–45
cooperatives, consumer, 96, 281n.90, 283n.136
cooperatives, production, 42, 45, 86–87, 165, 281n.88, 283n.135
Cord'homme, Charles, 199, 203, 232–33, 291n.34, 293n.77
corporatism, 39; corporate heritage, 102; corporate idiom, 44
corruption, 34, 37, 180

318 · Index